Essays in Anarchism and Religion: Volume 1

*Edited by Alexandre Christoyannopoulos &
Matthew S. Adams*

Published by
Stockholm University Press
Stockholm University
SE-106 91 Stockholm, Sweden
www.stockholmuniversitypress.se

Supporting Agency (funding): Department of Politics, History and International
Relations, Loughborough University, UK, Crowdfunding

First published 2017
Cover Illustration: Satan descends upon Earth. Illustration for John Milton's
"Paradise Lost", by Gustave Doré (1832–1883)
Reproduced by permission of Public domain
Cover designed by Karl Edqvist, SUP

Stockholm Studies in Comparative Religion (Online) ISSN: 2002–4606

ISBN (Paperback): 978–91–7635–043–0
ISBN (PDF): 978–91–7635–040–9
ISBN (EPUB): 978–91–7635–041–6
ISBN (Mobi/Kindle): 978–91–7635–042–3

DOI: https://doi.org/10.16993/bak

Suggested citation:
Alexandre Christoyannopoulos & Matthew S. Adams. 2017 *Essays in
Anarchism and Religion: Volume 1*. Stockholm: Stockholm University Press.
DOI: https://doi.org/10.16993/bak. License: CC-BY

To read the free, open access version of this book online,
visit https://doi.org/10.16993/bak or scan this QR code
with your mobile device.

Stockholm Studies in Comparative Religion

Stockholm Studies in Comparative Religion (SSCR) is a peer-reviewed series initiated by Åke Hultkrantz in 1961. While its earlier emphasis lay in ethnographic-comparative approaches to religion, the series now covers a broader spectrum of the history of religions, including the philological study of discrete traditions, large-scale comparisons between different traditions as well as theoretical and methodological concerns in the study of cross-cultural religious categories such as ritual and myth. SSCR strives to sustain and disseminate high-quality and innovative research in the form of monographs and edited volumes, preferably in English, but in exceptional cases also in French, German, and Scandinavian languages. SSCR was previously included in the series Acta Universitatis Stockholmiensis (ISSN 0562–1070). A full list of publications can be found here: http://www.erg.su.se/publikationer/skriftserier/stockholm-studies-in-comparative-religion-1.38944.

Editorial Board

Titles in the series

Peer Review Policies

Stockholm University Press ensures that all book publications are peer-reviewed in two stages. Each book proposal submitted to the Press will be sent to a dedicated Editorial Board of experts in the subject area as well as two independent experts. The full manuscript will be peer reviewed by chapter or as a whole by two independent experts.

A full description of Stockholm University Press' peer-review policies can be found on the website: http://www.stockholm universitypress.se/site/peer-review-policies/.

The Editorial Board of *Stockholm Studies in Comparative Religion* applies single-blind review during proposal and manuscript assessment.

Recognition for reviewers

We would like to thank all reviewers involved in this process. Special thanks to the two anonymous reviewers for meticulously peer reviewing of the manuscript of this book.

Contents

Acknowledgements

This book is available freely online and at a reduced price in print thanks to a successful crowdfunding campaign. We are very grateful to the following backers of the campaign for their generous support: Adam Adada; Agzenay Adel; Andrew Bradstock; Amanda McBride; Augusto Gayubas; Ben Geoghegan-Fittall; Ben Pauli; Bianca Maria Mennini; Brendon George; Brett Alan Gershon; Bryan Tucker; Carl Levy; Carole Clohesy; Christopher Rowland; Citlaly Barron; Colin Tyler; Conor Pattenden; Cris Baldwin; David Belcheff; David Carpenter; David Hatch; David McLellan; Eden Hyde Munday; Elyem Chej; Emilie Christoyannopoulos; Fanny Forest; Fernando Galván; Frankie Hines; Jacob Lester; Jana Wendler; James; Jennifer; Joel Martinell; John Probhudan; Jose Santiago Fernandez Vazquez; Joy Bose; Julia Sutterfield McKinney; Justin Anthony Stepney; Justin James Meggitt; Kate Birss; Kyle Gregory; Laura Galián; Lloyd Pietersen; Louis Swingrover; L. Wade Thompson; Marcus Peter Rempel; Marie-Hélène Forest; Marta Cedrés; Martin Pennington; Matthew Switzer; Matt Nyman; Michael Skazick; Miguel Ángel Aguilar Rancel; Miguel Torres; Niels Kjaer; Ole Birk Laursen; Oliver; Pascale Rougeron; Patrick McCarthy; Paul Cudenec; Paul Debu; Richard M. Allen; Robert M. McDonald; Robin Hanford; Ruy Llera Blanes; Salvatore Puma; Sam Underwood; Sergio Alvarez; Simon Podmore; Steven Shakespeare; Sydney Isaac; Tim Carter; Todd Grotenhuis; Truls Bjørvik; Tyler Martin; Vogelfrei; and a donor in honour of Mark Taylor.

The editors of this volume wish to thank the reviewers who commented on earlier drafts of the chapters presented here, the reviewers that read the manuscript for Stockholm University Press (SUP), and the staff at SUP for their enthusiastic support for this project. We also wish to acknowledge the generous financial support of Loughborough University's Department of Politics, History and International Relations, the broader School of Social, Political and Geographical Sciences, and the organisers of the Anarchist Studies Conference held at Loughborough in 2012 from which these papers emerged.

Anarchism and Religion: Mapping an Increasingly Fruitful Landscape

Alexandre Christoyannopoulos & Matthew S. Adams
Loughborough University, UK

Both anarchism and religion have enjoyed renewed academic attention since the end of the twentieth century: religion has been an increasingly visible aspect of political life; and anarchist ideas have suffused recent social and political movements to a striking degree. Scholars have therefore increasingly turned their attention to both of these trends, seeking to illuminate the causes of their resurgence, and the underlying debates that have informed this renewed prominence.[1] In line with these trends, the overlap between anarchism and religion has also attracted new interest.[2] In print, on social media, in the streets and in religious communities, religious anarchist analysis, and the analysis of religious anarchists, is gaining traction.[3]

Yet anarchism and religion have historically had an uneasy relationship. There are defined tensions between the two camps that are freighted with historical pedigree: many anarchists insist that religion is fundamentally incompatible with anarchism, while many religious adherents have grown suspicious of anarchists given a strain of anticlericalism that has sometimes sparked shocking violence.[4] At the same time, religious anarchists insist that their religious tradition embodies (or at least has the potential to embody) the very values that have historically accorded anarchism its unique place in the family of political ideologies.[5] Their religious beliefs, they argue, imply a rejection of the state, call for an economy of mutual aid, present a denunciation of oppressive authorities that often includes religious institutions, and embody

How to cite this book chapter:
Christoyannopoulos, A. and Adams, M. S. 2017. Anarchism and Religion: Mapping an Increasingly Fruitful Landscape. In: Christoyannopoulos, A. and Adams, M. S. (eds.) *Essays in Anarchism and Religion: Volume 1.* Pp. 1–17. Stockholm: Stockholm University Press. DOI: https://doi.org/10.16993/bak.a. License: CC-BY.

a quest for a more just society – despite, and indeed sometimes paradoxically *because* of, the acceptance of a god as 'master.'

However, despite the renewed attention devoted to the contested terrain between politics and religion, and despite the new prominence anarchism has enjoyed in radical politics post-1989, scholarship on the relation between anarchism and religion, on proponents of religious anarchism, and on their arguments, remains relatively rare. This is now changing. Whether emanating from academic, religious or activist circles, there is a growing literature, much of which centres on the Christian tradition, but is refreshed by an emerging focus on anarchism and Islam, Judaism, Buddhism, Hinduism and other religions and spiritualities.[6]

Building on this fertile work, this book aims to open a forum for the academic analysis of this contested field, to offer a critical space for the discussion of the theoretical, theological and historical overlaps between anarchism and religion, and to cast a probing light on the rich dialogue that these conflicts have created. While the issue of contemporary political relevance is one that runs through many of the chapters in this volume, the primary intention of this collection is scholarly: tracing the under-acknowledged resonances between anarchist politics and religious ideas, understanding the historical animus at the heart of this relationship, and highlighting examples of common action and concern.

It seems appropriate at this point to acknowledge our positionality. We – that is, both we the editors and most authors in these volumes – write from a predominantly Eurocentric, white, male and therefore privileged position. This was not intentional, but does reflect the continuing intersectional hierarchies present across the academic sector. We have attempted to solicit a mix of chapters with a more balanced gender mix, seeking contributions from both non-male authors and about non-male scholars. For instance, building on the origins of this first volume in the Anarchist Studies Network's (ASN) conference held at Loughborough University in 2012, we targeted the 2016 ASN conference, which had a central theme of anarcha-feminism. Future volumes will hopefully therefore go some way to addressing these issues, but the lack of voices belonging to women and non-white people in particular highlights enduring issues in higher education.

It goes without saying that we remain committed to broadening this ongoing research by considering such papers in the future, and indeed, are actively interested in encouraging contributions that either in authorship or content are not predominantly white, Eurocentric, or Christian (or post-Christian). Yet, as much as these volumes may reflect deeper structural biases at play in the contemporary scholarly world, each chapter makes an original and rigorous contribution to an important and emerging field, and these silences simply highlight the exciting work to done.

In what follows, we briefly stake out the current anarchism and religious studies landscape, and introduce the essays included in this volume.

Tentatively mapping the territory

The overlap between anarchism and religion can be studied in many ways, addressing different questions and using different methodologies rooted in different disciplinary conventions. While a detailed heuristic taxonomy of this burgeoning scholarship can be found elsewhere, a condensed summary nevertheless offers a useful compass.[7] Without meaning to force a limiting set of categories on to this literature, and noting that there are publications falling outside of this tentative classification, there seems to be four principal types of analysis typical in the scholarship examining the relation between anarchism and religion: anarchist critiques of religion, anarchist exegesis, anarchist theology, and histories of religious anarchists.

An anarchist critique of religion is apparent even in the earliest days of anarchism as a political tradition, and has tended to attack both religious claims and religious institutions.[8] The anarchist theoretician Peter Kropotkin is a quintessential example of this approach, portraying religious belief as an obstacle to a critical consciousness of social oppression, and depicting the organised church as a key ally of the nation-state in its efforts to dominate social life in the modern era.[9] The social role of religion has undergone significant transformations since the nineteenth century, but rarely have these changes been sufficient to convince anarchist critics that this critique is redundant. Even in Western

Europe where secularisation is most pronounced, religious institutions and religious mindsets continue to play important roles in public life, whether through moral conventions, established traditions or new spiritual and religious perspectives. For many anarchists, many criticisms of religion therefore still stand. Anarchists have thus condemned religion as, for instance: a source of inequality and suffering; a deluded and incoherent lie harmful to rational self-awareness; a hypnotic deception distracting the masses from revolutionary consciousness; an unnecessary, and perhaps harmful, basis for morality; an institution complicit in the perpetuation of injustice and slavery; and a residue from an arcane past. Yet not all anarchists have been this hostile, with some seeing positive elements in at least some religious claims and values, and acknowledging the contributions of dissenting religious groups who have challenged their orthodox counterparts.[10] Indeed many religious anarchists have themselves articulated sharp criticisms of religion, sometimes exhibiting a zealous anticlericalism of their own. All these anarchist critiques, and indeed any religious counter-arguments, constitute one category of analysis in the area.

The second principal category, religious exegesis, is not unconnected to the anarchist critique in that anticlerical arguments by religious anarchists have often been based precisely on the interpretation of religious scripture. Anarchist exegesis, however, does not stop with the development of anticlerical arguments. There are numerous examples of religious texts being interpreted as implying either direct or implicit criticism of the state, capitalism or other structures of oppression. At the same time, the focus of anarchist exegesis has more often been the *state* (and to some extent the church) rather than other oppressive structures or phenomena. Leo Tolstoy and Jacques Ellul are the most cited authors of such anarchist exegeses, though there are many others who each bring different angles of interpretation and focus on different varieties of scriptural texts. Many of those authors have been weaved together to articulate a more generic anarchist exegesis of Christian scripture in, for example, *Christian Anarchism: A Political Commentary on the Gospel.*[11] Yet there are many more anarchist interpretations of religious texts, many of which have been published in recent years, and not only with a Christian focus.[12] This category of analysis is vibrant in both religious and scholarly circles.

When religious communities have discussions on themes and issues as varied as war, poverty, injustice, charity and democracy, however, they do not necessarily always refer back to scripture. In other words, religious discussions are obviously not always reduced to exegesis, and those having discussions about social, political and economic issues based on their religious worldview will still use the grammar and referents of their religious tradition to articulate their reflections. When those religious reflections develop anarchist tropes, arguments or conclusions, what emerges is anarchist theology, the third category of analysis bridging anarchism and religion. The boundary between anarchist exegesis and anarchist theology is not rigid: theological discussions might evoke religious texts (without making these the sole basis of analysis) and exegetical discussions might develop broader reflections on social and political themes (without losing sight of scripture), but these remain rather different modes of inquiry, each with their anarchist advocates. Scholarly discussion of anarchist theology has been rarer than anarchist exegesis, yet the potential for anarchist theology is vast, and there is exciting research underway in this field.

Finally, there is also a defined strand of research, primarily historical, focusing on the lives and ideas of religious anarchist individuals and groups. The form of these enquiries varies considerably, from biographical investigations seeking to recover the activities of neglected figures from the tradition of religious anarchism, to the analysis of religious communities, and the dissection of currents of thought, identification of overlooked genealogies, and ideological filiations. As this implies, the sub-disciplines that characterise modern historical practice often cast a distinctive light on the intersections of religion and anarchism. It is a field populated by the intellectual, cultural, and social historian, as much as the historian of political thought and the historian of religion. What they share is a concern to recover, uncover or discuss the histories of religious anarchists and those who come close to fitting such a label.

It is worth noting that this tentative taxonomy, despite aiming to cover much of the area, does not in fact cover all possible approaches. Nor are these four categories mutually exclusive. Many studies in the present volume fruitfully combine elements of more than one category, and others take an approach that does not fit neatly into any of these traditions. Justin Meggitt's chapter, for instance, belongs primarily to the field of Bible studies – not quite exegesis, history or theology, yet arguably containing elements of each. There are also those such as Simon Critchley who adopt a Schmittian take on 'political theology' (where political discourses and institutions are understood as secularised theological ones) yet still discuss discernibly religious and anarchist themes – a case perhaps of anarchist theology, but not in the sense of 'theology' familiar to most theologians.[13] Or, to cite another example, there are interventions that read more as tracts, polemics or *plaidoyers*, perhaps eschewing a rigorously academic framework their authors consider constricting. These too are neither exegetical nor strictly theological in the traditional sense, yet they seek to develop and interrogate religious anarchist arguments from unconventional perspectives. This categorisation of *plaidoyer* is not intended to dismiss work that rejects the conventions of academic analysis, but, as a landmark on our tentative map of the territory, demonstrates the range of research currently underway examining the relationship between anarchist and religious ideas.

Our aim is to foster scholarly work on any of the above categories in a spirit of critical dialogue that is open to a range of perspectives not necessarily limited to the taxonomy outlined here. This also explains the sheer diversity of approaches, directions and methodologies in this volume. It also explains why some texts seem partly driven by an activist interest, and we recognise no problem in this method if the argument is rigorous. Our only criteria for us to consider a text for this project are that such work should examine the vexed overlap between religion and anarchism, and that it can pass the test academic peer-review. Of particular interest for the future, since particularly understudied thus far, are studies that deal with religions other than Christianity; analysis by authors outside the privileged demographic of white European males; further studies and reflections in anarchist theology; discussions of core accusations between anarchism and religion; and unwritten histories of important religious anarchists.

One of the surprises of working in this area is the true diversity of original research on religious anarchism, especially when these studies have emerged from different disciplinary areas and methodologies. Our aim with this multi-volume collection is to foster this variety, not encage it within a single direction or methodology.

How this book emerged

This book has a predecessor. The first major international conference organised by the then recently-founded ASN (as a specialist group of the United Kingdom's Political Studies Association) was held in Loughborough University in 2008. Out of a stream of that conference emerged *Religious Anarchism: New Perspectives*, a book which is unfortunately not available in open access and the chapters of which, although closely reviewed by its editor and peer-reviewed by the publisher, were ultimately not submitted to as rigorous a peer-reviewing process as the present book.[14]

All the essays in *this* volume have gone through such a process. There are many more papers still in the metaphorical pipeline, so we expect at least two more volumes in this collection – hopefully more if the volumes generate further interest. Any potential author interested in submitting a paper for consideration can contact either of the editors.

The essays in this volume

This first volume contains seven chapters of original scholarship on a variety of themes. Few are confined neatly to one of the aforementioned categories of analysis: most offer a range of perspectives and are inspired by diverse disciplinary approaches. Some are primarily historical interventions (Pauli, Blanes), others engage with anarchist theology by reflecting on notorious religious and anarchist thinkers (Podmore). Another considers the mystical anarchism of two thinkers not typically classed as religious anarchists (Hoppen), while one paper blends exegesis and history (Galvan-Alvarez). Other papers are rooted in Bible studies (Meggitt), and the last offers a philosophical discussion of the relevance of a particular anarchist critique of religion (Strandberg).

The first paper in this volume, by Benjamin Pauli, examines a group perhaps not unfamiliar to those with an interest in anarchist history: the Catholic Worker community. Founded in the United States by Dorothy Day and Peter Maurin in the early 1930s, in Pauli's analysis the group exemplifies the seeming tension at the heart of the overlap between religious ideas and anarchist politics: reconciling a religious faith apparently weighted down by a history of authoritarianism, with a politics whose first principle is a repudiation of hierarchy. Viewing the Catholic Worker movement through the lens of 'exemplarity', Pauli sees in Day and Maurin's efforts to offer leadership through the power of example rather than coercion, an intriguing model of political action directly inspired by an interpretation of central figures in the Christian pantheon. Rather than its Catholicism mutilating its anarchism, Pauli sees the Catholic Worker's religious attachments as 'enhancing' its anarchism, a reading that, he contends, is important even to those anarchist theorists who regard the claims of religion with scepticism.

In his contribution, Ruy Blanes similarly investigates how a specific historical moment in the history of Christianity, and a particular cultural manifestation of organised religious practice, was imbued with essentially anarchistic values. The Tokoist Church, which rose to prominence in the 1960s and 1970s in Angola as it became a key actor in the fight against Portuguese colonialism, continued this oppositional role as a critique of the country's post-independence People's Movement for the Liberation of Angola (MPLA) government. Offering a history of Simão or Simao Toko and his followers, Blanes examines the problems associated with peremptory rejection of religion that is characteristic of many anarchists, when the religious group itself initially embodied many anarchist principles: a commitment to horizontalism, a communal approach to leadership, faith in the powers of mutualism, and a burning desire to fight the forces of colonialism. At the same time, Blanes traces the process of 'hierarchization' that confronted the Tokoist movement, examining how these early principles were co-opted, and now often serve as fetters to 'processes of ideological and institutional innovation'.

Just as Blanes' contribution looks to the illumination of a fascinating but relatively unknown history as a means of interrogating the connections between anarchist politics and religion, Enrique Galván-Álvarez's chapter looks much further back, to Japan in the twelfth and thirteenth centuries, with a similar ambition. With the Buddhism of Shinran Shonin in mind, Galván-Álvarez looks to this tradition of Buddhist thought as especially relevant to contemporary anarchist practice. Through an analysis of Shinran's neglected writings, which offered a radical reading of the established sources of Buddhism, he sees Shinran offering a searching critique of political and religious hierarchies that has not only been neglected by historians, but retains its relevance nine centuries later as a fillip to those seeking to challenge hegemonic political forces.

Justin Meggitt's chapter interrogates the claim that 'Jesus was an anarchist' through a highly detailed exploration of both the history of anarchist thought, and a close reading of scriptural sources. Accepting the difficulties imposed by the heated debates concerning the very meaning of the label 'anarchist', and the issue of anachronism that might imperil efforts to associate Jesus with a political movement that emerged from social concerns and intellectual currents unleashed by industrial modernity, Meggitt nevertheless argues that there are good grounds for seeing Jesus through the lens of anarchism. Looking to Jesus' critique of existing power relations, and his quest for egalitarian and prefigurative forms of social life, Meggitt argues, echoing the reasoning of the anarchist Alexander Berkman, that Jesus was indeed an anarchist.

While Meggitt's contribution to this volume is notable for examining the perhaps unexpected connections between the historical Jesus and the anarchist tradition, Franziska Hoppen's chapter similarly sketches an original comparison in the work of two thinkers: Gustav Landauer and Eric Voegelin. Landauer's position in the anarchist canon is not in doubt, and his insightful and novel efforts to rethink the central claims of anarchist politics, while drawing on an idiosyncratic mysticism, are well established. Voegelin, however, a German academic with an interest in totalitarianism and political violence, is probably more unfamiliar to those inspecting the fault lines between anarchist theory and religious studies. This, Hoppen proposes, is a mistake, for considering the 'mystical anarchism' of Landauer and Voegelin in tandem reveals common threads in their vision of an 'anti-political community', in which the self is both a 'primary reality' and the starting point 'in the struggle for change'.

In this spirit of novel comparisons, the sixth chapter, written by Simon Podmore, unites the Danish philosopher and theologian Søren Kierkegaard with Pierre-Joseph Proudhon, the first thinker to wear the label of 'anarchist' as a badge of honour rather than a term of abuse. Podmore's paper reflects on the affinities between the two thinkers' negation of God and their paradoxical assertions about God implicit in that negation. Their anti-theism is thus compared and contrasted, showing that where Proudhon settles on the need to insist on the negation of the idea of 'God' in order to achieve justice, Kierkegaard's negation of God leads him to a *theological* affirmation of freedom. Juxtaposing these rather different thinkers therefore exposes interesting philosophical and theological parallels and differences.

Finally, Hugo Strandberg looks to another familiar figure in the anarchist pantheon, the German individualist Max Stirner, and uses his ideas to ponder the issue of whether religious belief demands servitude. He argues that, on reflection, it is egoism rather than religion which forces self-denial, because the egoist must harden their heart and renounce any social concern for others to submit to Stirner's ideal, whereas religion does not *necessarily* require servitude in submission to God, and can in principle be understood to affirm a kind of freedom primary to any political or religious institutions.

As this selection of papers demonstrates, there is an astounding intellectual vibrancy at the heart of contemporary scholarship on anarchism and religion. The range of perspectives encompassed in these contributions, their inherent interdisciplinarity, and the rich variety of thinkers, movements and ideas examined, all highlight the health of the field. Editing these papers and the many more to come in future volumes was both an intellectually stimulating and pleasurable experience, and we hope that readers will gain as much from them as we have.

Alexandre Christoyannopoulos &
Matthew S. Adams, September 2016

Notes

1. The literature on each of these is vast. For the resurgence of religion in politics, see for instance: Peter L. Berger, ed. *The Desecularization of the World: Resurgent Religion and World Politics* (Washington: W. B. Eerdmans, 1999); José Casanova, *Public Religions in the Modern World* (Chicago: University of Chicago Press, 1994); Jonathan Fox, *An Introduction to Religion and Politics: Theory and Practice* (Oxon: Routledge, 2013); Jeffrey Haynes, *An Introduction to International Relations and Religion* (Harrow: Pearson, 2007); Jeffrey Haynes, ed. *Routledge Handbook of Religion and Politics* (London: Routledge, 2009); Luca Mavelli and Fabio Petito, "The Postsecular in International Relations: An Overview," *Review of International Studies* 38, no. 5 (2012). For anarchist studies, see for instance: Uri Gordon, *Anarchy Alive!: Anti-Authoritarian Politics from Practice to Theory* (London: Pluto, 2008); Nathan J. Jun and Shane Wahl, eds., *New Perspectives on Anarchism* (Lanham, MD: Lexington, 2009); Ruth Kinna, ed. *The Continuum Companion to Anarchism* (London: Continuum, 2012); Carl Levy and Saul Newman, eds., *The Anarchist Imagination: Anarchism Encounters the Humanities and Social Sciences* (Routledge, forthcoming); Jonathan Purkis and James Bowen, eds., *Twenty-First Century Anarchism: Unorthodox Ideas for a New Millennium* (London: Continuum, 1997); Jonathan Purkis and James Bowen, eds., *Changing Anarchism: Anarchist Theory and Practice in a Global Age* (Manchester: Manchester University Press, 2004); Duane Rousselle and Süreyyya Evren, eds., *Post-Anarchism: A Reader* (London: Pluto, 2011).

2. For instance: Alexandre Christoyannopoulos, ed. *Religious Anarchism: New Perspectives* (Newcastle upon Tyne: Cambridge Scholars Publishing, 2009); Alexandre Christoyannopoulos, *Christian Anarchism: A Political Commentary on the Gospel* (Exeter: Imprint Academic, 2010); Alexandre Christoyannopoulos, "Religious Studies and Anarchism," in *The Anarchist Imagination: Anarchism Encounters the Humanities and the Social Sciences*, ed. Carl Levy and Saul Newman (tbc: Routledge, forthcoming); John A. Rapp, *Daoism and Anarchism: Critiques of State Autonomy in Ancient and Modern China*, Contemporary Anarchist Studies (London: Continuum, 2012); Mark Van Steenwyk, *That Holy Anarchist: Reflections on Christianity and Anarchism* (Minneapolis: Missio Dei, 2012);

A. Terrance Wiley, *Angelic Troublemakers: Religion and Anarchism in America*, ed. Laurence Davis, et al., Contemporary Anarchist Studies (London: Continuum, 2014); Tripp York, *Living on Hope While Living in Babylon: The Christian Anarchists of the Twentieth Century* (Cambridge: Lutterworth, 2009).

3. A full discussion and bibliography are available in Christoyannopoulos, "Religious Studies and Anarchism."; Alexandre Christoyannopoulos and Lara Apps, "Anarchism and Religion," in *A Companion to Anarchist Philosophy*, ed. Nathan Jun (tbc: Brill, forthcoming).

4. The Spanish Civil War provides the most frequently evoked case in point. On that, see for instance Manuel Pérez Ledesma, "Studies on Anticlericalism in Contemporary Spain," *International Review of Social History* 46, no. 02 (2001).

5. Michael Freeden, *Ideologies and Political Theory: A Conceptual Approach* (Oxford: Oxford University Press, 2008); Ruth Kinna, *Anarchism: A Beginner's Guide* (Oxford: Oneworld, 2005); David Miller, *Anarchism* (London: J. M. Dent, 1984).

6. For example: Harold B. Barclay, "Islam, Muslim Societies and Anarchy," *Anarchist Studies* 10, no. 1 (2002); Amedeo Bertolo, ed. *L'anarchico E L'ebreo: Storia Di Un Incontro* (Milan: Elèuthera, 2001); Furio Biagini, *Nati Altrove: Il Movimento Anarchico Ebraico Tra Mosca E New York* (Pisa: Biblioteca F. Serantini, 1998); Anthony T. Fiscella, "Imagining an Islamic Anarchism: A New Field of Study Is Ploughed," in *Religious Anarchism: New Perspectives*, ed. Alexandre Christoyannopoulos (Newcastle upon Tyne: Cambridge Scholars Publishing, 2009); Abdennur Prado, *El Islam Como Anarquismo Místico* (Barcelona: Virus, 2010); John A. Rapp, "Anarchism or Nihilism: The Buddhist-Influenced Thought of Wu Nengzi," in *Religious Anarchism: New Perspectives*, ed. Alexandre Christoyannopoulos (Newcastle upon Tyne: Cambridge Scholars Publishing, 2009); Rapp, *Daoism and Anarchism*; Kerry Thornley, "Zenarchy," IllumiNet Press and Impropaganda, http://www.impropa ganda.net/1997/zenarchy.html; Michael T. Van Dyke, "Kenneth Rexroth's Integrative Vision: Anarchism, Poetry, and the Religious Experience in Post-World War Ii San Francisco," in *Religious Anarchism: New Perspectives*, ed. Alexandre Christoyannopoulos

(Newcastle upon Tyne: Cambridge Scholars Publishing, 2009); Mohamed Jean Veneuse, "To Be Condemned to a Clinic: The Birth of the Anarca-Islamic Clinic," in *Religious Anarchism: New Perspectives*, ed. Alexandre Christoyannopoulos (Newcastle upon Tyne: Cambridge Scholars Publishing, 2009).

7. Christoyannopoulos, "Religious Studies and Anarchism."; Christoyannopoulos and Apps, "Anarchism and Religion."

8. For example, see: Mikhail Bakunin, *God and the State* (New York: Dover, 1970); Harold Barclay, "Anarchist Confrontations with Religion," in *New Perspectives on Anarchism*, ed. Nathan Jun and Shane Wahl (Lanham, MD: Lexington, 2010); Sébastien Faure, "Does God Exist? Twelve Proofs of the Non-Existence of God," The Anarchist Library, http://theanarchistlibrary.org/library/sebastien-faure-does-god-exist; Johann Most, "The God Pestilence," Anarchy Archives, http://dwardmac.pitzer.edu/Anarchist_Archives/bright/most/godpest.html; Nicolas Walter, "Anarchism and Religion," *The Raven: anarchist quarterly 25* 7, no. 1 (1994).

9. For this, consider: Matthew S. Adams, *Kropotkin, Read, and the Intellectual History of British Anarchism: Between Reason and Romanticism* (Basingstoke: Palgrave Macmillan, 2015), 54–56, 87–88.

10. For example: Barclay, "Anarchist Confrontations with Religion."; Gérard Bessière, *Jésus Selon Proudhon: La « Messianose » Et La Naissance Du Christianisme* (Paris: Cerf, 2007); John Clark, "Anarchism," in *Encyclopedia of Religion and Nature*, ed. Bron Taylor (London: Continuum, 2005); Peter Kropotkin, "'Anarchism'," Encyclopaedia Britannica, http://dwardmac.pitzer.edu/Anarchist_Archives/Kropotkin/britanniaanarchy.html.

11. Christoyannopoulos, *Christian Anarchism*.

12. See, for instance, the many sources listed in "Religious Studies and Anarchism."; Christoyannopoulos and Apps, "Anarchism and Religion."

13. Simon Critchley, "Mystical Anarchism," *Critical Horizons: A Journal of Philosophy and Social Theory* 10, no. 2 (2009); Ted Troxell, "Christian Theory: Postanarchism, Theology, and John Howard Yoder," *Journal for the Study of Radicalism* 7, no. 1 (2013).

14. Christoyannopoulos, ed. *Religious Anarchism*.

References

Adams, Matthew S. *Kropotkin, Read, and the Intellectual History of British Anarchism: Between Reason and Romanticism.* Basingstoke: Palgrave Macmillan, 2015.

Bakunin, Mikhail. *God and the State.* New York: Dover, 1970.

Barclay, Harold. "Anarchist Confrontations with Religion." In *New Perspectives on Anarchism,* edited by Nathan Jun and Shane Wahl, 169–85. Lanham, MD: Lexington, 2010.

Barclay, Harold B. "Islam, Muslim Societies and Anarchy." *Anarchist Studies* 10, no. 1 (2002): 105–18.

Berger, Peter L., ed. *The Desecularization of the World: Resurgent Religion and World Politics.* Washington: W. B. Eerdmans, 1999.

Bertolo, Amedeo, ed. *L'anarchico E L'ebreo: Storia Di Un Incontro.* Milan: Elèuthera, 2001.

Bessière, Gérard. *Jésus Selon Proudhon: La « Messianose » Et La Naissance Du Christianisme.* Paris: Cerf, 2007.

Biagini, Furio. *Nati Altrove: Il Movimento Anarchico Ebraico Tra Mosca E New York.* Pisa: Biblioteca F. Serantini, 1998.

Casanova, José. *Public Religions in the Modern World.* Chicago: University of Chicago Press, 1994.

Christoyannopoulos, Alexandre. *Christian Anarchism: A Political Commentary on the Gospel.* Exeter: Imprint Academic, 2010.

———, ed. *Religious Anarchism: New Perspectives.* Newcastle upon Tyne: Cambridge Scholars Publishing, 2009.

———. "Religious Studies and Anarchism." In *The Anarchist Imagination: Anarchism Encounters the Humanities and the Social Sciences,* edited by Carl Levy and Saul Newman, tbc. tbc: Routledge, 2016.

Christoyannopoulos, Alexandre, and Lara Apps. "Anarchism and Religion." In *A Companion to Anarchist Philosophy,* edited by Nathan Jun, tbc. tbc: Brill, 2016.

Clark, John. "Anarchism." In *Encyclopedia of Religion and Nature,* edited by Bron Taylor, 49–56. London: Continuum, 2005.

Critchley, Simon. "Mystical Anarchism." *Critical Horizons: A Journal of Philosophy and Social Theory* 10, no. 2 (August 2009): 272–306.

Faure, Sébastien. "Does God Exist? Twelve Proofs of the Non-Existence of God." The Anarchist Library, http://theanarchistlibrary.org/library/sebastien-faure-does-god-exist.

Fiscella, Anthony T. "Imagining an Islamic Anarchism: A New Field of Study Is Ploughed." In *Religious Anarchism: New Perspectives*, edited by Alexandre Christoyannopoulos, 280–317. Newcastle upon Tyne: Cambridge Scholars Publishing, 2009.

Fox, Jonathan. *An Introduction to Religion and Politics: Theory and Practice*. Oxon: Routledge, 2013.

Freeden, Michael. *Ideologies and Political Theory: A Conceptual Approach* Oxford: Oxford University Press, 2008.

Gordon, Uri. *Anarchy Alive!: Anti-Authoritarian Politics from Practice to Theory*. London: Pluto, 2008.

Haynes, Jeffrey. *An Introduction to International Relations and Religion*. Harrow: Pearson, 2007.

———, ed. *Routledge Handbook of Religion and Politics*. London: Routledge, 2009.

Jun, Nathan J., and Shane Wahl, eds. *New Perspectives on Anarchism*. Lanham, MD: Lexington, 2009.

Kinna, Ruth. *Anarchism: A Beginner's Guide*. Oxford: Oneworld, 2005.

———, ed. *The Continuum Companion to Anarchism*. London: Continuum, 2012.

Kropotkin, Peter. "'Anarchism'." Encyclopaedia Britannica, http://dwardmac.pitzer.edu/Anarchist_Archives/Kropotkin/britanniaanarchy.html.

Levy, Carl, and Saul Newman, eds. *The Anarchist Imagination: Anarchism Encounters the Humanities and Social Sciences*: Routledge, 2016.

Mavelli, Luca, and Fabio Petito. "The Postsecular in International Relations: An Overview." *Review of International Studies* 38, no. 5 (2012): 931–42.

Miller, David. *Anarchism*. London: J. M. Dent, 1984.

Most, Johann. "The God Pestilence." Anarchy Archives, http://dward mac.pitzer.edu/Anarchist_Archives/bright/most/godpest.html.

Pérez Ledesma, Manuel. "Studies on Anticlericalism in Contemporary Spain." *International Review of Social History* 46, no. 02 (2001): 227–55.

Prado, Abdennur. *El Islam Como Anarquismo Místico*. Barcelona: Virus, 2010.

Purkis, Jonathan, and James Bowen, eds. *Changing Anarchism: Anarchist Theory and Practice in a Global Age*. Manchester: Manchester University Press, 2004.

———, eds. *Twenty-First Century Anarchism: Unorthodox Ideas for a New Millennium*. London: Continuum, 1997.

Rapp, John A. "Anarchism or Nihilism: The Buddhist-Influenced Thought of Wu Nengzi." In *Religious Anarchism: New Perspectives*, edited by Alexandre Christoyannopoulos, 202–25. Newcastle upon Tyne: Cambridge Scholars Publishing, 2009.

———. *Daoism and Anarchism: Critiques of State Autonomy in Ancient and Modern China*. Contemporary Anarchist Studies. London: Continuum, 2012.

Rousselle, Duane, and Süreyya Evren, eds. *Post-Anarchism: A Reader*. London: Pluto, 2011.

Thornley, Kerry. "Zenarchy." IllumiNet Press and Impropaganda, http://www.impropaganda.net/1997/zenarchy.html.

Troxell, Ted. "Christian Theory: Postanarchism, Theology, and John Howard Yoder." *Journal for the Study of Radicalism* 7, no. 1 (2013): 37–60.

Van Dyke, Michael T. "Kenneth Rexroth's Integrative Vision: Anarchism, Poetry, and the Religious Experience in Post-World War Ii San Francisco." In *Religious Anarchism: New Perspectives*, edited by Alexandre Christoyannopoulos, 223–47. Newcastle upon Tyne: Cambridge Scholars Publishing, 2009.

Van Steenwyk, Mark. *That Holy Anarchist: Reflections on Christianity and Anarchism*. Minneapolis: Missio Dei, 2012.

Veneuse, Mohamed Jean. "To Be Condemned to a Clinic: The Birth of the Anarca-Islamic Clinic." In *Religious Anarchism: New Perspectives*, edited by Alexandre Christoyannopoulos, 249–79. Newcastle upon Tyne: Cambridge Scholars Publishing, 2009.

Walter, Nicolas. "Anarchism and Religion." *The Raven: anarchist quarterly 25* 7, no. 1 (Spring 1994): 3–9.

Wiley, A. Terrance. *Angelic Troublemakers: Religion and Anarchism in America*. Contemporary Anarchist Studies. edited by Laurence Davis, Nathan Jun, Uri Gordon and William Alexander Prichard London: Continuum, 2014.

York, Tripp. *Living on Hope While Living in Babylon: The Christian Anarchists of the Twentieth Century*. Cambridge: Lutterworth, 2009.

The Catholic Worker, Dorothy Day, and Exemplary Anarchism

Benjamin J. Pauli

Kettering University, USA

The Catholic Worker movement's fusion of anarchism and Catholicism is one of the most unusual hybrids in the history of the anarchist tradition and is sometimes dismissed as paradoxical or contradictory. In arguing that the pairing of these influences is not as counter-intuitive as it appears at first glance, this chapter seeks to explain the elective affinity of anarchism and Catholicism through the concept of exemplarity. The vision for the Catholic Worker devised by its founders Peter Maurin and Dorothy Day was, I argue, informed by interpretations of central Christian figures like Christ, the saints, and the "holy fool" that placed special emphasis on their exemplary qualities. Maurin and Day saw in the Catholic tradition of exemplarity a means of exercising leadership and authority through the power of examples and voluntary emulation rather than coercion, and within the context of the Catholic Worker movement the exemplary influence of Day in particular helped to reconcile the movement's need for coherence and direction with the autonomy and dignity of its members. In highlighting the Catholic Worker's "exemplary anarchism," this chapter not only reveals one of the ways in which the Worker's Catholicism actually enhanced its anarchism, but also points to the broader relevance of the concept of exemplarity to anarchist theory.

"I'm like everyone else: I admire people who have become outstanding."

—Dorothy Day

If one wanted to illustrate the proposition, recounted by Noam Chomsky in his introduction to Daniel Guerin's *Anarchism*, that

How to cite this book chapter:
Pauli, B. J. 2017. The Catholic Worker, Dorothy Day, and Exemplary Anarchism. In: Christoyannopoulos, A. and Adams, M. S. (eds.) *Essays in Anarchism and Religion: Volume 1.* Pp. 18–50. Stockholm: Stockholm University Press. DOI: https://doi.org/10.16993/bak.b. License: CC-BY

"anarchism has a broad back, like paper it endures anything," one could hardly do better than to point to the existence of the Catholic Worker movement.[1] Launched by Dorothy Day and Peter Maurin on May 1, 1933, when the first issue of the *Catholic Worker* was distributed to bemused radicals assembled in Union Square, Manhattan, the Catholic Worker movement has from its inception fused an anarchist sensibility with intense Catholic piety. Effecting that unlikely pairing required, to use the term employed by one of the movement's most perceptive scholars, nothing less than "inventing" Catholic radicalism in the United States, where Social Gospel Protestants had a near monopoly on faith-based social activism in the early 20th century.[2] If the mystery of its very existence were not enough, the unusual longevity of the Catholic Worker raises questions as to what deeper lessons about social movements might be contained in the Worker's seemingly idiosyncratic synthesis of disparate influences.

By no means can those lessons be illuminated comprehensively in the space of this chapter. Instead, in what follows I will attempt to draw attention to a feature of the movement that has garnered much comment but little systematic exposition, a feature that goes some way towards explaining how the Worker was able to find an affinity between anarchist ideas and a specifically Catholic version of the Christian faith. The concept that will underpin this discussion is the concept of "exemplarity," a concept whose flagging philosophical reputation has begun to revive thanks to recent scholarly work on the subject in the areas of philosophy, literary criticism, rhetoric, pedagogy, and legal studies.[3] Exemplarity, I will argue, played an instrumental role in shaping the Catholic Worker movement's self-conception and determining the manner of the movement's operation. After offering a brief history of the idea of exemplarity from its roots in ancient philosophy, history, and rhetoric to its incorporation into Christianity, I will examine its place in the founding vision for the Catholic Worker as fleshed out by Dorothy Day and Peter Maurin in the early 1930s. The ideal of contemporary sainthood that informed the Worker's activities was, I maintain, informed by interpretations of central Christian figures like Christ, the saints, and the figure of the "holy fool" that placed special emphasis on their exemplary qualities. I will then consider whether Day, the Worker's *de facto* leader, consistently adhered to the logic of exemplarity in her exercise of authority within the movement, given her reputation for authoritarianism and her occasional assertions of direct control over the New York Catholic Worker community and newspaper. Finally, I will argue that in a number of important respects the idea of exemplarity provides a more satisfactory framework than the Weberian theory of "charismatic" leadership for assessing Day's influence over the movement and the continued flourishing of the movement after her death.

In the course of this discussion I hope to deepen our understanding of the relationship of the Catholic Worker to the anarchist tradition by outlining one of the ways in which the Worker's Catholic faith was not, from an anarchist perspective, a liability but rather a resource. Most importantly, the connection to the exemplary tradition provided by Catholicism suggested a means of exercising leadership and authority through the power of examples and voluntary emulation rather than coercion. In this way, exemplarity brought to the movement coherence and direction that it might not otherwise have possessed, without compromising the autonomy and dignity of the movement's members. In highlighting the ability of exemplarity to reconcile these sometimes-competing priorities, I hope to use the example of the Catholic Worker movement to suggest some larger lessons for anarchist thought and practice.

The Christian *exemplum*

Although the concept of exemplarity found fertile soil in the Christian tradition, it did not originate there. In Greek thought it can be discerned in the notion of the *paradeigma*, a term first invested with philosophical significance by Plato. For Plato, *paradeigma* referred to a model derived from the transcendent Forms at the centre of his ontology. He used the term to connote a top-down, general-to-particular relationship involving the appearance of divine qualities in the world of phenomena, although sensible objects could partake of the Forms only imperfectly.[4] In Aristotle's work on rhetoric, by contrast, the idea of *paradeigma* was treated inductively, as a particular from which general conclusions could be derived.[5] The latter sense of the term, which gave *paradeigma* a functional role independent of larger ontological claims, was not far removed from the way in which early Greek historians like Herodotus and Thucydides began to conceive of the import of historical examples. In his *History of the Peloponnesian War*, Thucydides first made explicit an idea at best implicit in Herodotus' *Histories*: the study of history had utility in the present because it allowed one to learn from the examples—both good and bad—of one's historical predecessors, and to act with prudence in confronting situations similar to those they faced.[6] Later historians like Xenophon and Ephorus gave *paradeigma* an even more prominent role in their work by introducing an extradiegetic authorial voice meant to identify exemplary conduct unambiguously and ensure that it would be recognized as such by the reader. This innovation was increasingly put in the service of didactic and moralistic aims by the Greek historian Polybius, as well as historians of ancient Rome like Livy, for whom the Latin term corresponding to *paradeigma* was *exemplum*.[7] Aside from the prominent place accorded *exempla* in ancient histories, orators like Cicero helped to make *exempla* a standard feature of Roman rhetoric.[8]

In Roman thought and culture, the idea of the *exemplum* was closely linked to the figure that modern parlance knows as the *exemplar*, an individual whose body of accomplishments as a whole is considered exemplary and worthy of emulation. Romans memorialized great personages in a manner that linked their great deeds to an underlying greatness of character, as reflected in physical monuments like public statuary and *imagines* (images of ancestors displayed in the atria of noble residences), which often touted the high points of the individual's résumé in pictorial or even list form. Exemplarity became intertwined not just with specific acts, but with the overarching biographies of exceptional people, setting the stage for the exemplary personal narratives later associated with the venerated figures of Christendom. Unsurprisingly, given the dominant values of Roman society, *exemplars* tended to be revered politicians and military leaders, national heroes whose most admirable actions involved the subordination of self and personal relationships to patriotic duty. Despite the fact that these figures were, in some sense, prototypes for the Christian *exemplar*, the nationalistic morality they embodied was roundly excoriated by early Christians like Augustine, whose interpretation of the *exempla virtutis* emphasized allegiance to a transcendent order beyond the *saeculum*.[9]

Christians may have been critical of the particular ways in which exemplarity was manifested in pagan thought and culture, but the idea of exemplarity itself thrived within Christianity. For Christians, writes Peter Brown, "God Himself was proposed to man as the Exemplar behind all exemplars."[10] The exemplary relationship of God to man was facilitated by the idea that God, for all of His omniscience and omnipotence, was not an absolute Other to humanity. The creation myths of the early Hebrew Bible bequeathed to Christians the idea that human beings had been made in God's image and raised the prospect of a godly original condition or essential nature that could be discerned and promoted even within the context of a fallen world. "The result of this view," Brown continues, "was to present human history as containing a sequence of exemplars, each of which made real, at varying times and in varying degrees, the awesome potentiality of the first model of humanity." While precedents can be identified in the prophetic tradition of the Christian Old Testament, the gospel narratives brought this idea of exemplarity to its climax in the figure of Jesus Christ, in whom "the original beauty of Adam… blazed forth."[11] The precise nature of Christ—the relationship of His divine qualities to His human qualities—was of course one of the prickliest controversies within the early Church, and the significance of Christ's deeds was interpreted differently depending on where one placed emphasis. But as early as the Epistles of Paul there was suggestion that Christ's example was meant to be imitated by ordinary Christians: "Follow my example," Paul exhorted the Corinthians, "as I follow Christ's."[12] According to this conception of examples building upon examples, an apostolic disciple of Christ like Paul was, as John Howard Yoder writes, "merely an exemplary follower of the true example."[13]

Paul's words capture both the foundational quality of exemplarity within Christianity—Christ conceived, henceforth, as the ultimate exemplar, a point of reference for all who follow Him—and the self-replicating quality of *exempla*, in which present *exempla* spawn future *exempla* by referring back to past *exempla* (even Christ Himself referred back to the "perfection" of the "heavenly Father").[14] The proliferation of stories of saints in the Middle Ages attested to the potency of the exemplary idea, particularly among laypeople, for whom the vividness of a saintly example offered a concrete means of engaging with the teachings of the Church. In these stories, Christian principles were not transmitted in a dry, legalistic manner but instead embodied and dramatized in order to produce a visceral impact. It is probable, however, that the concretization of exemplarity in the tangible *deeds* of specific persons whose humanness was less in question than Christ's owed its appeal not only to its ability to make Christian doctrine more accessible, but to its vaguely subversive, anti-clerical quality. The *exempla* presented instances of self-sacrificing religious authenticity—sometimes associated with figures outside of the Church hierarchy—that were often meant to contrast with the privileged and hypocritical lives led by many Church officials. The *exempla* celebrated individual integrity rather than institutional position, proposing that individual holiness be judged on the basis of the way of life one adopted rather than the external trappings of religious authority. Accordingly, medieval authors like Chaucer and Gower placed emphasis on exemplarity "as doing, as *factum*, rather than *dictum*," a prioritization of *praxis* that the saints shared—or so it was claimed—with Christ. As Larry Scanlon explains, "If even Christ's *dicta* depend on his *facta,* then the textual authority of the clergy must always be secondary to their actual piety as a group of historical individuals." By this measure, most clergy did not merit the level of respect bestowed upon them.[15]

As has already been demonstrated, there were always grounds within the Christian tradition for putting stress on the similarities between God and His creation, between God's son and the creatures He was sent to redeem. Undoubtedly, the existence of these similarities helped to make plausible the suggestion that the characteristics and actions of God and Son stood in an exemplary relation to humanity, providing targets for aspiration and guides for action rather than being prohibitively transcendent. Nevertheless, until the rise of the mendicant orders in the 13th century, there was a general tendency to treat the idea of exemplarity metaphorically, to see in exceptional behaviour a moral lesson perhaps, but also the presence of something which, for the average person, was unreachably divine. As Christ began to be conceptualized less as an impossibly exalted, quasi-supernatural figure and more as the most perfect human being who ever lived, the idea that other human beings could live in "imitation" of Him became more influential. Figures like Saint Francis of Assisi adopted a more literal interpretation of what it meant to "imitate" Christ, aspiring not only to live up to His moral vision, but to replicate His voluntary poverty and His translation of neighbourly love into an *active* principle manifested in an ongoing commitment to good works. The godliness of Francis and those he himself inspired was expressed in a consistent and all-consuming pattern of life.[16]

Aside from what has already been canvassed in this necessarily brief overview, there are three further things to note about the Christian *exemplum* before assessing the way it was taken up by the Catholic Worker. First of all, the moral quality of Christian exemplarity was central—Christian *exempla* united not just universal and particular (as a more technical definition of *exemplum* might connote) but "ought" and "is." They fit that category of exemplarity identified by the critical theorist Alessandro Ferrara as overcoming the "dichotomic view of our world as split between *facts* and *values*, *facts* and *norms*, *Sein* and *Sollen*, *is* and *ought*." Exemplars, from this perspective, are "entities, material or symbolic, that are as they should be, atoms of reconciliation where *is* and *ought* merge and, in so doing, liberate an energy that sparks our imagination."[17] Secondly, it is important to note that within mainstream Christianity the notion of the "imitation" of Christ was invoked not as a binding moral commandment so much as an exemplary ideal. Understandings of just how relevant such an ideal was to everyday people evolved over the course of time. Isolated groups always existed in which individuals attempted to attain a state of Christ-like "perfection," but only gradually did similarly ambitious movements arise (like the Franciscans) that were strong enough to carve out an officially recognized place within the Church. Were we to carry the story of Christian exemplarity beyond the Catholic tradition specifically and into the

19th century, we would find a multiplication of groups aspiring to a Christ-like ideal and the increasing feeling that "sainthood" of a kind was within the reach of any committed practitioner of the Christian faith. Finally, we should highlight the tendency to see in the *exemplum* a kind of *authority* distinct from the law-like authority of Christian doctrine—authority that inspires imitation rather than commanding obedience. In some sense, *exempla* "compel" emulation, but they owe their influence principally to the voluntary actions of those who find their spirits stirred by them, not to feelings of obligation or threats of sanction for noncompliance.

Exemplarity and the origins of the Catholic Worker

There is ample evidence that the tradition of Christian exemplarity described above directly informed Dorothy Day's and Peter Maurin's visions for the Catholic Worker. It is in the nature of examples, however, that they tend to give rise to a multiplicity of interpretations, and it will be necessary not only to show that Day and Maurin found inspiration in the Christian *exempla* but to describe more precisely the manner in which they selectively appropriated the tradition for the sake of the movement. Both Day and Maurin, for instance, saw Christ's example as a model with great relevance to their own activities. But their understanding of His example placed heavy stress on His human qualities and lent credence to their own emphasis on anarchism, decentralism, and active ministry to the poor. Day argued that

> Philosophical anarchism, decentralism, requires that we follow the Gospel precept to be obedient to every living thing: "Be subject therefore to every human creature for God's sake." It means washing the feet of others, as Jesus did at the Last Supper. "You call me Master and Lord," He said, "and rightly so, for that is what I am. Then if I, your Lord have washed your feet, you also ought to wash one another's feet. I have set you an example; you are to do as I have done for you." To serve others, not to seek power over them. Not to dominate, not to judge others.[18]

Maurin, similarly, maintained that "Self-giving love…was the example Christ gave to his followers and was the consistent witness of Christians in the early Church." The implication was that the works of mercy articulated by Christ in Matthew 25 "must again become the Christian way of life."[19] Day's account of the *facta* of Christ's life in her autobiography *The Long Loneliness* highlighted His humble origins, His eschewal of political power, His closeness to the people and concern for their material welfare:

> He was born in a stable…He did not come to be a temporal King… He worked with His hands, spent the first years of His life in exile, and the rest of His early manhood in a crude carpentry shop in Nazareth. He fulfilled His religious duties in the synagogue and the temple. He trod the roads in His public life and the first men He called were fishermen, small owners of boats and nets. He was familiar with the migrant worker and the proletariat, and some of His parables dealt with them. He spoke of the living wage, not equal pay for equal work, in the parable of those who came at the first and the eleventh hour.[20]

Beyond the paramount example of Christ, the subsidiary exemplarity of the saints was frequently referenced by both Day and Maurin. Implicitly gesturing to the broader exemplary tradition, Maurin counselled Day early on in their collaboration that it was "better to know the lives of the saints than the lives of kings and generals."[21] The advice was, perhaps, superfluous: from an early age, Day had been impressed by saintly demonstrations of piety and driven to imitate them. Long before her conversion to Catholicism, Day's response to first hearing the story of a saint was to experiment with sleeping on the floor in her own attempt at asceticism.[22] As Day began to drift towards the Church, she was especially drawn to the life of Teresa of Avila, "a saint with whom [she] readily identified," as Day's biographer puts it.[23] The magnetic effect that Teresa and other saints had on Day was at first largely a consequence of their exemplary devotion, as Day struggled to transition from liberated bohemian to faithful adherent of the Church's teachings.[24] Maurin, however, encouraged Day to view the saints not just as exemplars of personal moral probity but as exemplars of radical social action who had pioneered strategies of translating Christian love into active care for the underprivileged.[25] Maurin helped Day to see that the answer to her well-known question—"Where were the saints to try to change the social order, not just to minister to the slaves but to do away with slavery?"—lay at least in part in forgotten and under-emphasized aspects of the Christian tradition itself.[26]

As important as Maurin's perspective was in encouraging Day to mine the Christian past for unexploded "dynamite," the fuller answer to her question was that the saintly precedents of Christian lore had to inspire analogous saintliness in the present. The movement Day and Maurin hoped to create would require, both realized, modern-day "saints," and although they were hesitant to claim the mantle of sainthood for themselves,[27] they were less reluctant to apply the designation to one another. As Jim Forest writes, Maurin believed that Day "had the potential of becoming a new Saint Catherine of Siena, the outspoken medieval reformer and peace negotiator who had counselled and reprimanded both popes and princes. What Saint Catherine had done in the fourteenth century, Peter believed Dorothy could do in the twentieth."[28] Day, likewise, regarded Maurin, who "lived the poverty he admired in St. Francis," as something of a saint.[29] Maurin's chief importance to the movement, in fact, may have been as an exemplar, as a "religious archetype and symbol."[30] As Mel Piehl explains:

> ultimately, Maurin's most important function for Day was that he provided her—and through her the Catholic Worker movement—with a personal symbol of traditional Catholic spirituality... Because he advocated and lived a life of absolute poverty and generosity based on Catholic ideals, Maurin expressed perfectly Day's most deeply held beliefs about religion and society. His humble appearance and openhearted simplicity brought to mind the saints she knew so well from her studies and suggested that sainthood was a present as well as a past reality.[31]

Day may indeed have had "an intuitive sense of saintliness, even when it came in strange disguises, and an intense desire to see the heroic potential of every person whom she met,"[32] but undoubtedly her exposure to Maurin played a substantial role in leading her to the conclusion that, in her own words, "There are many saints here, there and everywhere and not only the canonized saints that Rome draws to our attention." Referring back to Saint Paul's original call for Christians to live in imitation of Christ, Day held that "saints should be common" because "we are all called to be saints."[33]

As Day and Maurin interpreted them, then, the examples set by the saints were not to be regarded with passive awe but to be consulted as guides, not just by the "leaders" of the Catholic Worker movement, but by its rank-and-file, for whom it was not out of the question to aspire to saintliness in their own lives. The implication was that "the traditional 'counsels of perfection' applied to laypeople as well as to those in religious orders."[34] One means the Worker adopted of inculcating this view was through the sponsorship of annual weeklong retreats, inspired by the retreat movement of the Canadian Jesuit Father Onesimus Lacouture. These retreats

> offered a lofty vision of personal holiness, urging every Christian to aspire to the "counsels of perfection" that mainstream Catholicism enjoined only on members of religious orders. Participants were urged to take the Sermon on the Mount literally—to turn the other cheek and go the second mile—and to give up even minor indulgences if these stood in the way of loving Christ and the poor. In the retreat, Day explained, "We had to aim at perfection; we had to be guided by the folly of the Cross."[35]

Although their aims were in a sense "lofty," however, these retreats helped to convince Day of the wisdom of the "Little Way" advocated by one of her favourite saints, Saint Thérèse of Lisieux, who had modelled the possibility of sanctifying even the smallest and humblest acts. The greatness of Thérèse lay not in superhuman feats but in the plodding consistency with which she consecrated her life to God. While Day had initially been attracted to "spectacular saints who were impossible to imitate," she found in Thérèse a message "obviously meant for each one of us, confronting us with daily duties, simple and small, but constant."[36] The example of Thérèse illustrated the possibility of bridging the lowly and the transcendent within the context of everyday life, of planting modest "seeds" in one's own patch of ground that would ultimately bear fruit far beyond it in myriad, often unexpected ways. This idea was best captured, perhaps, in one of Day's favourite metaphors, the "loaves and fishes" of scripture: "we must lay one brick at a time, take one step at a time; we can be responsible only for the one action of the present moment. But we can beg for an increase of love in our hearts that will vitalize and transform all our individual actions, and know that God will take them and multiply them, as Jesus multiplied the loaves and fishes."[37]

The prospects of divine assistance aside, Day understood that in order for small actions to have this kind of multiplier effect they had to have propagandistic value, for actions cannot qualify as exemplary unless they command the attention of an audience.[38] This meant that some thought had to be given to the image that the Worker projected to those outside the movement. Rather than relying on the simplified, stereotypical imagery of traditional propaganda, however, the Worker consciously courted an image that looked, on the surface, counterintuitive and even contradictory. Workers challenged the idea that cleanliness was next to godliness through their "often ragtag appearance,"[39] they fought to eradicate poverty even as they embraced it themselves, and they preached the need for social action while adopting an approach that was strangely tolerant of failure. The upshot of the Worker's incongruous appearance was that it encouraged spectators to re-evaluate entrenched assumptions about the nature of holiness and the vocation of the saint. Day often appealed to the idea of the "holy fool" to capture this relationship between the quizzical spectator and the spectated.[40] A recurring character type within the Christian tradition sometimes attributed even to Christ Himself,[41] the holy fool is an individual whose outward bearing is contemptuous of social conventions, but whose actions hint at his underlying saintliness and superiority of character. The holy fool has sometimes been interpreted as engaging in wilful deceit, or at the very least in a complex performance meant both to conceal and reveal his true nature.[42] Day clearly liked the implication that immediate appearances can be deceiving, and that it was necessary to look for the deeper meaning in seemingly eccentric and provocative behaviour before passing judgment. There was no component of deliberate concealment in the Worker's actions, however: its departure from accepted notions of propriety was meant—in part, anyway—to expose the ways in which social and cultural conditions worked against genuine godliness, causing saints to appear peculiar, irrelevant, or even threatening. Within the context of the movement, therefore, the holy fool metaphor took on a significance aimed less at the exceptional qualities of the individuals in question, and more at the social structures that made such qualities *appear* exceptional. It also reinforced the "loaves and fishes" idea that the effects of one's actions were not rationally calculable, that the path of saintliness was not, therefore, the path of the so-called "rational actor," who is dependent upon conventional wisdom and focused on attaining immediate, tangible results within existing institutional structures.

Aside from the influence exerted on Day and Maurin by the figures of Christ, the saint, and the holy fool, the philosophy of personalism—a term which, for Maurin in particular, often served as a pithy encapsulation of the Worker's outlook—strengthened their attraction to the idea of exemplarity. While the concept of personalism is too complicated and capacious to be examined in detail here, a few ideas falling under that heading can be singled out as especially relevant. Like the exemplars of the Christian tradition, the notion of the "person," as formulated by early-20th century thinkers like Nikolai Berdyaev and Emmanuel Mounier, united the sacred with the secular. Personalism held that each person, in all of his or her uniqueness, was an absolute end, made in the image of God and therefore not to be sacrificed to any ostensibly "higher" cause. The same love and respect that one bestowed upon God was to be bestowed upon the least of His creatures as well. This helped to explain Day's determination "to meet Christ in the persons who came to her."[43] Personalism fostered a way of seeing that sensitized its exponents to the godly qualities of everyday people and held out the possibility that saintliness could be embodied not simply in abstract principles or Christian folklore but in living flesh and blood, in the here and now.

Aside from encouraging an exemplary way of seeing, personalism encouraged an exemplary way of acting. Rather than offloading social problems like poverty onto the impersonal, bureaucratic apparatus of the welfare state, Workers were expected to address them in a manner that not only established a direct relationship between benefactor and beneficiary (whose human dignity was violated by being termed a "client" or a "case") but that demanded personal sacrifice and fostered personal develop- ment. The Worker saw social change as inseparable from person- al change: thus, "While trying to transform society...a Catholic Worker was engaged in transforming himself as well."[44] The de- velopment of the self in this sense was personalistic rather than individualistic: cultivating the personality was supposed to result, in the words of the French philosopher and Catholic Worker sup- porter Jacques Maritain, in "the generous self of the heroes and saints."[45] The philosophy of personalism helped to enrich, there- fore, the links the Worker posited between exemplary personal qualities, the striving for saintliness in everyday life, and the strug- gle for social change.

Exemplarity, leadership, and authority

If the influence of the exemplary tradition on Day and Maurin has been well documented, less well understood is the relationship between exemplarity and the operation of leadership and author- ity within the Catholic Worker movement. In the third section of this chapter, I will argue that the concept of exemplarity is in many ways more useful than the Weberian concept of "charisma" in capturing these aspects of the movement as well as explaining the movement's ability to sustain itself in the absence of Day, who died in 1980. I hope to demonstrate that the Worker's emphasis on exemplarity created a functional model of leadership and au- thority which, by eschewing domination and coercion in favour of voluntary emulation, helped to reconcile these components of the movement with anarchist principles.

Before exploring these claims, however, it must be admitted that leadership and authority in the Catholic Worker movement were not always exerted in a strictly exemplary fashion, partic- ularly in the case of Day, whose influence was in a number of important instances both direct and, arguably, authoritarian. Day has, in fact, been described as something of a "benevolent dictator."[46] As Catholic Worker John Cort remembered: "I don't think I ever argued with her, so great was her authority among us.

What it came down to was that the Catholic Worker was an extraordinary combination of anarchy and dictatorship."[47] Michael Harrington, a member of the movement as a young man, had a similar impression: "we were living in a community where, whenever we made a decision, we all had a completely democratic, anarchist discussion, and then Dorothy made up her mind. The place was run on a führer concept, and Dorothy was the führer."[48] Day ensured that "certain convictions (pacifism, personalism, the centrality of the works of mercy) prevailed in the Worker publications as non-negotiable and publicly expressed values."[49] It was one of these convictions—pacifism—that inspired Day's most ambitious attempt to exercise control, not only over the New York Catholic Worker community, but over the movement as a whole: unflinching in her commitment to nonviolence during World War II, Day insisted that Catholic Worker communities throughout the country adopt a pacifist position in their publications or disassociate themselves from the movement.

Furthermore, Day often used her influence to ensure that her conservative orientation to Church theology and hierarchy predominated, in form if not in spirit. This was most evident, perhaps, in Day's approach to her role as overseer of the New York *Catholic Worker* paper. Day used this privileged position to supervise the hiring and activities of editors as well as the contributions of writers, closely monitoring the paper's content: "Day allowed her writers and editors creative freedom," Nancy Roberts writes, "but within what she perceived as Catholic Worker principles. She usually screened everything that went into the paper, with few exceptions." Rather than risk a quarrel with the matriarch, many writers resorted to "self-censorship."[50] This meant, for one thing, that no criticism of church officials was to be found in the paper. It also meant that the paper carried many articles espousing traditional roles for women and was prevented from becoming an active advocate for women's liberation after the emergence of the women's movement. Additionally, Day used the paper as a means of promulgating a very conservative view of abortion and birth control, labelling both "genocide."[51]

Finally, Day's *de facto* authority as watchful "mother and grandmother"[52] of the movement meant that "Certain behavioural assumptions pervaded life at the Catholic Worker." She would often chastise people whose conduct she disapproved of, as in the case of Jim Forest, whose "divorce and remarriage in 1967 moved Dorothy to request that Forest remove himself as head of the Catholic Peace Fellowship or she would remove her name from the list of sponsors."[53] On another occasion, she banned alcohol at Peter Maurin Farm. Her most forceful actions, however, consisted of the outright expulsion of individuals from the movement. The most notorious of these episodes took place in 1962, when "there were young people living in Worker house apartments whose standards were so at variance with traditional morality that Dorothy, in one of her moments of a towering righteous anger, threw them all out."[54]

Within her own Worker community in New York, Day's exercise of authority—as has often been remarked—was to a large extent modelled on the monastic role of the abbess, who exercised final sovereignty within an institution whose components functioned more or less autonomously on an everyday level. While many of the criticisms of Day's heavy-handedness by other Workers are undoubtedly justified, any explanation of Day's willingness to vest such authority in herself must take into consideration the fact that she felt a strong personal responsibility for the institutional survival of the New York Catholic Worker. Arguably, it was because Day voluntarily shouldered this burden and the complex and often painful problems of decision-making that came along with it that other figures within the movement—Maurin in particular—were able to lead lives of greater consistency, to adopt more literally "the values of smallness and openness to failure that Day espoused." As Dan McKanan points out, Maurin's "practice, during all the years he was associated with the movement, was simply to outline his 'program' and provide a personal example of a life of scholarship and manual labour, then leave it to others to follow suit or not."[55] Determined to build a movement, Day clearly felt that she could not afford the luxury of perfect exemplarity, and it was in New York more than elsewhere that the instrumentalities of movement-making stood out in her actions and gave them a more controlling aspect. It is crucial to acknowledge with McKanan, however, that whatever truth there is to claims about Day's authoritarian streak, "her authoritarianism had little influence on the movement beyond New York." In fact, "The one time she seriously tried to assert her authority on a national level"—the aforementioned effort to force other Worker communities to adopt a position of absolute pacifism or leave the movement— "the attempt backfired," resulting in a rash of defections by and dissolutions of Worker communities and even the burning of the New York *Catholic Worker*.[56]

However dictatorial some of Day's actions during her "long tenure as charismatic leader" may seem, Piehl is correct to argue that ultimately "the strength of Day's leadership was exercised as much through her role as spiritual writer and exemplar as through her position as head of the movement."[57] What I would like to suggest in evaluating that claim, however, is the utility of making a further distinction, a distinction between the concepts—both of which are invoked by Piehl—of "charisma" and "exemplarity." Piehl is far from alone in attaching the ideas of charisma and charismatic leadership to Day and to the Worker more generally. Aside from one full-length study of this connection,[58] it is frequently invoked in the secondary literature: Day's "charismatic leadership" has been described, for example, as "the glue of the movement," at least during her lifetime.[59] Max Weber's pioneering theory of charismatic leadership and authority—although it has been subjected to much critique and revision—remains the standard point of reference in this literature, and for this reason it is most useful to distinguish the concept of exemplarity from the concept of charisma as understood by Weber.[60]

There are at least three important respects in which Weber's theory of charisma and the concept of exemplarity would seem to be in tension. Firstly, Weber's understanding of charisma puts emphasis on the perception of special qualities in an exceptional individual. He describes charisma as "the surrender to the extraordinary...i.e., actual revelation or grace resting in such a person as a savior, a prophet, or a hero."[61] Charismatic leaders are seen as "the bearers of specific gifts of body and mind" that are so unusual they are "considered 'supernatural' (in the sense that not everybody could have access to them)."[62] Charisma is thus bound up with the specific person who bears it—it is "a highly individual quality" not easily reproduced because inaccessible to most.[63] The corollary of the idea that charisma is a scarce resource is that only a select few will possess the qualifications for leadership, sharply distinguishing them from those over whom they exercise their authority.

Secondly, although Weber gives charisma some strikingly anarchistic features, arguing that it "transforms all values and breaks all traditional and rational norms"[64] and, famously, that it is "the specifically creative revolutionary force of history,"[65] he ultimately makes it a handmaiden to political domination. The portrait Weber paints of the charismatic leader is of a figure who aspires to march at the head of a column of obedient disciples, a figure who out of a special sense of personal mission "seizes the task for which he is destined and demands that others obey and follow him."[66] While the charismatic leader's followers technically sign on to his cause voluntarily, in some sense "it is their *duty* to recognize his charisma."[67] In other words, his superior qualities generate a sense of obligation that takes on a compulsory aspect. The charismatic leader may begin by inspiring others, but he ultimately puts inspiration in the service of command. Weber envisioned this playing out quite literally in the realm of politics, where his personal preference was for strong but plebiscitarian leadership, combining wide executive prerogative with popular appeal. Charisma's political utility, as Weber saw it, was in its ability to secure the consent of the public to the exercise of power by elites and thus obviate the need for the naked exercise of political domination.

Thirdly, Weber saw charisma as inherently unstable and transitory. This was precisely because it is premised on the recognition of unique qualities in individuals. Even when the original charismatic leader is alive, he can only perpetuate his authority by "proving his powers in practice" again and again, by continuously working "miracles"—a feat few are able to sustain indefinitely.[68] When the charismatic leader dies, the group or movement built up around him almost inevitably experiences a severe crisis of succession, a desperate search for a replica of what cannot be replicated. To forestall such crises and ensure their survival, charismatic movements must "transform charisma and charismatic blessing from a unique, transitory gift of grace of extraordinary times and persons into a permanent possession of everyday life."[69] It is for this reason that charisma is subject to perennial decay: charismatic movements attempt to institutionalize the authority associated with the charismatic leader, adopting strategies of rationalization and bureaucratization that make authority stable and transmissible. While the organizations that evolve out of this process may continue to benefit from a lingering charismatic aura, on a day-to-day level their operations look much the same as those of any other rationalized enterprise and generally bear little resemblance to the charismatic leader's original vision.

Each of these three characteristics of charisma can be usefully contrasted with the characteristics I have associated with the concept of exemplarity. While exemplarity proposes that some individuals are especially accomplished, for example, it is less conducive to a rigid distinction between leader and follower, since examples must, in some sense, be accessible to those expected to imitate them. Rather than treating the exemplar as a quasi-divine figure in possession of unique qualities, exemplarity envisions people operating on a more or less equal plane of ability. Exemplarity presumes, in other words, that exceptional people do not have a monopoly on the qualities they exemplify, and that the proper response to exemplary behaviour is not genuflection or obedience, but an effort to discover and develop similar qualities in oneself. Both Day and Maurin, as we have seen, demurred when characterized by others as saints, and, like most exemplars, downplayed their own exemplarity by claiming merely to be imitating even worthier predecessors. Furthermore, they articulated an egalitarianism of aspiration according to which all members of the movement were invited to adopt saintliness as their own ideal. Day went even further, in fact, by consistently highlighting saintly qualities in the actions of figures outside the movement altogether, including the many secular radicals she counted as personal friends.

Exemplarity also differs from Weber's charisma in that it is, by its very nature, less likely to be employed as a means of legitimating domination. The actions of the exemplar, unlike the charismatic leader, have little to do with amassing and commanding followers.[70] The exemplar is generally content to exert an indirect influence, and imitation of the exemplar is voluntary rather than obligatory. The fact that the Catholic Worker used the idea of exemplarity to undermine rather than reinforce differences between leaders and led speaks to the fact that there was no general drive for domination within the movement. Although Day may have abused her authority at times, she also helped to ensure that the Worker remained "a voluntary organization eschewing credo and constitution."[71] Day actively promoted the idea that authority of all kinds—from exemplary authority to the authority of God[72]— must be willingly acceded to by the individuals subject to it, and she explicitly rejected—along with other Workers—the model of command and obedience epitomized by the state.

Finally, while charisma is distinguished by its incessant tendency to decay, exemplarity has a self-proliferating quality: exemplars, as already noted, tend to give rise to new exemplars, while charisma, bottled up in the exceptional few, is less communicable and thus shorter-lived. This fact may help to explain the Catholic Worker's failure to follow the trajectory Weber prophesied for charismatic movements that seek to overcome the mortality of their leaders and the resultant loss of charisma through routinization and bureaucratization. Even before Day's death the Catholic Worker's particular brand of exemplarity, which urged Workers to keep things "small" and to found autonomous communities in response to new needs, made it unusually indisposed to the idea of a large, bureaucratic organization. When Day's health began to decline in the 1970s, the movement did not suddenly abandon its principles in a frantic bid to institutionalize her authority. This is not to suggest that Day's role in the movement had been insignificant in holding things together over the years: her exemplarity did exert a kind of centripetal influence that helped imbue the loosely-organized Worker communities with a sense of common identity and the feeling that they were orbiting, however autonomously, around a common core. But there was no suggestion that the only way for the movement to survive was to become radically more centralized and rule-bound after her death. Rather, the movement has continued to favour centralization of a symbolic rather than an institutional kind. As McKanan notes, what is even more remarkable than the Worker's avoidance of bureaucratization, given its model of organization, is that "it has not simply disintegrated into hundreds of local houses and farms, without any sense of connection to a larger movement."[73] McKanan concludes, in line with the thesis being proposed here, that what accounts for this is largely that Day "modeled a practice of friendship" that fostered ties between diverse communities and even "reached beyond the boundaries of her movement."[74] With Day's death, Catholic Worker communities themselves took up the role that Day had exemplified, providing support and encouragement to one another and sustaining the movement's sense of identity.[75] It was the exemplary model of leadership and authority that Day brought to the Worker from its origins onward, in contradistinction to the charismatic leader's drive for domination, that allowed the movement as a whole to be "a multifaceted anarchist affair, with a variety of other leaders and tendencies."[76]

As the foregoing discussion makes clear, the Catholic Worker's reliance upon an exemplary model of leadership and authority has had the (largely intended) effect of enhancing the anarchist aspects of the movement. The concept of exemplarity has allowed the Worker to draw sustenance from contemporary and historical examples of excellence while simultaneously emphasizing the equality and the empowerment of all individuals within the movement, who are urged to think of themselves as having the capacity for self-determination as well as the capacity for selfless commitment to those in need. The Worker's emphasis on the noncoercive and indirect influence of examples rather than the coercive and direct influence of commands has meshed nicely with the traditional anarchist resistance to all forms of authority that are not voluntarily accepted. Finally, the concept of exemplarity has helped Workers to envision the possibility of a movement that opts for the centralization of common identity and purpose rather than the centralization of institutions, enabling Worker communities to develop autonomously while retaining ties of solidarity and support to the rest of the movement. It is not an exaggeration to say that for Day, Maurin, and the Catholic Worker, anarchism was not embraced as an abstract political ideology, but rather understood as the social arrangement that flowed logically out of exemplarity pushed to its limit. While this points to the counterintuitive conclusion that the Catholic Worker's Catholicism has—at least in some respects—enriched rather than undermined its anarchism, it also suggests that scholars of anarchism would do well to look more carefully at the potential for exemplarity to influence organizational structure and to serve as a binding agent within anarchist movements and communities. Exemplarity may help to separate authority from domination and to explain how the phenomenon that Paul McLaughlin labels "moral authority" may indeed be reconcilable with anarchist principles.[77]

Conclusion

In this chapter, I have attempted to use the concept of exemplarity to account for the affinity the Catholic Worker movement found between Catholicism's traditional celebration of saintly *exempla* and anarchism, the political philosophy that best describes the approach to organization the movement adopted internally, and promoted externally, through its social activism. More specifically, I have endeavoured to dissipate some of the "bewilderment" that many scholars have experienced in trying to make sense of Dorothy Day's "successful use of authority," by arguing that on the level of the movement as a whole she adopted an exemplary model of leadership that was ultimately more decisive than her occasionally authoritarian impulses.[78] This is not because I wish to exonerate Day of her shortcomings—indeed, I believe that she is open to criticism not only for overstepping her bounds with respect to the direct influence she exerted on the movement, but also for the example she set. In some ways, her exemplary authority, quite aside from whatever direct power she possessed, also served to close down possibilities within the movement that might otherwise have emerged.[79] Regardless of the manner in which Day wielded the exemplary leadership I have attributed to her, however, examining her relationship to the broader movement—in which, as Nancy Roberts writes, "Day's authority was most reinforced by the power of her own pristine example"[80]—can help us to discern the concept of exemplarity in action and to weigh its merits.

That Day should go down as the "inventor" of Catholic radicalism in the United States is instructive, for it teaches us one last, ironic, lesson about exemplarity. Exemplars are rarely the straightforward imitators of past greatness that they claim to be. Rather, in attempting to make the exemplary models of the past relevant to the present, they more often than not create something new. The chain of exemplary causation is as much about innovation as it is about the endless recycling of accomplishment. The greatest exemplars—those who liberate the sparks of the imagination rather than inspiring mere mimicry—are those whose deeds are familiar enough to bring to mind the best of the exemplary tradition, yet who steer the profound authority of that tradition into new channels.

Acknowledgement

The author would like to thank the anonymous reviewers, Alex Christoyannopoulos, Matt Adams, Christina Doonan, and Vivian Kao for helpful feedback, as well as Jeff Stout for his comments on an earlier version of this article.

Notes

1. The quote is from Octave Mirbeau. See the "Introduction" to Daniel Guerin, *Anarchism: From Theory to Practice* (New York: Monthly Review Press, 1970), vii.

2. Mel Piehl, *Breaking Bread: The Catholic Worker and the Origin of Catholic Radicalism in America* (Philadelphia, PA: Temple University Press, 1982), x.

3. Important examples of this strain of scholarship include Alexander Gelley, ed., *Unruly Examples: On the Rhetoric of Exemplarity* (Stanford, CA: Stanford University Press, 1995), Irene E. Harvey, *Labyrinths of Exemplarity: At the Limits of Deconstruction* (Albany, NY: State University of New York Press, 2002), Bryan R. Warnick, *Imitation and Education: A Philosophical Inquiry into Learning by Example* (Albany, NY: State University of New York Press, 2008), Dana Hollander, *Exemplarity and Chosenness: Rosenzweig and Derrida on the Nation of Philosophy* (Stanford, CA: Stanford University Press, 2008), Alessandro Ferrara, *The Force of the Example: Explorations in the Paradigm of Judgment* (New York: Columbia University

Press, 2008), Paul Fleming, *Exemplarity and Mediocrity: The Art of the Average from Bourgeois Tragedy to Realism* (Stanford, CA: Stanford University Press, 2009), and most recently Michele Lowrie and Susanne Ludemann, eds., *Exemplarity and Singularity: Thinking through Particulars in Philosophy, Literature, and Law* (Milton Park and New York: Routledge, 2015).

4. For a discussion of the complex role that the *paradeigma* plays in Plato's thought, see Stanley Rosen, *Plato's Republic: A Study* (New Haven, CT: Yale University Press, 2005), ch. 8.

5. For the Plato/Aristotle distinction, see the "Introduction" in Alexander Gelley, ed., *Unruly Examples: On the Rhetoric of Exemplarity* (Stanford, CA: Stanford University Press, 1995).

6. The connection between the past and the present implied by this view of history was rooted in a conception of history as cyclical, a repetitive sequence of events propelled by recurrent character types.

7. A helpful account of these developments is given in Jane D. Chaplin, *Livy's Exemplary History* (Oxford: Oxford University Press, 2000).

8. For an extended treatment of Cicero's use of *exempla*, see Henriette van der Blom, *Cicero's Role Models: The Political Strategy of a Newcomer* (Oxford: University of Oxford Press, 2010).

9. H. W. Litchfield, "National *Exempla Virtutis* in Roman Literature" *Harvard Studies in Classical Philology* 25 (1914): 1–71.

10. Peter Brown, "The Saint as Exemplar in Late Antiquity" *Representations* 2 (Spring 1983), 6. On the same page of Brown's article, the early Christian theologian Gregory of Nyssa is quoted describing Christianity as "an imitation of the divine nature."

11. Brown, "The Saint as Exemplar in Late Antiquity," 7.

12. 1 Cor. 10:33–34.

13. John Howard Yoder, *The Politics of Jesus* (Grand Rapids, MI: Wm. B. Eerdmans Publishing Co., 1994), 121. Similarly, in the Epistle to the Ephesians (whose authorship is disputed), the author writes "As God's dear children, try to be like him, and live in love as Christ loved you, and gave himself up on your behalf." (Eph. 5:1–2)

14. Matthew 5:48. We would be remiss not to mention as well the importance, within Catholicism in particular, of the "exemplary

holiness" of the Virgin Mary, who is conceived as the first and quint-essential disciple of Christ, the model of the Church, and a "living catechism." See, for example, the encyclicals *Marialis Cultus* and *Catechesi Tradendae*.

15. Larry Scanlon, *Narrative, Authority, and Power: The Medieval Exemplum and the Chaucerian Tradition* (Cambridge: Cambridge University Press, 1994), 9–10. It should be noted that Scanlon ultimately concludes that the *exempla*, as employed by Chaucer in particular, did not so much *subvert* Church authority as *appropriate* it.

16. Adolf von Harnack provides a helpful account of the novelty of Francis and the mendicants more generally in his *History of Dogma*, vol. VI (Boston: Little, Brown, and Company), ch. 2, pt. 1.

17. Ferrara, *The Force of the Example*, ix–x.

18. Day is quoted in Mel Piehl, "The Politics of Free Obedience," in Patrick G. Coy, ed., *A Revolution of the Heart: Essays on the Catholic Worker* (Philadelphia, PA: Temple University Press, 1988), 210.

19. Jim Forest, *All Is Grace: A Biography of Dorothy Day* (Maryknoll, NY: Orbis Books, 2011), 122.

20. Dorothy Day, *The Long Loneliness* (New York: Harper & Row, 1952), 204–5.

21. Maurin quoted in Forest, *All Is Grace*, 107.

22. Forest, *All Is Grace*, 14.

23. Forest, *All Is Grace*, 77.

24. As Piehl writes, Day's "commitment to Catholicism was closely attuned to the models she found in the early saints of the Church, whose spiritual illumination came through asceticism and prayer." *Breaking Bread*, 84.

25. Jim Forest describes, for example, how Maurin's idea for houses of hospitality (and, at a smaller level, rooms of hospitality, or "Christ Rooms") was inspired by Saint Basil's care for the poor in 4th-century Cappadocia. *All Is Grace*, 121.

26. Day, *The Long Loneliness*, 45.

27. One of Day's best-known quotes captures this reluctance: "Don't call me a saint. I don't want to be dismissed so easily." That Day

should resist the label of saint is perhaps more easily understood than her suggestion that recognition of sainthood would lead to her "dismissal." My own reading of this quote is that it reflects Day's determination to promote an image of herself as someone who was, like any other Catholic Worker, struggling towards sainthood rather than someone whose actions could be understood as saintly in an unqualified sense. The exemplarity she valued was that which kept the ideal in tension with the real, and therefore stimulated further action. To posit a too-literal saintliness in the present would have been to risk fostering complacency.

28. Forest, *All Is Grace*, 108.

29. Mark Zwick and Louise Zwick, *The Catholic Worker Movement: Intellectual and Spiritual Origins* (New York: Paulist Press, 2005), 16.

30. Piehl, *Breaking Bread*, 66.

31. Piehl, *Breaking Bread*, 65.

32. Dan McKanan, *The Catholic Worker Movement after Dorothy: Practicing the Works of Mercy in a New Generation* (Collegeville, MN: Liturgical Press, 2008), 34.

33. Forest, *All Is Grace*, 118.

34. McKanan, *The Catholic Worker Movement after Dorothy*, 49.

35. McKanan, *The Catholic Worker Movement after Dorothy*, 44.

36. Dorothy Day, *Loaves and Fishes* (Maryknoll, NY: Orbis Books, 1963), 127.

37. Day, *Loaves and Fishes*, 176.

38. For a discussion of how the concept of exemplarity factored in to the anarchist practice of "propaganda of the deed," see my "Pacifism, Nonviolence, and the Reinvention of Anarchist Tactics in the Twentieth Century," *Journal for the Study of Radicalism* 9.1 (Spring 2015). The Catholic Worker, I argue, played an important role in the development of propaganda of the deed into a form of "prefigurative exemplarity" by nonviolent anarchists in the 20th century.

39. William D. Miller, *A Harsh and Dreadful Love: Dorothy Day and the Catholic Worker Movement* (New York: Liveright, 1973), 6.

40. Aside from Day's references to the concept in print, one Worker confirms that "Dorothy was always talking about being fools for Christ" in Rosalie G. Riegle, *Dorothy: Portraits by Those Who Knew Her* (Maryknoll, NY: Orbis, 2006), 62.

41. Day, for example, liked to point out that by worldly standards, Christ was a fool and a failure. She drew from this fact a lesson for the movement: "What we do is so little we may seem to be constantly failing. But so did He fail. He met with apparent failure on the Cross. But unless the seed fall into the earth and die, there is no harvest." Day is quoted in McKanan, *The Catholic Worker after Dorothy*, 22.

42. See Sergey A. Ivanov, *Holy Fools in Byzantium and Beyond* (Oxford: Oxford University Press, 2006).

43. Zwick and Zwick, *The Catholic Worker Movement*, 9.

44. Piehl, *Breaking Bread*, 97.

45. Jacques Maritain, *The Person and the Common Good* (New York: Charles Scribner's Sons, 1947), 44.

46. Fred Boehrer, "Diversity, Plurality, and Ambiguity: Anarchism in the Catholic Worker Movement," in William Thorn, Phillip Runkel, and Susan Mountin, eds., *Dorothy Day and the Catholic Worker Movement: Centenary Essays* (Milwaukee, WI: Marquette University Press, 2001), 105.

47. John Cort, "My Life at The Catholic Worker" *Commonweal* 107 (1980): 367.

48. Michael Harrington quoted in Riegle, *Dorothy*, 61.

49. June O'Connor, *The Moral Vision of Dorothy Day: A Feminist Perspective* (New York: The Crossroad Publishing Company, 1991), 80.

50. Nancy L. Roberts, *Dorothy Day and the Catholic Worker* (Albany, NY: State University of New York Press, 1984), 99.

51. Dorothy Day, "On Pilgrimage – December 1972," *The Catholic Worker*, December 1972, 2, 8; available from http://www.catholicworker.org/dorothyday/daytext.cfm?TextID=526; Internet; accessed 12 August 2014.

52. Day, *Loaves and Fishes*, 142.

53. O'Connor, *The Moral Vision of Dorothy Day*, 80.

54. William D. Miller, *Dorothy Day: A Biography* (San Francisco, CA: Harper & Row, 1982), 484.

55. McKanan, *The Catholic Worker after Dorothy*, 23.

56. McKanan, *The Catholic Worker after Dorothy*, 24.

57. Piehl, *Breaking Bread*, 243.

58. Michele Teresa Aronica, *Beyond Charismatic Leadership: The New York Catholic Worker Movement* (Piscataway, NJ: Transaction Publishers, 1988).

59. McKanan, *The Catholic Worker after Dorothy*, 27.

60. Since the main objective here is determining the relationship of Day (and to a lesser extent Maurin) to the rest of the Catholic Worker movement, I focus on the mainstream, leader-centered reading of Weber's theory of charisma—the interpretation he emphasized towards the end of his life. I wish to acknowledge, however, the possibility of deriving from Weber's earlier work a theory of *collective* charisma in the form of charismatic social movements. See Andreas Kalyvas, *Democracy and the Politics of the Extraordinary: Max Weber, Carl Schmitt, Hannah Arendt* (Cambridge: Cambridge University Press, 2008).

61. Max Weber, *Economy and Society: An Outline of Interpretive Sociology* (Berkeley, CA: University of California Press, 1978), 954.

62. Weber, *Economy and Society*, 1112.

63. Weber, *Economy and Society*, 1113.

64. Weber, *Economy and Society*, 1115.

65. Weber, *Economy and Society*, 1117.

66. Weber, *Economy and Society*, 1112.

67. Weber, *Economy and Society*, 1113.

68. Weber, *Economy and Society*, 1114.

69. Weber, *Economy and Society*, 1121.

70. For some insightful comments to this effect see Garry Wills's chapter on Day in *Certain Trumpets: The Nature of Leadership* (New York: Touchstone, 1994).

71. Roberts, *Dorothy Day and the Catholic Worker*, 83.

72. In his autobiography, the Catholic Worker Ammon Hennacy recounts an interaction in which Day argued this point to a group of skeptical anarchist interlocutors. Day, Hennacy writes, "felt that man of his own free will accepted God or rejected God and if a man chose to obey the authority of God and reject the authority of the state it was not unethical to do so." *Autobiography of a Christian Anarchist* (New York: Catholic Worker Books, 1954), 129.

73. McKanan, *The Catholic Worker after Dorothy*, 22.

74. McKanan, *The Catholic Worker after Dorothy*, 23.

75. As McKanan writes, "Remarkably, no individual and no community presumed to step into the leadership vacuum that had been left by Dorothy Day. Yet perhaps it would be better to say that almost everyone did so: because so many individuals and communities took personal responsibility for some of the tasks needed to sustain a vital movement, there was no need for a central leader or bureaucratic structure to take charge of all of those tasks. In the last years of its founder's life, the Catholic Worker movement became what Dorothy Day had always said it was: an organism rather than an organization. And as such it has endured." *The Catholic Worker after Dorothy*, 28.

76. Piehl, *Breaking Bread*, 243.

77. On both the question of domination and the question of moral authority, McLaughlin's argument in his *Anarchism and Authority: A Philosophical Introduction to Classical Anarchism* (Aldershot, UK: Ashgate, 2007) is in tension with the idea of exemplary leadership and authority I have developed here. McLaughlin insists upon understanding authority as a "*dominative power*," entailing "*the right of A to issue directives and the correlative duty of B to follow them*." (54) While McLaughlin recognizes that authority can exert a kind of "normative" power, according to his definition it is always accompanied by an act of submission and obedience, which is what gives it the character of domination. Still, it is hard to make sense of his rather blunt contention that anarchists "reject moral authority," a conclusion

that apparently follows from the questionable assumption that moral authority is "held to be unquestionable." (62) Exemplarity, I believe, offers the potential of differentiating authority and domination as well as ensuring that exceptional people are able to exert a moral influence without necessarily compromising anarchist principles.

78. Roberts, *Dorothy Day and the Catholic Worker*, 84.

79. Former Catholic Worker Peggy Scherer attests to this influence: "I feel that some people, at least, want to act as if Dorothy is the ongoing authority. In my mind, that means they never do anything Dorothy didn't do, which means they're not responding to anything that's happening now." See Rosalie Riegle Troester, ed., *Voices from the Catholic Worker* (Philadelphia, PA: Temple University Press, 1993), 532. Day's lingering authority has proved especially consequential in relation to controversial issues like homosexuality. One-time New York Catholic Worker Richard Cleaver claims that the question of tolerance for gays and lesbians at the New York branch is particularly touchy because "Dorothy was not at all open to change on this subject...I think there are people who feel that it would be an affront to Dorothy to go against what were undoubtedly her wishes in this question." *Voices from the Catholic Worker*, 539. Feminism has also been a contentious issue, as Sr. Anna Koop explains: "I wouldn't exactly say feminism permeates the Worker movement. Dorothy was an incredibly traditional Catholic, and maybe we need more distance from Dorothy for it to flower." *Voices from the Catholic Worker*, 557.

80. Roberts, *Dorothy Day and the Catholic Worker*, 84.

References

Aronica, Michele Teresa, *Beyond Charismatic Leadership: The New York Catholic Worker Movement* (Piscataway, NJ: Transaction Publishers, 1988).

Brown, Peter, "The Saint as Exemplar in Late Antiquity," *Representations*, 2 (Spring 1983), 1–25.

Chaplin, Jane D., *Livy's Exemplary History* (Oxford: Oxford University Press, 2000).

Cort, John, "My Life at The Catholic Worker" *Commonweal*, 107 (1980), 361–7.

Coy, Patrick G., ed., *A Revolution of the Heart: Essays on the Catholic Worker* (Philadelphia, PA: Temple University Press, 1988).

Day, Dorothy, *Loaves and Fishes* (Maryknoll, NY: Orbis Books, 1963).

———, *The Long Loneliness* (New York: Harper & Row, 1952).

———, "On Pilgrimage – December 1972," *The Catholic Worker* (December 1972), 2, 8.

Ferrara, Alessandro, *The Force of the Example: Explorations in the Paradigm of Judgment* (New York: Columbia University Press, 2008).

Fleming, Paul, *Exemplarity and Mediocrity: The Art of the Average from Bourgeois Tragedy to Realism* (Stanford, CA: Stanford University Press, 2009).

Forest, Jim, *All Is Grace: A Biography of Dorothy Day* (Maryknoll, NY: Orbis Books, 2011).

Gelley, Alexander, ed., *Unruly Examples: On the Rhetoric of Exemplarity* (Stanford, CA: Stanford University Press, 1995).

Guerin, Daniel, *Anarchism: From Theory to Practice* (New York: Monthly Review Press, 1970).

Harvey, Irene E., *Labyrinths of Exemplarity: At the Limits of Deconstruction* (Albany, NY: State University of New York Press, 2002).

Hennacy, Ammon, *Autobiography of a Christian Anarchist* (New York: Catholic Worker Books, 1954).

Hollander, Dana, *Exemplarity and Chosenness: Rosenzweig and Derrida on the Nation of Philosophy* (Stanford, CA: Stanford University Press, 2008).

Ivanov, Sergey A., *Holy Fools in Byzantium and Beyond* (Oxford: Oxford University Press, 2006).

Kalyvas, Andreas, *Democracy and the Politics of the Extraordinary: Max Weber, Carl Schmitt, Hannah Arendt* (Cambridge: Cambridge University Press, 2008).

Litchfield, H. W., "National Exempla Virtutis in Roman Literature," *Harvard Studies in Classical Philology*, 25 (1914), 1–71.

Lowrie, Michele and Susanne Ludemann, eds., *Exemplarity and Singularity: Thinking through Particulars in Philosophy, Literature, and Law* (Milton Park and New York: Routledge, 2015).

Maritain, Jacques, *The Person and the Common Good* (New York: Charles Scribner's Sons, 1947).

McKanan, Dan, *The Catholic Worker Movement after Dorothy: Practicing the Works of Mercy in a New Generation* (Collegeville, MN: Liturgical Press, 2008).

McLaughlin, Paul, *Anarchism and Authority: A Philosophical Introduction to Classical Anarchism* (Aldershot, UK: Ashgate, 2007).

Miller, William D., *Dorothy Day: A Biography* (San Francisco, CA: Harper & Row, 1982).

———, *A Harsh and Dreadful Love: Dorothy Day and the Catholic Worker Movement* (New York: Liveright, 1973).

O'Connor, June, *The Moral Vision of Dorothy Day: A Feminist Perspective* (New York: The Crossroad Publishing Company, 1991).

Pauli, Benjamin J., "Pacifism, Nonviolence, and the Reinvention of Anarchist Tactics in the Twentieth Century," Journal for the Study of Radicalism, 9.1 (Spring 2015), 61–94.

Piehl, Mel, *Breaking Bread: The Catholic Worker and the Origin of Catholic Radicalism in America* (Philadelphia, PA: Temple University Press, 1982).

Riegle, Rosalie G., *Dorothy: Portraits by Those Who Knew Her* (Maryknoll, NY: Orbis, 2006).

———, ed., *Voices from the Catholic Worker* (Philadelphia, PA: Temple University Press, 1993).

Roberts, Nancy L., *Dorothy Day and the Catholic Worker* (Albany, NY: State University of New York Press, 1984).

Rosen, Stanley, *Plato's Republic: A Study* (New Haven, CT: Yale University Press, 2005).

Scanlon, Larry, *Narrative, Authority, and Power: The Medieval Exemplum and the Chaucerian Tradition* (Cambridge: Cambridge University Press, 1994).

Thorn, William, Phillip Runkel, and Susan Mountin, eds., *Dorothy Day and the Catholic Worker Movement: Centenary Essays* (Milwaukee, WI: Marquette University Press, 2001).

van der Blom, Henriette, *Cicero's Role Models: The Political Strategy of a Newcomer* (Oxford: University of Oxford Press, 2010).

von Harnack, Adolf, *History of Dogma, vol. VI* (Boston: Little, Brown, and Company).

Warnick, Bryan R., *Imitation and Education: A Philosophical Inquiry into Learning by Example* (Albany, NY: State University of New York Press, 2008).

Weber, Max, *Economy and Society: An Outline of Interpretive Sociology* (Berkeley, CA: University of California Press, 1978).

Wills, Garry, *Certain Trumpets: The Nature of Leadership* (New York: Touchstone, 1994).

Yoder, John Howard, *The Politics of Jesus* (Grand Rapids, MI: Wm. B. Eerdmans Publishing Co., 1994).

Zwick, Mark and Louise Zwick, *The Catholic Worker Movement: Intellectual and Spiritual Origins* (New York: Paulist Press, 2005).

Mutuality, resistance and egalitarianism in a late colonial Bakongo Christian movement

Ruy Llera Blanes
Institute of Heritage Sciences (CSIC), Spain

In this chapter I describe how a specific Christian movement (the 'Tokoist Church', a prophetic, reformist movement that emerged in late colonial Angola) incorporated anarchist values (mutualism, autonomism and egalitarianism) in its theology and praxis. Through a discussion of its posterior historical developments, I discuss how the introduction of hierarchical processes in its organisation contributed towards the current state of internal contestation it is experiencing. I argue that the case of the Tokoist Church exemplifies the existence of conflicting theologies within Christian thought.

The 'Tokoist Church' is an Angolan Christian prophetic movement that became a cornerstone of anti-colonial resistance in the 1960s and 1970s, and later opposed to the post-independence totalitarian MPLA government.[1] They became known in Angola for their peaceful resistance to the colonial endeavour, as well as for a particular sense of autochthon dignity they conveyed, which engaged ideologically in the rejection of prior political and religious establishments and the self-improvement towards a messianic new kingdom that they envisioned.[2] In the process, they cultivated a form of utopian mutualist egalitarianism that rejected imposed hierarchies and governmentalities. From this perspective, as I will describe throughout this chapter, in its first years of existence the Tokoist Church exemplified, through specific political utopian stances, a particular version of Christianity that, unlike other hierarchical traditions, reveals an understanding of Jesus Christ's

How to cite this book chapter:
Blanes, R. L. 2017. Mutuality, resistance and egalitarianism in a late colonial Bakongo Christian movement. In: Christoyannopoulos, A. and Adams, M. S. (eds.) *Essays in Anarchism and Religion: Volume 1*. Pp. 51–77. Stockholm: Stockholm University Press. DOI: https://doi.org/10.16993/bak.c. License: CC-BY

gospel as inherently anarchistic in its core values. This follows recent proposals that outline this understanding in the history of Christianity, while establishing a philosophical and political critique to historical processes of Christian institutionalization and hierarchization.[3] Here, I propose an ethnographic description of one such example from the Angola and Lower Congo region.

The movement emerged in the 1940s when its founder, Simão Gonçalves Toko (1918–1984), a former student and teacher in the Baptist missions of northern Angola (Kibokolo, Bembe), migrated to the capital of what was then the Belgian Congo, Léopoldville, and founded a musical choir (the 'Coro de Kibokolo') among the community of Angolan expatriates in the city.[4] This choir, after a series of spiritual events, eventually evolved into a religious movement, with its members preaching around the city about a new spiritual order. The first event was the participation of the choir in an international protestant missionary conference that took place in Léopoldville in 1946, which hosted missionaries, theologians and officials from several African, North American and European countries. In the conference Toko was given the chance of addressing the audience, and requested that *"the Holy Spirit may descend upon Africa and save it from darkness"*.[5] A second event took place in July 1949, when Toko organized a prayer vigil, in which himself and a group of his followers witnessed the descent of the Holy Spirit and began to speak in tongues, prophesy, engage in biblical acknowledgement and perform other miraculous events.[6] Immediately after this event, those present took the streets and began to preach the Bible throughout the city. It was not long before the Belgian authorities took notice of this unwarranted proselytism and eventually imprisoned and expelled them from the colony, deporting them back to Angola in early 1950. From this moment until Angolan independence in 1974, the story of the members of this movement was one of repression and suffering through imposed prison, forced labour, exile and other forms of violence; but it was also one of resistance and successful clandestine organization against the colonial apparatus, until it became officially recognized in the wake of the political transition to independency.

In the following pages, I will describe how the church's anti-colonialist moment was based on socio-political configurations of mutualism, egalitarianism and self-sovereignty vis-à-vis the metropolitan state, whilst promoting a non-hierarchical organization based on solidarity and respect – all of which core aspects of anarchistic thought and ethics. In the second part of the text, I will explain how the memory of this egalitarian and mutualist past reverberates today as an operative concept in the church's contemporary internal politics of dissent, after a historical process that has introduced diverse hierarchical structures in its social and political organization. I will also explore the ambiguities behind these configurations, namely in what concerns the autonomy of the believer versus the authority of both the state and God. This, as has been stated, has been a problematic question in the history anarchist political thought, considering the seemingly irreconcilable adherence to a supreme god and the rejection of all forms of authority that subdue the individual, as well as the traditional resistance of most (if not all) religious movements to conceive themselves in any way as 'anarchistic' (the Tokoists being no exception).[7] But the acknowledgement of egalitarian, resistant and utopian histories to be found in many of such cases has progressively pushed it into the centre of debate, as this volume exemplifies.

Resistance and political contestation in late colonial Congo

The fact that the Tokoist Church, despite being an Angolan based movement, emerged not in this territory but in the neighbouring Belgian Congo, was less a surprise as it could seem from the start. In fact, Simão Toko was but one of the many northern Angolans of Kongo ethnicity who crossed the colonial borders and headed towards the nearest metropolis. Despite the political frontier that separated, since the late nineteenth century, Portuguese, French and Belgian colonial endeavours, there was also a strong tradition of mobility, circulation and commercial exchange among the different Bakongo groups in the region that did not necessarily observe the juridical-political imposition on behalf of the Lisbon, Brussels and Paris metropolitan governments.[8] Therefore, a strong community of *zombo* (Angolans from the Maquela do Zombo region) expatriates concentrated in the suburbs of Leopoldville, namely the Quartier Indigène (Indigenous Neighbourhood) of the city. Likewise, other ethnicities and international expatriate communities concentrated around this urbanized portion around the river Congo.[9]

Thus, Leopoldville was everything but a restful city in the 1940s. In fact, many political and religious movements were becoming increasingly present in the local public scene, engaging progressively in the contestation of the colonial regime culminating in the Congolese independence in 1960. Political associations such as Joseph Kasa-Vubu's ABAKO (*Alliance des Bakongo*), which emerged in the 1950s, was one culmination of this political fervour.[10] Likewise, most political and paramilitary organisations that struggled towards Angolan independence were also found among exiled communities in this city, and the presence of Portuguese communist exiles – who fought the Estado Novo dictatorship in Portugal – in the region was a matter of fact.[11] Simultaneously, as Georges Balandier described, many religious movements that emerged in the particular 'colonial situation' of the Belgian Congo cultivated a messianistic ideology – usually concentrated around the figure of a leader or prophet who was at the same time a politician: Simon Kimbangu, Simon-Pierre Mpadi, Lassy Simon Zéphyrin, André Matswa and others – which typically evolved into specific nationalist ideologies that simultaneously contested the political state while addressing, more or less prophetically, new religious orders.[12] Such was the case of Simon Kimbangu (1887–1951), also a former Baptist student who, after a religious ministry of just months in the city, was arrested by the Belgian authorities and spent the rest of his life (thirty years) in prison in Élisabethville (today Lubumbashi) – but not before announcing prophetically to his followers that "*the white will become black and the black will become white*".[13] And in fact, as was observed in the decades after Congolese independence, movements such as the Kimbanguist Church would become referentials of the postcolonial nationalist projects. Another particularly interesting example in this respect was the movement known as *Amicalisme* – Société Amicale des Originaires de l'Afrique Equatorielle Française – founded in 1926 by André Matswa in

Paris as a self-improvement group for expatriates from French Equatorial Africa, through which money was collected to improve their condition as well as that of their original territories. This movement became largely influential in the Lower Congo region, and eventually evolved into a religious following known as 'Matswanism' after the founder's passing in 1942.[14] At the same time, in post-independence Congo his figure would become inspirational for several politicians.[15]

In this framework, the border between such religious and political movements was often more than blurry, or perhaps even irrelevant, conjured under concepts of charisma and utopia.[16] This was evident in the colonial setting, where such prophetic leaders were endogenously and exogenously construed as being politically agent – reason why they sojourned in local prisons more often than not – and in the postcolonial setting, where political movements such as Bundu Dia Kongo ("Union of the Kongo"), led by Ne Muanda Nsemi, have combined a struggle for the restoration of the ancient Kingdom of Kongo with religious ideologies, to the extent of clashing against state authorities.[17]

Apart from the religious/political conflation, such examples also highlight the emergence of a process of religiously mediated political disconnection – one between 'the state' (as an apparatus of government) and 'society', here conceived as the expression of autonomous collective organization, beyond externally imposed jurisdictions.[18] In other words, religious utopian and messianic ideals acted here against a hierarchical colonial system that had been imposed as a 'totalization' with no epistemological, political and moral alternative.[19] This emerged in a specific historical moment of political transformation in the African continent towards independency, through which the forces of production of the state were irrevocably undermined by grassroots mobilizations of diverse order: social, cultural, intellectual, political, military, religious, etc.[20] These processes of 'refracted governmentality', where a political, ideological and epistemological distinction is produced between the state and the will of its citizens, and also and ultimately implied a problem of (individual, collective, national) sovereignty and opened the ground for the consequent circulation of ideals of freedom and liberation.[21]

As a result, through such movements of contestation, specific ideas of sovereignty were being tested against a given socio-political order that was in a permanent process of self-construction as crystallized and unquestioned.[22] From this perspective, in their revolutionary mind-sets they conveyed a very 'Proudhonian' rejection of the state.[23] After the political transition into the postcolony, most of them, however, resulted in new socialist formations and political regimes that proved to be more totalitarian than the previous colonial regimes (Angola being a case in point). Likewise, movements such as Kimbanguism also evolved into complex, hierarchical state-like endeavours.[24] In the process, while many religious movements embarked successfully in the new political orders, others, like the Tokoist Church, remained until very recently marginal and ambiguous.

Spiritual and political formations

Considering the socio-political setting described above, one can imagine that it would be difficult to live in a place like 1940s Léopoldville and ignore its political effervescence. However, the emergence of Tokoist mutualist prophetism was also imbued with a theological formation, informed by the protestant covenantal ethos, by which the relationship between God and the believer is one of direct 'alliance', thus dispensing hierarchizing mechanisms of mediation. When Simão Toko arrived to Léopoldville in 1943, he was a young man (25 years old) with a pedagogic and spiritual training in the Baptist missions, where he began as a student and *empregado* (service boy) at the missionaries' houses. Due to his outstanding performance as a teenage student, he had been granted the possibility of moving to Luanda to obtain secondary education, sponsored by the missionaries. Upon its completion, he returned north, and was hired as a teacher in the Bembe mission – his last stop before his migration to the Belgian Congo.

However, after consecutive disagreements with the Baptist leaders, Toko began a process of estrangement that culminated in the irreversible emancipation and autonomization observed in Léopoldville. He disagreed on cases such as the salary received by indigenous teachers in the missions, and the fact that the students could not progress beyond a certain point in the study of the Bible. In a letter he wrote to the missionaries of the mission, he eventually asked to be released from the mission work: "*When consciousness talks, let it be truly heard. Here is my question: when someone offers a shirt or a loaf of bread to a beggar, what is his goal, and why? I'm not the one to tell you, but I think that it is to do the beggar good. (When consciousness speaks...)*" (circa 1942; my translation). Although his separation would only occur a few years later, one could observe how the process of moral and political detachment was already taking place.

From this perspective, Toko's political consciousness stemmed from a progressive acknowledgement of an unjust hierarchized system that was in itself contradictory with the notions of spiritual liberation taught by the Baptists; shortly before leaving to Léopoldville, Toko decides to organize a farewell party, inviting students, local elders and mission leaders. In the party, he appears wearing a sisal bag and singing a kikongo hymn that said: "*The turncoat has worn a bag, the turncoat has worn a bag, the turncoat has worn a bag*".[25] This was seen as an announcement of a future inversion of the state of affairs. It is said that by that time Toko also sang hymns in Kikongo where he summoned the Africans to "*open their eyes*"[26]– in what can be understood as a progressively public contestation to the work of the missionaries.

Once in Léopoldville, Toko would nevertheless continue his collaboration with the Baptist missions, teaching in the Itagar mission's Sunday school. As some elder Tokoists I interviewed in Luanda recall, his dominical classes were cramped with eager students, while the Baptists' church remained almost empty in their services. This situation provoked discomfort and growing suspicion in the Baptist leaderships. In parallel with the choir activities, he led an autonomous group of Bible students, known as the *Anciens Élèves*, who spent their free time reading and translating the Bible into the local language, kikongo, as well as learning other languages (namely English). During these meetings, Toko would introduce and discuss literature from other movements, such as the Jehovah's Witnesses and Watchtower (their proselytist branch) publications, a book called *Luz e Verdade* ("Light and Truth") that Toko had found in the rubbish bin in his previous visit to Luanda.

There was also another book known as *Vita Velela* ("Holy War"), used by the elder members of the group. Furthermore, in the 1946 missionary conference he met and engaged with representatives from different protestant churches, exchanging publications such as the Watchtower's *Sentinel* – engagements that progressively undermined his loyalty to the Baptist missionary endeavour and pushed him towards an independentist, liberationist movement.

This plural inspiration was, from a theological point of view, fundamental for the development of a utopian project, very much inspired by the Jehovah's Witnesses millenarian restorationist eschatology, in particular their belief in God's Kingdom as a literal government in heaven. This, therefore, implied a rejection of worldly government. As a Tokoist elder who followed him in the days of Léopoldville told me (February 2012), Toko would always tell them to be *"prepared to work their own land"* in the future, anticipating a new governmentality. But Toko also always called for a peaceful form of resistance to colonial oppression, which was simultaneously obedient with the established authorities but refused any form of externally imposed subjection, while explicitly denying any kind of involvement in violent resistance or guerrilla actions in the subsequent years.[27] This form of 'obedient resistance', however paradoxical as it may seem, was in fact rooted in two dispositions: an exegesis of Jesus' gospel as an essentially pacifist and love-informed preaching that prefigures a different image of God other than the old covenant autocratic, violent one[28] and simultaneously a strong sense of utopian expectation, a personal conviction of an imminent change that would proclaim their messianic victory over the soon-to-be defunct worldly government. In the first stance, one can appreciate a similar interpretation to that of Leo Tolstoy in *The Kingdom of God is Within You*, in which he points out the centrality of non-violent resistance in the Christian gospel, which he configured as a 'new theory of life'.[29] In the second, we observe a process de-totalization of the colonial system, the recognition of its fallibility, mediated by the inauguration of an expectation that questioned the 'victorious history' imposed by the colonial regime.[30]

One example of the irrevocability of the Tokoists' sovereign positioning can be found in the moment of their arrest in

Léopoldville. Upon the emergence of the choir members' door-to-door proselytism in the city, soon enough the Belgian authorities were tipped off by the Baptist missionaries concerning the dangers involved in their activities. A complaint filed in the local police station concerning an alleged robbery on behalf of one of these students/preachers gave the Belgian authorities the pretext to arrest Toko and the group of dozens of followers. As they were arrested, several other dozen followers voluntarily turned themselves in to the authorities, in order to remain closer to their leader. The police then conducted interrogatories to identify and build the case for a subsequent deportation. Every single interrogation followed the same script as this dialogue held by the interrogating official and 18-year-old G. Pierre:

> Q.- *Do you understand that you have been arrested for carrying the insignia of the Kibokolo choir?*
> R.- *Yes, because I am a member of that choir led by Simão Gonçalves Toko.*
>
> Q.- *Were you aware that that sect was forbidden?*
> R.- *Yes I was.*
>
> Q.- *Why then did you continue to be a part of that illegal movement, despite the interdiction?*
> R.- *Because it is about the will of God, to which I must submit myself.*
>
> Q.- *So one could say you follow firstly Toko's orders, and then those of the Government, is that right?*
> R.- *Yes, that is correct.*
>
> Q.- *Are you willing to give up on the Kibokolo choir movement?*
> R- *I am arrested, but I will never give up.*
>
> (Archives Ministère des Affaires Étrangères Bruxelles)[31]

As becomes clear, the arrested Tokoists would not recognize an authority that did not stem from Toko or God, and were willing to pay the price, suffering prison and deportation. And in fact, as Tokoists in Luanda recall, not only were these hundreds of singers arrested and expelled, but up to thousands of *zombo* voluntarily turned themselves in to the Belgian authorities, subjected themselves to prison and returned to Angola, inspired by Toko's liberationist message.[32] This refusal of allegiance to 'worldly government' brings us back once again to a critical point in the history of Christian Anarchist thought, from Tolstoy to Adin Ballou and Jacques Ellul: the problem of allegiance and subjection to 'authority'.[33] However, what cases like the Tokoist and others described by these authors show us is that the notion of subjection must be bracketed and considered in terms of how such movements understand and experience God – if as an autocratic source of domination or as an egalitarian source of 'love'.

Other examples of resistance would follow, namely during the subsequent decades in Angola. After being deported from the Belgian Congo in January 1950, Toko and his followers were subject to several measures of repression and control on behalf of the Portuguese authorities, which became increasingly suspicious of their political motivations. In order to exert control, they decided to separate the group into smaller teams, which would be dispersed into different labour camps, prisons, detention compounds or 'residence fixation' areas throughout the territory[34]. One such case took place in the *colonato* (plantation) of Vale do Loge (Uíge, northern Angola), to where a group of about one hundred Tokoists was sent to serve as enslaved labour for the construction and development of a coffee plantation. They sojourned in the plantation for about ten years, before fleeing into the bushes and the Congo at the outbreak of the independence war in 1961. Many of the survivors I interviewed described how they were able to establish a particular form of collective organization in which they would carry out the orders of the plantation chiefs in their own terms, where the fittest would cover for the weakest in the heaviest work, apparently with the complacency of the authorities that watched over them, allowing for their autonomy as long as the work was completed. Grenfell also describes how they refused to take up work that they deemed inhuman, and were encouraged by Toko to seek specific job training that would allow them to gain future economic autonomy. In any case, due to the relatively peaceful and orderly situation of the plantation, it became a model for the local authorities, who invited the Angolan General Governor, Silva Carvalho, in 1954 for a visit to appreciate the success of the agricultural venture.[35] But other episodes that took place in the plantation confirmed their irreducible autonomism. For instance, in 1955, they refused to accept the authorities' order of removing the symbols they invariably wore on their lapels (a red star), and confronted them, comparing their symbol with the official ranks the military and police wore in their own uniforms.[36] Another example took place in 1957, when a small Catholic church was built, to serve the local populations and the Portuguese colonists. The Bishop of Luanda was invited for the inauguration, and the Tokoists were summoned to attend the ceremony and sing Christian hymns. But they refused to take part of the event and escort the Bishop's vehicle.[37]

Mutual and solidary organization, resistance and liberation

The spiritual formations revealed above elicit a coupling of a utopian Christian eschatology and specific stances of resistance that enhanced their agency vis-à-vis the colonial states. But in his Léopoldville days Simão Toko had also engaged in several other social and political associations. While working as a portrait painter in the streets of Léopoldville and also as an apprentice of watchmaker, he also dedicated his time to the creation of a mutual self-help organization for the Zombo community, known as Nkutu a Nsimbani ("Mutual Help Fund"), in 1946.[38] This organization, located at number 41 of Luvua street in Léopoldville, congregated some members of the Coro, as well as other Zombo who worked in commercial activities. Their goal was to create a system of periodical donations for collective enterprises, which included helping new Zombo migrants arriving in the city, building houses, schools or medical facilities, or starting small commercial enterprises. Toko, who was constantly sought by newly arrived Zombo at his house for help, acted as chairman and treasurer of the association, collecting donations and organizing group meetings. The mutualist venture was very successful in its early stages, and acted as a hub for the Zombo community; but eventually a conflict broke between two groups, concerning the disappearance of part of the money collected, and led to the dissolution of the association by Toko himself in 1948.

This kind of mutual activity was not unheard of at the time. On the one hand, the Bakongo familial and kinship structure often engaged in similar collective enterprises. As many Zombo in Angola told me, migration from rural Maquela do Zombo to places like Léopoldville or Luanda were often covered by the collection of money through an extensive network of village and clan members.[39] But also in the urban, metropolitan setting of Léopoldville one could observe the influence of movements such as the Amicalist project, described above, and Kitawala (the autochthon version of the Watchtower). From this perspective, mutualism was in many ways engrained in Bakongo culture. But this specific project appeared as an expression of Christian mutualism, equally based in an ideal of religious communitarianism and libertarianism. This ideal in turn stemmed from a double, concomitant recognition of the inherently hierarchical and unjust version of Christianity imposed by the Western missionaries in the region, and the remembrance of a 'original' version of Christianity – that of the time of the apostles –, based on communality and solidarity.

Despite the failure of this specific mutualist project, Toko did not give up on his collectivist projects, and continued to push forward an agenda of a dignified, peaceful resistance. And, as many Bakongo in Luanda told me, Nkutu a Nsimbani in fact became a 'seed' out of which several other grassroots projects emerged. Toko's encouragement of "*communal solidarity, discipline in work and the learning of new skills*" had a considerable impact, and several former members of the Nkutu a Nsimbani engaged in new ventures.[40] Such was the case, for instance, of the ASSOMIZO (Asociation Mutuelle des Ressortissants de Zombo), a Zombo mutual aid society organized in 1956 by Emmanuel Kunzika and André Massaki which would eventually transform into a political party known as ALIAZO (Alliance Zombo) and later into the PDA (Partido Democrático de Angola) which, along with another paramilitary movement, the UPA, would form the FNLA (National Liberation Front of Angola, led by Holden Roberto). From this perspective, many Bakongo in Angola today see Nkutu a Nsimbani as a precursor of Angolan nationalism, at least in what concerned the capacity of creating a collective venture that disconnected from and fought against any state sponsored initiative of control. From this perspective, one could argue that this form of associativism implied a 'model for liberation', based simultaneously on religious notions of communality and transcendence, and on political ideals of autonomy and transformation.[41] However, as stated above, despite the common liberationist aspiration, the subsequent political transitions transformed many of these movements into socialist, Marxist-Leninist, communist and in many cases totalitarian endeavours. Furthermore, just like as I suggested above movements such as Kimbanguism engaged in similar processes of transformation that introduced hierarchy and inequality, Tokoist mutualism was also and eventually substituted by vertical forms of organization.

Refiguring vertical and horizontal organization in the post-colony

As a prophetic movement, Tokoism reflects forms of leadership that can be easily interpreted as prime examples of hierarchical ecclesiastical organization. It is not hard to agree with this, especially when one considers the moral, epistemological, political and spiritual 'dependence' that is detectable between Toko and his followers and is reproduced even today, decades after his physical passing. In fact, after the moments described above, the subsequent decades of demographic growth of the Tokoist Church witnessed a process of bureaucratization and administrative complexification that introduced particular steps towards a hierarchization of the entity, often against the will of the prophet founder himself. Considering that the following of Simão Toko began to transcend several ethnic and political boundaries, different administrative entities were created to address such processes. For instance, in the late 1950s, an internal organization of the church into "tribes", which implied the integration of an intermediary entity between believers and the leadership, was created, dividing them according to their original ethnicities.[42] Likewise, the creation of multiple entities with intermediate leaderships, such as counsels of elders, youths, etc, added to the complexity. This process of bureaucratization culminated after Toko's death in 1984, which implied, for the first time in the church's history, a process of political succession. This process was all but successful, as many different sectors of the church were not able to agree on who represented the legitimate authority, and, amidst several different kinds of mutual accusations, began a process of internal dismemberment. Throughout the 1980s and 1990s, what was a single entity was consecutively divided into several different Tokoist groups, some of which were able to obtain legal recognition (in 1992). Thus today one can no longer talk about a Tokoist Church, but instead of Tokoist Churches in plural.

This situation lasted roughly until the year 2000, when a series of events dramatically changed the church's political situation. One of the sectors began to be led by a man, Afonso Nunes, who claimed to have been visited and 'inhabited' by the spirit of Simão Toko and, after taking office, undertook a movement of reunification and transversal transformation – to the point that it is today one of the most successful churches in post-war Angola.[43] Apart from the dramatic reforms undertaken in the sector under Nunes' leadership, he also introduced a bureaucratic novelty: the inauguration of a bishopric, as a mechanism to solve the critical problem of leadership. Despite the contestation of many groups that remain somewhat marginal, Nunes' proposal can be considered a success, from an economic and political point of view, as he was also able to enact an almost complete reunification. Thus today, this sector appears in Angola as hegemonic in what concerns the public perception of Tokoism. Bishop Nunes and the Tokoist Church appear almost daily in the Angolan media, in a constant display of success and wealth – of which the majestic "Universal Cathedral", inaugurated in the summer of 2012 in eastern Luanda and congregating dozens of thousands of followers every week, is the ultimate example.

However, despite these processes of heightened hierarchization, through certain dimensions of the remembrance of Toko today we can see that the principles of mutuality and anti-hierarchical organization are still active to this day. One example is the way Toko is remembered as an individual and leader in the church by those who met him in person: like a humble person, consistently refusing any kind of moral, political or economic superiority vis-à-vis his own followers. For instance, he refused to be called *pai* ("father", a common form of deference to seniority or superiority in Angola and the Congo), preferring the term *dirigente* ("director"), and never distinguished among his followers through age, gender, socio-economic status, etc. Likewise, he would not accept as his own the recurrent offers that his wealthier followers would give him (cars, houses, etc.), and preferred to consider them collective property of the church. This portrait of Toko as an egalitarian leader is often conveyed as a critique of the church's current hegemonic version and the hierarchical structure it has imposed with the bishopric. Such is the case of one specific group known as the Twelve Elders, who are composed by survivors and descendants of the *zombo* who were expelled or voluntarily deported from the Belgian Congo, and who also sojourned in the Vale do Loge plantation. Frontally opposed to Nunes' leadership, they rely on this memory, as well as on the original mutualism and solidarity cultivated during the first years of the colony, in their contestations.

Another example can be found in the plural organizations that remain demographically marginal but proactive in the Tokoist universe. One such case is a small group based in Luanda, known as the Casa de Oração ("House of Prayer"). This group emerged in the late 1970s, a few years before Toko's death, as a group of youngsters (*na ngunza*, the "sons of the prophets") who circulated around the leader's residence and conducted daily prayer sessions. They became close to the leader and watched from a distance as the Tokoist movement began its process of internal combustion with the struggles for power occurring within. Today, they combine their weekly prayer meetings with their commitment to work for the reunification of the church. However, in contrast with other sectors of the church, they reject leadership as a way out of the conflict, and advocate a collegial solution, with no given leader, but a council of representatives who would decide upon the church's destiny. This form of political organization can also be understood as a form of horizontal organization that attempted to break through the hierarchical stratification developed on the meantime in the Tokoist venture. So far, they have not been successful in their attempts.

In any case, their critique, as that of the Twelve Elders, not only contests the hierarchization of the church's political organization, but also the moral implications of such transformations, which are seen as configuring a deviation from Simão Toko's preaching, thus implying a corruption of the egalitarian and mutualist principles.

Conclusion: liberation and freedom in Christian cultures

The apparent opposition between anarchism and religion has been historically construed as an irreconcilable one, especially considering the comments set forth by Mikhail Bakunin on the tyranny and coercion of theology and the idea of God as 'phantom', against the conviction of the intrinsic freedom of man.[44] Bakunin, who is seen as one of the most influential figures of anarchist thought, was also a self-proclaimed anti-theologian who deconstructed the 'absurd tales' of the doctrines extracted from the Bible in the history of Christian thought.[45] However, one could also argue that Bakunin's critique was ultimately directed not to the Bible or the idea of God per se, but rather to the posterior political construction that reduced, through control and exploitation, believers and citizens to ignorance and intellectual reduction.[46] From this perspective, throughout most of anarchist thought, church and state were the same agents of exploitation – and thus the anarchist aspiration of 'abolishment' must concern extrinsic government and God alike. This classic positioning, as Paul-François Tremlett has pointed out, has historically placed the debate of religion in anarchist thought into the fringes.[47]

However, as several authors mentioned in this chapter point out, the contradiction only emerges in the process of political exegesis and translation into religious institution; and in fact, both religion and anarchism share, more often than not, a utopian ambition. Thus, the problem with the debate was not so much the lack of ability (or will) to surpass the epistemological conundrum between God and anarchism, but instead perhaps a concentration of understanding of 'religion' as 'institution' on behalf of particular strands of anarchist thought and the consequent lack of interest in surveying the implications of religious experience in the believers, both in spiritual and political terms. Likewise, a similar position has been assumed on behalf of a clear majority of theologians who refused to accept the possibility of an anarchist political framing in their own conceptions, also due to a restricted, biased understanding of its implications.

In this chapter, I attempted to describe one such movement of a religious configuration that is self-conceived as political, collectivist, egalitarian and liberationist. In many ways, its historical emergence revealed the confluence of ideals and practices that are equally shared by anarchistic thought and activity. Namely: the initial association under the framework of mutualist organization; the development of a utopian, idealist spirit based on ideas of freedom; the practice of 'obedient resistance' against colonial domination; and the establishment of a 'horizontal', communal leadership. In a way, Toko's initial activity in Léopoldville, both in religious and political terms, shared Bakunin's will of rebellion against subjugation against the 'empire' (political, epistemological, philosophical). The developments which occurred after his passing in 1984 implied a process of revision that ultimately corrupted the initial ideals by introducing hierarchizing processes. In this respect, if in the first years of the movement egalitarianism was a practical principle through which Toko and his followers devised an autonomist project, today it seems to have become a somewhat marginal moralizing statement deployed as a tool of contestation against processes of ideological and institutional innovation. The contestation that emerged against such processes of innovation and hierarchization, stemming from the memory of the egalitarian past, illustrates the dilemmas of the coupling of religion (Christianity) and anarchism.

Notes

1. This text is part of an anthropological study of the Tokoist Church debating problems of memory, temporality and politics. The ethnographic research has been taking place since 2007 in Luanda, Northern Angola and Lisbon, where I attended religious services, conducted interviews with church elders and prophets, and visited sacred sites with the church's members. It has also been complemented with historical research in colonial archives in Lisbon and Brussels. I would like to thank Alexandre Christoyannopoulos and Matthew Adams, as well as the anonymous reviewers, for helping me improve this text significantly.

2. James Grenfell, 'Simão Toco: An Angolan Prophet', *Journal of Religion in Africa*, 28:2, (1998), 210–226.

3. See Vernand Eller, *Christian Anarchy: Jesus' Primacy over the Powers* (Grand Rapids, MI: Eerdmans Publishing, 1987); Jacques Ellul, *Anarchy and Christianity* (Grand Rapids, MI: Eerdmans Publishing, 1991); Harold Barclay, 'Anarchist Confrontations with Religion', in *New Perspectives on Anarchism*, ed. by Nathan Jun and Shane Wahl (Lanham: Lexington Books, 2010), 169–88; and Alexandre Christoyannopoulos, 'Christian Anarchism: A Revolutionary Reading of the Bible', in *New Perspectives on Anarchism*, ed. by Nathan Jun and Shane Wahl (Lanham: Lexington Books, 2010), 149–68.

4. The Coro de Kibokolo (named as such in honour of the Baptist mission in which Toco grew up), sang religious hymns, mostly from the Baptist hymnal, but was also composed of members from other churches, such as the Salvation Army, Jehovah's Witnesses, etc., and also sung new hymns composed by Toco. The choir begun as a group of twelve youngsters led by Toco, but soon became a movement of hundreds of singers, notorious in the religious circles of the city for their organization and musical performances. However, the vast majority was not only Angolan and Bakongo but also originating from the same region in Angola: the Maquela do Zombo prefecture, in Uíge. For this reason they were known as *zombos*.

5. See Grenfell 'Simão Toco'; and Ruy Blanes, *A Prophetic Trajectory. Ideologies of Time and Space in an Angolan Religious Movement* (Oxford and New York: Berghahn Books, 2014).

6. Ibid.

7. See e.g. Paul-François Tremlett, 'On the Formation and Function of the Category "Religion" in Anarchist Writing', *Culture and Religion* 5:3 (2004), 367–381; and Alexandre Christoyannopoulos, 'Christian Anarchism'.

8. One could in fact affirm that most Bakongo observed – and observe today – a different political map, that of the ancient Kingdom of Kongo, which was one of the largest state structures in Africa for many centuries, and saw its demise confirmed in the early twentieth century, with the effective occupation of the territory on behalf of the Portuguese, Belgian and French empires. From this perspective, the memory of the Kingdom of Kongo is still very present and agent

in several contemporary political and religious movements in the region. Concomitantly so is the desire or expectation to one day restore it. See René Pélissier, 'A la Recherche d'un Dieu Anti-Colonialiste', in *La Colonie du Minotaure. Nationalismes et Révoltes en Angola (1926–1961)* (Orgeval: Éditions Pélissier, 1978); and Ramon Sarró, Fátima Viegas and Ruy Blanes, 'La Guerre en temps de Paix. Ethnicité et Angolanité dans l'Église Kimbanguiste de Luanda', *Politique Africaine* 110 (2008), 84–101.

9. Georges Balandier, 'Messianismes et Colonialismes en Afrique Noire', *Cahiers Internationaux de Sociologie* 14 (1952), 1–65; Alfredo Margarido, 'The Tokoist Church and Portuguese Colonialism in Angola', in *Protest and Resistance in Angola and Brazil. Comparative Studies*, ed. by R. Chilcote (Berkeley and London: University of California Press, 1972), 29–52; Wyatt MacGaffey, *Religion and Society in Central Africa: The BaKongo of Lower Zaire* (Chicago: University of Chicago Press, 1986); Jean-Luc Vellut, 'The Congo Basin and Angola', in *General History of Africa, VI, Africa in the Nineteenth Century until the 1880s*, VV.AA. (London: James Currey & UNESCO, 1989); and Luena Pereira, 'Os Bakongo de Angola: Religião, Política e Parentesco num Bairro de Luanda', PhD Thesis, Department of Anthropology, University of São Paulo, 2004.

10. The ABAKO, one of the first grassroots autochthon political associations in the region, was one of the main protagonists of Bakongo nationalism against the Belgian colony.

11. Edmundo Rocha also notes that Léopoldville also harboured many Portuguese Catholic priests, critical of the colonial endeavour and the role played by the Catholic hierarchies in the process. They were certainly inspired by the Catholic worker unions that developed in Europe and North America. Edmundo Rocha, *Contribuição ao Estudo da Génese do Nacionalismo Moderno Angolano: período de 1950–1964: testemunho e estudo documental* (Luanda: Kilombelombe, 2003). See also Mary Segers, 'Equality and Christian Anarchism: The Political and Social Ideas of the Catholic Worker Movement', *The Review of Politics* 40, 2 (1978), 196–230; and Maria Inácia Rezola, *O Sindicalismo Católico no Estado Novo* (Lisbon: Estampa, 1999).

12. Georges Balandier, 'Messianismes et Colonialismes en Afrique Noire'; and *Sociologie Actuelle de l'Afrique Noire* (Paris: Presses Universitaires de France, 1955).

13. See Ramon Sarró, 'Kongo en Lisboa: un ensayo sobre la reubicación y extraversión religiosa', *Introducción a los Estudios Africanos*, ed. by Yolanda Aixelá et al., (Barcelona: CEIBA, 2009), 115–129. Despite this temporal framing, the Lower Congo region bears a long history of prophetic movements with a political impact, which are recurrently remembered by the followers of these contemporary movements. For instance, one transversal historical reference is Dona Beatriz Kimpa Vita, a late 17th century prophetess who promoted an Afro-centered re-reading of Christianity known as Antonianism. See John Thornton, *The Kongolese Saint Anthony: Dona Beatriz Kimpa Vita and the Antonian Movement, 1684–1706* (Cambridge: Cambridge University Press, 1998).

14. See e.g. Martial Sinda, *Le Messianisme Congolais et ses Incidences Politiques. Kimbanguisme, Matsouanisme, Autres Mouvements* (Paris: Payot, 1972).

15. As one of the reviewers of this text rightly pointed out, these traditions of leadership in the Bakongo culture bear an interesting paradox, namely when we consider the 'acephalousness' of the Bakongo segmentary system, where the idea of the collective is primary. Within this framework, Christian theology was not so much responsible for the introduction of hierarchy and individuality, but instead worked along this paradox, combining logics of leadership and egalitarian communitarianism.

16. Ruy Blanes, 'Extraordinary Times: Charismatic Repertoires in Contemporary African Prophetism', in *Ecstasies and Institutions: The Anthropology of Religious Charisma*, ed. by Charles Lindholm (New York: Palgrave Macmillan, 2013), 147–168.

17. Denis Tull, 'Troubled State-Building in the DR Congo: The Challenge from the Margins', *The Journal of Modern African Studies* 48, 4 (2010), 643–661.

18. See Bertram Turner and Thomas Kirsch (eds.), *Permutations of Order: Religion and Law as Contested Sovereignties* (Aldershot: Ashgate, 2008).

19. On hierarchy and totalization, see Knut Rio and Olaf Smedal (eds.), *Hierarchy. Persistence and Transformation in Social Formations* (Oxford and New York: Berghahn, 2009).

20. On independency in Africa, see Robert Rotberg and Ali A. Mazrui (eds.), *Protest and Power in Black Africa* (New York: Oxford University Press, 1970). On the production of the state, see Bruce Kapferer and Christopher Taylor, 'Forces in the Production of the State', in *Contesting the State. The Dynamics of Resistance and Control*, ed. by Angela Hobart and Bruce Kapferer (Wantage: Sean Kingston, 2012), 1–20.

21. On refracted governmentality, see António Tomás, 'Refracted Governmentality: Space, Politics and Social Structure in Contemporary Luanda', PhD Thesis, Anthropology, Columbia University (2012). On state and citizenship, see James Scott, *Seeing Like a State: How Certain Schemes to Improve the Human Condition Have Failed* (New Haven: Yale University Press, 1998), 283–323; and Bruce Kapferer and Bjorn Bertelsen, 'Introduction: The Crisis of Power and Reformations of the State in Globalizing Realities', in *Crisis of the State: War and Social Upheaval*, edited by Bruce Kapferer and Bjorn Bertelsen (Oxford: Berghahn, 2009), 1–26.

22. Ruy Blanes, 'Da Confusão à Ironia. Expectativas e Legados da PIDE em Angola', *Análise Social* XLVIII, 1 (203), 30–55.

23. I am referring here to Pierre-Joseph Proudhon's well-known suspicion (perhaps obsession) vis-à-vis the State as a form of government that is ultimately a mechanism of control, abuse and theft of the autonomous individual. One such argument appears in his famed manifesto *Idée Générale De La Revolution Au XIXe Siecle*, published in 1851. See Daniel Guerin, *Anarchism. From Theory to Practice* (New York: Monthly Review Press, 1970).

24. Wyatt MacGaffey, *Modern Kongo Prophets. Religion in a Plural Society*, (Bloomington, IN: Indiana University Press, 1983); Anne Mélice, 'Prophétisme, héterodoxie et dissidence. L'imaginaire kimbanguiste en mouvement', PhD Thesis, Social and Political Sciences, University of Liège, 2011.

25. Pedro Agostinho, *Simão Gonçalves Toco e os Tocoistas no Mundo* (Luanda: Edição de Autor, n.d.), my translation.

26. Ibid.

27. James Grenfell, 'Simão Toco'.

28. See Vernand Eller, *Christian Anarchy*; Harold Barclay, 'Christian Confrontations'; Alexandre Christoyannopoulos, 'Christian Anarchism', and *Christian Anarchism: A Political Commentary on the Gospel* (Exeter: Imprint Academic, 2010).

29. Leo Tolstoy, *The Kingdom of God is Within You* (New York: Cassell, 1894).

30. Ruy Blanes, 'Extraordinary Times'.

31. Q.- Reconnaissez-vous avoir été arrêté, portant sur la poitrine l'insigne du « Chœur de Kibokolo » ?
R.- Oui, parce que je suis membre du chœur, dirigé par Toko Simao Goncalves.

Q.- Ignoriez-bous que cette secte est interdite ?
R.- Je ne l'ignore pas.

Q.- Pourquoi alors, malgré l'interdiction, vous avez maintenu votre participation à ce mouvement irrégulier ?
R.- Parce qu'il s'agit là d'un ordre de Dieu auquel je dois me soumettre.

Q.- C'est comme qui dirait d'abord les ordres donnés par Toko, ensuite le Gouvernement, n'est-ce-pas ?
R.- En effet, c'est bien ainsi.

Q.- Etes-vous disposé à abandonner le mouvement « Chœur de Kibokolo » ?
R- Je suis arrêté, je n'abdiquerai jamais.

32. Ruy Blanes, *A Prophetic Trajectory*.

33. Harold Barclay, 'Christian Confrontations'.

34. Ruy Blanes, 'Da Confusão à Ironia'; Ruy Blanes and Abel Paxe, 'Atheist Political Cultures in Independent Angola', *Social Analysis* 59, 2 (2015), 62–80.

35. In the 1950s, there was a strong investment on behalf of the Portuguese government towards exploring the natural resources in its colonies, creating several agricultural and industrial projects. Coffee and cotton production became main export products in the Angolan colony during this period, but also the loci of the first anti-colonial rebellions, considering the enslaved conditions in which the autochthon labour worked.

36. The conflict would be eventually resolved by Toko himself, asking his followers to remove the symbol in order to prevent further physical confrontation, and reminding them that the 'true symbol' was in their foreheads and hearts – not in their clothes.

37. Grenfell also describes how the group that was sent to Luanda at the time refused to pay taxes when they were forced to work for half pay. James Grenfell, 'Simão Toco', 219.

38. The full name of the movement was *Nkutakani a Nsumbani ya Aklisto Minkwikizi mia Ntoto wa Zombo*, Association Mutuelle Chrétienne du Plateau du Zombo.

39. This form of micro-saving venture is a version of a common form of economic organization that in fact persists today in Angola/Congo and elsewhere in Africa. In Angola, the *kixikila* is an example of this, where groups of 5–10 women associate and create micro-enterprises. I see these ventures as informal, grassroots forms of mutualism in many ways similar to the ventures described above. See e.g. Henda Lucia Ducados and Manuel Ennes Ferreira, 'O financiamento informal e as estratégias de sobrevivência económica das mulheres em Angola: a Kixikila no município do Sambizanga (Luanda), CEsA Documentos de Trabalho 53 (1998), Working Paper.

40. Grenfell, 'Simão Toco', 220.

41. Kenneth Surin, *Freedom Not Yet. Liberation and the Next World Order* (Durham and London: Duke University Press, 2009).

42. Thus for instance, believers in the Tokoist churches also belong to the 'Northern' or 'Southern' tribes.

43. Ruy Blanes, 'Unstable Biographies: The Ethnography of Memory and Historicity in an Angolan Prophetic Movement', *History and Anthropology* 22, 1 (2011), 93–119; and *A Prophetic Trajectory*.

44. Mikhail Bakunin, *God and the State* (New York: Dover Publications, 1970 [1871]).

45. Mikhail Bakunin, *God and the State*, 11.

46. Mikhail Bakunin, *God and the State*, 16–17.

47. Paul-François Tremlett, 'On the Formation and Function'.

References

Agostinho, Pedro, *Simão Gonçalves Toco e os Tocoistas no Mundo* (Luanda: Edição de Autor, n.d.).

Bakunin, Michail, *God and the State* (New York: Dover Publications, 1970 [1871]).

Balandier, Georges, *Sociologie Actuelle de l'Afrique Noire* (Paris: Presses Universitaires de France, 1955).

_____. 'Messianismes et Colonialismes en Afrique Noire', *Cahiers Internationaux de Sociologie* 14 (1952), 41–65.

Barclay, Harold, 'Anarchist Confrontations with Religion', in *New Perspectives on Anarchism* (Lanham: Lexington Books, 2010), edited by Nathan and Shane Wahl, pp. 169–88.

Blanes, Ruy, *A Prophetic Trajectory. Ideologies of Time and Space in an Angolan Religious Movement* (Oxford: Berghahn, 2014).

_____. 'Extraordinary Times: Charismatic Repertoires in Contemporary African Prophetism', in Lindholm, in *Ecstasies and Institutions: The Anthropology of Religious Charisma*, edited by Charles Lindholm. New York: Palgrave Macmillan, 2013), pp. 147–168.

_____. 'Da Confusão à Ironia. Expectativas e Legados da PIDE em Angola', *Análise Social* XLVIII, 1 (2013), 30–55.

_____. 'Unstable Biographies: The Ethnography of Memory and Historicity in an Angolan Prophetic Movement', *History and Anthropology* 22, 1 (2011), 93–119.

Blanes, Ruy and Abel Paxe, 'Atheist Political Cultures in Independent Angola', *Social Analysis* 59, 2 (2015), 62–80.

Christoyannopoulos, Alexandre, *Christian Anarchism: A Political Commentary on the Gospel* (Exeter: Imprint Academic, 2010).

_____. 'Christian Anarchism: A Revolutionary Reading of the Bible', in *New Perspectives on Anarchism*, edited by Nathan Jun and Shane Wahl (Lanham: Lexington Books, 2010), pp. 149–68.

Ducados, Henda Lucia and Manuel Ennes Ferreira, 'O financiamento informal e as estratégias de sobrevivência económica das mulheres em Angola: a Kixikila no município do Sambizanga (Luanda), *CEsA Documentos de Trabalho* 53 (1998), Working Paper.

Eller, Vernand, *Christian Anarchy: Jesus' Primacy over the Powers* (Grand Rapids, MI: Eerdmans Publishing, 1987).

Ellul, Jacques, *Anarchy and Christianity* (Grand Rapids, MI: Eerdmans Publishing, 1991).

Grenfell, James, 'Simão Toco: An Angolan Prophet', *Journal of Religion in Africa* 28, 2 (1998), 210–226.

Guerin, Daniel, *Anarchism. From Theory to Practice* (New York: Monthly Review Press, 1970).

Kapferer, Bruce and Bjorn Bertelsen, 'Introduction: The Crisis of Power and Reformations of the State in Globalizing Realities', in *Crisis of the State: War and Social Upheaval*, edited by Bruce Kapferer and Bjorn Bertelsen (Oxford: Berghahn, 2009), pp. 1–26.

Kapferer, Bruce and Christopher Taylor, 'Forces in the Production of the State', in *Contesting the State. The Dynamics of Resistance and Control*, edited by Angela Hobart and Bruce Kapferer (Wantage: Sean Kingston, 2012), pp. 1–20.

MacGaffey, Wyatt, *Religion and Society in Central Africa: The BaKongo of Lower Zaire* (Chicago: University of Chicago Press, 1986).

_____. *Modern Kongo Prophets. Religion in a Plural Society* (Bloomington, IN: Indiana University Press, 1983).

Margarido, Alfredo, 'The Tokoist Church and Portuguese Colonialism in Angola', in *Protest and Resistance in Angola and Brazil. Comparative Studies*, edited by Ronald Chilcote (Berkeley & London: University of California Press, 1978) 29–52.

Mélice. Anne, 'Prophétisme, héterodoxie et dissidence. L'imaginaire kimbanguiste en mouvement', PhD Thesis, Social and Political Sciences, University of Liège (2011).

Pélissier, René, 'A la Recherche d'un Dieu Anti-Colonialiste', in *La Colonie du Minotaure. Nationalismes et Révoltes en Angola (1926–1961)* (Orgeval: Éditions Pélissier, 1978).

Pereira, Luena, 'Os Bakongo de Angola: Religião, Política e Parentesco num Bairro de Luanda', PhD Thesis, Department of Anthropology, University of São Paulo (2004).

Rezola, Maria, *O Sindicalismo Católico no Estado Novo* (Lisbon: Estampa, 1999).

Rio, Knut and Olaf Smedal, eds, *Hierarchy. Persistence and Transformation in Social Formations* (Oxford and New York: Berghahn, 2009).

Rocha, Edmundo, *Contribuição ao Estudo da Génese do Nacionalismo Moderno Angolano: período de 1950–1964: testemunho e estudo documental* (Luanda: Kilombelombe, 2003).

Rotberg, Robert & Ali A. Mazrui, eds, *Protest and Power in Black Africa* (New York: Oxford University Press, 1970).

Sarró, Ramon, Ruy Blanes and Fátima Viegas, 'La Guerre en temps de Paix. Ethnicité et Angolanité dans l'Église Kimbanguiste de Luanda', *Politique Africaine* 110 (2008), 84–101.

Sarró, Ramon, 'Kongo en Lisboa: un ensayo sobre la reubicación y extraversión religiosa', in *Introducción a los Estudios Africanos*, edited by Yolanda Aixelá et al. (Barcelona: CEIBA, 2009), pp. 115–129.

Scott, James C., *Seeing Like a State: How Certain Schemes to Improve the Human Condition Have Failed* (New Haven: Yale University Press, 1998), pp. 283–323.

Segers, Mary 'Equality and Christian Anarchism: The Political and Social Ideas of the Catholic Worker Movement', *The Review of Politics* 40, 2 (1978), 196–230.

Sinda, Martial, *Le Messianisme Congolais et ses Incidences Politiques. Kimbanguisme, Matsouanisme, Autres Mouvements* (Paris: Payot, 1972).

Surin, Kenneth, *Freedom Not Yet. Liberation and the Next World Order* (Durham and London: Duke University Press, 2009).

Thornton, John. *The Kongolese Saint Anthony: Dona Beatriz Kimpa Vita and the Antonian Movement, 1684–1706* (Cambridge: Cambridge University Press, 1998).

Tomás, António, 'Refracted Governmentality: Space, Politics and Social Structure in Contemporary Luanda', PhD Thesis, Anthropology, Columbia University (2012).

Tremlett, Paul-François, 'On the Formation and Function of the Category "Religion" in Anarchist Writing', *Culture and Religion* 5, 3 (2004), 367–381.

Tolstoy, Leo. *The Kingdom of God is Within You* (New York: Cassell, 1894).

Tull, Denis, 'Troubled State-Building in the DR Congo: The Challenge from the Margins', *The Journal of Modern African Studies* 48, 4 (2010), 643–661.

Turner, Bertram & Thomas Kirsch, eds, *Permutations of Order: Religion and Law as Contested Sovereignties* (Aldershot: Ashgate, 2008).

Vellut, Jean-Luc. 'The Congo Basin and Angola', in *General History of Africa, VI, Africa in the Nineteenth Century until the 1880s*, VV.AA. (London: James Currey & UNESCO, 1989).

Why Anarchists Like Zen? A Libertarian Reading of Shinran (1173–1263)

Enrique Galván-Álvarez
Universidad Internacional de La Rioja (UNIR), Spain

Most attempts to formulate a Buddhist anarchism in the West take Zen Buddhism as their reference point, often disregarding other Buddhist traditions and their anarchic/libertarian potential. In response to these early Western formulations I propose an alternative pathway for Buddhist anarchism based on a radically different Buddhist tradition, that of Shinran Shonin (1173–1263). Shinran's thought can arguably contribute to contemporary Buddhist anarchism some of the elements that it seems to be lacking: a self-critique that is not devoid of social criticism, a deconstruction of Buddhist power and an historical awareness. For this purpose, I will first outline some of the anti-authoritarian traits in Shinran's writings, which have so far not been read from an explicitly anarchist angle. Then I will look closely at Shinran's critical view of humanity and human relations through his concept of mappo, drawing out the egalitarian and subversive implications of Buddhist eschatology. In so doing I show how Shinran's radical re-reading of the Buddhist canon, and the self-understanding it yields, bring into question some important narratives that legitimize and construct the established, politico-religious order.

1. Why Anarchists Like Zen –Introduction.

Most attempts to formulate a Buddhist anarchism in the West take Zen Buddhism as their reference point, often disregarding other Buddhist traditions and their anarchic/libertarian potential. This is partly to do with the way in which Zen has been presented

How to cite this book chapter:
Galván-Álvarez, E. 2017. Why Anarchists Like Zen? A Libertarian Reading of Shinran (1173–1263). In: Christoyannopoulos, A. and Adams, M. S. (eds.) *Essays in Anarchism and Religion: Volume 1*. Pp. 78–123. Stockholm: Stockholm University Press. DOI: https://doi.org/10.16993/bak.d. License: CC-BY

to the West, by individuals such as D.T. Suzuki or Alan Watts, and also due to a relative ignorance about Asian anarchisms and their links with various forms of (both Zen and non-Zen) Buddhism.[1] It is not uncommon to read that Gary Snyder was the first Buddhist anarchist, a view that despite being popular does no justice to the longer history of Buddhist anarchism.[2] Although Snyder is likely to have been the first to have used the term 'Buddhist anarchism,' in his homonymous 1961 essay (he is certainly the first one to use the term in English), the first self-identified Buddhist anarchists are to be found in the turbulent histories of early 20th century Japan, Korea and China. Buddhist anarchism first emerged as a Buddhist response to colonial domination (Korea), industrialization, war and the totalitarian state (Japan) and the various authoritarian regimes that followed the fall of the Qing dynasty (China).[3] Many participants in the North American Counterculture had an interest in both Buddhism and anarchism, but they were largely oblivious to the fact that the two traditions had already been brought together in Asia.

Snyder's rhetoric of "[t]he mercy of the West [being] social revolution" and "the mercy of the East [being] individual insight into the basic self / void," hints that not only he is setting himself up as a pioneer by merging the two "mercies" but also that the West lacks "insight" and the East "social revolution".[4] Although Snyder has long moved away from this orientalist discourse, some of the problematic aspects of his Buddhist anarchism still haunt many of the representations of Buddhist anarchism in the West. Although Zen is certainly not incompatible with anarchism (in fact one of the first self-identified Buddhist anarchists was the Japanese Soto Zen monk Uchiyama Gudo, 1874–1911), the way in which Zen and anarchism have been combined in the West often lacks a thorough critique of Buddhist power, historical awareness and the willingness to confront authoritarian aspects within the Zen tradition.[5] Furthermore, Suzuki's conception of "pure Zen", still popularly accepted in most Western countries, as a "rational" practice completely devoid of rituals, doctrine or philosophy, is not only "ahistorical [and] formless"; it is also crafted in a political context that is far from libertarian.[6] Suzuki's "pure Zen" is an attempt to marry Zen exceptionalism to state-sponsored Japanese

nationalism and to offer "an exceptional gift of the Japanese people to the world", especially to an ailing West, "overtly determined
by its rationalistic materialism".[7]

Although Suzuki's Zen is a perfectly valid formulation within
the Zen tradition, to claim that all historical manifestations of Zen
are 'pure Zen' or that Zen is the most rational form of Buddhism
and therefore the one closest to radical thinking, is problematic.
At best such a claim is a misguided bow to Zen narratives of
self-legitimation and at worst a colonial ordering of Buddhist
traditions according to European criteria and needs, which mirrors the British discovery of Buddhism in the 19th century.[8] The
discovery and construction of (Theravada) Buddhism by early
British orientalists reflects an analogous pattern to the modern
construction of Zen in so far as it tries to identify a "pure" and
"original" Buddhism that is palatable for the rational ethos of the
post-enlightenment. By stripping this "original" Buddhism from
"irrational" and "religious" elements, Buddhism is rendered abstract, philosophical and ahistorical, thus fulfilling the needs of a
certain European consumer.

The aim of this chapter is to propose an alternative pathway
for Buddhist anarchism based on a radically different Buddhist
formulation, that of Shinran Shonin (1173–1263). Shinran's
thought can arguably contribute to contemporary Buddhist
anarchism some of the elements that it seems to be lacking: a
self-critique that is not devoid of social criticism, a deconstruction of Buddhist power and some form of historical awareness.
For this purpose, I will first outline some of the anti-authoritarian traits in Shinran's writings, which have so far not been
read from an explicitly anarchist angle. Then I will look closely at Shinran's critical view of humanity and human relations
through his concept of *mappo*, drawing out the egalitarian and
subversive implications of Buddhist eschatology. In so doing I
show how Shinran's radical re-reading of the Buddhist canon,
and the self-understanding it yields, bring into question some
important narratives that legitimize and construct the established, politico-religious order. Finally, I explore the ethical and
political implications of Shinran's actions, assessing what Jodo
Shinshu (i.e. Shinran's Buddhism) can contribute, not just to

the deconstruction, but also to the articulation of a Buddhist anarchist project.[9]

2. Rebellion Beyond Zen: Shinran's Buddhism

The most significant and central feature of Shinran's thought is the logic of *tariki*, often translated as other-power.[10] Whereas in most Buddhist traditions, including Zen, the individual is meant to strive through some form of disciplined practice regime in order to reach a given soteriological goal, Shinran formulated a Buddhism based on a radical negation of self-effort and self-reliance as a means to insight. In fact he harmonized means and ends by arguing that if the end (becoming a Buddha) is a state of naturalness and spontaneity (Jp. *jinen*, Ch. *ziran*) the means (the path towards Buddhahood) must also reflect and be guided by those qualities. Shinran's formulation of *tariki* represented a significant departure from the more conventional and established forms of Buddhism and, consequently, had important social implications. Shinran lived during the turbulent Kamakura period (1185–1333), at a time when other Japanese Buddhist 'reformers', such as Shinran's own teacher, Honen (1133–1212), as well as Dogen (pioneer of Japanese Soto Zen, 1200–1253) or Nichiren (1222–1282), were often critical of the established socio-religious order and substantially reformulated existing ideas about Buddhist practice, social relations and hierarchy. In order to explore the anarchic potential of Shinran's thought I will first discuss how Zen has been (mis) construed as the most anarchist of Buddhisms.

Paraphrasing Christmas Humphreys and John Clark, Peter Marshall refers to Zen as "the apotheosis of Buddhism" and the Buddhism that "developed its libertarian potential to the fullest".[11] The libertarian thrust of Zen lies in its iconoclastic statements and the often playful, absurdist and rhizomatic dynamics that animate many of the narratives of the Zen lore.[12] However, most Zen anarchists or anarchists with Zen Buddhist sympathies present Zen in an ahistorical, uncritical and decontextualized fashion, sometimes enshrining meditation as an inherently revolutionary tool for social change.[13] The self-legitimizing discourse of Zen is also often taken at face value leaving unquestioned the histories of the

Zen tradition and institutions in a context of competition with other Buddhist schools and discourses.[14] The lack of self-criticism and the adoption of an absolutist Zen discourse renders these attempts at formulating a Buddhist anarchism self-referential and unconvincing.

Thus, formulations of Zen anarchism, such as Max Cafard's (a.k.a. John Clark) *Zen Anarchy* or Kerry Thornley's *Zenarchy* often present Zen as being "more anarchic than anarchism" or "hold Universal Enlightenment a prerequisite to abolition of the state".[15] The complete identification of Zen and anarchism leads to a dismissal of authoritarian elements in the Zen tradition, which are either ignored or explained away by using Zen's own self-legitimating narratives. An example of this tendency can be found not only among Zen anarchists but also in Marshall, who presents Zen's disciplinary regime of practice in a mildly sympathetic fashion by using much of Zen's own discourse. The authority of the teacher is justified because students need someone "to help them break out of their everyday perceptions and intellectual habits".[16] Analogously, the strict discipline of Zen monasteries, including the ritual of using the *keisaku* for hitting the shoulder, is presented as "ways of shaking people out of their habitual way of seeing" and as a method to "develop the pupil's character from within and increase his or her moral sense".[17] Although Marshall acknowledges that these forms of authority and externally half-imposed, half-consented discipline are "aimed at creating self-disciplined freedom, not dependence on masters" he does not question the seeming dissonance between means and ends.[18] Many of these formulations take as premise the anarchic nature of Zen, which if left unquestioned result in celebratory discourses that lack a reflective and critical self-assessment. Whereas the Zen tradition does not lack elements of self-reflection and self-deconstruction, it is true that those elements are very rarely engaged with in Western Zen anarchist writings. Hence, Shinran's understanding of Buddhism through the logic of *tariki* and the self-critical awareness it yields, can contribute a thorough critique of Buddhist histories of power, which is essential to any Buddhist anarchism. In order to make Shinran's anarchic potential explicit I now turn to outline the antiauthoritarian implications of *tariki* in the context of the Pure Land tradition.

3. The Liberative Promise of *Tariki*

An important task in the formulation of any Buddhist anarchism is to examine the social relations that a given set of Buddhist ideas inspires or produces. The fact that most Buddhist institutions throughout history have tended to mimic and adopt the authoritarian patterns present in their societies does not mean that all formulations of the Buddhist teachings automatically lead towards oppressive social formations. Moreover, institutionalization is unequally regarded in the various Buddhist traditions; it might be seen as an essential and necessary feature enshrined as part of the doctrine (e.g. the role of the teacher in Tantric Buddhism) or it might be conceptualized as a historical and situational development that is somehow useful but also contingent (e.g. the institutions claiming to preserve Shinran's legacy), with a broad range of positions in between.[19] Any Buddhist anarchism would favour more decentralized forms of organization that do not consider social hierarchy as a requisite for Buddhist practice. Arguably, the teachings of Shinran or Jodo Shinshu lean towards the more libertarian side, despite being used, after his death, to create highly hierarchical and rigid systems of authority.[20] In his radical reformulation of Buddhist doctrine Shinran demolishes many of the premises that legitimated the Buddhist authorities and hierarchies of his time. The debunking of established Buddhist rituals, moral and meditative disciplines and the monastic regime is accomplished through the logic of *tariki*.

The *tariki* principle involves, in Shinran's own words, "entrusting ourselves to the Primal Vow and our birth becoming firmly settled; hence it is altogether without one's working".[21] The "Primal Vow" refers to the 18th among Dharmakara Bodhisattva's 48 vows, who promised not to attain enlightenment (and therefore become Amida Buddha) unless all beings could be born in his Pure Land by simply calling his name with a trusting mind. "Birth", the soteriological goal of Shinran's Buddhism, is thus accomplished by trusting the Buddha's vow and not through the practitioners "own working", that is her or his efforts, designs or meritorious practice. The practical implication of this principle is a cancellation of the polarity of good and evil: "on one hand, you should not be anxious that Tathagata [Amida Buddha] will not receive you because you do wrong [...] On the other hand you should not think that you deserve to attain birth because you are good".[22] The irrelevance of moral or spiritual abilities for attaining the soteriological goal renders the institutions, disciplinary regimes and authority figures that act as guiding examples of moral or spiritual accomplishment also irrelevant. In fact, Shinran does not stop at considering good and evil people equal in regards to realizing entrusting to the vow, but goes as far as enshrining the evil person, as the true object of the Buddha's promise: "Amida made the Vow, the essential intent of which is the evil person's attainment of Buddhahood".[23]

In this way, Shinran does not only transcend the established Buddhist morality but also subverts its implicit hierarchy, arguing that the "good" person is likely to rely on her or his own abilities to achieve Buddhahood and therefore is less likely to entrust to the vow, whereas "evil" people are more receptive to the vow since they are more aware of their limitations. In this new framework the notions of good and evil are relativized and redefined, affecting the social relations based on their polarity. "Good" people are those who think of themselves as good and do not realize their "evilness". The logic of Amida's vow makes both good and evil contingent, rendering the authority figures associated with good unnecessary and preventing a clear-cut hierarchy based on the deliberate cultivation of good acts or states of mind. Therefore, hierarchical institutions devised for the purpose of cultivating good and avoiding evil (e.g. the monastic community) can also be made redundant. Although new institutions could be created to promote "entrusting to the Primal Vow", such institutions can never be said to mediate or cultivate the experience of entrusting. Shinran's strong emphasis on *tariki* characterizes entrusting or *shinjin* as spontaneous experience that cannot be achieved through practice, therefore any religious institution is rendered contingent.

The traditional authority of the master over the disciples is also redefined if not dissolved altogether. Though Shinran regarded Honen as his master, and the presence of Amida in the world, he claims to have not had "even a single disciple". There were many who looked up to Shinran as an example to follow, but Shinran's logic is based on his understanding of *tariki*: "if I brought people to say the nembutsu [Amida's name] through my own efforts, then they might be my disciples. But it is indeed preposterous to call persons 'my disciples' when they say the nembutsu having received the working of Amida".[24] Consequently, Shinran regards the idea that "going against a teacher" mars one's path to enlightenment as both "arrogant" and "absurd".[25] Students and teachers meet and part because of their conditions and conditionings (in Sanskrit: *karma*), and gratitude is a spontaneous feeling, not something to be cultivated by the student or to be used as a form of controlling mechanism on the part of the teacher. By shifting the focus to an individual relationship between the practitioner and the Buddha, the traditional disciplinary regime of Buddhist practice is dismantled and translated to a subjective and personal realm, which does not necessitate social relationships of authority. Shinran preserves some of those relationships (e.g. his regard for his teacher and leadership before his students, his loose monastic identity) in a symbolic way but their original hierarchical content is emptied or radically redefined.

Shinran's ideas are a development within Pure Land Buddhism, a stream of Buddhism focused on the goal of birth in the Pure Land of Amida Buddha, the realm of effortless enlightenment, through a variety of devotional and often non-monastic, non-meditative practices. Unlike other forms of Buddhism, which prescribe meditative exercises and a monastic lifestyle in order to achieve the Buddha's enlightenment in this life, Pure Land Buddhism aims to create the necessary conditions for emerging in a realm where enlightenment will naturally happen after death. However, as I will argue later, the transcendent/inherent nature of the Pure Land as a post-mortem/this life realm varies greatly in different Pure Land Buddhist contexts. Pure Land Buddhism originated in India and later developed in various ways in China, Tibet, Korea, Vietnam and Japan. Pure Land Buddhism was first organized as a separate tradition or school in 13th century Japan, through Honen's movement and the many lineages established by his disciples. However, Pure Land practices and ideas pervade Mahayana Buddhism in all its manifestations across South, Central and East Asia. The Pure Land movement represented a simplification of Buddhist practice, making its eventual goal accessible for lay people who had no time for meditation or a contemplative lifestyle. It is based on the idea that everybody can be reborn in Amida's Pure Land (understood differently across the Buddhist world but generally equated with Buddhahood or the effortless attainment of Buddhahood) by doing a variety of relatively simple practices that differ slightly depending on historical and geographical setting, but that all have in common the recitation of the Buddha's name (in Japanese: *nenbutsu*). This practice is based on the story of the Buddha Amida who promised to bring all beings to his realm if they call the Buddha's name and aspire to be born in the Pure Land.

However, the Buddha's vow and his joyous realm have been interpreted in myriad ways across the Buddhist world, from symbolic interpretations that equate the Pure Land with enlightenment and refer to it as the practitioner's pure mind (Zen) to readings of the Pure Land as a realm reached fully only after death (common among most Pure Land Buddhists) or as a visionary display that can be accessed through meditation (Tibetan and Chinese Pure Land meditative-visionary traditions).[26] Analogously, within Pure Land Buddhism, interpretations of the practical implications of the Buddha's vow range from the requirement to adhere to (monastic or lay) precepts and arduously engage in constant recitation of the *nenbutsu* up to the crucial moment of death (most Chinese and some Japanese traditions) to an emphasis on the mind that calls the *nenbutsu* and understands recitation as an expression of mindfulness or gratitude towards the Budhha (Shinran).

Over and above being central to Pure Land Buddhists, the Pure Land narrative also pervades all forms of Mahayana Buddhism. It can be said to be a Buddhist utopia or ideal world, as it represents the social application of the Buddha's insight. In so far as it stands for the world that unfolds from a Buddha's enlightenment it expresses the Buddhist virtues of compassionate detachment, equality and all-inclusiveness and, consequently, has a history of being construed as heterotopia, an alternative social order.[27] The Pure Land of Amida Buddha is sometimes described in the Sutras in ways that lend themselves to a radical egalitarian reading. As a realm of egolessness, all beings share in the same qualities and have only nominal status, their wishes are fulfilled and their needs are met.[28] Also, the absence of greed, hatred and ignorance involves the lack of property or possession, violence, war and, indeed, government.[29] Though the Buddha is often referred to as the lord or king of the land, he does not seem to rule it in any way and appears more as a *primus inter pares* in a society of Buddhas. Neither the sutras nor Shinran elaborate on the Pure Land in the explicitly political way described above, however, the latent anti-authoritarian potential of the Pure Land narrative can contribute a utopian referent to any Buddhist anarchist imagination.

Though never overtly political, Shinran's reading of the Pure Land is not devoid of social implications. Emphasizing compassion, the Pure Land is not seen as the ultimate destiny of the practitioner, but as a transformative stage leading to his or her return to the realm of suffering to liberate all beings. Thus, the world ought to be first escaped, but only for the purpose of being later revisited and transformed. Shinran's spacio-temporal conception of the Pure Land is a complex and debated matter within Jodo Shinshu which falls beyond the scope of this chapter. Suffice to say that interpretations of Shinran's thought range from an otherworldly Pure Land located in a mythical West and reached only after death to an immanent Pure Land that interpenetrates, irrupts and transforms our world.[30] This diversity of readings is enabled by Shinran's reluctance to accept there were living Buddhas among his fellow humans but also his certainty that "There is no need to wait in anticipation for the moment of death, [since] at the time shinjin [entrusting] becomes settled, birth too becomes settled".[31] This means, paradoxically, that the person who entrusts in the Buddha's vow is "equal to Tathagatas" and "is in the rank of succession to Buddhahood" and yet they remain "foolish beings possessed of blind passions".[32] This double awareness (in Japanese: *nishu jinshin*, literally "two kinds of deep confidence"), involving both assurance and self-criticism, constitutes the structure of liberative entrusting, rendered in Shinran's writings as *shinjin* (true or trusting mind) or *anjin* (peaceful mind).

Shinjin plays a key role in Shinran's thought, as the expression of realization of the Buddha's vow which assures the practitioner unfailing enlightenment. It is the mind of *shinjin* what makes *nenbutsu*, or the calling of the name, effective, as it accomplishes birth in the Pure Land. Thus, Shinran deemphasizes any inherent magical power in the name (*Namu Amida Butsu*, as pronounced in Japanese) and focuses on the mind that leads one to recite the name. This is a mind that understands the paradoxical nature of the human condition (both steeped in defilement and assured of enlightenment) and expresses itself by the verbal act of entrusting in the Buddha. Most importantly, this is not a mind that could be cultivated or brought about through a prescribed method, it is a mind that comes about through *tariki* or *jinen* (naturalness, spontaneity).[33] In this way the practitioner is liberated from a strict regime of practice, in which the only requirement is the spontaneous recitation of the name, understood not as the practitioner's but as the Buddha's practice. This approach to practice reflects the naturalness or spontaneity of the Pure Land, implicitly modelling the lifestyle of the person of *shinjin* in the free and effortless life of the Pure Land. When translated to the discourse of anarchism this mirroring offers an example of prefiguration or harmonizing means and ends. The duality running through Shinran's thought enables this awareness to be at once (self-)critical and (self-)confident, providing a valuable model for any utopian project.

Furthermore, the centrality of spontaneous *tariki*, and the absence of anxiety about "performing good acts" or "despair[ing] of the evil they commit" allows the practitioners to act with a large degree of freedom.[34] The ethics emerging out of this logic can be neither legalistic nor finalist, since the violation of any given code represents no hindrance and there is no goal that has not been accomplished in the mind of entrusting.[35] Not surprisingly, the open-ended formulation of ethical behavior became a highly controversial issue in the early Jodo Shinshu communities, who often used this new discovered freedom in ways that transgressed conventional moralities. Although Shinran admonished his followers against "excusing acts that should not be committed, words that should not be said and thoughts that should not be harbored" he never mentions what those acts might be.[36] Similarly, he does not regard any bad deed as powerful enough to outdo the liberating effectiveness of the Buddha's vow and considers wrongdoing the norm among "foolish beings possessed of blind passions".[37] Paradoxically again, Shinran's vision of human defilement and radical evil enables, in Fabio Rambelli's words, "radical Amidists [...] to offer an alternative vision –an essentially egalitarian one".[38] Although Rambelli does not consider Shinran a "radical Amidist" *per se* he acknowledges him as an intellectual bridge that enables subversive Pure Land Buddhists to deconstruct and mock the established politico-religious order.[39]

Consequently, Galen Amstutz calls Shinran "one of the most shrewdly and profoundly rebellious individuals in East Asian history" since his reinterpretation of Buddhist doctrine issues "a challenge to the mythos of monastic Buddhism and its authority".[40] This is accomplished largely through *tariki,* which posits a primordial, enlightened agent (the Amida Buddha) who acts directly on the practitioner without mediation or validation from religious authorities. In this way, by regarding the Buddha as the primordial and ultimate agent, the practitioner becomes, in a complex and paradoxical manner, empowered as one assured of enlightenment, freed from religious institutions and disciplines but deeply indebted to the Buddha. By entrusting practitioners' autonomy over practices that involve training, skill and learning, the social framework of Buddhist practice can be dismantled or radically redefined, since there is no need for spiritual hierarchy. However, a flexible conscience ordered according to Buddhist sensibilities is not altogether absent, though shifted to the individual's subjective sphere, as I will discuss in the fourth section of this chapter. The libertarian implications of this peculiarly Shinranian notion offer a paradigm of Buddhist individuality and freedom that can be developed in an anarchist direction as a basis for self-reliance and non-conformity. Nonetheless, *tariki* is embedded and needs to be seen within the narrative of *mappo*, the degenerate last days of the Buddhist teaching (dharma) in which beings are incapable of being morally good or accomplishing Buddhist practices.

4. Egalitarian Hopelessness, Collective Transformation

Shinran's revered teacher Honen (1133–1212) was a pioneer in advocating exclusive reliance on the *nenbutsu* as the only effective practice in the age of *mappo*.[41] However, Honen was not guided by a teacher but by reading the Buddhist scriptures over and over, eagerly seeking a path to enlightenment that could be available to all, not just the intellectual, moral, contemplative, economic or social elites. Honen was the first Buddhist in Japan to regard the Pure Land teaching as a doctrine that could stand on its own; its practices and motifs had always been part of larger systems or the chosen personal practice of certain individuals or small groups. Following his egalitarian concern Honen attracted people from all the social classes, who despite largely retaining their social positions were linked by a new religious consciousness that made no distinctions among them. Honen's exclusive focus on an easy practice that was available to anyone is deeply rooted in the narrative of *mappo*, since it is in the latter days that beings need more than ever a simple means to Buddhahood. An idea rooted in Buddhist eschatology with distinctly negative teleological implications can be engaged for opening up an egalitarian and liberative horizon. As history moves away from the time the Buddha appeared in the world, beings also move away from the possibility of becoming enlightened. It is this deeply relational notion of *mappo* that allows Shinran to challenge the political and Buddhist authorities of his time, and to re-conceptualize all sentient beings in a horizontal relationship to each other in relation to the Buddha's compassion. Horizontality is founded in interdependence among deluded beings and between beings and their times. If all beings are the product of their times and the times are corrupt, there is no room for positing a spiritual vanguard that transcends its *zeitgeist*. Rambelli further spells out the subversive possibilities of this idea:

> There is no distinction between the enlightened, morally pure elites and their ignorant and corrupt subordinates: in the final period only evil, common folk exist. Those who think that they are better than others are actually worse than the worst criminals because while sinners are aware of being sinners, elites delude themselves by believing in their innate goodness [...] Evil became the essential characteristic of all beings: the *kenmitsu*'s [established Buddhism] lowest are now the anthropological paradigm.[42]

Shinran's conception of *mappo* is also intensely personal, and what is sometimes interpreted as a negative self-image is in fact

Shinran's self-awareness of being a product of his time. The discovery of the degenerate age is primarily existential in Shinran's writings, and it expresses a given historical consciousness through personal insight. From a Buddhist philosophical standpoint, it is impossible to separate the subjects living in a given context and the context itself, since they both create each other. Thus, living in *mappo* is being *mappo*. Shinran discovers this reality in himself and declares: "This self is false and insincere; / I completely lack a pure mind".[43] Although most of the time Shinran expresses this critical awareness in relation to himself, he is not oblivious to the fact that others are equally a product of the corrupt times: "Each of us in outward bearing, /Makes a good show of being good, wise and dedicated / But so great are our greed, anger, perversity and deceit / That we are filled with all forms of malice and cunning".[44] This severe perception of humanity complicates any attempt to claim religious or moral authority. Shinran undermines his own authority in an un-self-legitimizing way when he exposes his position as religious leader or teacher as a farce: "I am such that I do not know right and wrong / And cannot distinguish false and true, / I lack even small love and small compassion, / And yet, for fame and profit, enjoy teaching others".[45]

Self-reflective statements such as this along with the *tariki*-infused claim "I do not have a single disciple" further complicate Shinran's identity as a teacher.[46] However self-deprecatory his rhetorical self reveals itself to be at times, this perception did not stop Shinran from sharing his ideas and writing until the end of his life. Neither did it stop him from occasionally using his loosely defined form of authority when he felt his message was compromised, sometimes in a hierarchical or authoritarian fashion.[47] Although the narrative of *mappo* can lead to a quietist acceptance of the established order, its highly relational nature also entails a subversive promise. The interdependent relation between beings and their times can be applied politically to yield a Buddhist, relational analysis of domination, which can be disrupted if the relational agents shift.[48] Social relations are also reflections of the age and beings' mindsets and so can be imagined to be governed by the same relational principles. Moreover, it should not be forgotten that even in the dark latter days, even if traditional (and more hierarchical) Buddhist disciplines are no longer available, the (horizontal) *tariki* way is still available to all. Therefore, the dystopian reality of *mappo* can be disrupted, exited or transformed.

Against the empty authorities of *mappo*, based on greed and deception, Shinran posits the community of those who have entrusted themselves to Amida, who are in a sense awake but who also remain entangled in the vicissitudes of their era. In a posthumous biography Shinran is recorded renouncing again his teacher role because of its incompatibility with *tariki* and further arguing that "As we are all the disciples of the Tathagatha, all of us stand on a par as "fellow seekers [*ondobo ondogyo*]".[49] *Ondobo ondogyo*, often rendered in English as "fellow practitioners", "Dharma friends", "fellow companions" or "fellow travelers", is imagined by Shinran as a body of equals galvanized by a common purpose: that of journeying together towards the Pure Land. Though never developed in explicitly socio-political terms by Shinran, this horizontal model can be said to fulfil a double purpose: to mirror the Pure Land, the realm where all beings are equal, and to offer a liberative alternative to the hierarchical and corrupt world of *mappo*. In this sense, *ondobo ondogyo* represents a prefiguration of ideal equality like the undisciplined and "natural" lifestyle of the entrusting person. The community of fellow practitioners exists in between a hierarchical world and an egalitarian ideal, a position that could potentially turn them into a transformative agent. The egalitarian ideal of the Pure Land does not only provide a "principle of social criticism" but can also shape non-hierarchical formations in a hierarchical society.[50]

This model resembles, structurally, Shinran's negotiation of the paradox of defilement and assurance as one of opposition but also of dialectic transformation. Thus, while practitioners remain "in this [defiled] world" their *shinjin* or entrusting heart is "equal to the hearts and minds of all Buddhas".[51] Assurance of enlightenment presumes a transformative and liberative process that unfolds with the awakening of *shinjin*, since "Through the benefit of the unhindered light [*tariki*], / We realize shinjin of vast, majestic virtues, / And the ice of our blind passions necessarily melts / Immediately becoming the water of enlightenment".[52] Although the particular signs of this transformative process remain a contested issue within Jodo Shinshu, it seems clear that Shinran's view of *mappo* is not ultimately fatalistic as it entails the promise of liberation or transformation. Another phrase commonly used by Shinran to refer to assurance of Buddhahood is "the stage of no-retrogression" implying that people of *shinjin* are on a continuous journey forward towards enlightenment.[53] From a Buddhist anarchist perspective, the dialectic of self-criticism / transformative assurance offers a paradigm of critical progression that never stops questioning itself, as I will elaborate at length later.[54]

Furthermore, in social terms, *ondobo ondogyo* or the people of *shinjin* can become an embodied space of transformation and resistance to the empty hierarchies of *mappo*. The fellow practitioner's heart-minds are already beyond the control of both state and monastic authority, being equal with the Buddhas and having received assurance of reaching the Pure Land. Consequently the actions flowing from such hearts, despite being often filtered and expressed through selfish delusion, can introduce a disruptive and spontaneous element within a network of hierarchical relationships. Gustav Landauer's insight into the relational nature of the state is very relevant to this analysis, along with his idea that revolution comes from within and moves expansively outwards.[55] The same principle is expressed in the poetical formulation of the Spanish anarchist Buenaventura Durruti, who when asked about the ruins that a destructive revolution would leave behind replied: "*Llevamos un mundo nuevo en nuestros corazones y ese mundo está creciendo en este instante*" [We carry a new world in our hearts and that world is growing right now].[56] Although the world in Durruti's heart is different from the Pure Land, his utopian imagination runs parallel to Shinran's imagining of the relationship between the Pure Land and the person assured of birth in the Pure Land.

The strong relational quality that animates Shinran's conception of *mappo* and the interplay between the realms of enlightenment and delusion has structural similarities to certain formulations of anarchist thought and if translated to the realm of politics can be read in an anti-authoritarian direction. Because of these features Shinran's thought has the potential to contribute to Buddhist anarchist discourses a model for a community of equals and some

form of blueprint for imagining the interaction between a dystopian consciousness and a utopian one. As confidence is ever
coupled with severe self-criticism and an aspiration for ongoing
transformation, any project modelled in Shinran's thought ought
to remain self-questioning and suspicious about its owns claims
and authority. This critical spirit is an important element missing
in many current Buddhist anarchist discourses. While not fully
anarchist, Shinran's political statements and social identity also
contain many subversive elements that offer a number of interpretive possibilities.

5. Neither Monk Nor Layman: An Ethic of Resistance?

In 1207 Honen's exclusive *nenbutsu* movement was banned by
the imperial court, at the request of the state-supporting and state-
supported Buddhist institutions. In the banning petition against
Honen and his followers, the established Buddhist orders argued
not only over contentious points of doctrine but also warned of the
undesirable social implications of letting the Pure Land movement
grow unchecked. The popularity of Honen's movement posed a
threat to the status of the traditional schools, in terms of social and
financial support from the laity, but it was also an implicit threat to
the larger socio-political order.

Two of the accusations levelled against the Pure Land movement concerned the imperial order (in)directly. The first involved
setting up a new Buddhist school without imperial permission
and the second charged the movement with being disrespectful
or neglectful towards the *kami*, the native deities of Japan whose
worship is intimately connected to the cult of the emperor[57]. These
alleged crimes set a dangerous precedent: Buddhist institutions
could exist without state control and might, directly or indirectly,
challenge its authority.

A few members of the Pure Land movement were executed,
and others like Shinran or Honen were exiled and / or disrobed.
The ban and the diaspora it created seems to have strengthened
the movement in two fundamental ways: on one hand, it allowed
Honen's ideas to spread to remote areas of Japan far from Kyoto,
and on the other it reinforced the nonconformist attitudes of those

punished. As an exile stripped of his monastic status, Shinran found himself in an in-between position which he playfully appropriated through the term *hiso hizoku* (literally, neither monk nor layman). This term has been read in myriad ways by both sectarian and non-sectarian scholars; however, it seems unquestionable that the phrase denotes a gesture of resistance towards the state who disrobed him. By being *hiso hizouku* Shinran can be seen as denying both state and Buddhist authority. By claiming he is not a layman he resists the state's forceful disrobement, while by claiming he is not a priest or monk he refuses to submit to the monastic community and its hierarchy. Shinran's self-proclaimed marginality thus becomes an exilic space, a space of resistance to various entangled and established orders.

The phrase *hiso hizoku* also appears in the postscript of the *Kyogyoshinsho*, Shinran's *opus magna*, in which he openly criticizes the emperor and his ministers. In his (in)famous diatribe he accuses them of "acting against the dharma and violating human rectitude" when they become "enraged and embittered".[58] This dystopian portrayal of the political authorities resonates with the rhetoric of *mappo*, which, needless to say, also applies to the rulers of the latter age (*mappo*). If the emperor and his ministers act against both Buddhist and Confucian principles, which are meant to legitimize their rule in the first place, how can they use those same principles to justify their rule? Shinran does not ask such a question directly, but his invective implicitly hints at the rulers' hypocrisy. Even if Shinran does not develop this criticism to encompass all forms of political authority, his message seems to be that rulers can be challenged and held to certain standards. Furthermore, as Shinran finds in his rulers the same "blind passions" and duplicity he finds in himself and others around him, the implicit legitimacy of the rulers as moral examples or superior beings is seriously compromised.

Despite Shinran's relatively few explicit pronouncements about political issues, many scholars have explored the political implications of his message. Thus, the "shrewdly" and "rebellious" individual whom Amstutz sees using "the masks of technical interpretation and his own self-deprecation" Christopher Goto-Jones construes as "stretching way off the 'permissive' end of Shotoku's political constitution" into some "kind of anarchism".[59] Shinran stretches some of the more liberal aspects of the Japanese politico-religious tradition but he also sets himself apart from it by refusing to present *buppo* (i.e. the Buddhist teaching) and *obo* (i.e. the law of the king) as necessary or inherently complementary. This separation is put forward in a letter in which Shinran's disavows his son Jishin-bo for misrepresenting his ideas:

> If you accept what Jishin-bo is saying –that I have instructed people to spread the nembutsu by relying on outside people as powerful supporters, which I have never said- it will be an unmitigated error. [...] You must not in any way design to spread the nembutsu by utilizing outside people for support. The spread of the nembutsu in that area must come about through the working of the revered Buddha.[60]

By refusing any kind of interference or help from "outside people" or "powerful supporters", which referred to government officials, Shinran can be said to resist the cooptation of his community. However, by using the principle of *tariki* once again he disrupts an old Japanese concept: the mutual or necessary dependence between *buppo* and *obo*. The coupling of *buppo* and *obo* goes back to the introduction of Buddhism in Japan and served to provide a symbiotic relationship for state and Buddhist institutions. Thus, the monks protect the state through rituals and in turn the state protects them through naked power.[61] This relationship enabled the rulers to be legitimized by Buddhist ideology and to be able to use that ideology to rule their subjects; on the other hand the Buddhist teachings were officially endorsed and spread by the rulers. Shinran explicitly challenges the logic of this model when refusing external support.[62] Although he does not reject the idea that practicing the *nenbutsu* might benefit the nation in some sense, Shinran is firmly opposed to provide or receive the "benefit" the state expected from Buddhist establishments.

The possibility of benefiting the nation, and others at large, is expressed in another letter to Shoshin-bo, a follower who was about to undergo litigation because of his involvement with Shinran's movement. In it Shinran identifies as part of a persecuted community, "people of the Pure Land nembutsu", and shares his experience as an exile. Towards the end he also encourages the community to say the *nenbutsu* "not with thoughts of themselves, but for the sake of the imperial court and for the sake of the people of the country". He also recommends people whose *shin-jin* is settled to say it "with the wish, 'May there be peace in the world, and may the Buddha's teaching spread'".[63] This fragment has been used to imply that Shinran paid homage to the emperor and implicitly endorsed the *obo-buppo* ideology.[64] However, the wish for the teachings to spread and the saying of the *nenbutsu* "for the sake of the imperial court" are not explicitly connected in the letter. Moreover, saying the *nenbutsu* for the court is an act of ambiguous devotion. As much as it could signify a bow to the emperor's authority, we should not forget that Shinran frequently encouraged his followers to say the *nenbutsu* for their enemies (e.g. those obstructing the *nenbutsu*).

Using a language that resembles that of his diatribe against the emperor and his minister, Shinran speaks of those authorities who persecuted his movement as "people lacking eyes" and "people lacking ears" because they "perform deeds that will bring about the suppression of the nembutsu and act out of malice toward people of the nembutsu".[65] Shinran's advice on how to deal with *nenbutsu* opponents is thus articulated for his followers: "without bearing any ill toward such persons, you should keep in mind the thought that, saying the nembutsu, you are to help them".[66] The fact that Shinran encourages his followers to say the *nenbutsu* for a given individual does not necessarily mean that homage is paid to that individual, as the second instance clearly shows. Far from paying respects or accepting the authority of "people lacking ears" and "people lacking eyes", Shinran's response is a clear gesture of resistance couched in the all-inclusive language of Buddhist compassion. The reference to the imperial court does not necessarily signify an implicit relationship of mutual dependence or cooperation, but an expression of the Buddha's compassion, which embraces friends and enemies alike.

By drawing this basic separation between *buppo* and *obo*, Shinran can be said to on one hand preempt the emergence of a Jodo Shinshu fundamentalist politics with aspirations to take over the state, and on the other resist state interference aimed at turning the religious teachings and community into a mechanism of social control. Shinran's refusal to entrust the spreading of his religious ideas to the state is also rooted and legitimated through the logic of *tariki*. Since no person can make or train another to entrust to Amida, how can anybody claim the role of spreading the teaching?

The logic of *tariki* does not only affect the relationship between the community and the state but Shinran's self-perception and relations within and across the religious community. In a manner that resembles the Buddha of the *Kalama Sutta* Shinran is recorded saying in the *Tannisho:* the "Vow of Amida [...] was entirely for the sake of myself alone" and addressing his audience: "whether you take up and accept the nembutsu or whether you abandon it is for each of you to determine."[67] The first statement should not be read as an ontological assertion of Shinran's specialness, but as an experiential appraisal of the individual experience of entrusting to the Buddha. Shinran can only speak for himself and therefore, as far as he is concerned, the vow is for himself alone. Although he shares the teaching and his interpretation of it with others he cannot speak for others or impose his beliefs on them. This non-coercive and individualistic approach further confirms why a coercive and homogenizing structure like the state could never be in charge of spreading or propagating the teaching.

A laissez-faire attitude towards divergence from his teachings is also observed in his letters, except when certain individuals claim Shinran's authority while misrepresenting his message for their own purposes (e.g. his son Jishin-bo). This attitude of non-interference can be found in statements such as "I cannot accept what your fellow practicers are saying, but there is nothing to be done about it".[68] Shinran's tone is more severe when he condemns slandering of parents, teachers or fellow-practicers, as in the case of Zenjo-bo from whom Shinran takes distance: "I had no close feelings for him and did not encourage him to come and see me".[69] In other letters, Shinran advises his followers to "keep a respectful distance and not become familiar with those given to wrongdoing".[70] Although this can be read as an informal kind of excommunication, Shinran systematically refused to take back the sacred objects given to his followers (the very procedure that signifies excommunication in Japanese Buddhist communities) denying that he has any power over the objects or the students.[71]

It is impossible to determine the exact power relations at work in the many disputes that took place in Shinran's community, however there seems to be a difference in the way he deals with difference of opinion in doctrinal matters and the way he addresses aggressive or deceitful behaviour that compromised Shinran or disrupted the community. Furthermore, the advice to not become familiar with "wrongdoers" ambiguously reads in context both as an informal excommunication and as a refusal to impose his views on those antagonizing them.[72] Among fellow practitioners, the slander of the three treasures (teacher –freely used to refer to Honen, Shinran or the Buddha– the teachings and the community of fellow practitioners) is likely to have been regarded as expressing the wish to leave the community and Shinran's "respectful distance" can thus be read as a tacit acknowledgment of that wish. In any case, the correspondence recording these disputes never goes into detail as to what specific acts or words entailed "slander" or were deemed beyond the pale.

Shinran is at his most severe when he disowns his son, who had been claiming his father's authority to seemingly create his own power base in the Eastern provinces. In this case, Shinran resorts to his social authority as a father, rather than his loosely defined authority as a teacher, to curtail his son's attempt to speak on his behalf. However, neither in Jishin-bo's case nor in the other instances that involve conflict, Shinran issues any form of spiritual condemnation. No pronouncement is made about his opponents' future destiny, although he at times rationalizes their behaviour in the following manner: "such thoughts arise because they fail to entrust themselves to the Buddha dharma".[73] Ultimately, however, Shinran seems to regard relations with his loosely defined followers as ruled by karmic conditions, which escape both the student and the teacher's conscious will: "We come together when conditions bring us to meet and part when conditions separate us. In spite of this, some assert that those who say the nembutsu having turned from one teacher to another cannot attain birth. This is absurd".[74]

An analogous use of the *tariki* logic for deconstructing social relationships of authority and obedience can be found in the thirteenth chapter of *Tannisho*, in which Shinran first assumes the mask of authoritarianism to later debunk it by offering a radical critique of obedience. The chapter opens with an unusual request of obedience from Shinran to Yuien-bo: "Yuien-bo, do you accept all that I say? [...] Then you will not deviate from whatever I tell you?" -Yuien-bo swiftly promises to comply.[75] However, the unusual request for obedience is followed by a further bizarre command: "Now, I want you to kill a thousand people. If you do, you will definitely attain birth".[76] Yuien-bo's response is again swift, but negative: "Though you instruct me thus, I'm afraid it is not in my power to kill even one person".[77] To which Shinran ironically retorts: "Then why did you say that you would follow whatever I told you?"[78] Shinran then elaborates on how hard it is to act according to our wishes, since we are often at the mercy of our karmic histories, and how the "good" or "evil" in our hearts has no weight in our attainment of birth in the Pure Land. In this way, not only "good" and "evil" are once again relativized when seen from the all-inclusive and non-discriminating compassion of the Buddha, but the very possibility of obedience (whether to one's own will or to another's) is revealed to be an illusion.

By adopting the mask of authoritarianism Shinran demonstrates the absurdity of obedience and implicitly sets a precedent for questioning authority. As his own unreasonable request shows, the fact that we respect or agree with certain people does not mean that we should or could blindly follow their instructions.[79] Although the focus of Shinran's argument is our inability to act coherently and, consequently, how no behavioural requirements (including social or religious compliance) should be added to *shinjin*, the implication of his exchange with Yuien-bo also implies that compliance is both irrelevant and irrational. Even though this brief exchange needs to be understood as part of a Buddhist polemic, it offers a paradigm and logic of nonconformity that can be engaged in a subversive manner. However, by making obedience illusory and not just irrelevant or unnatural, Shinran implicitly equates deliberate conformity and conscious nonconformity as absurd designs. In other words, one might argue that obedience is an illusion but complying with it while being aware of its illusory nature does not present a problem. Seeing the absurdity of authority does not necessarily involve rebellion, as one might choose to cynically or playfully comply with it. After all, obedience is deconstructed along with free will or the ability to act according to our wishes and, since we are prisoners of our karmic histories, neither rebellion nor compliance are really our choice.[80] Thus, whereas Shinran's playful debunking of his own authority could be interpreted in an antiauthoritarian direction, it can also be used for justifying an ironic and self-aware form of compliance.[81]

In fact, this problem has long haunted the political history of Buddhism and the formulation of any kind of Buddhist anarchism. The relativistic character of most Buddhist thought, including Jodo Shinshu, can produce a sort of cynical passivity that, despite being critical of government, also lets governments rule. The paradigmatic example of the Buddhist-influenced Daoist text *Wu Nengzi* (9th century) in China demonstrates how Buddhist relativity can lend itself to an ironic acceptance and collaboration with the government.[82] Although there might be a critical and self-cynical element in collaborating with authority, such approach, far from destabilizing or disrupting that authority, ensures its smooth functioning. Suzuki (in)famously wrote about Zen, and Buddhism at large I would argue, can be "wedded to anarchism or fascism, communism or democracy".[83] The history of Jodo Shinshu certainly confirms that Suzuki's statement also applies to the teachings of Shinran, which have been interpreted from a broad range of ideological perspectives from socialism to liberalism and from Japanese imperial nationalism to eco-pacifism.[84]

To claim that Shinran is inherently anarchistic is as anachronistic and misleading as claiming Zen philosophy and discourse as being "more anarchistic than anarchism". However, Shinran, like Zen philosophy, can be read anarchically and provide a Buddhist foundation to an anarchist project. Furthermore, Shinran's critical and historical awareness and his critique of both Buddhist and state authority can help contemporary Buddhist anarchisms to critically examine their own history and the history of Buddhism at large. Whether seen as reformist or revolutionary, Shinran's attempts to redefine his own authority in a decentralizing way, and his nonconformist attitude towards what he perceived as corrupt secular and religious powers, can inspire a fruitful reflection about the social relations at work in Buddhist anarchist communities and their relationship to their larger societies. Moreover, as Buddhist anarchism grapples with its own relationship to the state, the history of Buddhists who wrestled with the state and kept a respectful but resistant distance can yield many poetical and political lessons. In these ways, the critical and rebellious side of Shinran can be extrapolated and re-engaged for resisting other and more recent practices of domination and oppression.

6. Concluding Thoughts

This discussion of the libertarian potential of Shinran fulfills a dual purpose: to reveal the more anarchistic aspects of Shinran's teaching, using them for formulating a Jodo Shinshu Buddhist anarchism; and to offer some of his insights as a counterbalance to the privileging of an orientalist and ahistorical conception of Zen in recent Buddhist anarchist rhetoric. Offering an alternative, though not necessarily incompatible, Buddhist foundation for forging a different Buddhist anarchism, could enable the Western Buddhist anarchist tradition to question its own assumptions and histories of power. Furthermore, Shinran's emphasis on trust and devotional language destabilizes Buddhist anarchist orientalist imaginings of Buddhism as exclusively meditative, non-religious and, in a post-enlightenment sense, rational. However, a Shinran-based anarchism shows how Buddhist anarchism need not be couched in the language of exceptionalism that regards Buddhism as "the religion of no-religion".[85]

A clear example is the logic of *tariki*, which is grounded in Buddhist rationality and philosophy, but which sits awkwardly with a purely meditative Buddhism stripped of "religious" elements. Nonetheless, *tariki* frees up the Buddhist practitioner from traditional Buddhist regimes of practice, which often involved hierarchical and disciplinary elements. Since the unmediated agency of the Amida Buddha acts directly on the practitioner it might be said to be a Buddhist "right of private judgment", enabling the practitioner to discern in relation to his or her experience of *tariki*. As William Godwin's work proves, the notion of a "private judgment" can be developed into a critique of state authority and authority at large. Also, *tariki* accomplishes the equalization of all beings, since in the last days of *mappo* no one can be said to not need the Buddha's help. These parallel equalities, which offer complementary visions of entanglement and liberation, enable social criticism and can be engaged for militating against hierarchy. Most importantly, the notion of *mappo* has a strong relational flavor that identifies the dark age with the dark minds of the beings living through them, which are equally and mutually entangled in darkness. Thus, the relational awareness of being deeply involved in the oppressive realities of *mappo* can trigger the wish to rebel and transform.

If we were to apply Shinran's insight into the ruler's corruption, following the same historical logic that makes him imagine the *nenbutsu* as the most central and universal Buddhist practice and also the most appropriate for *mappo*, it could be argued that in the latter days' hierarchy has become corrupting and ineffective and ought to give way to an alternative social paradigm. The alternative could be inspired in Shinran's *ondobo ondogyo*, the community of fellow travelers, which resists hierarchical formations and the ethos of *mappo*. The horizontal social formation embodied in the equal discipleship to the Buddha can, thus, be construed, like the *nenbutsu,* as the most fundamental Buddhist social model and in the latter age of *mappo*, the only viable one. This model can add to the Buddhist anarchist project a focus on historical suitability and sensitivity, which does not need to be rooted in Buddhist eschatology, to balance the emphasis on the philosophical and ahistorical similarity between Buddhism and anarchism. Though Shinran's view of history is rooted in Buddhist teleological narratives, his critical awareness of his *zeitgeist* and attention to historical context and suitability (rooted also in Buddhist ideas of causation) are helpful tools that can be translated to other conceptions of history.

The interaction between the age of *mappo* and the Pure Land is Shinran's formulation of the basic Mahayana doctrine of the mutual dependence of *samsara* and *nirvana*, however it can also be engaged for negotiating notions of dystopia and utopia in a political context. At the heart of the relationship between *mappo* and the Pure Land lies a concern about harmonizing means and ends. In so far as the corrupted self of *mappo* cannot affect liberation, any more than the state can orchestrate its own vanishing, release comes from a radically different realm and is expressed in actions that mimic or instantiate the utopian end. By decentralizing the Buddhist community and freeing it from traditional regimes of discipline, the Pure Land can be said to be prefigured in the age and world of *mappo*. However, such a prefigured community ought to remain extremely cautious about its own motives, as it is still under the influence of *mappo*. The fact that Shinran sees both *mappo* and the Pure Land at work within himself introduces a critical element of self-questioning accompanied by self-confidence and assurance. This dual awareness provides a paradigm for articulating the interplay between a critical or dystopian consciousness and a hopeful or utopian one. Shinran's complex notion of birth in the Pure Land, as something that is at once fully settled in the middle of ordinary life and also only entirely realized in the future, presents a living utopia that can irrupt and affect our present world while being ever deferred to the future. These dynamics offer a model of constant progression that can never look at itself in a self-satisfied manner, claiming to have achieved the final goal.

Furthermore, the temporal and simultaneous immanence and transcendence of birth in the Pure Land introduces a critical gap between the utopian ideal and the embryonic awareness that embodies it absent in formulations of Buddhist anarchism that see anarchy already fulfilled in the realm of Zen rhetoric or the practice of meditation. However, the main problem in Shinran's thought is agency or, more precisely, a rebellious agency that can transform the dystopian realm of *mappo*. Such an agency is never articulated by Shinran, but his actions, which can be read as an extension of his teachings, show that neither the *tariki* logic nor the teleology of *mappo*, rendered him submissive or passive. Even though he calls into question his own ability to discern between good and evil, Shinran acts in accordance to his relative judgment, which at times includes vehemently contesting what he regarded as unacceptable behavior (e.g. the ban on *nenbutsu*).

Thus, Shinran's example proves how an awareness of the ultimate relativity of morality does not involve a necessary bow to the established order, but can also be used to challenge it and, arguably, transform it. In the same way that Shinran stands up against what he judges to be injustice, the Jodo Shinshu anarchist can use her or his relative judgment to articulate strategies of resistance.

Following the analogy of the Christian "right of private judgment" the relative judgment of Shinran or the practitioner is informed or infused by the subjective experience of *tariki*. A subversive agency ought to come about as an interplay of both the enlightened design of the Buddha and the relative and contingent design of the practitioner. Shinran's actions can be said to provide an instance of that interplay of wills or agencies. Whereas his relationships reflect a freer and more decentralized spirit founded in *tariki*, he also considers pragmatic implications and acts in relation to an implicit and culturally received moral sensibility. The particular content of this moral sensibility is not crucial to the formulation of a Shinran based anarchism as it belongs to the realm of provisional judgment, to which Shinran refuses to confer any ultimate validity, and could be replaced or reformulated. However, this interplay of agencies offers a model for trying to live in the spirit of an ideal world while having to deal with a dystopian one.

Most importantly, Shinran's refusal to enter a symbiotic relationship with the state can trigger a Buddhist anarchist reassessment of the long history of Buddhist cooptation and collaboration with the state, to which the Jodo Shinshu tradition is no exception. If Buddhism is not inherently authoritarian, its long history of entanglement with government across the Buddhist world needs to be acknowledged and critically explored. In order to articulate a Buddhism that can be anarchist, it is essential to first understand how Buddhism has not, by and large, been anarchistic. Further, by exploring oppressive histories many instances of resistance can be discovered and creatively re-appropriated. Shinran's historical awareness and his creative re-engagement of the Buddhist textual tradition extend an invitation to re-interpret and re-read. Such re-reading, which is understood as one of the Latin etymologies of the word religion (*re-legere*, literally read again), is central to any Buddhist anarchism that aims to *religiously* re-read the world and itself. Thus Shinran contributes a thorough and critical model for re-reading Buddhist history, the Buddhist canon and the (Buddhist) readers themselves.

Acknowledgement

This research was partially enabled by the research group Culturas, Religiones y Derechos Humanos (CRDH-GdI-01) at the International University of La Rioja (Universidad Internacional de La Rioja-UNIR). The author would like to thank the project for the generous material and institutional support which contributed to the completion of this chapter.

Notes

1. Perhaps the best example of a Buddhist anarchist who did not rely (exclusively) on Zen ideas in order to construct his Anarcho-Buddhism is that of the Chinese monk Taixu (1890–1947). Taixu's main Buddhist practice was connected to the millenarian tradition of Maitreya and it shares many of the devotional aspects of Japanese Pure Land thinking discussed in this chapter. For a thorough discussion of Taixu's thought see Justin Ritzinger, *Anarchy in the Pure Land: Tradition, Modernity, and the Reinvention of the Cult of Maitreya in Republican China* (Ann Arbor, Michigan: ProQuest, 2010).

2. An example of the tendency to consider Gary Snyder the first Buddhist anarchist can be found in this blog entry by Ian Mayes, which constitutes one of the more articulate contemporary formulations of Buddhist anarchism in the West: "Envisioning a Buddhist Anarchism" in *The Implicit & Experiential Rantings of a Person* (http://parenthesiseye.blogspot.co.uk/2011/11/envisioning-buddhist-anarchism.html, 2010)

3. Gary Snyder, "Buddhist Anarchism", in *Bureau of Public Secrets*, (http://www.bopsecrets.org/CF/garysnyder.htm, 2002 [1961]).

4. Ibid.

5. An account of Gudo's work and some of his manuscripts can be found in Fabio Rambelli. *Zen Anarchism. The Egalitarian Dharma of*

Uchiyama Gudo (Berkeley: Institute of Buddhist Studies, 2013). Also, instances of the tendency to present Zen as an inherently anarchist philosophy separated from its history can be found in the writings of John Clark, Kerry Thornley, Brad Warner and to some extent Gary Snyder.

6. For Suzuki's own account of the Zen tradition see Daisetz Suzuki, *Zen and Japanese Culture* (Princeton: Princeton University Press, 1993), pp. 3–18. Griffith Foulk, 'Ritual in Japanese Zen Buddhism', in *Zen Ritual. Studies of Zen Buddhist Theory in Practice, ed. by Steven Heine and Dale Wright* (Oxford: Oxford University Press, 2008), p. 36.

7. James Brown. "The Zen of Anarchy: Japanese Exceptionalism and the Anarchist Roots of the San Francisco Poetry Renaissance". *Religion and American Culture: A Journal of Interpretation,* 19.2 (Summer 2009) p. 214.

8. For a brief discussion of this historical tendency see Rachelle Scott, *Nirvana for Sale. Buddhism, Wealth and the Contemporary Dharmakaya Temple in Contemporary Temple* (Albany: State University of New York Press, 2009), pp. 8–11.

9. Shinran uses the term Jodo Shinshu (literally 'the true Pure Land way') to refer to his own doctrine, which in his view is a restatement of what his teacher Honen taught. However, Shinran developed Honen's thought and substantially reinterpreted and enriched it in a number of ways, as Alfred Bloom discusses at length in "Honen and Shinran: Loyalty and Independence", in *Shindharmanet* (http://www.shindharmanet.com/wp-content/uploads/2012/pdf/Bloom-Loyalty.pdf, 2012). Throughout this chapter, I will be using the term Jodo Shinshu as synonymous with Shinran's thought and not as referring to any specific institutional denomination.

10. To make clear that the term *tariki,* literally "other power", is not meant to imply a power completely external to the individual but simply other to her or his conscious self, Mark Blum offers these suggestions for the translation of the term: "*Tariki,* also called *butsuriki* [buddha-power] or *ganriki* [vow-power], denotes the transcendent power of a buddha, but because of the ambiguity inherent in the relationship between buddha and self in the *tathagatagarbha* [literally buddha-seed, but generally translated as buddha nature] doctrines, which have always been close to Pure Land thought, 'spiritual power beyond the known self' is a more apt gloss for this term" (Blum, p. 8).

11. Peter Marshall, *Demanding the Impossible. A History of Anarchism* (London: Harper Perennial, 2008), p. 61.

12. Many of the more anarchistic stories correspond to the early age of Chinese Zen (Chan) which corresponds to the Tang period (618–907). This age has been construed by Zen anarchists, from Uchiyama Gudo to John Clark as a golden era in which the antiauthoritarian spirit of Zen is fully expressed, as I have argued elsewhere (see Galvan-Alvarez, Enrique, "Meditative Revolutions? Orientalism and History in the Western Buddhist Anarchist Tradition in *Enlightened Anarchism*, Forthcoming). A representative cycle of stories about the Zen of this period is the collection of *koan* of Rinzai patriarch Linji, see Fuller Sasaki, Ruth, trans., *The Record of Linji* (Honolulu, University of Hawai'i Press: 2009).

13. Discourses that construct meditation as an inherently progressive tool that might even be indispensable to social revolution can be found across Western Zen anarchist writings. These include Snyder's characterization of meditation as having "nation-shaking implications" ("Buddhist Anarchism"), Warner's implicit construction of Zen and *zazen* as a form "inner anarchy" (pp. 28–30) or Thornley's statement that "Zenarchy is the Social Order which springs from Meditation" (p. 13). These attempts to "meditate the state away" obscure the history of practices like *zazen* being used to support the state and further its ends as Brian Victoria's work demonstrates and fails to answer how the mere practice of Buddhist meditation has so far failed to produce an anarchist society despite being widely practiced across the history and geography of Buddhism. See Victoria, Brian Daizen. *Zen at War.* (Oxford: Rowman and Littleman Publishers, 2006).

14. In finding Zen the most anarchist of Buddhisms, Zen anarchists collude with a certain Zen Buddhist discourse that presents Zen as the superior and ultimate form of Buddhism. Whereas this exceptionalist discourse is common across Buddhist traditions, which often competed against each other and unfailingly presented themselves as the best option, incorporating it to a Buddhist anarchism is problematic. Presenting Zen unmediated as the "Apotheosis of Buddhism" (Marshall p. 61) or asserting that "it did not degenerate into superstition [unlike other forms of Buddhism]" are ahistorical claims that ignore the power struggles and politics at work in the self-legitimation of Zen. For an account of the political implications

of this self-legitimation see Park, Jin Y. *Buddhism and Postmodernity. Zen, Huayan and the Possibility of Buddhist Postmodern Ethics.* Plymouth: Lexington Books, 2008, pp.135–143.

15. John Clark [Max Cafard]. "Zen Anarchy" [2006]. *The Anarchist Library.* August 14th 2009, p.4 http://theanarchistlibrary.org/library/max-cafard-zen-anarchy; Thornley, Kerry. "Zenarchy" [1991]. *The Anarchist Library.* December 19th 2009, p. 13. http://theanarchistlibrary.org/library/kerry-thornley-zenarchy

16. Marshall, p. 61.

17. Peter Marshall, p. 62. It ought to be said that the Zen practice of using the *keisaku,* a long flat stick used for hitting the shoulders of practitioners while in meditation, is not necessarily always used as a form of disciplinary punishment but also as a form of relieving muscle tension around the shoulders when sitting in meditation for long periods of time. In Soto Zen the meditator has to request to be hit, but in the Rinzai 'school' or 'tradition' the stick-holder (*jikijitsu*) might choose who to hit and when. Whatever the purpose, the atmosphere created by someone menacingly carrying a stick behind your back (Zen practitioners sit facing the wall and so they cannot see the movements of the stick-holder) is certainly one of disciplinary rigor, if not mild coercion.

18. Ibid. The same can be said about one of Gary Snyder's early poems which combines spiritual and political vanguardism in imagining a future revolution: "Revolution in the Revolution in the Revolution", in *Regarding Wave* (New York: New Directions Books, 1970), p. 39.

19. The practice of Buddhist *tantra* is traditionally regarded as impossible outside a hierarchical teacher-student relationship. In a recent study, Singh expresses it in these terms: "The *Guru* alone can be the guide and the pathfinder. Without taking refuse [sic] in a *Guru* and getting proper initiation from him any effort to understand transcendental reality and infinite unity would be ludicrous efforts of emptying the ocean with the help of a shell. […] It is *Guru* and *Guru* alone who can help us in transcending our being", Lalan Prasad Singh. *Buddhist Tantra: A Philosophical Reflection and Religious Investigation.* (New Delhi: Concept Publishing Company, 2010), pp. 117–118. James Dobbins analyses the emergence of doctrinal authority within Shinran's community and the contending institutions that claimed it, shortly after Shinran's death in great detail in *Jodo Shinshu: Shin*

Buddhism in Medieval Japan (Hawai'i: University of Hawai'i Press: 2002), pp. 63–98.

20. For a history of the development of the Jodo Shinshu institution(s) after Shinran's death see Dobbins (pp. 63–156) and its later and increasingly authoritarian character see Carol Richmond Tsang. *War and Faith. Ikko Ikki in Late Muromachi Japan.* (London: Harvard University Press, 2007). Although Shinran relativized good and evil and disregarded notions of auspiciousness or ritual purity, his later followers developed new criteria for "separating the pure from the polluted" (Jessica Main. *Only Shinran Will Not Betray Us. Takeuchi Ryo'on (1891–1967), the Otani-ha Administration and the* Burakumin. (Thesis Presented at McGill University, April 2012), p. 80), enshrining Shinran's bloodline as the locus of purity and mimicking the imperial model of kin(g)ship.

21. Lamp for the Latter Ages. *Mattosho* II in Shinran, *Collected Works of Shinran,* Dennis Hirota, trans. (Kyoto: Jodo Shinshu Hongwanji-ha, 1997), p. 525. From now on *Collected Works of Shinran* will be referred to as *CWS.*

22. Ibid., pp. 525–6.

23. A Record in Lamenting Divergences. *Tannisho* III, *CWS,* p. 663.

24. A Record in Lamenting Divergences. *Tannisho* VI, *CWS,* p.664.

25. Ibid.

26. A few of these interpretations are analyzed in Tanaka and Payne, eds., *Approaching the Land of Bliss. Religious Praxis of Amitabha* (Honolulu: University of Hawai'i Press, 2004), which explores different approaches to the Pure Land ideal throughout Buddhist history and geography.

27. Curley explicitly discusses the pre-modern conception of the Pure Land "as a heterotopia –an enacted utopia, or an immanent space of difference, neither strictly transcendent nor strictly immanent", Curley, Ann Marie *Know That We Are Not Good Persons: Pure Land Buddhism and the Ethics of Exile* (PhD Thesis presented at McGill University, June 2009), p. 7. More modern and politically oriented readings feature Takagi Kemmyo's construction of the Pure Land as "the place in which socialism is truly practiced", Takagi Kemmyo, "My Socialism", in *Living in Amida's Universal Vow,*

Alfred Bloom, ed., (Bloomington, Indiana: World Wisdom, 2004), p. 191. Takagi Kemmyo (1864–1914) was a Jodo Shinshu cleric from Higashi Hongaji, expelled from the order because of his involvement in the socialist-anarchist movement. He was tried and convicted for seemingly fabricated charges of conspiring against the emperor's life and died in prison, allegedly at his own hand.

28. The *Larger Sutra*, the Buddhist sutra privileged by Shinran as the most important, describes the beings born in the Pure Land as being "all of a single kind with no distinction in appearance. The words 'humans' and 'devas' [Sanskrit, gods] are used simply in accordance with the forms of existence in other worlds [...] all receive the body of naturalness, of emptiness and of boundlessness", Inagaki Hisao, ed. *The Three Pure Land Sutras, Volume II. The Sutra on the Buddha of Immeasurable Life.* (Kyoto: Jodo Shinshu Hongwanji-Ha, 2009), p.46. Furthermore, "the sentient beings born in that land all possess the thirty two major physical characteristics [of a Buddha]. Their wisdom having been completely perfected, they penetrate deeply into the reality of all things" (Inagaki, p. 60). Again the *Larger Sutra* describes the Pure Land as a place where "Palaces to dwell in, clothes, food and drink, many kinds of beautiful flowers and incense, and other ornaments that are provided to them [those born in the Pure Land] arise out of spontaneity" (Inagaki, p.45).

29. The *Larger Sutra* further describes the inhabitants of the Pure Land: "With respect to the myriad things in that land, they harbor neither a sense of 'mine' nor any sense of attachment. Free and unrestricted, their minds are unattached in going and coming, proceeding and staying. They do not discriminate between those with whom they are close and those with whom they are not. They have no thought of self and other, nor of competition and dispute" (Inagaki, pp. 62–63).

30. For the recent and modern history of some of these interpretations see Curley (pp. 133–177). For an outline of some of the earlier patterns of interpretation of Shinran's teaching see Shigaraki Takamaro. *Heart of the Shin Buddhist Path*. David Matsumoto, trans. (Boston: Wisdom Publications, 2013), pp. 76–80.

31. Lamp for the Latter Ages. *Mattosho* I. *CWS,* p. 523.

32. Lamp for the Latter Ages. *Mattosho* IV. *CWS,* p. 528, 529. A Record in Lament of Divergences. *Tannisho* IX. *CWS,* p. 665.

33. Shinran elaborates on this originally Daoist idea of spontaneity for explaining the workings of *tariki* agency in "On Jinen Honi", *CWS*, p. 427–428. In his own words *jinen* or spontaneity (Chinese, *ziran*) means both the "supreme nirvana" (p.428) and the lack of concern "about being good or bad" (pp. 427–428). Thus, the goal of Buddhist practice mirrors the means that attain it. Above all *jinen* means that entrusting and realization do not happen "through the practicer's calculation" but "through the working of the Tathagata's vow" (p.427), therefore, "no working is true working" (p. 428).

34. A Record in Lament of Divergences. *Tannisho* I. *CWS*, p. 661.

35. Bloom discusses Shinran's moral approach on the one hand "not advocat[ing] a repressive ethic emphasizing abstention from any worldly activity simply because it is worldly" and, on the other, "suggest[ing] an ethic of displacement in which contemplation of the Vow and the recitation of Nembutsu infuses an awareness of Amida's compassion" which in turn inspires compassionate action. See Bloom, "Shin Buddhism in the Modern Ethical Context", in *Shindharmanet* (http://shindharmanet.com/course/c24/).

36. Lamp for the Latter Ages. *Mattosho* XX. *CWS*, p. 553.

37. A Record in Lament of Divergences. *Tannisho* IX. *CWS*, p. 665

38. Rambelli, Fabio. "Just Behave as You Like; Prohibitions and Impurities Are Not a Problem. Radical Amida Cults and Popular Religiosity in Premodern Japan" in Kenneth Tanaka and Richard Payne *Approaching the Land of Bliss. Religious Praxis in the Cult of Amitabha*. Honolulu: University of Hawai'i Press, 2004, p.176.

39. In fact, Rambelli presents Shinran simultaneously being considered by others to be an *ichinengi*, one of the streams of Pure Land Buddhism that he labels as "radical Amidism", but also being "very critical of this alternative interpretation of Amidist orthodoxy and orthopraxy" (p. 179)

40. Amstutz, "Shinran and Authority," p. 150.

41. The idea of *mappo* is based on some Buddhist sutras that posed that humanity will progressively degenerate as time elapsed from the historical Buddha's disappearance from the world (fifth century BCE). The most popular Japanese calculations located the beginning of the last and most degenerate age circa 1050.

42. Rambelli, "Just Behave, p. 176.

43. Hymns of the Dharma Ages. *Shozomatsu Wasan* LXLIV. *CWS*, p. 421.

44. Hymns of the Dharma Ages. *Shozomatsu Wasan* LXLV. *CWS*, p. 421.

45. Hymns of the Dharma Ages. *Shozomatsu Wasan* CXVI. *CWS*, p. 429.

46. A Record in Lament of Divergences. *Tannisho* VI. *CWS*, p. 664.

47. The best example is Shinran's disowning of his son Jishin-bo in 1256. Jishin-bo had deceived Shinran by claiming in front of his students that he had received new and secret teachings. The new teachings divided the community between those who remained faithful to Shinran's original teaching and those who espoused Jishin-bo's purported secret and new teaching. Although the actual content of Jishin-bo's doctrines is largely a matter of speculation, it seems to have contained the idea that the community ought to enter a symbiotic relationship with the political authorities and powerful patrons. A thorough account of the dispute and disowning can be found in Bloom. "The Life of Shinran Shonin: The Journey to Self-Acceptance" in Paul Williams, ed., *Buddhism in China, East Asia and Japan*. Vol II (Abingdon, Oxon: Routledge, 2005), pp. 87–93.

48. This moment of negative self-discovery and its social implications can be compared to Max Stirner's notion of *empörung*, since they both represent a turning point that begins within the individual but that ultimately has social consequences. Both notions also lead to a debunking of inner and outer authorities, as De Ridder explains in relation Stirner in his essay "Max Stirner: The End of Philosophy and Political Subjectivity", in *Max Stirner,* ed. by Saul Newman (London: Palgrave Macmillan, 2011), p. 160.

49. *Kudensho* VI in Bloom, ed. *The Essential Shinran. A Buddhist Path of True Entrusting* (Boston: World Wisdom, 2007), p. 20.

50. Ugo Dessi discusses "The Pure Land as a Principle of Social Criticism" in *Japanese Religions,* 33 (1 & 2), 75–90.

51. Lamp for the Latter Ages. *Mattosho* VII. *CWS*, p. 532.

52. Hymns of the Pure Land Masters. *Koso Wasan* XXXIX. *CWS*, p. 371.

53. For a letter that discusses the implications of this concept see Lamp for the Latter Ages. *Mattosho* XIII. *CWS*, p. 540.

54. Shinran kept this attitude of self-questioning and self-criticism until the end of his life as a he writes at 85 the following reflection: "[W]e are full of ignorance and blind passion. Our desires are countless, and anger, wrath, jealousy, and envy are overwhelming, arising without pause; to the very last moment of life they do not cease, or disappear, or exhaust themselves". Notes on Once-Calling and Many-Calling. *Ichinen tanen mon'i. CWS*, p. 488.

55. Landauer in Martin Buber, *Paths in Utopia* (Syracuse, New York: Syracuse University Press, 1950), p. 49.

56. Alberto Márquez, *León Duarte* (Montevideo: Editorial Compañero, 1993), p. 27

57. In fact, the teaching of Shinran was used to legitimize countless peasant uprisings two centuries later, during the fifteenth and sixteenth centuries (*Ikko-ikki*). Even as the socially subversive potential of his thought was thus demonstrated, the largest and emerging institution claiming to represent Shinran's legacy at the time (the Hongan-ji) had a mixed approach to the revolts, not meeting them with suppressive measures but admonishing the insurgents against drawing easy social implications from Shinran's message. A thorough discussion of this period and the attitude of the Jodo Shinshu institution can be found in James Dobbins, pp. 132–156 and Carol Tsang, pp. 44–156. Ambivalence about the revolts still pervades Jodo Shinshu discourses. However, modern Jodo Shinshu scholars and clerics, like Alfred Bloom (1926) have appreciated the liberatory dimension of the *Ikko-ikki*: "The outcome was the emancipation of the peasants from spiritual oppression, based on the fear of *batchi* or divine retribution in forms of punishment if they did not obey the demands of their overlords, the temples, shrines, and *daimyo* (local warlords), who represented the divine power on the land. Their release from superstition later led to the single minded peasant revolts (*Ikko ikki)*", Bloom, Alfred. "Introduction" in *Honen the Buddhist Saint: Essential Writings and Official Biography* (Bloomington, Indiana: World Wisdom, 2006), p. xxxvii.

58. *Kyogyoshinsho* VI, 117. *CWS*, p.289.

59. Amstutz, *Shinran and Authority*, p. 150. Christopher Goto-Jones, *Political Philosophy in Japan. Nishida, the Kyoto School,*

and Co-Prosperity (Oxford: Oxford University Press, 2005), p. 35. The semi-legendary prince Shotoku Taishi (574–622) is credited for having brought Buddhism and literacy to Japan. Shinran's relationship with the crown prince is a complex and nuanced one. On the one hand Shotoku serves to legitimate Jodo Shinshu as stemming from the founding father of Japanese Buddhism (through Shinran's dream-visions of Shotoku as Bodhisattva Kannon), but on the other, "Shinran's focus on the karmic and spiritual lineage [connecting Shinran and his teaching to Shotoku], undermined the authority of the emperor, who gained his symbolic power through his imperial lineage to Prince Shotoku", Kenneth Doo Young Lee, *The Prince and the Monk. Shotoku Worship in Shinran's Buddhism.* (Albany: State University of New York Press, 2007), p. 124.

60. A Collection of Letters VII. *CWS*, p. 568.

61. These dynamics are discussed at length in Neil McMullin, *Buddhism and the State in Sixteenth-Century Japan* (Princenton, New Jersey: Princeton University Press, 1984).

62. See Tokunaga Michio, "Buddha's Law and King's Law: The Bifurcation of Shinran's Teaching," in *Shin Buddhism: Monograph Series* (Los Angeles: Pure Land Publications, 1993).

63. A Collection of Letters II. *CWS*, p. 560.

64. This interpretation was particularly preeminent during the period stretching from the Meiji Ishin (1868) and the end of World War II (1945). A good example is the testament of the 20th Monshu of Nishi Honganji, Konyo Ohtani (1798–1871), which explicitly identifies the emperor with Amida, and argues that gratitude ought to be expressed as obedience. Shinran's teaching had thus come full circle, from denouncing the rulers' hypocrisy to becoming their ultimate source of legitimacy. Konyo's text can be found, along with thorough analyses in Curley (p. 140–147) and in Rogers, Minor and Ann Rogers. "The Honganji: Guardian of the State (1868–1945)". *Japanese Journal of Religious Studies* 17 (1990): 1–26. As the Japanese state became increasingly militarized and imperialistic, Shinshu scholars scanned Shinran's writing in order to find passages that could legitimate Japan's many wars. This process has been called "The Mobilization of Doctrine" and is discussed by Christopher Ives in more detail in "The Mobilization of Doctrine: Buddhist Contributions to Imperial

Ideology in Modern Japan," *Japanese Journal of Religious Studies* 26 (1999), pp. 83–106. Moreover, in the early 1910s, the Shinshu socialist and pacifist Takagi Kemmyo strongly criticized the reading of Shinran's injunction to say the *nenbutsu* for the sake of the imperial court as advocating subservience. He points out how later in the same letter Shinran encourages the fellowship to recite the *nenbutsu* "with the wish 'May there be peace in the world and may the Buddha's teaching spread'". This latter injunction seems to contradict the violent and repressive policies of "the imperial court" (at Takagi's time) and cannot be understood as implying obedience, but simply as a wish for the wellbeing of all, including those opposed to the *nenbutsu*. The increasingly militarized Japanese state of the early 20th century seems to sit awkwardly with the wish for peace and so Takagi refuses to imagine that compliance with its policies could be justified in any way through Shinran's teaching. Takagi thus confronts the Shinshu scholars who legitimate the imperial polity through this particular letter: "Although the passage above is a gospel for peace, have people mistaken it for the sound of a bugle commanding us to attack the enemy? Or did I mistake the bells and drums of battle for injunctions for peace?" Takagi Kemmyo, "My Socialism", in *Living in Amida's Universal Vow,* Alfred Bloom, ed., (Bloomington, Indiana: World Wisdom, 2004), p. 193.

65. A Collection of Letters V. *CWS,* p. 565.

66. Ibid.

67. A Record in Lament of Divergences. *Tannisho,* Postcript. *CWS,* p. 679; A Record in Lament of Divergences. *Tannisho* II. *CWS,* p. 662. The *Kalama sutta* from the Pali canon features the historical Buddha exhorting his audience not to rely on authority, received tradition, or well-sounding words. The Buddha insists that every individual should question and test everything they hear and then decide for themselves whether it is true or not. See Tannisaro Bikku, trans., *Kalama Sutta: To the Kalamas* (http://www.accesstoinsight.org/tipitaka/an/ano3/ano3.065.than.html, 1994).

68. Lamp for the Latter Ages. *Mattosho* XVIII. *CWS,* p. 549.

69. Lamp for the Latter Ages. *Mattosho* XIX. *CWS,* pp. 551–552. Some of the actions described in these letters comprised what East Asian Mahayana Buddhism considered the acts carrying the worst

karmic consequences, namely the five grave offenses and the misuse or slander of the dharma [Buddhist teaching]. The five gravest offenses are enumerated divergently in different canonical sources but usually involve the killing or attacking of parents, a Buddha, the Buddhist community, Arahats or Bodhisattvas. Although the *Larger Sutra* mentions that the easy practice of *nenbutsu* is not available to "those who commit the five grave offenses and slander the right Dharma" (Inagaki, p. 22), the latter Pure Land tradition from Shan Tao (613–681) onwards, including Shinran, considered this as a deterrence to commit those actions and not as an actual clause of exclusion. Thus, Shinran reads this exclusion as oblique inclusion. The purpose of the exclusion clause is to show "the gravity of these two evil kinds of wrongdoing", which he sees at work in himself, a confirmation that sentient beings cannot liberate themselves and that the Buddha's vow is for their sake. Thus the deterrence to commit evil is seen as a form of reassurance, which "make[s] us realize that the sentient beings throughout the ten quarters, without a single exception, will be born in the Pure Land". Notes on the Inscription on the Sacred Scrolls. *CWS*, p. 494.

70. Lamp for the Latter Ages. *Mattosho* XX. *CWS*, p. 554.

71. When asked why does he not demand the sacred objects given to a follower who has now left the community, Shinran is recorded to have thus reasoned against it: "When differences of opinion arise in this world, the land becomes raucous with complaints to return the *Honzon* scroll and sacred writings, to return the titles, to return the true entrusting they've gotten. […] The *Honzon* scroll and sacred writings are forms of skilful means meant to benefit sentient beings. Even if someone were to decide to cut their ties with me and to enter someone else's community, I have no special monopoly on these sacred writings, for what the Tathagata teaches has currency throughout all communities". *Kudensho* V. Bloom, ed., *The Essential,* pp. 20–21.

72. In the same letter in which Shinran advices to "keep a respectful distance and not become familiar" with wrongdoers, he also reasons that they ought to be left alone since their conversion "is not our design" as it needs to be "awakened through the Buddha's working", Lamp for the Latter Ages. *Mattosho* XX. *CWS*, p. 554.

73. Lamp for the Latter Ages. *Mattosho* XX. *CWS*, p. 554.

74. A Record in Lament of Divergences. *Tannisho* VI. *CWS*, p. 664.

75. A Record in Lament of Divergences. *Tannisho* XIII. *CWS*, p. 670.

76. Ibid.

77. Ibid.

78. Ibid.

79. A structurally similar argument is put forward by Kiyozawa (1863–1901) who regards moral codes as ultimately unrealistic and unattainable. At a time when the Jodo Shinshu institutions were advocating an ethic of obedience to the state, Kiyozawa regards morality as a teaching aimed "at enabling someone to appreciate the *impossibility* of moral praxis" (Kiyozawa Manshi, "Negotiating Religious Morality and Common Morality" in Mark Blum and Robert Rhodes ed., *Cultivating Spirituality. A Modern Shin Buddhist Anthology*, (Albany: State University of New York Press, 2011), p. 82). Not unlike Shinran's relativization of morality, Kiyozawa's could equally be appropriated for a libertarian agenda that interrogates the state and its ethics but also as a quiet injunction to let it be as it is and focus on the absolute experience of *shinjin*. Consequently readings of Kiyozawa both as accommodating and as resistant are equally abundant (Curley, pp. 148–153).

80. Shinran is at his most deterministic in *Tannisho* XIII, arguing that it is not our good or bad intentions what determine our actions, but our karmic histories, over which we have no power. However, this view can be interpreted, as Bloom does, as implying that another form of agency, through *tariki*, is possible since "[t]he reality of the Vow and its compassion illuminates and determines our [karmic] experience. Our experience does not limit the Vow", *Strategies for Modern Living. A Commentary with the Text of the Tannisho*. (Berkeley: Numata Centre, 1992), p. 120.

81. For instance, Amstutz characterizes Jodo Shinshu values during the Tokugawa period (1603–1868) as "emphasizing hard work, frugality, obedience to the government, conservative protectiveness of one's family group or business […], honesty, moderation, courtesy, restraint, observance of social hierarchy and, above all, self-confidence" (*Interpreting* 24). This enumeration shows how Jodo Shinshu did not develop in an antiauthoritarian direction and how Shinran's rhetoric of equality and spontaneity did not translate, and does not necessarily translate, into social equality and individual freedom. Thus, a long

history of cooptation and cooperation with the state does not render Jodo Shinshu essentially conservative any more than an early history of subversion and social criticism makes it inherently antiauthoritarian.

82. A detailed commentary of text from an anarchist perspective can be found in Rapp, John. "Anarchism or Nihilism: The Buddhist-Influenced Thought of Wu Nengzi" in Alexandre Christoyannopoulos *Religious Anarchism: New Perspectives*. Newcastle: Cambridge Publishing Scholars, 2009), pp. 202–225.

83. Although a younger Suzuki had written in 1938 that Zen could be "wedded to anarchism or fascism, communism or democracy, atheism or idealism, or any political or economic dogmatism" (Suzuki in Victoria, p. 63), towards the end of his life he said at a public lecture that "anarchism is best" (Brown, p. 214).

84. A socialist reading can be found in Takagi (see note 28), a liberal one in Kiyozawa (see note 81), a Japanese imperialist reading corresponds to the war time doctrines discussed in note 66 and elements of eco-pacifism can be said to pervade the official discourse of the two largest Jodo Shinshu institutions: the Nishi and Higashi Honganjis. The addresses of the 24th Monshu of the Nishi Honganji, Sokunyo Koshin Ohtani (1945), reflect on "peace issues and environment concerns" and offers a Buddhist analysis of "armed conflicts and climate change" and ethics of moderation and mutuality. Sokunyo Ohtani Koshin. "Immesurable Light and Life -2008 New Year's Message from the Monshu" in *Manitoba Buddhist Temple*. (http://www.manitoba buddhistchurch.org/blog_files/1cbf020d5e607cce8a4ce4a2c63b8c11–46.html).

85. The phrase, widely used to describe Buddhism in popular culture, can also be found in the title of Alan Watts' *Buddhism the Religion of No-Religion* (Boston: Tuttle Publishing, 1999).

References

Amstutz, Galen, *Interpreting Amida. History and Orientalism in the Study of Pure Land Buddhism* (Albany: State University of New York, 1997).

Amstutz, Galen, "Shinran and Authority in Buddhism", in *Living in Amida's Universal Vow. Essays in Shin Buddhism, ed. by Alfred Bloom* (Bloomington, Indiana: World Wisdom, 2004), pp. 143–154.

Bloom, Alfred "Honen and Shinran: Loyalty and Independence", in *Shindharmanet,* 2012 (http://www.shindharmanet.com/wp-content/uploads/2012/pdf/Bloom-Loyalty.pdf)

Bloom, Alfred, "Introduction", in Fitzgerald et al., eds., *Honen the Buddhist Saint: Essential Writings and Official Biography* (Bloomington, Indiana: World Wisdom, 2006), pp. xxiii-xxxvii.

Bloom, Alfred, "Shin Buddhism in the Modern Ethical Context", in *Shindharmanet* (http://shindharmanet.com/course/c24/)

Bloom, Alfred. *Strategies for Modern Living. A Commentary with the Text of the Tannisho.* (Berkeley: Numata Centre, 1992).

Bloom, Alfred. "The Life of Shinran Shonin: The Journey to Self-Acceptance" in Paul Williams, ed., *Buddhism in China, East Asia and Japan.* Vol II (Abingdon, Oxon: Routledge, 2005), pp. 87–93.

Bloom, Alfred, ed., *The Essential Shinran. A Buddhist Path of True Entrusting* (Boston: World Wisdom, 2007).

Blum, Mark. *The Origins and Development of Pure Land Buddhism: A Study and Translation of Gyonen's* Jodo Homon Genrusho. Oxford: Oxford University Press, 2002.

Brown, James. "The Zen of Anarchy: Japanese Exceptionalism and the Anarchist Roots of the San Francisco Poetry Renaissance". *Religion and American Culture: A Journal of Interpretation,* 19.2 (Summer 2009) p. 214.

Buber, Martin, *Paths in Utopia* (Syracuse, New York: Syracuse University Press, 1950).

Clark, John [Max Cafard]. "Zen Anarchy" [2006]. *The Anarchist Library.* August 14th 2009, (http://theanarchistlibrary.org/library/max-cafard-zen-anarchy)

Curley, Melissa Anne-Marie, *Know That We Are Not Good Persons: Pure Land Buddhism and the Ethics of Exile* (PhD Thesis presented at McGill University, June 2009).

De Ridder, Widdukind, "Max Stirner: The End of Philosophy and Political Subjectivity", in, *Max Stirner,* ed. by Saul Newman (London: Palgrave Macmillan, 2011), pp. 143–164.

Dessi, Ugo, "The Pure Land as a Principle of Social Criticism", *Japanese Religions,* 33 (1 & 2): 75–90.

Dobbins, James *Jodo Shinshu: Shin Buddhism in Medieval Japan* (Hawai'i: University of Hawai'i Press: 2002).

Esho Shimazu, "The Sangowakuran Incident and its Significance for Engaged Buddhism", in *Muryoko. Journal of Shin Buddhism.* (http://www.nembutsu.info/sangowakuran.htm)

Foulk, Griffith, 'Ritual in Japanese Zen Buddhism', in *Zen Ritual. Studies of Zen Buddhist Theory in Practice,* ed. by Steven Heine and Dale Wright (Oxford: Oxford University Press, 2008), pp. 21–82.

Fuller Sasaki, Ruth, trans., *The Record of Linji* (Honolulu, University of Hawai'i Press: 2009).

Galvan-Alvarez, Enrique. "Meditative Revolutions? Orientalism and History in the Western Buddhist Anarchist Tradition in *Enlightened Anarchism.* Forthcoming.

Goto-Jones, Christopher, *Political Philosophy in Japan. Nishida, the Kyoto School, and Co-Prosperity* (Oxford: Oxford University Press, 2005).

Inagaki Hisao, ed. *The Three Pure Land Sutras, Volume II. The Sutra on the Buddha of Immeasurable Life.* (Kyoto: Jodo Shinshu Hongwanji-Ha, 2009)

Ives, Christopher, "The Mobilization of Doctrine: Buddhist Contributions to Imperial Ideology in Modern Japan", *Japanese Journal of Religious Studies* 26 (1999): 83–106.

Kiyozawa Manshi, "Negotiating Religious Morality and Common Morality" in Mark Blum and Robert Rhodes ed., *Cultivating Spirituality. A Modern Shin Buddhist Anthology,* (Albany: State University of New York Press, 2011), pp. 77–91.

Main, Jessica. *Only Shinran Will Not Betray Us. Takeuchi Ryo'on (1891–1967), the Otani-ha Administration and the* Burakumin, (Thesis Presented at McGill University, April 2012).

Márquez, Alberto, *León Duarte* (Montevideo: Editorial Compañero, 1993).

Marshall, Peter, *Demanding the Impossible. A History of Anarchism,* (London: Harper Perennial, 2008).

Mayes, Ian "Envisioning a Buddhist Anarchism", in *The Implicit & Experiential Rantings of a Person,* 2011, (http://parenthesiseye. blogspot.co.uk/2011/11/envisioning-buddhist-anarchism.html).

McMullin, Neil, *Buddhism and the State in Sixteenth-Century Japan* (Princenton, New Jersey: Princeton University Press, 1984).

Park, Jin Y. *Buddhism and Postmodernity. Zen, Huayan and the Possibility of Buddhist Postmodern Ethics. (*Plymouth: Lexington Books, 2008).

Rambelli, Fabio. "Just Behave as You Like; Prohibitions and Impurities Are Not a Problem. Radical Amida Cults and Popular Religiosity in Premodern Japan" in Kenneth Tanaka and Richard Payne, eds., *Approaching the Land of Bliss. Religious Praxis in the Cult of Amitabha.* (Honolulu: University of Hawai'i Press, 2004), pp. 169–201.

Rambelli. Fabio. *Zen Anarchism. The Egalitarian Dharma of Uchiyama Gudo* (Berkeley: Institute of Buddhist Studies, 2013).

Rapp, John. "Anarchism or Nihilism: The Buddhist-Influenced Thought of Wu Nengzi" in Alexandre Christoyannopoulos *Religious Anarchism: New Perspectives.* Newcastle: Cambridge Publishing Scholars, 2009), pp. 202–225.

Ritzinger, Justin, *Anarchy in the Pure Land: Tradition, Modernity, and the Reinvention of the Cult of Maitreya in Republican China* (Ann Arbor, Michigan: ProQuest, 2010).

Rogers, Minor and Ann Rogers. "The Honganji: Guardian of the State (1868–1945)". *Japanese Journal of Religious Studies* 17 (1990): 1–26

Scott, Rachelle. *Nirvana for Sale. Buddhism, Wealth and the Contemporary Dharmakaya Temple in Contemporary Temple* (Albany: State University of New York Press, 2009).

Shigaraki Takamaro. *Heart of the Shin Buddhist Path.* David Matsumoto, trans. (Boston: Wisdom Publications, 2013).

Shinran, *Collected Works of Shinran,* Dennis Hirota, trans., (Kyoto: Jodo Shinshu Hongwanji-ha, 1997).

Snyder, Gary, "Buddhist Anarchism", in *Bureau of Public Secrets,* (http://www.bopsecrets.org/CF/garysnyder.htm, 2002 [1961])

Snyder, Gary "Revolution in the Revolution in the Revolution", in *Regarding Wave* (New York: New Directions Books, 1970), p. 39.

Sokunyo Ohtani Koshin. "Immesurable Light and Life -2008 New Year's Message from the Monshu" in *Manitoba Buddhist Temple*. (http://www.manitobabuddhistchurch.org/blog_files/1cbf020d5e6 07cce8a4ce4a2c63b8c11–46.html)

Suzuki, Daisetz, *Zen and Japanese Culture* (Princenton: Princenton University Press, 1993).

Takagi Kemmyo, "My Socialism", in *Living in Amida's Universal Vow,* ed. Alfred Bloom (Bloomington, Indiana: World Wisdom, 2004), pp.189–196.

Tanaka Kenneth and Richar Payne, eds., *Approaching the Land of Bliss. Religious Praxis of Amitabha* (Honolulu: University of Hawai'i Press, 2004.

Tannisaro Bikku, trans., *Kalama Sutta: To the Kalamas* 1994 (http://www.accesstoinsight.org/tipitaka/an/an03/an03.065.than.html).

Thornley, Kerry. "Zenarchy" [1991]. *The Anarchist Library.* December 19th 2009. (http://theanarchistlibrary.org/library/kerry-thornley-zenarchy)

Tokunaga, Michio, "Buddha's Law and King's Law: The Bifurcation of Shinran's Teaching", in *Shin Buddhism: Monograph Series* (Los Angeles: Pure Land Publications, 1993), pp. 145–156.

Tsang, Carol Richmond, *War and Faith. Ikko Ikki in Late Muromachi Japan.* (London: Harvard University Press, 2007).

Victoria, Brian Daizen, *Zen at War.* (Oxford: Rowman and Littleman Publishers, 2006).

Warner, Brad, *Hardcore Zen: Punk Rock, Monster Movies & The Truth About Reality* (Somerville, Massachusetts: Wisdom Publications, 2003).

Watts, Alan, *Buddhism the Religion of No-Religion* (Boston: Tuttle Publishing, 1999)

Young Lee, Kenneth Doo. *The Prince and the Monk. Shotoku Worship in Shinran's Buddhism.* (Albany: State University of New York Press, 2007)

Was the historical Jesus an anarchist? Anachronism, anarchism and the historical Jesus

Justin Meggitt
University of Cambridge, UK

The claim that Jesus was an anarchist has been made by a variety of individuals and movements throughout history. Although there have been significant differences in what has been meant, it is possible to determine the validity of such a judgement. Once initial questions about historicity, methodology, and definition have been addressed, it is apparent that there are a number of recurrent, dominant, motifs within our earliest sources about the figure of Jesus that can legitimately be judged anarchist. The 'Kingdom of God' for example, a concept that pervades the earliest data, includes the active identification and critique of coercive relations of power, and the enactment of new, egalitarian and prefigurative modes of social life, as well as a reflexive, undetermined, and self-creative praxis. The pedagogy of the historical Jesus also appears to have been predominately prefigurative and non-coercive. Although the picture certainly is not uniform, and there are early motifs that can be judged authoritarian and hierarchical, claims that the historical Jesus was an anarchist are legitimate, defensible and valuable.

It is true that if we could follow the precepts of the Nazarene this would be a different world to live in. There would then be no murder and no war; no cheating and lying and profit-making. There would be neither slave nor master, and we should all live like brothers, in peace and harmony. There would be neither poor nor rich, neither crime nor prison, but that would not be what the church wants. It would be what the Anarchists want.[1]

How to cite this book chapter:
Meggitt, J. 2017. Was the historical Jesus an anarchist? Anachronism, anarchism and the historical Jesus. In: Christoyannopoulos, A. and Adams, M. S. (eds.) *Essays in Anarchism and Religion: Volume 1.* Pp. 124–197. Stockholm: Stockholm University Press. DOI: https://doi.org/10.16993/bak.e. License: CC-BY

1. Preliminary issues

The claim that Jesus was an anarchist is one that has been made by a variety of individuals and movements since the term "anarchist" itself first began to be commonly used from the 1840s onwards.[2] Nietzsche,[3] is probably amongst the most culturally significant to have given Jesus this label, though other prominent figures have made more or less the same claim, including Berdyaev,[4] Tolstoy,[5] and Wilde,[6] as have a host of lesser known figures. It has been most common amongst groups and networks that are overt in their espousal of some form of Christian anarchism, such as the Catholic Worker Movement,[7] the Jesus Radicals,[8] the Brotherhood Church,[9] and the Union of the Spiritual Communities of Christ,[10] but could also be said to be implied in movements that have been identified as containing implicit anarchist characteristics, such as those associated with some forms of liberation theology[11] and related contextual theologies.[12] The anarchist potentiality of the historical Jesus was even recognised by classical anarchist thinkers, most prominently Proudhon,[13] but also, to varying degrees, Bakunin,[14] Kropotkin,[15] and Stirner.[16]

Of course, what exactly is meant when someone calls Jesus an "anarchist" is not self-evident and there is sometimes little, if anything, that such claims have in common. Authors assume a range of different interpretations of the figure of Jesus and also of anarchism itself in making their judgments. This paper is not a criticism of any such estimations of Jesus but rather an attempt to bring a little more clarity to the subject and to see if, historically speaking, there is any analytical value in talking in such a way about Jesus. More specifically, I would like to examine whether the historical Jesus can legitimately be called an anarchist.

By using the expression "the historical Jesus" I am assuming a distinction, common in Biblical scholarship since the nineteenth century,[17] between the historical figure of Jesus and the Christ of Christian faith, a distinction that assumes that the two are not necessarily the same (a distinction that not all the writers that might be labeled Christian anarchist would share). My concern is not whether the Christ of Christian faith, that believers claim is known from the Christian Bible, doctrine and experience was (or indeed, for them, *is*) an anarchist but whether the man called Jesus of Nazareth, who lived and died about two thousand years ago, could usefully be called such.

I should also make it clear that I am specifically interested in whether Jesus can be called an "anarchist". This is not necessarily the same as saying that he simply had anti-authoritarian tendencies nor that he was a violent insurrectionist of some kind – something that received considerable attention some decades ago and which has recently been revived.[18] Nor is it the same as deciding that he was a "revolutionary" of some other kind, something that has been a particular interest in contemporary scholarship, especially amongst those concerned with trying to demonstrate that the historical Jesus was an "inclusive" figure of some sort.[19] Ideas about what might constitute "politics" have become increasingly nuanced, under the influence of such things as postcolonial and gender theory,[20] and the ideological contexts of both the historical Jesus and New Testament scholars themselves have come under extensive scrutiny.[21]

However, before we can attempt to answer the question we have posed, there are a number of preliminary matters that need to be addressed. In asking whether the historical Jesus can be usefully labeled an anarchist I am conscious that many anarchists may be familiar with material, academic and otherwise, which maintains that Jesus of Nazareth never existed,[22] and they may think that my question is a pointless one to try to answer. Although no questions should be ignored in the critical study of religion, the arguments of those who doubt the existence of the historical Jesus are unpersuasive.[23] None of the opponents of early Christianity, although they found numerous grounds for criticising the life and teaching of Jesus, doubted his existence,[24] and, to put the matter concisely, the existence of Jesus of Nazareth is by far the most plausible way of explaining the traditions we have about a first-century, charismatic, Jewish peasant of that name. Traditions that, culturally speaking, cohere with what we know about the religious and cultural environment of Palestine at the time and which combine to form a picture of a specific and distinctive individual within it – not a banal and fanciful composite. Of course, these sources need to be handled with critical caution, as they have been since the Enlightenment, as most are composed by followers of Jesus.[25] However, this in itself is not surprising: the poor in the Roman empire – and pictures of Jesus from antiquity are universal in placing him in this category[26] – like the poor in most of history, had little and left less behind. Very few, mostly through accident rather than design, left anything, so thoroughgoing has been what E. P. Thompson called "the enormous condescension of posterity".[27] Jesus' significance, to those other than his immediate followers, was only evident in retrospect and so we should not be surprised that there is little in the way of non-Christian documentary or literary evidence for this life and that our analysis will have to rely on extensive and diverse but largely Christian sources.[28]

However, having accepted that it is possible to talk about a historical Jesus, how should we go about determining whether it is reasonable to label him an anarchist or not? The current literature that has touched on this is of little assistance. Many of those claiming that Jesus was an anarchist are often doing little more than constructing a mythology to give authority to a movement, as Woodcock has suggested.[29] Some have arrived at their interpretation of Jesus through a more critical, ostensibly historical approach to the sources; Tolstoy's anti-supernaturalist reading of the gospels, which had no place for the miraculous "rotten apples"[30] is perhaps the most famous example. However, there has been little systematic or coherent engagement with critical scholarship concerned with the study of the historical Jesus and the problems it has tried to address, and most readings by those who want to label Jesus an anarchist are characterised by rather literalistic and hermeneutically naive approaches to Biblical texts,[31] as the analysis of Christoyannopoulos has recently demonstrated.[32] The teachings of the historical Jesus are, for example, often assumed to be easily accessible. For some, this is just a matter of rescuing Jesus from Paul (and often, by implication, the later church), but however rhetorically appealing it is to many Christian anarchists for whom Paul can be a rather uncomfortable figure,[33] this is not a defensible approach as Paul is the author of the earliest Christian literature that we possess and provides us with data about the historical Jesus, which, limited though it is, actually predates the gospels.[34]

A number solve the conundrum by giving priority to the Sermon on the Mount (Matthew 5.3–7.27), seeing it as the authoritative epitome of Jesus' teaching,[35] but in so doing they ignore its redactional character; it is, to a large extent, the construction of the author of the gospel in which it is found and cannot be said to go back to the historical Jesus.[36] Even if the sermon is composed of elements that early Christians thought originated with Jesus, many of which are paralleled in the so-called Sermon on the Plain (Luke 6:20–49), and can also be seen in the epistle of James and the early Christian text, the *Didache*,[37] there is much about its structure and content that clearly owes itself to the author of the Gospel of Matthew and those who brought together and transmitted the sources from which he created his final text. Of course, there has been a handful of scholars who have been practitioners of critical biblical scholarship and who have also shown an interest in Christian anarchism, most notably Vaage[38] and Myers,[39] but these are relatively few and, to date, there has been no critical and programmatic attempt to answer the question we have asked. In the light of this it is necessary to sketch, in a little detail, a valid method for scrutinizing the sources we have for the historical Jesus that might provide us with some plausible results.

But before I do this, I should add some caveats about my own historical approach here. I am very conscious that in asking questions about the historical Jesus I might well be doing something that strikes some as epistemologically naive – even if a lot of people do it – and I could be accused, along with others who engage one way or another with the "Quest"[40] for the historical Jesus, of making oddly positivist assumptions about the nature of historical knowledge and how it can be arrived at.[41] However, my aims are quite modest: I am not claiming to uncover the "real" Jesus,[42] nor even a useful one, but to make some provisional but, I hope, plausible suggestions about how this figure could be understood if examined in the light of the assumptions, aspirations, and praxis characteristic of anarchism. In asking this question I am not assuming anything about the significance of what follows or its implications: my interest in the historical Jesus is not in uncovering a figure, or an aspect of a figure, that is somehow determinative for Christians or anyone else. The shifting sands of historical reconstruction are not really a very useful foundation for anything much that matters – though many biblical scholars enjoy their time in the sandpit and make quite remarkable claims about the ephemeral edifices that they fashion.[43]

Before I turn to the question of historical method it is also important to address an initial objection to the question this paper tries to answer, which might, in the eyes of some, like the question of Jesus' existence, prevent them proceeding any further: the problem of Jesus' theism. I am conscious that it might be argued that the theism of the historical Jesus precludes him from being considered an anarchist. Most of the words or actions ascribed to him, in one way or another, either reference or are predicated upon belief in God.[44] For example, the arrival of God's rule and its implication for humans seems to have preoccupied him and is at the heart of whatever socio-political vision he may have had, as we shall see.[45] However, it is not the case that anarchism necessarily implies atheism. Atheism is central to many forms of classical anarchism. One need only think of Bakunin's famous *God and the State,* Faure's *Les douze preuves de l'inexistence de dieu*[46] or the infamous anti-clerical massacres carried out by anarchist units in the Spanish Civil War.[47] Such atheism is often predicated upon the need to reject the tyranny assumed to be inherent in the idea of an omnipotent God (powerfully expressed in Bakunin's famous remark, "If God really existed, it would be necessary to abolish him").[48] However, it is also driven by the desire to oppose the oppression that is thought to result from the social consequences of belief in God, both that oppression caused by religious institutions themselves and the power that they exert, and also the oppression which results from the support such religious institutions, in turn, provide to the state, the prime focus of the anarchist critique of exploitation (Bakunin famously called the state, "the Church's younger brother").[49] Indeed, the apparent demise of religion – even if anarchism has often been rather premature in its claims about this – has been taken by some anarchists as evidence of the likely demise of the state:

> The history of religion is a model for the history of government. Once it was thought impossible to have a society without God;

now God is dead. It is still thought impossible to have a society without the state; now we must destroy the state.[50]

The atheism of anarchism can be so intense as to spill over into misotheism, not just a denial of the existence of God but an active hatred of God.[51] However, as the influential chronicler of anarchism, Peter Marshall has noted, "Anarchism is not necessarily atheistic any more than socialism is."[52] And it is clear from the existence of religious anarchists of various kinds, some of which we have already mentioned, that this is the case.[53] However eccentric they might appear, religious anarchists are not normally considered outside the anarchist fold in studies of the field (unlike, for example, anarcho-capitalists[54] or far-right national anarchists[55]). It would be, for example, an unusual history of anarchism that did not make at least some mention of Tolstoy or the Catholic Worker Movement.[56] Therefore the theism of Jesus should not preclude him from being labelled an anarchist.

These observations aside, let us now turn to the question of historical method.

2. Constructing the historical Jesus

Until recently there was a general agreement on the historical method used by most of those studying the figure of Jesus.[57] There was a rough consensus on the range of historical-critical tools that should be employed and the sources that were deemed relevant.[58] In addition, most scholars also agreed on the need to apply so-called "criteria of authenticity" to the data in order to distinguish between "authentic" and "inauthentic" traditions about Jesus.[59] Five criteria were given particular weight in reconstructions: embarrassment, dissimilarity, multiple attestation, coherence and crucifiability, and these, explicitly or implicitly, have underpinned most of the critical studies of Jesus that have appeared in the last few decades.[60] However, the field is now experiencing something of a crisis. Consensus on historical method has not produced agreement on the results[61] and we have, instead, seen a proliferation of widely divergent reconstructions of the historical Jesus.[62] There is a growing recognition that, despite attempts to rectify their weaknesses,[63] some of which have long been noted,[64] the criteria of authenticity are inadequate for the task, and should be abandoned. The discipline is now (or perhaps, once again) much more alert to the challenges posed by such things as memory[65] and has a greater awareness of the problems inherent in talking about "authenticity". A recent essay by Dale Allison, a leading historical-Jesus scholar, in which he chronicled his own growing disillusionment with the way in which the subject has been approached, is emblematic of the current state of the field.[66]

My own position is similar to that at which Allison has recently arrived.[67] There is much about Jesus that remains impossible to substantiate if we treat it with the same kind of scepticism that one would responsibly use if you were, for example, trying to establish the details of the life of other figures who were significant in antiquity, such as Socrates,[68] Apollonius of Tyana,[69] or Rabbi Akiva,[70] and to say with any certainty what they may have said or done or what ideas that they might have had. Only a limited amount of information can be ascertained about the historical Jesus with anything approaching confidence, and that, for the most part, is of a general rather than specific kind. The significant creativity evident amongst those who first repeated and recorded traditions about Jesus, and the lack of evidence that the early Christians were discerning in their transmission of stories about him,[71] makes such a position unavoidable. Most of the data we have about Jesus can only provide us with *impressions* of the man but these impressions are relatively trustworthy and reflect the enduring effect he had upon his earliest followers. They remain valid irrespective of the historicity of any particular unit of tradition, regardless of the abbreviation, elaboration, conflation, embellishment and fabrication evident within the sources.[72] So, for example, as I have noted elsewhere, when we look at the relevant texts:

> The virtues that Jesus exhibited in the face of death, of both forebearance and submission, and his refusal to return violence with violence, seem to have been recurring motifs in the pictures of Jesus that emerge from these traditions and tell us something about the enduring impression his personality made on his followers.[73]

And there are, I believe, many larger patterns evident in the sources, patterns that are sufficiently robust so as to still hold true even if the data that they are derived from includes material that was invented. Indeed, as Allison has said, even "fiction can bring us facts ... some of the traditions about Jesus which are, in the strict sense, not historical, surely give us a faithful impression of the sort of person he was or the sort of thing he typically did."[74] The temptation narratives, for example, despite being highly legendary depict Jesus as someone who shows disdain for personal political power, a motif that recurs a number of times in our sources.[75] And so I would go along with Allison, albeit for slightly different reasons, and say:

> So, in the matter of Jesus, we should start not with the parts but with the whole, which means with the general impression that the tradition about him, *in toto*, tends to convey. The criteria of authenticity are, for this endeavour, simply in the way.[76]

It is the working assumption of this text that beyond a small cluster of incidents – such as his crucifixion – the details of the life of Jesus are historically elusive although the general picture, and recurrent motifs, are discernible and historically reliable.

It follows, therefore, that I am not going to engage in detailed exegesis of specific texts, even those that look particularly relevant to our theme. For example, the "Render unto Caesar" incident,[77] something central to most studies of the politics of Jesus,[78] will not be the focus of detailed scrutiny because the best that can be said about individual traditions of this kind is that they were the kind of thing Jesus' followers[79] thought Jesus might have said. Our business is about seeing the patterns and determining what was characteristic of the figure, not to be too concerned with the historicity of the details. Such an approach also has the advantage of resembling the way that ancient biographies – which to a large extent the gospels are[80] – would have been understood in antiquity.[81]

3. The meaning and utility of the term "anarchist"

If we want to determine whether the historical Jesus can be termed an "anarchist" we need to determine not only how we can arrive at knowledge about the figure than might allow us to make such a judgement but also what we mean by the term "anarchist" when we attempt such an evaluation. In addition, we will need to address two potential criticisms of the business of determining whether the term "anarchist" is a fair one to apply to Jesus: that the term "anarchist" is anachronistic and ethnocentric.

Any attempt to define anarchism has to deal with the problem of its popular image. The notion that anarchism is about the absence of order rather than the absence of government, that it is synonymous with chaos and senseless violence, has persisted since the Victorian period[82] and was made famous by such works as Joseph Conrad's *The Secret Agent*.[83] Of course, there are some forms of insurrectionary anarchism that appear to fit this stereotype – one needs only think of the recent activities of the *Federazione Anarchica Informale*[84] – but counter to the popular image, the use of violence[85] is, for most anarchists, subject to considerable constraints, and most would eschew anything that could be deemed to be coercive violence against persons, even if outright pacifism is a minority position.[86] Far from being senseless and destructive, most anarchists would consider themselves engaged in a constructive project consisting of "reconstructive visions, pre-figurative politics and self-organisation".[87]

But once we move past the problem of the popular image of anarchism, and try to define anarchism more accurately, we still face a number of acute challenges. There are, for example, a range of terms commonly used to qualify the word "anarchist", such as collectivist, communist, individualist, liberal, life-style, mutualist, poststructuralist, primitivist, social, and syndicalist, the diversity of which seems, at first sight, to indicate something that is so pluriform that it resists definition. But whilst such labels, and more, are clearly significant, it is possible to have what has been called "an anarchism without adjectives",[88] some kind of anarchism that is roughly representative of what most forms of anarchism have in common and true to its varied but essentially ecumenical character.[89] Although it is customary to begin such fundamental definitions with an etymological point about the Greek word *anarchos,* from which the term anarchism is derived,[90] and to point out that it means "without a ruler", this does not get us very far, and saying something more is challenging, not least because anarchism is profoundly anti-dogmatic.[91] Nonetheless, the definition of the anthropologist Brian Morris is one that is helpful for our purposes, encapsulating both its critical and constructive programme.

> Anarchists are people who reject all forms of government or coercive authority, all forms of hierarchy and domination [...] But anarchists also seek to establish or bring about by varying means, a condition of anarchy, that is, a decentralised society without coercive institutions.[92]

However, it might also be helpful to keep in mind, in what follows, the suggestion by David Graeber, that any definition of the term anarchist has to encompass a range of interrelated and overlapping meanings. He notes that generally speaking, people, ideas or institutions are labelled anarchist if they endorse an explicit doctrine, display a particular attitude, or engage in specific practices. That is, anarchists include those who are heirs of the intellectual tradition that began in the nineteenth century which is characterised by "a certain vision of human possibilities";[93] those that display a particular "attitude" which "reject[s] government and believe[s] that people would be better off in a world without hierarchies";[94] and those that engage in practices and forms of social organisation that are broadly egalitarian in ethos[95] (seen, for example in what Evans-Pritchard called the "ordered anarchy" of the Nuer).[96] No definition of "anarchist" will ever be satisfactory but Graeber's remarks remind us that whilst we should be careful not to make our understanding of the term so broad as to be meaningless (it will not do, for example, to label anyone who is anti-authoritarian an anarchist) we should be aware that the term is an expansive, dynamic and necessarily malleable one.

However, having briefly explored the question of what an "anarchist" might be usefully said to be, we now need to address whether it is anachronistic or ethnocentric to ask if the historical Jesus can be usefully described in this way.

The charge of anachronism seems, at face value, a damning one. To many anarchism may seem clearly wedded to a specific historical moment, its character determined by its formal origins in the nineteenth century, or the brief periods of prominence it enjoyed with the Maknovists in Ukraine,[97] the CNT-FAI in Republican Spain,[98] its prominence in events in France in May 1968,[99] or its more recent re-emergence within anti-capitalist and anti-globalisation movements, and anarchist volunteers contributing to the defense of the Rojava revolution in north Syria/West Kurdistan.[100] All these are a long way from first-century Palestine and so it seems legitimate to ask whether it is just downright anachronistic to even pose the question whether the historical Jesus was an anarchist. If it is then we are wasting our time.

However, the problem of using contemporary terminology to describe and elucidate past realities is not a new one and obviously not limited to the study of the historical Jesus (although scholars of the historical Jesus often behave as though they were engaged in a unique endeavour). Given the opprobrium that has faced those who have maintained that the historical Jesus can be usefully described as a Jewish Cynic,[101] a not unreasonable suggestion given the clear resemblances between Jesus and the philosophical movement of that name active in the early Roman empire, and a suggestion that at least had the virtue of applying to the historical Jesus a term that was current in the first-century world,[102] to ask whether Jesus could usefully be called an "anarchist" seems unwise. However, it is a term that is, generally speaking, particularly amenable to being used of a figure in the past. As Graeber has noted, the founding ideologues of anarchism, such as Proudhon, "did not think of themselves as having invented anything particularly new. The basic principles of anarchism – self-organization, voluntary association, mutual aid – referred to forms of human behaviour they assumed it had been around about as long as humanity."[103] It is certainly a less problematic term to use than, say, "Marxist". The latter has always been associated with high theory and the fundamental project of analysis begun with Karl Marx, whilst anarchism is, again in the words of Graeber, "more a moral project"[104] and the only thing that really changed in the nineteenth century was that it acquired a name.[105] Such thinking lies behind, for example, Robert Graham's recent documentary chronicle of anarchism, which begins at 300CE,[106] or Peter Marshall's *Demanding the Impossible*, a substantial and influential history of anarchism that traces the origins of anarchism back to Taoism and the sixth century BCE, and, like Graham, contains extensive discussion of pre-nineteenth century movements. Indeed, not just historians of anarchism but historians working in other fields have believed that anarchism can have analytic purchase when talking about the past. Patricia Crone, for example, a key figure in the study of Islamic origins, has argued that some Mu'tazilites and members of the Najadāt sub-sect of Khārijites, should be termed anarchists and included in histories of anarchism as they believed that society could, indeed *should,* function without a government or what we would call a state.[107] Similarly, Norman Cohn used it to describe various millenarian movements in medieval Europe, most notably Taborites of Bohemia.[108] Likewise, the anthropologist James C. Scott has used the term in his history of the peoples of Zomia, a region of upland Southeast Asia which has, until relatively recently, resisted the "internal colonialism" of state-making in the area and whose inhabitants had successfully practiced the art of not being governed for centuries.[109] And similarly, fellow anthropologist Brian Morris has considered it an appropriate designation for Lao Tzu.[110] We should not, therefore, be reluctant to use the term "anarchist" to describe the figure of Jesus, if he merits such a designation.

Nonetheless, the problem of anachronism is not necessarily dealt with so easily: for much of its history anarchism has been associated with opposition to both capitalism and the state, which are usually seen as inseparable objects that mutually re-enforce one another, are irredeemably coercive,[111] and neither of which might strike someone as obviously present in the first-century, pre-industrial world; something that might undermine its utility for our purposes. However, anarchists have not always seen capitalism and the state as the sole causes of inequalities of power and creations of hierarchy,[112] and critiques of all forms of domination, whatever their source and in whatever domain, are common, something particularly evident in the articulations of anarchism that have come to the fore in recent years. It is also the case that the terms "capitalism" and "state" can have some explanatory power for making sense of antiquity and the world within which the historical Jesus lived. First, it has proven useful for those engaged in the study of antiquity to characterise the economy of the early Roman empire as one of political capitalism,[113] in the Weberian sense, an economy that consisted of "the exploitation of the opportunities for profit arising from the exercise of political power";[114] it may have been a market economy of sorts[115] but profit-making was in the hands of the political elite within the empire and its retainers. Secondly, whilst there was little analogous to the modern state in antiquity, the Roman government did monopolise ultimate military, fiscal, legislative and judicial power within the regions it ruled (even if also allowed considerable autonomy). Although the Roman empire of the first century CE was relatively light on administrative functionaries[116] and military personnel,[117] given the extent of territory controlled,[118] it certainly meets a minimal definition of a state where a state is understood as a social organization "capable of exerting a considerable degree of power [...] over large numbers of people, and for sustained periods".[119] Indeed, the Rome empire fulfilled the classic definition of the state as that which "lays claim to the monopoly of legitimate physical violence within a territory".[120]

We also need to address the related problem of ethnocentrism. If we call Jesus an "anarchist" are we employing a term that has no interpretative value outside of the modern European or North American context within which anarchism first emerged as a self-conscious movement, employing a concept that impedes rather than assists our understanding of a figure from a different cultural and historical context?[121] One that might be said to carry with it the superior presumptions of Western modernity (or, indeed, post-modernity) within which anarchism was born and thrives? Not only would such a judgment be wrong because anarchism itself has a long history of formal existence outside of Europe or North America (one thinks, for example, of the history of formal anarchist movements in Africa,[122] China,[123] Korea, Japan[124] and elsewhere),[125] but also because, as we have noted, it has been used by those engaged in the description and interpretation of non-European cultures, famously by Evans-Pritchard but also by other anthropologists acutely aware of such criticisms.[126] Harold Barclay has made perhaps the most thoroughgoing defence of the use of the term cross-culturally. He recognises that it the use of the term "anarchy" might be viewed as:

Ethnocentric and confuses ideology with social classification. It is to take a highly emotionally charged word, one with a very clear ideological connotation, identified with Euro-American cultural traditions, and to apply it cross-culturally, when those in other cultures would clearly lack the ideology and values of the anarchist. Thus, not only is the word distorted but also is the meaning of those cultures.

But quite rightly he notes that:

> If this is true of the word 'anarchy', it applies equally to the use of such words as 'democratic', 'government', 'law' [...] and a host of others employed daily by social scientists, yet derived from ordinary speech. Social sciences is full of terms in common usage which are applied to social contexts in other cultures. There are certainly dangers to such a procedure. It is easy to carry extraneous ideological baggage along with the term. On the other hand, if we cannot at all make such cross-cultural transfers, we are left with a proliferation of neologisms which become pure jargonese, enhancing obfuscation rather than clarification.[127]

So the question of whether the historical Jesus was an anarchist is one that can be asked and one to which we can expect a meaningful answer of some kind. Let us now sketch a response.

4. Was the *historical* Jesus an anarchist?

As we discussed earlier, any attempt to talk about the *historical* Jesus will need to concern itself with impressions and motifs rather than detailed exegesis of specific traditions. Even within these constraints there is much that could be said but for the purposes of this essay I would like to focus a prominent motif present within a large quantity of traditions associated with the figure of Jesus: the kingdom of God. A "kingdom", of whatever kind, does not, of course, sound a very anarchist thing but it should be noted, from the outset, that the Greek term *basileia*, which is translated into English as "kingdom", can be understood as having a territorial or geographical meaning but it can also refer to royal power or sovereignty; it can be understood as "reign" or "rule" as well as "realm". This is also true of the Hebrew and Aramaic word *malkūth* which probably underlies the use of the Greek term.[128] So, although we shall use the expression "kingdom of God", as this phrase remains the best-known rendering into English of the Greek phrase *basileia tou theou* found in early Christian sources and associated with the figure of Jesus, it can also be thought of as the "reign of God" or "rule of God".

In our sources, references to the kingdom of God saturate not just Jesus' teaching but his activity too.[129] The phrase, or the term "kingdom" by itself, is prominent in the canonical gospels of Matthew, Mark and Luke (customarily referred to as the Synoptic gospels) and the non-canonical gospel of Thomas,[130] a text which is considered by most scholars in the field to contain early traditions about Jesus comparable to those of the Synoptics[131] (the gospel of John is usually judged to be somewhat later and of little value in the study of the historical Jesus).[132] The "kingdom" is all pervasive. It appears at the outset of accounts of the life of Jesus, as the subject of his preaching, and remains a preoccupation throughout his ministry. For example, at the beginning of his public activity, according to Matthew and Mark, Jesus proclaims:

> The time is fulfilled, and the kingdom of God has come near; repent, and believe in the good news.[133]

And, it remains a preoccupation to the end, a subject of discussion at his final meal[134] and even his words from the cross.[135] It was determinative of the content and character of his ethics. For example, renunciation of wealth appears a prerequisite for entrance to the kingdom.

> It is easier for a camel to go through the eye of a needle that for someone who is rich enter the kingdom of God.[136]

The kingdom is also directly linked to Jesus' role as a healer and exorcist, something that is a particularly prominent characteristic of his portrayal in our sources (and although unusual, not exceptional, in the cultural context of the early empire and first-century Judaism).[137] He is presented, for example, as declaring that his exorcisms are proof of the kingdom's arrival:

> But if it is by the Spirit [finger] of God that I cast out demons, then the kingdom of God has come to you.[138]

The theme of the kingdom is also present in a range of forms of tradition from which our sources about Jesus are composed, including aphorisms, apocalyptic sayings, pronouncement stories, miracle stories, legends and parables.[139] Indeed, parables, "the characteristic form of Jesus' teaching",[140] seem particularly associated with this idea. Not only are we told that the interpretation of the parables requires hearers to know "the secret of the kingdom of God"[141] but a number of parables are introduced with direct reference to the kingdom and most function to explicate some aspect of its character.[142] The Gospel of Thomas, for example, regularly presents the parables it contains as concerned with the nature of the kingdom. In a tradition that does not have a direct parallel with anything in the Synoptic tradition, the reader is told:

> (97) Jesus said: The kingdom of the [Father] is like a woman, carrying a jar full of meal and walking a long way. The handle of the jar broke; the meal poured out behind her on the road. She was unaware, she knew not her loss. When she came into her house, she put down the jar (and) found it empty.

Whilst the introductions to the parables, which tie them so clearly to the theme of the kingdom, might well be redactional and not go back beyond the final composition of the gospels themselves, they are so commonplace that it seems fair to conclude that the parables – or at least most of them – were central to whatever Jesus wished to convey about the kingdom of God.

So we seem on safe grounds in saying that the kingdom or reign of God reflects the main concern of the historical Jesus, as most historical Jesus scholars agree, even if they disagree quite sharply about what exactly this might imply.[143] As Markus Bockmuehl puts it, "The favourite and important subject of Jesus' teaching is clearly the Kingdom of God."[144]

What exactly the historical Jesus may have had in mind when he spoke of the kingdom is notoriously difficult to determine definitively not just because close antecedents to this idea are not easy to identify, even if it clearly draws upon concepts common in the Hebrew Bible and later Jewish literature,[145] but also because the form of teaching used by Jesus to talk about the kingdom of God, the parable,[146] is both terse and figurative – most parables appear to be extended metaphors or similes[147]– and, as a result their meaning is, to an extent, open and polyvalent (though clearly not arbitrary).[148] Their meaning cannot be crudely reduced to a single referent or point;[149] the symbol of the kingdom in the parables of Jesus is allusive, tensive and experiential.[150] But the meaning of the kingdom in the teaching of Jesus has also been hampered by the preoccupations of scholarship. Discussion of the theme of the kingdom in the study of the historical Jesus is often effectively constrained by questions of chronology that are often rather narrowly conceived. Did he believe its arrival was imminent?[151] Or that it was already present?[152] Or both?[153] Or are such temporal judgments predicated on culturally inappropriate assumptions about the nature of time and language?[154] This is not the place to rehearse such debates which have preoccupied scholars of the historical Jesus since the inception of the so-called "Quest",[155] though I would say that both tendencies can be found throughout the data, and so it seems unreasonable to deny that one or other did not go back in some form to the figure of Jesus, as has recently been the fashion.[156] Rather, I am here more interested in the question of the *character* of the reign of God envisioned by Jesus (although I am aware that this is deeply entwined with the question of eschatology).[157] That is, I would like to make some observations about what the historical Jesus is likely to have understood by the rule of God and the nature of human response to it, and in particular, a number of motifs that may legitimately and usefully be described as anarchist – although what follows is not a comprehensive analysis of the possibilities but an indicative treatment of the subject.

a. The kingdom of God is characterized by the active identification and critique of coercive relations of power, and the enactment of new, egalitarian modes of social life.

This is seen, perhaps most acutely, in the recurrent, general motif of reversal which is typical of traditions associated with Jesus. The theme of reversal is more than a rhetorical characteristic of his teaching. As the leading scholar of New Testament ethics, Richard Hays, has noted:

> The theme of *reversal* seems to have been pervasive in his thought [...] This reversal motif is built into the deep structure of Jesus' message, present in all layers of the tradition [...] a foundational element of Jesus' teaching.[158]

The socio-political nature of much of this reversal[159] is obvious to a modern reader without knowledge of the specific political, religious and cultural context of first-century Palestine – though such knowledge is necessary for a fuller exploration of its implications.[160] In Jesus' vision, the kingdom belonged to the poor, not the rich;[161] to the hungry, not those who were full;[162] to the tax-collectors and prostitutes not chief priests and the aristocrats;[163] to children not adults;[164] to sinners and not the righteous.[165] Its values were exemplified by foreigners,[166] beggars,[167] and impoverished widows not the religiously, politically and economically powerful.[168] We find this theme in aphorisms,[169] commandments,[170] and sayings[171] ascribed to the historical Jesus, but, perhaps above all, in the parables. For example, in the Parable of the Wedding Feast,[172] the eventual guests at the banquet are those that one would least expect to be there – in Luke's version it is "the poor, the crippled, the blind and lame."[173] In the Parable of the Rich Man and Lazarus, it is the beggar Lazarus who "longed to satisfy his hunger with what fell from the rich man's table" who goes to be with Abraham and the angels, whilst the rich man who has "dressed in purple and fine linen and who feasted sumptuously every day" is in Hades.[174] In the Parable of the Sheep and the Goats, the manner in which someone has treated the "least" in society, those who are hungry, thirsty, naked, imprisoned, sick, or foreign, provides the criterion by which their life is ultimately judged.[175] In the Parable of the Rich Fool, the selfish accumulation of wealth during his life leaves the rich man impoverished when he dies.[176] But perhaps the most compelling evidence of socio-political reversal in traditions associated with Jesus is the recurrent portrayal of his own praxis, as someone who lived with the outcasts and the socially marginal,[177] and in an almost constant state of conflict with those who were not.[178] The theme of reversal functions not just to expose a number of inequitable relationships, but also to make visible and valorise the powerless within them, and their needs and their desires.

In addition to the theme of reversal we can see a significant cluster of traditions in which exploitation, whether economic,[179] legal,[180] theocratic,[181] military,[182] or medical,[183] is exposed and condemned, and responses advocated or made available that affirm both the agency of the oppressed and their capacity to resist such oppression. An example of this is seen, for example, in the tradition of how one should respond to being pressed into service by the occupying forces in Judea to carry their equipment.[184] The command that the victim carry the equipment further than was demanded, if acted upon, would have resulted in striking and unexpected behaviour that could function not just to restore the power of agency to the victim but also to non-violently undermine the assumption, on the part of the soldier, that he, and the colonial regime which he represented, had ultimate authority – a response that could be seen to enact the command to love enemies,[185] an idea particularly associated with Jesus in our sources.[186] The concern to restore agency to those deprived of it can also be seen, though in a rather different way, in the stories in which individuals gain healing from Jesus by actively demanding it from him or even seizing it for themselves – tactics which he seems to not just to have tolerated but to have encouraged.[187]

New models of social relationship are enacted that present alternative, largely egalitarian ways of living. For example, there are a number of traditions associated with historical Jesus that contain sharp criticisms of familial relationships and obligations,[188] and whilst it would be wrong to see these as part of a programmatic attack on patriarchy (significant numbers of women were drawn to the movement but there is no evidence of a "critical feminist impulse" in traditions about Jesus),[189] the traditional form of the family is eclipsed and a much more inclusive, fictive, family, where membership is not conditional on ties of marriage and blood, but on shared purpose, is advocated and comes into being amongst Jesus' followers.[190] Social relations and obligations are no longer structured according to reciprocity, whether symmetrical or asymmetrical, which requires someone to have the means to "repay"[191] but instead an ethos of generosity is expected, where debts are forgiven and those with resources are told to be free with them and not to keep account.[192]

Traditions of Jesus' teaching and praxis also regularly involve a distinctive approach to dining, something that was central to the literal and symbolic maintenance of inequitable relationships of power in antiquity, and also, in the case of first-century Palestine, created significant, inequitable divisions.[193] He advocated and demonstrated what Crossan calls "open commensality",[194] that is "eating together without using table as a miniature map of society's vertical discriminations and lateral separations."[195] This was a significant motif in Jesus' practice,[196] so much so that he was mocked as "a glutton and a drunkard"[197] and someone who ate with "tax collectors and sinners",[198] but it is also present in the teaching traditions ascribed to Jesus,[199] particularly the parable traditions,[200] as well as miracle traditions,[201] and is even in an apocalyptic vision of the future kingdom: "I tell you, many will come from east and west and will eat with Abraham and Isaac and Jacob in the kingdom of heaven"[202] – something that indicates that the aspirations and concerns of the kingdom envisaged by the historical Jesus were ultimately universal[203] and could even be said to come close to a form of cosmopolitanism,[204] a concept central to anarchism.[205]

The historical Jesus also appears to have modelled a form of social interaction that ignored expectations of deference,[206] probably rooted in the expectation that the behaviour of those in the kingdom should reflect the character of God, and God was for Jesus, and other Jews of the time, "no respecter of persons".[207] This was something both egalitarian in itself but also revealed and challenged the structures and presumptions of power symbolised by such deference; to those who were beneficiaries of stratification and hierarchy, it presented a disruptive rhetoric of impoliteness.[208]

However, whilst there are sufficient clusters of data to make it plausible to see the historical Jesus as a figure known for confronting coercive and hierarchical relationships, and advocating alternative models of social life, there are aspects of the teaching and actions of Jesus that do not easily fit with this picture, are equally prominent in our sources, and need to be addressed.

First, it is quite clear that although the figure of Jesus is characteristically associated with the powerless, he enjoyed the support of those who facilitated and benefited from political and economic exploitation, supported by the largess of the rich and socializing with the agents of imperial rule, such as tax-collectors and the military – something sufficiently prominent in our sources that it cannot be dismissed as redactional, an invention of Christians who were comfortable within the empire and wished to legitimate their experience.[209] Such a picture is difficult to reconcile with a figure engaged in a thoroughgoing and confrontational response to non-egalitarian forms of social life. Was he, perhaps, so inclusive that this somehow transcended, or less positively, undermined the political vision we have observed? This seems unlikely. As Bockmuehl quite rightly notes, Jesus was *not* an inclusive figure. "Jesus of Nazareth includes a remarkably wide diversity of the marginalized, yet he also marginalizes an uncomfortably diverse range of the religiously or socio economically included."[210] It is probably best to explain this apparent tension by reference to the theme of repentance, something regularly associated with the notion of the kingdom of God. Repentance was not concerned with contrition but rather the idea that individuals should return to God[211] and do what God expects of those who wish to be righteous.[212] In our sources those responding to the call of Jesus, whoever they are, are expected to imitate Jesus' praxis, including such things as open commensality, and there is also evidence, from the story of Zaccheus, the tax collector but also in the story of the rich ruler, that the rich were also expected to make restitution and return what they had extracted by exploitation.[213]

Secondly, it should be noted that the historical Jesus does not appear straightforwardly or consistently anti-authoritarian or anti-hierarchical. It would be unfair to ignore the considerable range of data where Jesus is presented as either claiming an authoritative or pivotal role,[214] or where it is implied,[215] and this observation stands regardless of other questions about Jesus self-estimation and "Christology" which have attracted so much attention because of their obvious theological consequences.[216] Of

course, anarchists have not been averse to leaders, albeit often for
tactical reasons, one thinks of the prominence of Nestor Makhno,
Errico Malatesta, or Emma Goldman, but this claim appears to
be of a rather different kind. The historical Jesus initiated a hierarchical organisation through the appointment of twelve disciples, something which he did not envisage as temporary[217] and
his own authority was predicated upon coercion through the pronouncement of future judgement upon those who rejected it.[218] It
is usually assumed that where leadership exists within anarchism
it is "a continual exchange of mutual, temporary, and, above all,
voluntary authority and subordination"[219] but evidently the type
of leadership modelled and advocated by the historical Jesus was
somewhat different.

In response to this it could be said that the nature of the leadership shown by Jesus and expected of the Twelve was, somewhat
paradoxically, an inversion of hierarchical expectations, epitomized in the repeated motif that leaders must be servants and the
deliberate contrast of the model of power within the community with that which was characteristic of the empire, indeed, on
which the empire was built and sustained, to the detriment of the
latter.[220] And so, in Mark, chapter ten, we read:

> 42 So Jesus called them and said to them, 'You know that among
> the Gentiles those whom they recognize as their rulers lord it over
> them, and their great ones are tyrants over them. 43 But it is not
> so among you; but whoever wishes to become great among you
> must be your servant, 44 and whoever wishes to be first among
> you must be slave of all.[221]

It could also be said – though this is perhaps a little less evident –
that in choosing twelve disciples the historical Jesus was using a
symbol of a pre-monarchical Israel, when it existed as a confed-
eration of tribes, to represent his vision of the kingdom, something that Ched Myers has said "bears some resemblance to
'anarcho-syndicalist' vision in modernity";[222] recalling a time before the people of Israel decided to be like other nations and have
a king, rejecting God's direct rule.[223]

The activities of healing and teaching that are so characteristic
of the representation of Jesus in our sources also have little to do

with authoritarian forms of kingly, messianic leadership that were dominant at the time.[224] Indeed, given that the historical Jesus seems to have expected those around him to be empowered to carry out similar actions,[225] it might not be too fanciful to agree with Gerd Theissen that the historical Jesus may well have envisaged his followers collectively taking on messianic tasks, enacting a kind of group messiahship. If this is the case, it would have meant that the historical Jesus effectively played down his own significance and so could be seen as advocating a kind of distributed, non-authoritarian form of leadership.[226]

Similarly, the traditions about his death are uniform in presenting a figure who remained consistent in not using or endorsing violence against enemies and for whom physical violence by humans against humans was anathema.[227] It was not a form of leadership in which authority was equated with a superior sense of personal value. Indeed, it appears to have been the opposite.

b. The kingdom of God is prefigurative.

As we have noted, the kingdom motif is not just associated with judgement but also with new forms of social life, and these are not just advocated but practiced. It can therefore be usefully understood as prefigurative and, more specifically, prefigurative in a way that resembles anarchist ethics. In most forms of anarchist ethics, the means are consistent with the desired ends, that is "the outcomes are *prefigured* by the methods".[228] The practice of anarchists is assumed to have immediate consequences and to resemble the outcome that is desired. As James Guillaume, a colleague of Bakunin, said, in his famous critique of statist socialists, "How could one want an egalitarian and free society to issue from authoritarian organisation? It is impossible."[229]

The ethics of Jesus could be seen as analogous to this and in many ways this helps makes sense of the notion that the kingdom is already present, and being enacted, even if in an initially insignificant way, in a manner that resembles and is related to its final form. One thinks, of example, of the Parable of the Mustard Seed[230] or the practice of open commensality we have touched upon.

Indeed, I do not think it is pushing things too far to speak of the prefigurative ethics of the kingdom as necessitating a form of direct action, something characteristic of anarchism and something that involves "acting as if the state's representatives have no more rights to impose their views of the rights or the wrongs of the situation than anybody else."[231] A number of the activities of Jesus seem to have this characteristic, whether it is the tradition of his action in the Temple,[232] or his response to the question about the payment of taxes to Caesar,[233] or his behaviour at his trial,[234] in all of which he appears to show no concern for the consequences of his actions. Indeed, just as direct action is sometimes "playful and the carnivalesque",[235] so, often, are the forms of behaviour ascribed to Jesus or advocated by him.[236] As Peter Marshall rightly observes, Jesus consistently "held political authority up to derision",[237] demystifying and mocking the power it claimed.

c) The vision of the kingdom is not utopian but reflexive, undetermined, and self-creative

It is surprisingly difficult to describe, with any detail, the forms of social life expected within the new reality enacted and proposed by the historical Jesus. Although, as we have noted, it can be characterised by certain practices, such as open commensality, there is much that is not spelled out. There certainly is no obvious utopian blueprint, and despite the arguments of Mary Ann Beavis, it is not useful to characterise the vision of the kingdom held by the historical Jesus as utopian.[238] As we have noted, the main mode of teaching employed by Jesus, the parable, is figurative and by its nature allusive, resisting simple explanation and allowing a range of indeterminate, experiential responses. Parables do not communicate a specific plan. Indeed, it seems more helpful to think of Jesus as anti-utopian, a quality that resonates with anarchist thinking even if anarchists are popularly assumed to be driven by utopian visions. Although utopias can have their uses – they can inspire, encourage, provide a pleasurable escape[239] – they can also be coercive and that is why, on the whole, they have been resisted by anarchists; utopianism enforces others to live in a certain way, and a utopia envisaged as a single, totalising endpoint will necessitate manipulation to fit a predetermined plan. As Marie Louise Berneri demonstrated in her analysis of utopian thought from Plato to Huxley, they are inherently authoritarian.[240] For anarchists, the details of such social order need to be determined by those that that are dominated. Their ethics are:

> Reflexive and self-creative, as they do not assess practices against a universally prescribed end-point, as some utopian theorists have done, but through a process of immanent critique.[241]

Some might feel uneasy about this alleged similarity between the historical Jesus and anarchism because it is often assumed that the historical Jesus had a clear idea of his intentions and understanding of the implications of the kingdom of God from the outset. However, such thinking is an imposition upon the records of subsequent doctrinal assumptions. Our sources indicate a figure open to reflection and revision in the light of events and encounter with others. An example of this is the story of the Syrophoenian woman in which a gentile argues a reluctant Jesus into healing her daughter,[242] and the incidents at Nazareth[243] and Caesarea Philippi[244] which likewise seem to indicate moments which were critical in his self-understanding.[245] The possibility that the historical Jesus' own life was one characterised by reflexivity and a mutable understanding of his mission, should not come as a surprise even if it may be surprising to some. As Henry Cadbury observed many decades ago:

> Probably much that is commonly said about the general purpose of Jesus' life and the specific place in that purpose of detailed incidents is modern superimposition upon a nearly patternless life and upon nearly patternless records of it.[246]

d. The pedagogy of the kingdom is prefigurative and non-coercive.

There are also significant parallels between the distinctive pedagogy associated with the kingdom and the non-coercive, prefigurative pedagogy of anarchism. Although the latter is, as Judith Suissa has argued, surprisingly under theorised,[247] pedagogy has been something of considerable significance in anarchism. This is largely, as Justin Mueller has suggested, because unlike other political philosophies

aimed at social transformation, "education has never been simply
the means to achieve a new social order"[248] but rather part of the
prefigurative practice that is central to all forms of anarchism,
a prefigurative practice characterised by non-coercion, and the
inculcation of solidarity and fellow-feeling, rather than competition and domination, the encouragement of active empathy and
identification with others.[249] Some of Jesus' teaching does seem to
have taken the form of commands, such as the command to love
enemies[250] or the prohibition on divorce,[251] but by far the largest
quantity of his teaching comes in the form of parables, which are
figurative and affective, a form that does not compel the hearer
to arrive at a narrowly predetermined understanding of what is
being conveyed. Many parables could also be said to function in
some way to directly encourage empathy and identification with
others,[252] and most could be said to contribute to this indirectly
by, amongst other things, intensifying the significance placed upon
the praxis of the kingdom.

However, before we conclude our discussion it is important to
note that some grounds on which Jesus is often considered an anarchist should not be part of any attempt to answer the question,
despite their popularity. For example, some might be surprised
that there has been no mention of Jesus' death in the preceding
analysis. As Christoyannopoulos has noted, this is often seen as
the climax of Jesus' ministry, as confirmation of the character of
his mission:

> For most Christian Anarchists, Jesus is the saviour precisely be-
> cause he accepted the cross – *that* is the revolution. He is the mes-
> siah because he consistently responds to injustice with unwavering
> love, forgiveness and non-resistance. He does not seek to lead yet
> another revolutionary government, but instead points to the true
> kingdom beyond the state. Therefore the crucifixion is indeed the
> glorious climax of Jesus' messianic ministry.[253]

For many, there is something "inevitable" about this conclusion
to the life of Jesus, it is "the concrete consequence" of his teaching
and practice.[254] Christian anarchists and others who believe that
Jesus deserves the label of anarchist, are not so unusual in seeing
Jesus' death as a necessary consequence of his teaching. In modern

historical-Jesus scholarship, as we have mentioned, one of the criteria used to determine which traditions are likely to go back to the historical Jesus is the criterion of 'crucifiability'[255] – that is, if a tradition can explain Jesus' execution then it is judged likely to be "authentic". However, given the ubiquity of crucifixion in the empire, and the casual manner in which it could be imposed on the poor and inconsequential, it is likely that the Roman authorities did not give the killing of Jesus much thought and he need not have done anything much, in their eyes, for them to put him to death. For example, as A. E. Harvey plausibly suggested:

> Jesus could have been one of those innocent victims who are picked up by police action at a time when peace-keeping has become difficult and the forces of law and order are over-stretched, and then arbitrarily put to death.[256]

The *titulus*,[257] placed on the cross by the Romans, which seems to indicate that Jesus was killed because of a kingly claim of some kind, might well be no more than evidence that, from the perspective of the Romans, they were executing a deluded madman who talked of invisible kingdoms – something that would be in keeping of what we know about their treatment of others they believed to fall into this category.[258]

5. Conclusion

To return to our question: was the historical Jesus an anarchist? Any answer depends upon the definition of "anarchist" used and how much room such a definition has for anarchism to be judged to exist outside of a formal political movement composed of self-declared anarchists. It would, however, be an inadequate definition that limited itself solely to the likes of Proudhon – and one that would not be true to their own understanding of the perennial nature of the doctrine they espoused. Instead, the suggestion of Graeber, that definitions of anarchism should also be inclusive of those who display anarchist attitudes and practices, as well as those who endorse a specific ideological position, has far more merit.

However, if we decide that Jesus might well meet the rather broader definition of "anarchist" of the kind offered by Graeber, we will need to accept some things that, at least to many contemporary anarchists, appear incompatible with anarchism. For example, as Kathleen Corley has noted, Jesus does not appear to have criticised patriarchy,[259] and our sources are silent about his thoughts on slavery, something ubiquitous in the empire. Even his proclamation of the kingdom of God could be seen to replicate elements of the imperialism that appears anathema to it.[260] But such problems should not preclude us using the label "anarchist" for Jesus. As Harold Barclay has observed in his study of ethnographic accounts of stateless and governmentless societies, we cannot expect contemporary anarchists to necessarily approve of such societies, which though highly decentralised, can, for example, be highly conformist, patriarchal, gerontocracies,[261] yet the use of the term anarchist is clearly legitimate for them. So, our use of the term "anarchist" outside of the modern context, where individuals and movements may display characteristics that are similarly unappealing to contemporary anarchists, has to be generous.

There is enough in what we can know about the historical Jesus, of the impressions of the man and his vision that have left their mark on our sources, to reveal someone not just intensely anti-authoritarian but also concerned with a prefigurative, non-coercive reality which would both confront existing inequity and be transformative of the lives of those oppressed by it. It may be pushing the evidence too far to say that Jesus of Nazareth was "a major political thinker",[262] but it is no surprise, to return to the quote with which we began, that Alexander Berkman believed Jesus to be an anarchist. He was right.[263]

Notes

1. Alexander Berkman, *Now and After: The ABC of Communist Anarchism* (New York: Vanguard Press, 1929), p. 61.

2. The term "anarchist" had been used before this date but was employed solely to refer to someone who sought to create disorder rather than an advocate of a political ideology. It acquired the additional meaning following the publication of Pierre-Joseph Proudhon, *Qu'est-ce que la propriété? Ou recherches sur le principe du droit et du gouvernment* (Paris: Librairie de Prévot, 1840).

3. Friedrich Wilhelm Nietzsche, 'Der Antichrist', in *Nietzsches Werke: Der Fall Wagner; Götzen-Dämmerung; Nietzsche contra Wagner; Der Antichrist; Gedichte* (Leipzig: C. G. Naumann, 1895), VIII, 211–313.

4. See, for example, Nicolai Berdyaev, *Slavery and Freedom* (New York: Charles Scribner's Sons, 1944), pp. 140–148.

5. See, for example, Leo Tolstoy, '*The Kingdom of God Is within You*': *Christianity Not as a Mystic Religion but as a New Theory of Life*, trans. by Constance Garnett, 2 vols. (London: William Heinemann, 1894). However, it is important to note that Tolstoy did not explicitly call Jesus an "anarchist". This is probably explained by the close association between anarchism and violence in Tolstoy's mind, something that almost certainly accounts for his reticence in using the label for himself too. See Brian Morris, *Ecology and Anarchism: Essays and Reviews on Contemporary Thought* (Malvern: Images Publishing, 1996), p. 159.

6. Likewise, Wilde did not use the term "anarchist" for Jesus but that he believed him to be such is a reasonable inference from such works as *The Soul of Man Under Socialism* (London: Privately Printed, 1891), in which Jesus is presented as the model of socialist individualism. See Kristian Williams, 'The Soul of Man Under . . .Anarchism?', *New Politics*, 8 (2011) <http://newpol.org/content/soul-man-under-anarchism> [accessed 31 July 2015]. For the anarchism of Wilde see David Goodway, *Anarchist Seeds Beneath the Snow: Left-libertarian Thought and British Writers from William Morris to Colin Ward*, 2nd edn (Oakland: PM Press, 2011), pp. 62–92.

7. Mary C. Segers, 'Equality and Christian Anarchism: The Political and Social Ideas of the Catholic Worker Movement', *The Review of Politics*, 40 (1978), 196–230 and Frederick Boehrer, 'Christian Anarchism and the Catholic Worker Movement: Roman Catholic Authority and Identity in the United States' (unpublished PhD, New York: Syracuse University, 2001).

8. See www.jesusradicals.com (accessed 31 July 2015).

9. Charlotte Alston, *Tolstoy and His Disciples: The History of a Radical International Movement* (London: I.B. Tauris, 2014).

10. See, for example, the official website of the Union of the Spiritual Communities of Christ, the main body of Doukhobors today (http://www.usccdoukhobors.org/faq.htm#faq2. Accessed 31 July 2015).

11. Linda H. Damico, *The Anarchist Dimension of Liberation Theology* (Pieterlen: Peter Lang, 1987).

12. See, for example, Keith Hebden, *Dalit Theology and Christian Anarchism* (London: Ashgate, 2011).

13. Proudhon's most substantial work on the subject was *Jésus et les origines du christianisme* (Paris: G. Havard fils, 1896), though see also *Ecrits sur la religion*, ed. by M. Ruyssen (Paris: M. Rivière, 1959). For a comprehensive treatment of Proudhon's views on Jesus see Georges Bessière, *Jésus selon Proudhon: la « messianose » et la naissance du christianisme* (Paris: Cerf, 2007) and Henri de Lubac, *Proudhon et le christianisme* (Paris: Editions du Seuil, 1945).

14. Mikhail Bakunin, *God and the State* (London: Freedom Press, 1910 [1882]), p. 54.

15. Peter Kropotkin, *Ethics: Origin and Development* (Bristol: Thoemmes Press, 1993 [1924]), pp. 118–119.

16. Max Stirner, *The Ego and His Own* (New York: Benj. R. Tucker, 1907), pp. 178–179,

17. This distinction is usually attributed to Martin Kähler, and became common following the publication of his *Der sogenannte historische Jesus und der geschichtliche, biblische Christus* (Leipzig: A. Deichert, 1892), although it was employed to describe something that most scholars of the historical Jesus would argue was common from the work of Herman Reimarus and the posthumous publication of his *Fragmente eines Ungenannten* beginning in 1774.

18. See, for example, S. G. F. Brandon, *Jesus and the Zealots: a Study of the Political Factor in Primitive Christianity* (Manchester: Manchester University Press, 1967) and the comprehensive response edited by Ernst Bammel and C. F. D. Moule, *Jesus and the Politics of His Day* (Cambridge: Cambridge University Press, 1984). Amongst recent contributions those of Fernando Bermejo-Rubio are of greatest consequence; see, for example, 'Jesus and the Anti-Roman Resistance', *Journal for the Study of the Historical Jesus*, 12 (2014), 1–105 and 'Jesus as a Seditionist: The Intertwining of Politics and Religion in his Teaching and Deeds', in *Teaching the Historical Jesus: Issues and Exegesis*, ed. by Zev Garber (London: Routledge, 2015), pp. 232–243.

19. See, for example, John Dominic Crossan, *The Historical Jesus: The Life of a Mediterranean Jewish Peasant* (San Francisco: HarperSanFrancisco, 1991), and *Jesus: A Revolutionary Biography* (San Francisco: HarperSanFrancisco, 1994), Richard A. Burridge, *Imitating Jesus: An Inclusive Approach to New Testament Ethics* (Grand Rapids: Eerdmans, 2007) and Marcus Borg, *Jesus in Contemporary Scholarship* (London: Continuum, 1994), pp. 97–126. For a trenchant critique of attempts to present the historical Jesus as "inclusive" see Markus Bockmuehl, 'The Trouble with the Inclusive Jesus', *Horizons in Biblical Theology*, 33 (2011), 9–23.

20. See, for indicative examples, Colleen M. Conway, *Behold the Man: Jesus and Greco-Roman Masculinity* (New York: Oxford University Press, 2008); Anna Runesson, *Exegesis in the Making: Postcolonialism and New Testament Studies* (Leiden: Brill, 2010) and Michael J. Sandford, *Poverty, Wealth, and Empire: Jesus and Postcolonial Criticism* (Sheffield: Sheffield Phoenix Press, 2014).

21. For significant contributions in this area see *Jesus Beyond Nationalism: Constructing the Historical Jesus in a Period of Cultural Complexity*, ed. by Ward Blanton, James G. Crossley and Halvor Moxnes (London: Equinox, 2010), James G. Crossley, *Jesus in an Age of Terror: Scholarly Projects for a New American Century* (London: Equinox, 2008) and *Jesus in an Age of Neoliberalism: Quests, Scholarship and Ideology* (London: Equinox, 2012).

22. For the most recent, comprehensive statement of this position see Richard Carrier, *On the Historicity of Jesus: Why We Might Have Reason for Doubt* (Sheffield: Sheffield Phoenix Press, 2014). See also *Is This Not the Carpenter?: The Question of the Historicity of the Figure of Jesus*, ed. by Thomas L. Thompson and Thomas S. Verenna (Sheffield: Equinox, 2012).

23. See, for example, Maurice Casey, *Jesus: Evidence and Argument or Mythicist Myths?* (Bloomsbury T&T Clark, 2014) and Bart D. Ehrman, *Did Jesus Exist?: The Historical Argument for Jesus of Nazareth* (San Francisco: HarperOne, 2012).

24. See, for example, Craig A. Evans, 'Jesus in Non-Christian Sources', in *Studying the Historical Jesus: Evaluations of the State of Current Research*, ed. by Bruce Chilton and Craig A. Evans (Leiden: Brill, 1998), pp. 443–478. See also John Granger Cook, *The Interpretation*

of the New Testament in Greco-Roman Paganism (Peabody: Hendrickson Publishers, 2002).

25. For a useful survey of non-canonical sources of various kinds see James H. Charlesworth and Craig A Evans, 'Jesus in the Agrapha and Apocryphal Gospels', in *Studying the Historical Jesus: Evaluations of the State of Current Research*, ed. by Bruce Chilton and Craig A. Evans (Leiden: Brill, 1994), pp. 479–534.

26. See, for example, the pagan critic Celsus in Origen, *Contra Celsum* 1.28.

27. E. P. Thompson, *The Making of the English Working Class* (London: Victor Gallancz, 1963), p. 12.

28. For the inconsequential nature of Jesus' life from the perspective of the Romans see Justin J. Meggitt, 'The Madness of King Jesus', *Journal for the Study of the New Testament*, 29 (2007), 379–413.

29. George Woodcock, *Anarchism*, 2nd edn (Harmondsworth: Penguin, 1986), p. 36.

30. Alexandre Christoyannopoulos, *Christian Anarchism: A Political Commentary on the Gospel* (Exeter: Imprint Academic, 2010), p. 19.

31. Few, if any, have paid attention to non-canonical sources despite their significance in contemporary scholarship concerned with the figure of the historical Jesus. For example, as Patterson rightly notes, "anyone who writes today on the historical question of what Jesus said or did must deal with the issue of the Gospel of Thomas" (Stephen J. Patterson, 'The Gospel of Thomas and Historical Jesus Research', in *Coptica – Gnostica – Manichaica*, ed. by Louis Painchaud and Paul-Hubert Poirier [Quebec: Les Presses de l'Université Laval, 2006], p. 663).

32. Christoyannopoulos, *Christian Anarchism*, pp. 15, 295.

33. Tolstoy, for example, called him "the lover of authoritarian teaching" and held him chiefly responsible for Christianity's departure from Jesus' vision. See Leo Tolstoy, *Church and State and Other Essays: Including Money; Man and Woman: Their Respective Functions; The Mother; A Second Supplement to the Kreutzer Sonata* (Boston: B. R. Tucker, 1891), p. 17.

34. James D G. Dunn, 'Jesus Tradition in Paul', in *Studying the Historical Jesus: Evaluations of the State of Current Research*, ed. by Bruce Chilton and Craig A Evans (Leiden: Brill, 1994), pp. 155–178.

35. Christoyannopoulos, *Christian Anarchism*, pp. 43–81.

36. See, for example, Hans Dieter Betz and Adela Yarbro Collins, *The Sermon on the Mount: A Commentary on the Sermon on the Mount, Including the Sermon on the Plain (Matthew: 5:3–7:27 and Luke 6:20–49)* (Minneapolis: Augsburg Fortress, 1995); W. D. Davies and D. C. Allison, *A Critical and Exegetical Commentary on the Gospel According to Saint Matthew. Volume I. Introduction and Commentary on Matthew I-VII* (Edinburgh: T. & T. Clark, 1988), pp. 429–731; Ulrich Luz, *Matthew 1–7: a Commentary*, 2nd edn (Minneapolis: Fortress Press, 2007).

37. Huub van de Sandt and Jürgen K. Zangenberg, *Matthew, James, and Didache: Three Related Documents in Their Jewish and Christian Settings* (Atlanta: Society of Biblical Literature, 2008); *Matthew and his Christian Contemporaries*, ed. by David C. Sim and Boris Repschinski (Edinburgh: T&T Clark, 2008). It is no surprise that Tolstoy was keen on the Didache which was only rediscovered in his lifetime. See E. B. Greenwood, 'Tolstoy and Religion', in *New Essays on Tolstoy*, ed. Malcolm Jones (Cambridge: Cambridge University Press, 1978), pp. 149–74 (p. 166).

38. See, for example, Leif E. Vaage, 'Beyond Nationalism: Jesus the "Holy Anarchist"? : the Cynic Jesus as Eternal Recurrence of the Repressed', in *Jesus Beyond Nationalism: Constructing the Historical Jesus in a Period of Cultural Complexity*, ed. by Halvor Moxnes, Ward Blanton and James G. Crossley (London: Equinox, 2009), pp. 79–95.

39. Although I am not aware of Ched Myers identifying himself as a Christian anarchist, his commentary on Mark's gospel, *Binding the Strong Man: A Political Reading of Mark's Story of Jesus* (Maryknoll: Orbis Books, 1988), has been extremely influential on a number of contemporary Christian anarchists (Christoyannopoulos, *Christian Anarchism*, pp. 39–40), and in the supportive preface that he recently wrote to Van Steenwyk's primer on Christian anarchism he endorses the notion that the Bible contains "anarchist tendencies" (*That Holy Anarchist: Reflections on Christianity & Anarchism* [Minneapolis:

Missio Dei, 2012], p. 9) and suggests that "the anarchist vision may yet be a key to the renewal of church and society" (*Holy Anarchist*, p. 11).

40. It has become customary to refer to the study of the historical Jesus as the "Quest" for the historical Jesus, following the publication of the English translation in 1910 of Albert Schweitzer's influential *Von Reimarus zu Wrede: eine Geschichte der Leben-Jesu-Forschung* (Tübingen: Mohr ,1906) which was entitled *The Quest of the Historical Jesus: a Critical Study of Its Progress from Reimarus to Wrede* (London: A. and C. Black, 1910).

41. See, for example, the criticisms of Bernard C. Lategan, 'Questing or Sense-Making? Some Thoughts on the Nature of Historiography', *Biblical Interpretation: A Journal of Contemporary Approaches*, 11 (2003), 588–601.

42. For a still useful, albeit confessional, critique of such undertakings see Luke Timothy Johnson, *The Real Jesus: The Misguided Quest for the Historical Jesus and the Truth of the Traditional Gospels* (San Francisco: HarperSanFrancisco, 1996).

43. See, for example, N. T. Wright, *Jesus and the Victory of God* (London: SPCK, 1996), p. xv.

44. Although characterizing the historical Jesus' understanding of God as a matter of "belief" is, perhaps, unhelpful. "Belief" has a distinctive and specific place in some forms Christianity but cannot be said to be a significant organizing or nodal concept within the religious life of most humans, ancient or modern. See, for example, Malcolm Ruel, *Belief, Ritual and the Securing of Life: Reflective Essays on a Bantu Religion* (Leiden: Brill, 1997), pp. 36–59.

45. For example, Mark 1.15 and Matthew 4.17 (see also Luke 4.43); Luke 17.20–21, Thomas 3, 113; Matthew 11.11–12, Luke 5.28, 16.16, Thomas 46; Mark 10.15, Matthew 18.3, Luke 18.17; Mark 10.23–25, Matthew 19.23–24, Luke 18.24–25; Luke 11.20, Matthew 12.28; Matthew 13.44; Thomas 109; Matthew 13.45–46, Thomas 76; Mark 3.22–27, Matthew 12.29–30, Luke 11.21–23; Mark 9:1 (see also Matthew 16.28, Luke 9.27); Mark 14.25, Matthew 26.29 (cf. Luke 22.18); Matthew 8.11, Luke 13.28–30; Matthew 6.10, Luke 11.2 and Didache 8.2.

46. Sébastien Faure, *Les douze preuves de l'inexistence de Dieu,* (Paris: Librairie sociale, 1908).

47. See, for example, Paul Preston, *The Spanish Holocaust: Inquisition and Extermination in Twentieth-century Spain* (London: HarperPress, 2012), pp. 221–258

48. Bakunin, *God and the State,* p. 28. For similar sentiments see Emma Goldman, *Anarchism and Other Essays* (New York: Mother Earth Publishing Association, 1911), p. 22.

49. Saul Newman, *From Bakunin to Lacan: Anti-Authoritarianism and the Dislocation of Power* (Lanham: Lexington Books, 2001), p. 26.

50. Nicholas Walter, *About Anarchism*, 2nd edn (London: Freedom Press, 2002), p. 43.

51. Bernard Schweizer, *Hating God: The Untold Story of Misotheism* (Oxford: Oxford University Press, 2010), p. 34.

52. Peter Marshall, *Demanding the Impossible: A History of Anarchism* (Oakland: PM Press, 2010), p. 75.

53. For examples see *Religious Anarchism: New Perspectives*, ed. by Alexandre Christoyannopoulos (Newcastle: Cambridge Scholars, 2009) and Christoyannopoulos, *Christian Anarchism.*

54. Such ideas "are described as anarchist only on the basis of a misunderstanding of what anarchism is" (Jeremy Jennings, 'Anarchism', in *Contemporary Political Ideologies*, ed. by Roger Eatwell and Anthony Wright, 2nd edn [London: Continuum International Publishing Group, 1999], p. 142).

55. Graham D. Macklin, 'Co-opting the Counter Culture: Troy Southgate and the National Revolutionary Faction', *Patterns of Prejudice*, 39 (2005), 301–326.

56. Both are mentioned a number of times in such standard histories as Marshall, *Demanding;* Robert Graham, *Anarchism: From Anarchy to Anarchism (300CE to 1939). Volume 1: A Documentary History of Libertarian Ideas* (Montreal: Black Rose Books, 2005); and Woodcock, *Anarchism.* However, some surveys do pass over Christian anarchism. It is absent from, for example, Michael Schmidt's *Cartography of Revolutionary Anarchism* (Oakland: AK Press, 2013).

57. There are, of course, notable exceptions. See, for example, David Flusser and R. Steven Notley, *The Sage from Galilee: Rediscovering Jesus' Genius*, 4th edn (Grand Rapids: Eerdmans, 2007 [1968]).

58. See the survey of the so-called "Third Quest" in John P. Meier, 'The Present State of the "Third Quest" for the Historical Jesus: Loss and Gain', *Biblica*, 80 (1999), 459–487. There have been significant differences of opinion on the relative weight that should be placed upon non-canonical sources in reconstructions. Contrast, for example, the use of non-canonical texts in Crossan, *The Historical Jesus*, with that in John P. Meier, *A Marginal Jew: Rethinking the Historical Jesus* (New York: Doubleday, 1991).

59. For a useful introduction to these see Meier, *A Marginal Jew* and *Handbook for the Study of the Historical Jesus. Volume 1: How to Study the Historical Jesus*, ed. by Tom Holmén and Stanley E. Porter, 4 vols. (Leiden: Brill, 2010).

60. These criteria are not new but have been used, in various forms, since the 1920s. See Stanley E. Porter, *The Criteria for Authenticity in Historical-Jesus Research: Previous Discussion and New Proposals* (Sheffield: Sheffield Academic Press, 2000), pp. 63–102.

61. Joel Willitts, 'Presuppositions and Procedures in the Study of the Historical Jesus: Or, Why I Decided Not to Be a Historical Jesus Scholar', *Journal for the Study of the Historical Jesus*, 3 (2005), 61–108.

62. For a helpful survey of these see Helen K. Bond, *The Historical Jesus: A Guide for the Perplexed* (London: T&T Clark, 2012), pp. 19–36; David B. Gowler, *What Are They Saying About the Historical Jesus?* (New York: Paulist Press, 2007).

63. Porter, *Criteria*, and Gerd Theissen and Dagmar Winter, *The Quest for the Plausible Jesus: the Question of Criteria* (Louisville: Westminster John Knox Press, 2002).

64. M. D. Hooker, 'Christology and Methodology', *New Testament Studies*, 17 (1971), 480–487.

65. Dale C. Allison, *Constructing Jesus: Memory, Imagination, and History* (Grand Rapids: Baker Academic, 2010); Anthony Le Donne, *The Historiographical Jesus: Memory, Typology, and the Son of David* (Waco: Baylor University Press, 2009) and *Historical Jesus: What Can We Know and How Can We Know It?* (Grand Rapids:

Eerdmans, 2011); Alexander J. M. Wedderburn, *Jesus and the Historians* (Tübingen: Mohr Siebeck, 2010), pp. 189–224.

66. Dale C. Allison, 'It Don't Come Easy: a History of Disillusionment', in *Jesus, Criteria, and the Demise of Authenticity*, ed. by Chris Keith and Anthony Le Donne (London: T&T Clark, 2012), pp. 186–199.

67. Although I place greater weight on the role of invention within the tradition associated with Jesus. See Justin J. Meggitt, 'Popular Mythology in the Early Empire and the Multiplicity of Jesus Traditions', in *Sources of the Jesus Tradition: Separating History from Myth*, ed. by R. Joseph Hoffmann (Amherst: Prometheus, 2010), pp. 53–80.

68. See, for example, Louis-André Dorion, 'The Rise and Fall of the Socratic Problem', in *The Cambridge Companion to Socrates*, ed. by Donald R. Morrison (Cambridge: Cambridge University Press, 2011), pp. 1–23.

69. See, for example, Maria Dzielska, *Apollonius of Tyana in Legend and History* (Rome: L'Erma di Bretschneider, 1986).

70. As Fonrobert and Jaffee note about Rabbi Akiva, one of the key founders of Rabbinic Judaism, the nature of the sources make it impossible to know, "with any degree of historical certainty", whether he really said what is attributed to him (Charlotte Fonrobert and Martin S. Jaffee, 'Introduction: The Talmud, Rabbinic Literature, and Jewish Culture', in *The Cambridge Companion to the Talmud and Rabbinic Literature* [Cambridge: Cambridge University Press, 2007], pp. 1–14 [p. 2]).

71. Meggitt, 'Popular Mythology'.

72. A similar idea can be found in C. H. Dodd, *History and the Gospel* (London: Nisbet, 1938) although it was passed over by subsequent work in the field.

73. Justin J. Meggitt, 'Psychology and the Historical Jesus', in *Jesus and Psychology*, ed. by Fraser Watts (London: Darton,Longman & Todd, 2007), pp. 16–26 (p. 24). Also quoted in Allison, *Constructing Jesus*, p. 433.

74. Dale C. Allison, 'Behind the Temptations of Jesus : Q 4:1–13 and Mark 1:12–13', in *Authenticating the Activities of Jesus*, ed. by Bruce Chilton and Craig A. Evans (Leiden: Brill, 1999), pp. 195–213.

75. Matthew 4.8–10; Luke 4.5–8 (Mark 1.12–13). See Matthew 20.26–27, 23.11–12, Mark 9.35, 10.43–44, Luke 14.11, 18.14b, 22.26; Matthew 6.29, Luke 12.27; Luke 13.32; Matthew 27.11, Mark 15.2, Luke 23.3; Luke 22.25; Luke 23.9; John 18.33–38; John 6.15.

76. Allison, 'It Don't Come Easy', p. 198. Although it could be said that this approach, albeit in an attenuated form, makes use of two familiar criteria, those of multiple attestation and, to a lesser extent, coherence.

77. Matthew 22.15–22:22; Mark 12.13–17; Luke 20.20–26; Thomas 100.

78. See, for example, Richard Bauckham, *The Bible in Politics: How to Read the Bible Politically*, 2nd edn (London: SPCK, 2011).

79. Or rather the dominant group amongst those claiming this identity and which probably equated, more or less, with what the pagan critic Celsus called the "great church" (Origen, *Contra Celsum* 5.59).

80. For the gospels as biographies see Richard A. Burridge, *What Are the Gospels?: a Comparison with Graeco-Roman Biography*, 2nd edn (Grand Rapids: Eerdmans, 2004) and Dirk Frickenschmidt, *Evangelium als Biographie: Die vier Evangelien im Rahmen antiker Erzählkunst* (Tübingen: Francke, 1997).

81. Though obviously there was considerable variation. See Thomas Hägg, *The Art of Biography in Antiquity* (Cambridge: Cambridge University Press, 2012).

82. Haia Shpayer-Makov, 'Anarchism in British Public Opinion 1880–1914', *Victorian Studies*, 31 (1988), 487–516 (p. 487).

83. Joseph Conrad, *The Secret Agent* (London: J. M. Dent, 1907).

84. See, for example, 'Italian Anarchists Kneecap Nuclear Executive and Threaten More Shootings', *The Guardian*, 2012 <http://www.guardian.co.uk/world/2012/may/11/italian-anarchists-kneecap-nuclear-executive> [accessed 31 July 2015]. See also Richard Bach Jensen, *The Battle against Anarchist Terrorism: An International History, 1878–1934* (Cambridge: Cambridge University Press, 2013) and John M. Merriman, *The Dynamite Club: How a Bombing in Fin-de-Siècle Paris Ignited the Age of Modern Terror* (London: JR Books, 2009).

85. Though what constitutes "violence" is itself far from self-evident. For a discussion of definitional problems see Willem Schinkel, *Aspects of Violence: A Critical Theory* (Basingstoke: Palgrave, 2010), pp. 16–83.

86. See Ruth Kinna, *Anarchism: A Beginner's Guide* (Oxford: Oneworld Publications, 2009), pp. 158–164. See also Peter Gelderloos, *How Nonviolence Protects the State* (Cambridge: South End Press, 2007) and Uri Gordon, *Anarchy Alive!: Anti-Authoritarian Politics From Practice to Theory* (London: Pluto Press, 2008), pp. 78–108.

87. See, for example, Cindy Milstein, *Anarchism and its Aspirations* (Oakland: AK Press, 2010).

88. George Richard Esenwein, *Anarchist Ideology and the Working-Class Movement in Spain: 1868–1898* (Berkeley: University of California Press, 1989), p. 135.

89. Murray Bookchin, *Social Anarchism Or Lifestyle Anarchism: An Unbridgeable Chasm* (Oakland: AK Press, 1996), p. 4.

90. E.g. Woodcock, *Anarchism*, p. 8.

91. A point made by Marshall, *Demanding*, p. 3.

92. Brian Morris, *Anthropology and Anarchism: Their Elective Affinity* (London: Goldsmiths College, 2005), p. 6.

93. David Graeber, *Direct Action: An Ethnography* (Oakland: AK Press, 2009), p. 214.

94. Graeber, *Direct Action*, p. 214.

95. For Graeber, anarchism does not equate to any of these things and is best thought of "as that movement back and forth between these three." (*Direct Action*, p. 215).

96. E. E. Evans-Pritchard, *The Nuer: A Description of the Modes of Livelihood and Political Institutions of a Nilotic People* (Oxford: Oxford University Press, 1940), p. 6.

97. Peter Arshinov, *History of the Makhnovist Movement, 1918–21*, 2nd edn (London: Freedom Press, 2005).

98. Murray Bookchin, *To Remember Spain: The Anarchist and Syndicalist Revolution of 1936* (Oakland: AK Press, 1995); Stuart Christie, *We the Anarchists: A Study of the Iberian Anarchist*

Federation (FAI) 1927–1937 (Oakland: AK Press, 2008); José Peirats, *The CNT in the Spanish Revolution*, ed. by Chris Ealham, 3 vols. (Oakland: PM Press, 2011).

99. Michael Seidman, *The Imaginary Revolution: Parisian Students and Workers in 1968* (New York: Berghahn Books, 2004).

100. For the centrality of anarchism in new movements of dissent see Giorel Curran, *21st Century Dissent: Anarchism, Anti-Globalization and Environmentalism* (London: Palgrave Macmillan, 2006). For anarchists fighting in Rojava see http://rabble.org.uk/kobane-interview-with-an-anarchist-fighter/ [accessed 3 August 2015]

101. For a very helpful survey of the debate see F. Gerald Downing, 'Jesus and Cynicism', in *Handbook for the Study of the Historical Jesus. Volume 2. The Study of Jesus*, ed. by Tom Holmén and Stanley E. Porter, 4 vols. (Leiden: Brill, 2010), pp. 1105–1136.

102. For an attempt to explain the vitriolic response that this suggestion has elicited from some historical-Jesus scholars who see it as somehow denying Jesus' Jewishness, see William E. Arnal, *The Symbolic Jesus: Historical Scholarship, Judaism and the Construction of Contemporary Identity* (London: Equinox, 2005) and 'The Cipher "Judaism" in Contemporary Historical Jesus Scholarship', in *Apocalypticism, Anti-Semitism and the Historical Jesus: Subtexts in Criticism*, ed. by John S. Kloppenborg and John Marshall (London: Continuum, 2005), pp. 24–54.

103. David Graeber, *Fragments of an Anarchist Anthropology* (Chicago: Prickly Paradigm Press, 2004), p. 3.

104. Graeber, *Direct Action*, p. 211. It is unsurprising that Kropotkin's final, unfinished work was *Ethics, Origin and Development*.

105. Graeber, *Direct Action*, p. 216.

106. Graham, *Anarchism*.

107. Patricia Crone, 'Ninth-Century Muslim Anarchists', *Past & Present*, 167 (2000), 3–28. See also *Medieval Islamic Political Thought*, 2nd edn (Edinburgh: Edinburgh University Press, 2005).

108. Norman Cohn, *The Pursuit Of The Millennium: Revolutionary Millenarians and Mystical Anarchists of the Middle Ages* (London: Pimlico, 2004), pp. 214–222.

109. James C. Scott, *The Art of Not Being Governed: an Anarchist History of Upland Southeast Asia* (New Haven: Yale University Press, 2009).

110. Morris, *Ecology and Anarchism,* p. 51.

111. See, for example, Brian Morris, *Kropotkin: The Politics of Community* (Amherst: Humanity Books, 2003), pp. 202–203.

112. Todd May, *The Political Philosophy of Poststructuralist Anarchism* (University Park: Pennsylvania State University Press, 1994).

113. See, for example, John R. Love, *Antiquity and Capitalism: Max Weber and the Sociological Foundations of Roman Civilization* (London: Routledge, 1991).

114. Love, *Antiquity and Capitalism,* p. 4. Max Weber, *The Theory of Economic and Social Organizations,* trans. by A. M. Henderson and Talcott Parsons (New York: Free Press, 1964), p. 280.

115. See, for example, Peter Temin, *The Roman Market Economy* (Princeton: Princeton University Press, 2012).

116. Particularly in comparison with China. See, Keith Hopkins, *Death and Renewal. Volume 2: Sociological Studies in Roman History* (Cambridge: Cambridge University Press, 1985). However, see Walter Scheidel, 'From the "Great Convergence" to the "First Great Divergence": Roman and Qin-Han State Formation and Its Aftermath', in *Rome and China: Comparative Perspectives on Ancient World Empires,* ed. by Walter Scheidel (Oxford: Oxford University Press, 2009), pp. 11–23 (p. 19).

117. Although its size fluctuated somewhat, the Roman army of the early empire probably numbered around 300,000. Ramsay MacMullen, 'How Big Was the Roman Imperial Army?', *Klio,* 62 (1980), 451–60. See Tacitus, *Annals* 4.5.

118. The population of the Roman empire as a whole is difficult to calculate but a figure of about 50 million would be accepted by most in the field. See Keith Hopkins, 'Taxes and Trade in the Roman Empire (200 B.C.-A.D. 400)', *The Journal of Roman Studies,* 70 (1980), 101–125 (p. 118). However, Frier cautions that estimates of the gross population of the empire can be not more than a guess. See

Bruce W. Frier, 'More Is Worse: Some Observations on the Population of the Roman Empire', in *Debating Roman Demography*, ed. by Walter Scheidel (Leiden: Brill, 2001), pp. 139–160 (p. 139).

119. David Christian, 'State Formation in the Inner Eurasian Steppes', in *Worlds of the Silk Roads: Ancient and Modern*, ed. by David Christian and Craig Benjamin (Turnhout: Brepols, 1998), pp. 51–76 (p. 53).

120. Max Weber, *Weber: Political Writings*, ed. by Peter Lassman and Ronald Spiers (Cambridge: Cambridge University Press, 1994), p. 310. Although such a definition famously has its weaknesses; see Timothy Mitchell, 'The Limits of the State: Beyond Statist Approaches and Their Critics', *The American Political Science Review*, 85 (1991), 77–96.

121. For the perils of ethnocentrism in historical-Jesus scholarship see Richard L. Rohrbaugh, 'Ethnnocentrism and Historical Questions About Jesus', in *The Social Setting of Jesus and the Gospels*, ed. by Wolfgang Stegemann (Minneapolis: Augsburg Fortress, 2003), pp. 27–43.

122. Sam Mbah, and I. E. Igariwey, *African Anarchism: A History and Analysis* (Tucson: See Sharp Press, 1997).

123. Arif Dirlik, *Anarchism in the Chinese Revolution* (Berkeley: University of California Press, 1991); Graham, *Anarchism*, pp. 336–366.

124. Graham, *Anarchism*, pp. 367–89; Sho Konishi, *Anarchist Modernity: Cooperatism and Japanese-Russian Intellectual Relations in Modern Japan* (Cambridge: Harvard University Press, 2013).

125. *No Gods, No Masters, No Peripheries: Global Anarchisms*, ed. by Raymond Craib and Barry Maxwell (Oakland: PM Press, 2015).

126. Evans-Pritchard, *Nuer*. See, for example, Harold Barclay, *People Without Government: An Anthropology of Anarchy* (London: Kahn & Averill, 1990); Scott, *The Art of Not Being Governed;* Joanna Overing, 'Images of Cannibalism, Death and Domination in a "Nonviolent" Society', *Journal de la Société des Américanistes*, 72 (1986), 133–156.

127. Barclay, *People Without Government*, p. 18.

128. Maurice Casey, *Jesus of Nazareth: An Independent Historian's Account of His Life and Teaching* (London: Continuum, 2010), p. 212. For a survey of the kingdom of God in critical scholarship see Bruce Chilton, 'The Kingdom of God in Recent Discussion', in *Studying the Historical Jesus: Evaluations of the State of Current Research*, ed. by Craig A. Evans and Bruce Chilton (Leiden: Brill, 1998), pp. 255–280.

129. A largely comprehensive presentation of the canonical data relating to the kingdom can be found in Joachim Jeremias, *New Testament Theology: The Proclamation of Jesus*, trans. by John Bowden (London: SCM Press, 1971), pp. 31–35. See also Wright, *Jesus and the Victory of God*, pp. 663–670.

130. Thomas 3, 54, 57, 76, 82, 96, 97, 98, 99, 107, 109, 113.

131. For a critical evaluation see Simon Gathercole, *The Gospel of Thomas* (Leiden: Brill, 2014), pp. 112–127.

132. For a critical evaluation of the historicity of John see Maurice Casey, *Is John's Gospel True?* (London: Routledge, 1996). For re-assessments of its historical value see *John, Jesus, and History, Volume 1: Critical Appraisals of Critical Views*, ed. by Paul N. Anderson, Felix Just and Tom Thatcher (Atlanta: Society of Biblical Literature, 2007); *John, Jesus, and History, Volume 2: Aspects of Historicity in the Fourth Gospel*, ed. by Paul N. Anderson, Felix Just and Tom Thatcher (Atlanta: Society of Biblical Literature, 2009).

133. Mark 1.15 and Matthew 4.17; see also Luke 4.43.

134. Matthew 26.29, Mark 14.25.

135. Luke 23.41–42.

136. Matthew 19.24; Mark 10.25; Luke 18.25.

137. For a critical introduction to the evidence and current state of scholarship on the subject, see Eric Eve, *The Healer from Nazareth: Jesus' Miracles in Historical Context* (London: SPCK, 2009). For indicative examples of others believed to be healers and exorcists at the time, see Josephus, *Antiquities* 8.45–8; Lucian, *Philopseudes* 11, 16; Origen, *Contra Celsum* 1.68.

138. Matthew 12.28, Luke 11.20.

139. For a useful introduction to these see James L. Bailey and Lyle D. Vander Broek, *Literary Forms in the New Testament: A Handbook* (Louisville: Westminster John Knox Press, 1992).

140. Gerd Theissen and Annette Merz, *The Historical Jesus: a Comprehensive Guide* (London: SCM Press, 1998), p. 316.

141. Matthew 13:11, Mark 4:11, Luke 8:10.

142. See, for example, Matthew 13.24, 31, 33, 44, 45, 47; 18.23, 20.1; 22.2, 25.1. The phrase "kingdom of heaven", generally preferred by Matthew to "kingdom of God", is identical in meaning (compare Matthew 13.11, Mark 4.11, and Luke 8.10).

143. For a the surprising degree of agreement on this between scholars with quite different ideological positions, see, for example, Dale C. Allison, *Jesus of Nazareth: Millenarian Prophet* (Minneapolis: Fortress, 1998), p. 46; Casey, *Jesus of Nazareth*, p. 212; Crossan, *Historical Jesus*, p. 266; Bart D. Ehrman, *Jesus: Apocalyptic Prophet of the New Millennium* (Oxford: Oxford University Press, 1999), p. 142; Paula Fredriksen, *From Jesus to Christ: the Origins of the New Testament Images of Christ*, 2nd edn (New Haven: Yale University Press, 2000), p. 3; Robert W. Funk, *Honest to Jesus: Jesus for a New Millennium* (New York: Polebridge, 1996), p. 41; Craig S. Keener, *The Historical Jesus of the Gospels* (Grand Rapids: Eerdmans, 2009), p. 196; Gerd Lüdemann, *Jesus After Two Thousand Years: What He Really Said and Did* (London: SCM Press, 2000), p. 689; E. P. Sanders, *Jesus and Judaism* (London: SCM Press, 1985), p. 139; Geza Vermes, *The Religion of Jesus the Jew* (London: SCM Press, 1993), pp. 119–151; Wright, *Jesus and the Victory of God*, p. 11.

144. Markus N. A. Bockmuehl, *This Jesus: Martyr, Lord, Messiah* (Edinburgh: T. &T. Clark, 1994), p. 81.

145. The phrase "kingdom of God" does not appear in the Hebrew Bible. However, the kingship or reign of God is a major theme (e.g. Exodus 15.1–18; Isaiah 6.5–9; Psalm 99.1–5) and is also present in some non-canonical Jewish texts (e.g. *Sibylline Oracles* 3:46f; *Assumption of Moses* 10; Dead Sea Scrolls 1 QM 2.7, 6.6). A related idea, that of the "Day of the Lord", in which God was expected to intervene directly in history to judge both Israel and her enemies is a common motif in prophetic literature (e.g. Isaiah 13.6–9, Joel 2, Malachi 4.1–6).

146. The Greek work for parable, παραβολή, is used in the following texts: Matthew 13.3, 10, 18, 24, 31, 35, 53; 15.15; 21.33, 45; 22.1; Mark 3.23, 4.2, 10, 11, 13, 30, 33, 34; 7.17; 12.1, 12; Luke 5.36; 6.39; 8.4, 9, 10, 11; 12.16, 41; 13.6; 14.7; 15.3; 18.1, 9; 19.11; 20.9, 19; 21.2. Most relate, either directly or indirectly, to the kingdom of God/heaven.

147. This is true of most parabolic material but not all (see, for example Mark 7.17; Luke 14.7). We should be wary of approaches to the parables of Jesus that do not take account of such diversity (see Peter Dschulnigg, 'Positionen des Gleichnisverständnisses im 20. Jahrhundert. Kurze Darstellung von fünf Wichtigen Positionen der Gleichnistheorie (Jülicher, Jeremias, Weder, Arens, Harnisch)', *Theologische Zeitschrift*, 45 (1989), 335–351 (p. 347).

148. Ruben Zimmermann, 'How to Understand the Parables of Jesus: A Paradigm Shift in Parable Exegesis', *Acta Theologica*, 29.1 (2009), 157–182 (p. 175).

149. The sayings that conclude a number of parables are often allusive and are usually thought to be secondary additions. For example, the saying "the first will be last and the last first" is found as a conclusion to the Parable of the Householder in Luke (13.23–30) but appears as the conclusion to the Parable of the Labourers in the Vineyard in Matthew (20.1–16), as well as in non-parabolic material (Matthew 19.30, Mark 10.31).

150. Bernard Brandon Scott, *Hear Then the Parable: A Commentary on the Parables of Jesus* (Philadelphia: Fortress Press, 1989), p. 58. For surveys of the parables of Jesus in critical scholarship see Dschulnigg, 'Positionen des Gleichnisverständnisses', pp. 335–351; David B. Gowler, *What Are They Saying About the Parables?* (New York: Paulist Press, 2000); Klyne Snodgrass, 'From Allegorizing to Allegorizing: a History of the Interpretation of the Parables of Jesus', in *The Challenge of Jesus' Parables*, ed. by Richard Longenecker (Grand Rapids: Eerdmans, 2000), pp. 3–29.

151. Indicated by such sayings as: "The time is fulfilled, and the kingdom of God has come near; repent, and believe in the good news" (Matthew 4.17 and Mark 1.15; see also Luke 4.43) and, "And he said to them, 'Truly I tell you, there are some standing here who will not taste death until they see that the kingdom of God has come with power.'" (Mark 9.1; see also Matthew 16.28, Luke 9.27).

152. Indicated by such sayings as: "Once Jesus was asked by the Pharisees when the kingdom of God was coming, and he answered, 'The kingdom of God is not coming with things that can be observed; 21 nor will they say, "Look, here it is!" or "There it is!" For, in fact, the kingdom of God is among you.'" (Luke 17.20–21; cf. Thomas 3, 113); "But if it is by the Spirit [finger] of God that I cast out the demons, then the kingdom of God has come to you" (Matthew 12:28; Luke 11.20.); and "Truly I tell you, among those born of women no one has arisen greater than John the Baptist; yet the least in the kingdom of heaven is greater than he. 12 From the days of John the Baptist until now the kingdom of heaven has suffered violence, and the violent take it by force"(Matthew 11.11–12; Luke 5.28, 16.16; Thomas 46.).

153. For useful surveys of the problem see Heinz Giesen, *Herrschaft Gottes, heute oder morgen?: Zur Heilsbotschaft Jesu und der Synoptischen Evangelien* (Regensburg: Pustet, 1995).

154. Bruce J. Malina, 'Christ and Time: Swiss or Mediterranean?', *Catholic Biblical Quarterly*, 51 (1989), 1–31. However, *contra* Malina, there is evidence that some people in the early empire were quite literal and linear (or "Swiss" as Malina puts it) in their interpretation of future-oriented language. See, for example, 1 Thessalonians 4.13–18; 2 Peter 3.4; Cook, *The Interpretation of New Testament*, p. 192.

155. See Benedict Viviano, 'Eschatology and the Quest for the Historical Jesus', in *Oxford Handbook of Eschatology*, ed. by Jerry L. Walls (New York: Oxford University Press, 2008), pp. 73–90.

156. Contrary to the position of, for example, Crossan, *The Historical Jesus*; Borg, *Jesus*, pp. 47–96; Stephen J. Patterson, *The God of Jesus: The Historical Jesus and the Search for Meaning* (Valley Forge: Trinity Press International, 1998). For a helpful analysis of the question see *The Apocalyptic Jesus: A Debate*, ed. by Robert J. Miller (Santa Rosa, California: Polebridge Press, 2001).

157. The degree of imminence can, for instance, affect both the character and content of the ethical demands of Jesus. For example, Albert Schweitzer claimed that Jesus' ethic was an "interim-ethik", temporary and transitory; "completely negative [...] not so much an ethic as a penitential discipline" undertaken in preparation for

the arrival of the kingdom (*Quest of the Historical Jesus*, p. 239). Peabody's criticisms of Schweitzer remain pertinent: "it is difficult to see in it [Jesus' ethics] a predominating quality of indifference to the world's affairs or of complete preoccupation with a supernatural catastrophe" (Francis Peabody, 'New Testament Eschatology and New Testament Ethics', *Harvard Theological Review*, 2 [1909], 50–57 [p. 54]).

158. Richard B. Hays, *The Moral Vision of the New Testament: Community, Cross, New Creation* (Edinburgh: T&T Clark, 1996), p. 163. For the theme of reversal in the ethics of Jesus see Allen Verhey, *The Great Reversal: Ethics and the New Testament* (Exeter: Paternoster, 1984).

159. The theme of reversal is not solely concerned with things that can be reasonably categorized in this way. See, for example, Luke 6.21, 25.

160. For a general guide to the cultural context of the data relating to the historical Jesus see *The Oxford Handbook of Jewish Daily Life in Roman Palestine*, ed. by Catherine Hezser (Oxford: Oxford University Press, 2010). See also *The Historical Jesus in Context*, ed. by Amy-Jill Levine, Dale C. Allison and John Dominic Crossan (Princeton: Princeton University Press, 2006).

161. See Luke 6.20, 24 (cf. Matthew 5.3). See also Matthew 19.16–24; Mark 10:17–25; Luke 18.18–25.

162. Luke 6.21; see also Matthew 6.11, Luke 11.3; Matthew 15.32, Mark 8.3;

163. Matthew 21.31–32 (Matthew 9.9, Mark 2.14, Luke 5.28; Luke 18.10, 19.2). The elders were a non-priestly group who, with the scribes and chief priests, made up the Sanhedrin. They were the local aristocracy and consisted of "the heads of the most influential lay families" (Joachim Jeremias, *Jerusalem in the Time of Jesus: an Investigation into Economic and Social Conditions During the New Testament Period* [London: SCM Press, 1969], p. 223).

164. Matthew 18.3, 19.14; Mark 10.14; Luke 10.21, 18.16.

165. See Luke 15.11–32; Matthew 18.10–14, Luke 15.3–7; Matthew 10.6; Matthew 15.24. The term "sinner" can have a range of meanings but is best understood, in this period, as including those "who

act as if there is no God, people who do not observe the [Jewish] Law (or certain interpretations of the Law), people who were effectively outside of God's covenant with Israel, and people contrasted with the 'righteous'" (James G. Crossley, *Reading the New Testament: Contemporary Approaches* [London: Routledge, 2010], p. 91).

166. Matthew 9.21–22, Luke 10.13–14; Luke 10.25–37; Luke 17.11–19; Matthew 8.5–13, Luke 7.1–10 cf. John 4.1–42; though see Matthew 15.21–28, Mark 7.24–30; Matthew 6.32, Luke 12.30; Matthew 10.5; cf. Luke 9.52.

167. Mark 10.46, Luke 18.35.

168. Mark 12.41–44, Luke 21.1–4.

169. Most famously, "many who are first will be last, and the last will be first" (Matthew 19.30; see also Matthew 20.16; Mark 10.31; Luke 13.30; Mark 9.35; Thomas 4).

170. For example, "When you give a luncheon or a dinner, do not invite your friends or your brothers or your relatives or rich neighbours, in case they may invite you in return, and you would be repaid. 13 But when you give a banquet, invite the poor, the crippled, the lame, and the blind." (Luke 14.12–13).

171. For example, "Truly I tell you, the tax-collectors and the prostitutes are going into the kingdom of God ahead of you." (Matthew 21.31).

172. Matthew 22.1–14, Luke 14:15–24, Thomas 64.

173. Luke 14.21.

174. Luke 16:19–31 – yet a rich person might normally be assumed, like Abraham, to be blessed by God (Genesis 13:2; Proverbs 10:22).

175. See Matthew 25:31–46. For the interpretation of verse 45 see W. D. Davies and Dale C. Allison, *A Critical and Exegetical Commentary on the Gospel According to Saint Matthew. Volume III. Commentary on Matthew XIX-XXVIII* (Edinburgh: T&T Clark, 1997), pp. 428–429. It should be emphasised that in one sense the reversal here is a typical one within first-century Judaism (see, for example 2 Esdras 2.20–23). Concern for the "least" was a consistent feature of Jewish ethical thinking, from the earliest prophetic texts onwards (see, for example, Amos 2.6–8, 4.1–3, 5.10–13, 8.4–6; Malachi 3.5).

176. Luke 12.16–21; Thomas 63.

177. For example: Mark 2.4, 15–17; Luke 7.36–48, 8.2; 19.2–10; John 7.53–8.11.

178. The theme of conflict is so pervasive that "conflict stories" constitute a distinctive and widely distributed form of the traditions associated with the historical Jesus. See, for example, Arland J. Hultgren, *Jesus and His Adversaries: The Form and Function of the Conflict Stories in the Synoptic Tradition* (Minneapolis: Augsburg, 1979).

179. There is a pervasive theme of hostility to wealth in the Jesus tradition (see, for example, Matthew 6.24, Luke 16.13; Luke 12.13–21; Matthew 6.29, Luke 12.27; Matthew 19.24, Mark 10.25, Luke 18.25; Matthew 24.17, Mark 13.15; Luke 17.31; cf. Luke 16:14–15). Real treasure is said to be located in heaven (Matthew 6.20; Luke 12.33; Matthew 19.21, Mark 10.21, Luke 18.22; Matthew 6.2, Luke 16.13; Luke 12.13–14, cf. Thomas 72). The recurrent attacks on the rich show that this hostility to wealth is not motivated by asceticism but an assumed relationship between poverty and wealth (see Luke 19.1–9; Matthew 19.21, Mark 10.21, Luke 18.22). An indication of such thinking might be visible in Mark 10.19 where the command not to defraud is added to a series of commandments otherwise taken from the Ten Commandments cf. Luke 19.8; James 5.4; Deuteronomy 5.6–11, Exodus 20.1–17.

180. Matthew 5.40, Luke 6.29 cf. Luke 18.2–6.

181. Matthew 15.5, Mark 7.11; Matthew 23.1–36, Mark 12.37b–40, Luke 20.45–47; Mark 12.41–13.4, 21.1–7.

182. See Matthew 5:41.

183. Note, for example, the destitution that resulted from illness: "She had endured much under many physicians, and had spent all that she had; and she was no better, but rather grew worse" (Mark 5.26, Luke 8.43); "I was a mason, earning a living with my hands; I beg you, Jesus, restore my health to me, so that I need not beg for my food in shame." (Gospel of the Nazareans in Jerome, *Commentary on Matthew* 12.13). The free nature of the healing offered by Jesus and his followers was clearly significant (Matthew 10.5).

184. Davies and Allison, *Matthew. Volume I,* pp. 546–47. Cf. Mark 15.21; Epictetus, *Discourses* 4.1.79.

185. Walter Wink, 'Neither Passivity nor Violence: Jesus' Third Way (Matt 5:38//Luke 6:29–30)', in *The Love of Enemy and Non-Retaliation in the New Testament*, ed. by Willard M. Swartley (Louisville: Westminster John Knox Press, 1992), pp. 102–125 (p.111).

186. Matthew 5.44; Luke 6.27, 35; Romans 12.12–21. See William Klassen, 'The Authenticity of the Command : "Love Your Enemies"', in *Authenticating the Words of Jesus*, ed. by Bruce Chilton and Craig A. Evans (Leiden: Brill, 1999), pp. 385–407. Such non-violent resistance was a significant strand within first-century Judaism. See Gordon Zerbe, *Non-retaliation in Early Jewish and New Testament Texts: Ethical Themes in Social Contexts* (Sheffield: JSOT, 1993). For examples, see Josephus, *Antiquities* 18:55–59, *War* 2.175–203.

187. In the case with the woman with the hemorrhage, in the earliest rendering of this tradition, her healing comes about as a result of her own decision and action not that of Jesus (Mark 5.29, Luke 8.44; cf. Matthew 9.22). In the case of the Syrophoencian woman it is her arguments that convince a reluctant Jesus to heal her daughter (Matthew 15.21–28, Mark 7.24–30). See also Matthew 9.1–8, Mark 2.1–12, Luke 5.17–26 ; Matthew 8.28–34, Mark 5.1–20, Luke 8.26–39.

188. See, for example, the command to "hate" families (Luke 14.26–27, cf. Matthew 10.37–39). See also Matthew 12.46–50, Mark 3.31–35, Luke 8.19–21; Matthew 19.29; Mark 10.29, Luke 18.29b; Matthew 8.21–22, Luke 9.59–60. However, cf. Matthew 19.19, Mark 10.19, Luke 18.20; Matthew 15.4, Mark 7.10.

189. Fiorenza, *In Memory of Her*, p. 107. For a persuasive and important criticism of Fiorenza and similar attempts to present the Jesus as a critic of patriarchy, see Kathleen E. Corley, *Women and the Historical Jesus: Feminist Myths of Christian Origins* (Santa Rosa: Polebridge Press, 2002).

190. Matthew 12.46–50, Mark 3.31–35, Luke 8.19–21; Matthew 19.19, Mark 10.30, Luke 18.30.

191. Luke 14.12.

192. Matthew 5.42, Luke 6.30; Matthew 6.12–13, Luke 11.4; Matthew 18.21–35; Luke 12.33; Matthew 19.21, Mark 10.21, Luke 18.22; Luke 14.33, Matthew 6.4, 20; Luke 6.34–35.

193. See David Kraemer, 'Food, Eating and Meals', in *The Oxford Handbook of Jewish Daily Life in Roman Palestine*, ed. by Catherine Hezser (Oxford: Oxford University Press, 2010), pp. 403–419 and *Jewish Eating and Identity Throughout the Ages* (New York: Routledge, 2007). However, there were always means of enabling commensality, however constrained. See Jordan D. Rosenblum, *Food and Identity in Early Rabbinic Judaism* (Cambridge: Cambridge University Press, 2010).

194. For a description of this see Crossan, *The Historical Jesus*, pp. 261–264.

195. John Dominic Crossan, *Jesus: a Revolutionary Biography* (San Francisco: HarperSanFrancisco, 1994), p. 69.

196. See, for example, Matthew 9.10, Mark 2.15, Luke 5.29; Matthew 26.6, Mark 14.3; Thomas 61.

197. Matthew 11:19, Luke 7.34.

198. Matthew 9.11, Mark 2.16, Luke 5.30.

199. Luke 14.12–14.

200. Matthew 22.1–14, Luke 14.16–24, Thomas 64; Matthew 25.10 (cf. Matthew 9.15, Mark 2.19, Luke 9.34); Luke 12.37, 15.23.

201. The feeding of the five thousand: Matthew 14.13–21, Mark 6.30–44, Luke 9.10–17. The feeding of the four thousand: Matthew 15.32–39, Mark 8.1–10.

202. Matthew 8.11, Luke 13.29. It is, perhaps, unsurprising that a symbolic meal, associated with the kingdom, would become the central rite in early Christianity and was legitimized, probably with good reason, by appeal to an event in the life of the historical Jesus. See Matthew 26.26–29, Mark 14.22–25, Luke 22.15–20; 1 Corinthians 11.23–25. Cf. Justin, *First Apology* 66.3.

203. Something that owed itself to the universal tradition within Judaism. See Jacob Neusner, *Recovering Judaism: The Universal Dimension of Jewish Religion* (Fortress Press, 2001). Second Temple Jewish literature shows a range of ideas about the ultimate fate of the gentiles some of which involved their inclusion in salvation. See E. P. Sanders, *Judaism: Practice and Belief, 63 BCE-66 CE* (London: SCM Press, 1992), pp. 289–298. The tradition found in Matthew

8.11, Luke 13.29 may not be as self-evidently universal as it is often assumed, as Allison quite rightly notes ('Who Will Come from East and West? Observations on Matt. 8.11–12 = Luke 13.28–29', *Irish Biblical Studies*, 11 [1989], 158–170) but the implication is certainly there. See Michael F. Bird, 'Who Comes from the East and the West? Luke 13.28–29/Matt 8.11–12 and the Historical Jesus', *New Testament Studies*, 52 (2006), 441–457.

204. For cosmopolitanism see A. A. Long, 'The Concept of the Cosmopolitan in Greek & Roman Thought', *Daedalus*, 137 (2008), 50–58; Catherine Lu, 'The One and Many Faces of Cosmopolitanism', *Journal of Political Philosophy*, 8 (2000), 244–267.

205. Carl Levy, 'Anarchism and Cosmopolitanism', *Journal of Political Ideologies*, 16 (2011), 265–278.

206. See, for example, Matthew 22.16, Mark 12.14, Luke 20.21; Matthew 7.21, Luke 6.46. Jesus' initial silence when questioned by the high priest (Matthew 26.63, Mark 14.61), Herod (Luke 23.9), and Pilate (Matthew 27.11–14, Mark 15.1–4, Luke 23.2–5) could be interpreted as deliberately insolent. See also the exchange in Matthew 21.23–27, Mark 11:27–33, Luke 20.1–8.

207. Such impartiality is regarded as characteristic of God in the biblical tradition (e.g. Leviticus 19.15 cf. Acts 10.34, Rom. 2.11) and appears to be particularly associated with the rule of God in the New Testament (Matthew 5.45; cf. also Matthew 5.44, Luke 6.27, 35; Matthew 6.14, Luke 11:4).

208. For understanding the implications of departing from cultural expectations of deference and the problems of "face" it would raise, see Penelope Brown and Stephen C. Levinson, *Politeness: Some Universals in Language Usage* (Cambridge University Press, 1987). See also Richard Bauman, *Let Your Words Be Few: Symbolism of Speaking and Silence Among Seventeenth-century Quakers* (Cambridge: Cambridge University Press, 1983).

209. Luke 8.3; Matthew 9.9–13, Mark 2.13–17, Luke 5.27–32; Luke 19.2; Matthew 8.5, Luke 7.2.

210. Bockmuehl, 'Inclusive Jesus', p. 14.

211. See, for example, Casey, *Jesus of Nazareth,* p. 200. See Matthew 4.17, Mark 1.15; Mark 6.7, 12; Luke 15.11–32; Matthew 18.10–14,

Luke 15.3–7; Matthew 12.38–42; Luke 11:29–32; Luke 13.1–9. Contra Sanders, *Jesus and Judaism*, pp. 106–113 (cf. Casey, *Jesus of Nazareth,* pp. 282–84).

212. It is related to the idea in the Hebrew Bible that a sinful Israel needs to return to God (Isaiah 44.22, 55.7), a common theme, particularly in traditions concerned with the Day of the Lord (e.g. Joel 2.32)

213. See Luke 19.1–9; Matthew 19.21, Mark 10.21, Luke 18.22. For the expectation of restitution see Leviticus 6.1–5, Numbers 5.5–7.

214. See, for example, Matthew 12.28, Luke 11.20; Matthew 10.34–36, Luke 12.49–56; Matthew 11.2–6, Luke 7.18–23.

215. See, for example, Luke 5.32; Matthew 9.13; Matthew 5.21, 27, 33, 39, 44.

216. H. J. de Jonge, 'The Historical Jesus' View of Himself and of His Mission', in *From Jesus to John*, ed. by Martinus de Boer (Sheffield: JSOT, 1993), pp. 21–37; Theissen and Merz, *The Historical Jesus*, pp. 512–567; Wedderburn, *Jesus and the Historians,* pp. 275–322; Ben Witherington, *The Christology of Jesus* (Philadelphia: Fortress, 1990).

217. For example, Matthew 10.1–5; Mark 3.16–19, 4.10, 6.7, 9.35; Luke 6.13–16; John 6.67; Acts 1.13, 6.2; 1 Corinthians 15.5.

218. For example, Luke 10:9–16, Matthew 10:7–16; Luke 12:8–9 and Matthew 12:32–33.

219. Bakunin, *God and the State,* p. 33. See Simon Western, 'Autonomist Leadership in Leaderless Movements: Anarchists Leading the Way', *Ephemera: Theory & Politics in Organization,* 14 (2014), 673–698.

220. See Richard P. Saller, *Personal Patronage Under the Early Empire* (Cambridge: Cambridge University Press, 2002).

221. Mark 10.42–44; see also Matthew 20.20–28, Luke 22.24–27; Matthew 18.1–5, Mark 9.33–37, Luke 9.46–48; see John 13.1–11.

222. Myers in Van Steenwyk, *Holy Anarchist,* p. 8.

223. 1 Samuel 8.7. 1 Samuel 8.10–18 includes a stinging critique of the exploitation that results from monarchy.

224. The idea that the messiah would be identified by the healings he carried out, assumed in the tradition of Jesus' answer to John the Baptist (Matthew 11.2–6, Luke 7.18–23) is almost entirely absent from our sources for Jewish messianic expectations at the time. It can only be found in Dead Sea Scroll 4Q521. See Lidija Novakovic, '4Q521: The Works of the Messiah or the Signs of the Messianic Time?', in *Qumran Studies*, ed. by Michael Thomas Davis and Brent A. Strawn (Cambridge: Eerdmans, 2007), pp. 208–231.

225. E.g. Matthew 10.8, Luke 10.9.

226. Matthew 19.28, Luke 22.28–30. Cf. Psalms of Solomon 17.26. Gerd Theissen, 'Gruppenmessianismus: Überlegungen zum Ursprung der Kirche im Jüngerkreis Jesu', *Jahrbuch für Biblische Theologie*, 7 (1992), 101–123.

227. This is most obvious in the arrest narratives. See Matthew 26:47–56, Mark 14:43–52, Luke 22:47–53, John 18:1–11.

228. Benjamin Franks, *Rebel Alliances: The Means and Ends of Contemporary British Anarchisms* (Edinburgh: AK Press, 2006), p. 93.

229. Franks, *Rebel Alliances,* p. 98.

230. Matthew 13.31, Mark 4.31; Luke 13.18–19, Thomas 20.

231. Graeber, *Direct Action,* p. 203.

232. Matthew 21.13, Mark 11.15–19, Luke 19.45–48, John 2.13–17.

233. Matthew 22.15–22, Mark 12.13–17, Luke 20.20–26, Thomas 100, Egerton Papyrus 2.

234. Matthew 26.57–27.26, Mark 14.53–15.15, Luke 22.54–25, John 18.12–19.16.

235. Graeber, *Direct Action*, p. 114.

236. See, for example, Matthew 17.19–27; Matthew 18.3, Mark 9.15, Luke 18.17.

237. Marshall, *Demanding,* p. 75.

238. Justin J. Meggitt, 'Review of Mary Ann Beavis, *Jesus & Utopia: Looking for the Kingdom of God in the Roman World*', *Utopian Studies*, 18 (2007), 281–284.

239. See, for example, the use of a fictional anarchist utopia in Ursula Le Guin, *The Dispossessed: An Ambiguous Utopia* (New York: HarperPrism, 1974).

240. See the classic anarchist critique Marie Louise Berneri, *Journey Through Utopia* (London: Freedom Press, 1982).

241. Franks, *Rebel Alliances,* p. 99.

242. Matthew 15.21–28, Mark 7.24–30.

243. Mark 13.53–58, Mark 6.1–6a; cf. Luke 4.16–30.

244. Matthew 16.13–23, Mark 8.27–33, Luke 9.18–22.

245. See, for example, Bockmuehl, *This Jesus,* p. 86.

246. Henry Joel Cadbury, *The Peril of Modernizing Jesus* (New York: Macmillan, 1937), p. 141.

247. Judith Suissa, *Anarchism and Education: A Philosophical Perspective*, 2nd edn (Oakland: PM Press, 2010), p. 149.

248. Justin Mueller, 'Anarchism, the State, and the Role of Education', in *Anarchist Pedagogies: Collective Actions, Theories, and Critical Reflections on Education*, ed. by Robert H. Haworth (Oakland: PM Press, 2012), pp. 14–31 (p. 14).

249. Mueller, 'Anarchism', pp. 18–19.

250. Matthew 5.44; Luke 6.27, 35 (Romans 12.12–21).

251. Matthew 19.3–12, Mark 10.2–12; Matthew 5.31–32; Luke 16.18 (1 Corinthians 7.10).

252. For example, Matthew 22.1–14, Luke 14.15–24, Thomas 64; Matthew 25.31–46; Luke 10.25–37; 15.11–32; 16.19–31.

253. Christoyannopoulos, *Christian Anarchism,* p. 118.

254. Myers, *Binding the Strong Man,* p. 383.

255. For the use of the term see Wright, *Jesus and the Victory of God,* pp. 86, 98.

256. A. E. Harvey, *Jesus and the Constraints of History* (London: Duckworth, 1982), p. 16.

257. Matthew 27.37, Mark 15.26, Luke 23.38, John 19:19, 21.

258. For further discussion of this, see Meggitt, 'Madness'.

259. Corley, *Women and the Historical Jesus*. Jesus' message clearly appealed to some women, who were significant in the early movement, but probably because it embodied the more liberative tendencies visible in some forms of Judaism of the time, and elsewhere in the empire, or because of what it offered the poor and oppressed more generally.

260. A point forcefully made by James Crossley, *Jesus and the Chaos of History: Redirecting the Life of the Historical Jesus* (Oxford:Oxford University Press, 2015), pp. 64–95.

261. Barclay, *People Without Government,* p. 18.

262. Paul Chambers, 'Review of *Christian Anarchism: A Political Commentary* by Alexandre Christoyannopoulos', *Anarchist Studies*, 20 (2012), 109–111 (p. 110).

263. For those who reject such a capacious understanding of the term 'anarchist', at the very least there is sufficient evidence here to say that the historical Jesus displayed "an anarchist sensibility", and can legitimately be ranked alongside other figures like Aurobindo, Berdyaev, Blake, Gandhi and Tolstoy who are descibed in such a way by Brian Morris. See Brian Morris, 'Review of Paul Cudenec, *The Anarchist Revelation: Being What We Are Meant to Be*', *Anarchist Studies*, 23 (2015), 111–15 (p. 112).

References

Allison, Dale C., 'Who Will Come from East and West? Observations on Matt. 8.11–12 = Luke 13.28–29', *Irish Biblical Studies*, 11 (1989), 158–170.

Allison, Dale C., *Jesus of Nazareth: Millenarian Prophet* (Minneapolis, MN: Fortress, 1998).

Allison, Dale C., 'Behind the Temptations of Jesus : Q 4:1–13 and Mark 1:12–13', in *Authenticating the Activities of Jesus*, ed. by Bruce Chilton and Craig A. Evans (Leiden: Brill, 1999), pp. 195–213.

Allison, Dale C., *Constructing Jesus: Memory, Imagination, and History* (Grand Rapids, MI: Baker Academic, 2010).

Allison, Dale C., 'It Don't Come Easy: a History of Disillusionment', in *Jesus, Criteria, and the Demise of Authenticity*, ed. by Chris Keith and Anthony Le Donne (London: T&T Clark, 2012), pp. 186–199.

Alston, Charlotte, *Tolstoy and His Disciples: The History of a Radical International Movement* (London: I.B. Tauris, 2014).

Anderson, Paul N, Felix Just and Tom Thatcher, eds, *John, Jesus, and History, Volume 1: Critical Appraisals of Critical Views* (Atlanta, GA: Society of Biblical Literature, 2007).

Anderson, Paul N, Felix Just and Tom Thatcher, eds, *John, Jesus, and History, Volume 2: Aspects of Historicity in the Fourth Gospel* (Atlanta, GA: Society of Biblical Literature, 2009).

Arnal, William E., *The Symbolic Jesus: Historical Scholarship, Judaism and the Construction of Contemporary Identity*, Religion in Culture: Studies in Social Contest and Construction (London: Equinox, 2005).

Arnal, William E., 'The Cipher "Judaism" in Contemporary Historical Jesus Scholarship', in *Apocalypticism, Anti-Semitism and the Historical Jesus: Subtexts in Criticism*, ed. by John S. Kloppenborg and John Marshall (London: Continuum, 2005), pp. 24–54.

Arshinov, Peter, *History of the Makhnovist Movement, 1918–21*, 2nd edn (London: Freedom Press, 2005).

Bailey, James L., and Lyle D. Vander Broek, *Literary Forms in the New Testament: A Handbook* (Louisville, KY: Westminster John Knox Press, 1992).

Bakunin, Mikhail, *God and the State* (London: Freedom Press, 1910 [1882]).

Bammel, Ernst and C. F. D. Moule, eds, *Jesus and the Politics of His Day* (Cambridge: Cambridge University Press, 1984).

Barclay, Harold B., *People Without Government: An Anthropology of Anarchy* (London: Kahn & Averill, 1990).

Bauckham, Richard, *The Bible in Politics: How to Read the Bible Politically*, 2nd edn (London: SPCK, 2011).

Bauman, Richard, *Let Your Words Be Few: Symbolism of Speaking and Silence Among Seventeenth-century Quakers* (Cambridge: Cambridge University Press, 1983).

Berdyaev, Nicolai, *Slavery and Freedom* (New York, NY: Charles Scribner's Sons, 1944).

Berkman, Alexander, *Now and After: The ABC of Communist Anarchism* (New York, NY: Vanguard Press, 1929).

Bermejo-Rubio, Fernando, 'Jesus and the Anti-Roman Resistance', *Journal for the Study of the Historical Jesus*, 12 (2014), 1–105.

Bermejo-Rubio, Fernando, 'Jesus as a Seditionist: The Intertwining of Politics and Religion in his Teaching and Deeds', in *Teaching the Historical Jesus: Issues and Exegesis*, ed. by Zev Garber (London: Routledge, 2015), pp. 232–243.

Berneri, Marie Louise, *Journey Through Utopia* (London: Freedom Press, 1982).

Bessière, Georges, *Jésus selon Proudhon: la « messianose » et la naissance du christianisme* (Paris: Cerf, 2007).

Betz, Hans Dieter and Adela Yarbro Collins, *The Sermon on the Mount: A Commentary on the Sermon on the Mount, Including the Sermon on the Plain (Matthew: 5:3–7:27 and Luke 6:20–49)* (Minneapolis, MN: Augsburg Fortress, 1995).

Bird, Michael F., 'Who Comes from the East and the West? Luke 13.28–29/Matt 8.11–12 and the Historical Jesus', *New Testament Studies*, 52 (2006), 441–457.

Blanton, Ward, James G. Crossley, and Halvor Moxnes, eds, *Jesus Beyond Nationalism: Constructing the Historical Jesus in a Period of Cultural Complexity* (London: Equinox, 2010).

Bockmuehl, Markus, *This Jesus: Martyr, Lord, Messiah* (Edinburgh: T&T Clark, 1994).

Bockmuehl, Markus, 'The Trouble with the Inclusive Jesus', *Horizons in Biblical Theology*, 33 (2011), 9–23.

Boehrer, Frederick, 'Christian Anarchism and the Catholic Worker Movement: Roman Catholic Authority and Identity in the United States' (unpublished PhD, New York: Syracuse University, 2001).

Bond, Helen K., *The Historical Jesus: A Guide for the Perplexed* (London: T&T Clark, 2012).

Bookchin, Murray, *To Remember Spain: The Anarchist and Syndicalist Revolution of 1936* (Oakland, CA: AK Press, 1995).

Bookchin, Murray, *Social Anarchism Or Lifestyle Anarchism: An Unbridgeable Chasm* (Oakland, CA: AK Press, 1996).

Borg, Marcus, *Jesus in Contemporary Scholarship* (London: Continuum, 1994).

Brandon, S. G. F., *Jesus and the Zealots: a Study of the Political Factor in Primitive Christianity* (Manchester: Manchester University Press, 1967).

Brown, Penelope and Stephen C. Levinson, *Politeness: Some Universals in Language Usage* (Cambridge: Cambridge University Press, 1987).

Burridge, Richard A., *What Are the Gospels?: a Comparison with Graeco-Roman Biography*, 2nd edn (Grand Rapids, MI: Eerdmans, 2004).

Burridge, Richard A. *Imitating Jesus: An Inclusive Approach to New Testament Ethics* (Grand Rapids, MI: Eerdmans, 2007).

Cadbury, Henry Joel, *The Peril of Modernizing Jesus* (New York, NY: Macmillan, 1937).

Carrier, Richard, *On the Historicity of Jesus: Why We Might Have Reason for Doubt* (Sheffield: Sheffield Phoenix Press, 2014).

Casey, Maurice, *Is John's Gospel True?* (London: Routledge, 1996).

Casey, Maurice, *Jesus of Nazareth: An Independent Historian's Account of His Life and Teaching* (London: Continuum, 2010).

Casey, Maurice, *Jesus: Evidence and Argument or Mythicist Myths?* (London: T&T Clark, 2014).

Chambers, Paul, 'Review of *Christian Anarchism: A Political Commentary* by Alexandre Christoyannopoulos', *Anarchist Studies*, 20 (2012), 109–111.

Charlesworth, James H. and Craig A Evans, 'Jesus in the Agrapha and Apocryphal Gospels', in *Studying the Historical Jesus: Evaluations of the State of Current Research*, ed. by Bruce Chilton and Craig A. Evans (Leiden: Brill, 1994), pp. 479–534.

Chilton, Bruce, 'The Kingdom of God in Recent Discussion', in *Studying the Historical Jesus: Evaluations of the State of Current Research*, ed. by Craig A. Evans and Bruce Chilton (Leiden: Brill, 1998), pp. 255–280.

Christie, Stuart, *We the Anarchists: A Study of the Iberian Anarchist Federation (FAI) 1927–1937* (Oakland, CA: AK Press, 2008).

Christian, David, 'State Formation in the Inner Eurasian Steppes', in *Worlds of the Silk Roads: Ancient and Modern*, ed. by David Christian and Craig Benjamin (Turnhout: Brepols, 1998), pp. 51–76.

Christoyannopoulos, Alexandre, ed., *Religious Anarchism: New Perspectives* (Newcastle: Cambridge Scholars Publishing, 2009).

Christoyannopoulos, Alexandre, *Christian Anarchism: A Political Commentary on the Gospel* (Exeter: Imprint Academic, 2011).

Cohn, Norman, *The Pursuit Of The Millennium: Revolutionary Millenarians and Mystical Anarchists of the Middle Ages* (London: Pimlico, 2004).

Conrad, Joseph, *The Secret Agent* (London: J. M. Dent, 1907).

Conway, Colleen M., *Behold the Man: Jesus and Greco-Roman Masculinity* (New York: Oxford University Press, 2008)

Cook, John Granger, *The Interpretation of the New Testament in Greco-Roman Paganism* (Peabody, MA: Hendrickson Publishers, 2002).

Corley, Kathleen E., *Women and the Historical Jesus: Feminist Myths of Christian Origins* (Santa Rosa, CA: Polebridge Press, 2002)

Craib, Raymond and Barry Maxwell, eds, *No Gods, No Masters, No Peripheries: Global Anarchisms* (Oakland, CA: PM Press, 2015).

Crone, Patricia, 'Ninth-Century Muslim Anarchists', *Past & Present*, 167 (2000), 3–28.

Crone, Patricia, *Medieval Islamic Political Thought*, 2nd edn (Edinburgh: Edinburgh University Press, 2005).

Crossan, John Dominic, *The Historical Jesus: The Life of a Mediterranean Jewish Peasant* (Edinburgh: T&T Clark, 1992).

Crossan, John Dominic, *Jesus: A Revolutionary Biography* (San Francisco, CA: HarperSanFrancisco, 1994).

Crossley, James G., *Jesus in an Age of Terror: Scholarly Projects for a New American Century* (London: Equinox, 2008).

Crossley, James G., *Reading the New Testament: Contemporary Approaches* (London: Routledge, 2010).

Crossley, James G., *Jesus in an Age of Neoliberalism: Quests, Scholarship and Ideology* (London: Equinox, 2012).

Crossley, James G., *Jesus and the Chaos of History: Redirecting the Life of the Historical Jesus* (Oxford: Oxford University Press, 2015).

Curran, Giorel, *21st Century Dissent: Anarchism, Anti-Globalization and Environmentalism* (London: Palgrave Macmillan, 2006).

Damico, Linda H., *The Anarchist Dimension of Liberation Theology* (Pieterlen: Peter Lang, 1987).

Davies, W. D., and D. C. Allison, *A Critical and Exegetical Commentary on the Gospel According to Saint Matthew. Volume I. Introduction and Commentary on Matthew I-VII* (Edinburgh: T&T Clark, 1988).

Davies, W. D., and Dale C. Allison, *A Critical and Exegetical Commentary on the Gospel According to Saint Matthew. Volume III. Commentary on Matthew XIX-XXVIII* (Edinburgh: T&T Clark, 1997).

Dirlik, Arif, *Anarchism in the Chinese Revolution* (Berkeley, CA: University of California Press, 1991).

Dodd, C. H., *History and the Gospel* (London: Nisbet, 1938).

Dorion, Louis-André, 'The Rise and Fall of the Socratic Problem', in *The Cambridge Companion to Socrates*, ed. by Donald R. Morrison (Cambridge: Cambridge University Press, 2011), pp. 1–23.

Downing, F. Gerald, 'Jesus and Cynicism', in *Handbook for the Study of the Historical Jesus. Volume 2. The Study of Jesus*, ed. by Tom Holmén and Stanley E. Porter, 4 vols. (Leiden: Brill, 2010), pp. 1105–1136.

Dschulnigg, Peter, 'Positionen des Gleichnisverständnisses im 20. Jahrhundert. Kurze Darstellung von fünf Wichtigen Positionen der Gleichnistheorie (Jülicher, Jeremias, Weder, Arens, Harnisch)', *Theologische Zeitschrift*, 45 (1989), 335–351.

Dunn, James D. G., 'Jesus Tradition in Paul', in *Studying the Historical Jesus: Evaluations of the State of Current Research*, ed. by Bruce Chilton and Craig A Evans (Leiden: Brill, 1994), pp. 155–178.

Dzielska, Maria, *Apollonius of Tyana in Legend and History* (Rome: L'Erma di Bretschneider, 1986).

Ehrman, Bart D., *Jesus: Apocalyptic Prophet of the New Millennium* (Oxford: Oxford University Press, 1999).

Ehrman, Bart D., *Did Jesus Exist?: The Historical Argument for Jesus of Nazareth* (San Francisco, CA: HarperOne, 2012).

Esenwein, George R., *Anarchist Ideology and the Working-Class Movement in Spain, 1868–1898* (Berkeley, CA: University of California Press, 1989).

Evans, Craig A., 'Jesus in Non-Christian Sources', in *Studying the Historical Jesus: Evaluations of the State of Current Research*, ed. by Bruce Chilton and Craig A. Evans (Leiden: Brill, 1998), pp. 443–478.

Evans-Pritchard, E. E., *The Nuer: a Description of the Modes of Livelihood and Political Institutions of a Nilotic People* (Oxford: Clarendon Press, 1940).

Eve, Eric, *The Healer from Nazareth: Jesus' Miracles in Historical Context* (London: SPCK, 2009).

Faure, Sébastien, *Les douze preuves de l'inexistence de Dieu*, (Paris: Librairie sociale, 1908).

Fiorenza, Elizabeth Schüssler, *In Memory of Her: A Feminist Theological Reconstruction of Christian Origins*, 2nd edn (London: SCM, 2009).

Flusser, David and R. Steven Notley, *The Sage from Galilee: Rediscovering Jesus' Genius*, 4th edn (Grand Rapids: Eerdmans, 2007 [1968]).

Fonrobert, Charlotte, and Martin S. Jaffee, 'Introduction: The Talmud, Rabbinic Literature, and Jewish Culture', in *The Cambridge Companion to the Talmud and Rabbinic Literature*, ed. by Charlotte Fonrobert and Martin S. Jaffee, (Cambridge: Cambridge University Press, 2007), pp. 1–14.

Franks, Benjamin, *Rebel Alliances: The Means and Ends of Contemporary British Anarchisms* (Edinburgh: AK Press, 2006).

Fredriksen, Paula, *From Jesus to Christ: the Origins of the New Testament Images of Christ*, 2nd edn (New Haven, CT: Yale University Press, 2000).

Frickenschmidt, Dirk, *Evangelium als Biographie: Die vier Evangelien im Rahmen antiker Erzählkunst* (Tübingen: Francke, 1997).

Frier, Bruce W., 'More Is Worse: Some Observations on the Population of the Roman Empire', in *Debating Roman Demography,* ed. by Walter Scheidel (Leiden: Brill, 2001), pp. 139–160.

Funk, Robert W., *Honest to Jesus: Jesus for a New Millennium* (New York, NY: Polebridge, 1996).

Gathercole, Simon, *The Gospel of Thomas* (Leiden: Brill, 2014).

Gelderloos, Peter, *How Nonviolence Protects the State* (Cambridge, MA: South End Press, 2007).

Giesen, Heinz, *Herrschaft Gottes, heute oder morgen?: Zur Heilsbotschaft Jesu und der Synoptischen Evangelien* (Regensburg: Pustet, 1995).

Goodway, David, *Anarchist Seeds Beneath the Snow: Left-libertarian Thought and British Writers from William Morris to Colin Ward,* 2nd edn (Oakland, CA: PM Press, 2011).

Gordon, Uri, *Anarchy Alive!: Anti-Authoritarian Politics From Practice to Theory* (London: Pluto Press, 2008).

Gowler, David B., *What Are They Saying About the Parables?* (New York: Paulist Press, 2000).

Gowler, David B., *What Are They Saying About the Historical Jesus?* (New York, NY: Paulist Press, 2007).

Graeber, David, *Fragments of an Anarchist Anthropology* (Chicago, IL: Prickly Paradigm Press, 2004).

Graeber, David, *Direct Action: An Ethnography* (Oakland, CA: AK Press, 2009).

Graham, Robert, *Anarchism: From Anarchy to Anarchism (300CE to 1939)* V. 1: *A Documentary History of Libertarian Ideas* (Montreal: Black Rose Books, 2005).

Greenwood, E. B., 'Tolstoy and Religion', in *New Essays on Tolstoy*, ed. Malcolm Jones (Cambridge: Cambridge University Press, 1978), pp. 149–174.

Hägg, Thomas, *The Art of Biography in Antiquity* (Cambridge: Cambridge University Press, 2012).

Harvey, A. E., *Jesus and the Constraints of History* (London: Duckworth, 1982).

Hays, Richard B., *The Moral Vision of the New Testament: Community, Cross, New Creation* (Edinburgh: T&T Clark, 1996).

Hebden, Keith, *Dalit Theology and Christian Anarchism* (London: Ashgate, 2011).

Hezser, Catherine, ed., *The Oxford Handbook of Jewish Daily Life in Roman Palestine* (Oxford: Oxford University Press, 2010).

Holmén, Tom and Stanley E. Porter, eds, *Handbook for the Study of the Historical Jesus. Volume 1: How to Study the Historical Jesus* (Leiden: Brill, 2010).

Hooker, M. D., 'Christology and Methodology', *New Testament Studies*, 17 (1971), 480–487.

Hopkins, Keith, 'Taxes and Trade in the Roman Empire (200 B.C.-A.D. 400)', *The Journal of Roman Studies*, 70 (1980), 101–125.

Hopkins, Keith, *Death and Renewal. Volume 2: Sociological Studies in Roman History* (Cambridge: Cambridge University Press, 1985).

Hultgren, Arland J., *Jesus and His Adversaries: The Form and Function of the Conflict Stories in the Synoptic Tradition* (Minneapolis, MI: Augsburg, 1979).

Jennings, Jeremy, 'Anarchism', in *Contemporary Political Ideologies*, ed. by Roger Eatwell and Anthony Wright, 2nd edn (London: Continuum, 1999), pp. 131–151.

Jensen, Richard Bach, *The Battle against Anarchist Terrorism: An International History, 1878–1934* (Cambridge: Cambridge University Press, 2013).

Jeremias, Joachim, *Jerusalem in the Time of Jesus: an Investigation into Economic and Social Conditions During the New Testament Period* (London: SCM Press, 1969).

Jeremias, Joachim, *New Testament Theology: The Proclamation of Jesus*, trans. by John Bowden (London: SCM Press, 1971).

Johnson, Luke Timothy, *The Real Jesus: The Misguided Quest for the Historical Jesus and the Truth of the Traditional Gospels* (San Francisco, CA: HarperSanFrancisco, 1996).

Kähler, Martin, *Der sogenannte historische Jesus und der geschichtliche, biblische Christus* (Leipzig: A. Deichert, 1892).

Keener, Craig S., *The Historical Jesus of the Gospels* (Grand Rapids, MI: Eerdmans, 2009).

Kinna, Ruth, *Anarchism: A Beginner's Guide* (Oxford: Oneworld Publications, 2009).

Klassen, William, 'The Authenticity of the Command : "Love Your Enemies"', in *Authenticating the Words of Jesus*, ed. by Bruce Chilton and Craig A. Evans (Leiden: Brill, 1999), pp. 385–407.

Konishi, Sho, *Anarchist Modernity: Cooperatism and Japanese-Russian Intellectual Relations in Modern Japan* (Cambridge, MA: Harvard University Press, 2013).

Kraemer, David, 'Food, Eating and Meals', in *The Oxford Handbook of Jewish Daily Life in Roman Palestine*, ed. by Catherine Hezser (Oxford: Oxford University Press, 2010), pp. 403–419.

Kraemer, David, *Jewish Eating and Identity Throughout the Ages* (London: Routledge, 2007).

Kropotkin, Peter, *Ethics: Origin and Development* (Bristol: Thoemmes Press, 1993 [1924]).

Lategan, Bernard C., 'Questing or Sense-Making? Some Thoughts on the Nature of Historiography', *Biblical Interpretation: A Journal of Contemporary Approaches*, 11 (2003), 588–601.

Le Donne, Anthony, *The Historiographical Jesus: Memory, Typology, and the Son of David* (Waco, TX: Baylor University Press, 2009).

Le Donne, Anthony, *Historical Jesus: What Can We Know and How Can We Know It?* (Grand Rapids, MI: Eerdmans, 2011).

Le Guin, Ursula, *The Dispossessed: An Ambiguous Utopia* (New York, NY: HarperPrism, 1974).

Levine, Amy-Jill, Dale C. Allison and John Dominic Crossan, eds, *The Historical Jesus in Context* (Princeton, NJ: Princeton University Press, 2006).

Levy, Carl, 'Anarchism and Cosmopolitanism', *Journal of Political Ideologies*, 16 (2011), 265–278.

Long, A. A., 'The Concept of the Cosmopolitan in Greek & Roman Thought', *Daedalus*, 137 (2008), 50–58.

Love, John R., *Antiquity and Capitalism: Max Weber and the Sociological Foundations of Roman Civilization* (London: Routledge, 1991).

Lu, Catherine, 'The One and Many Faces of Cosmopolitanism', *Journal of Political Philosophy*, 8 (2000), 244–267.

Lubac, Henri de, *Proudhon et le christianisme* (Paris: Editions du Seuil, 1945).

Lüdemann, Gerd, *Jesus After Two Thousand Years: What He Really Said and Did* (London: SCM Press, 2000).

Luz, Ulrich, *Matthew 1–7: a Commentary*, 2nd edn (Minneapolis, MN: Fortress Press, 2007).

Macklin, Graham D., 'Co-opting the Counter Culture: Troy Southgate and the National Revolutionary Faction', *Patterns of Prejudice*, 39 (2005), 301–326.

MacMullen, Ramsay, 'How Big Was the Roman Imperial Army?', *Klio*, 62 (1980), 451–460.

Malina, Bruce J., 'Christ and Time: Swiss or Mediterranean?', *Catholic Biblical Quarterly*, 51 (1989), 1–31.

Marshall, Peter, *Demanding the Impossible: A History of Anarchism*, 4th edn (Oakland, CA: PM Press, 2010).

May, Todd, *The Political Philosophy of Poststructuralist Anarchism* (University Park, PA: Pennsylvania State University Press, 1994).

Mbah, Sam and I. E. Igariwey, *African Anarchism: A History and Analysis* (Tucson, AZ: See Sharp Press, 1997).

Meggitt, Justin J. 'The Madness of King Jesus', *Journal for the Study of the New Testament*, 29 (2007), 379–413.

Meggitt, Justin J., 'Review of Mary Ann Beavis, *Jesus & Utopia: Looking for the Kingdom of God in the Roman World*', *Utopian Studies*, 18 (2007), 281–284.

Meggitt, Justin J., 'Psychology and the Historical Jesus', in *Jesus and Psychology*, ed. by Fraser Watts (London: Darton,Longman & Todd, 2007), pp. 16–26.

Meggitt, Justin J., 'Popular Mythology in the Early Empire and the Multiplicity of Jesus Traditions', in *Sources of the Jesus Tradition: Separating History from Myth*, ed. by R. Joseph Hoffmann (Amherst, NY: Prometheus, 2010), pp. 53–80.

Meier, John P., *A Marginal Jew: Rethinking the Historical Jesus* (New York, NY: Doubleday, 1991).

Meier, John P. 'The Present State of the "Third Quest" for the Historical Jesus: Loss and Gain', *Biblica*, 80 (1999), 459–487.

Merriman, John M., *The Dynamite Club: How a Bombing in Fin-de-Siècle Paris Ignited the Age of Modern Terror* (London: JR Books, 2009).

Miller, Robert J., *The Apocalyptic Jesus: A Debate* (Santa Rosa, CA: Polebridge Press, 2001).

Milstein, Cindy, *Anarchism and its Aspirations* (Oakland, CA: AK Press, 2010).

Mitchell, Timothy, 'The Limits of the State: Beyond Statist Approaches and Their Critics', *The American Political Science Review*, 85 (1991), 77–96.

Morris, Brian, *Ecology and Anarchism: Essays and Reviews on Contemporary Thought* (Malvern: Images Publishing, 1996).

Morris, Brian, *Kropotkin: The Politics of Community* (Amherst, NY: Humanity Books, 2003)

Morris, Brian, *Anthropology and Anarchism: Their Elective Affinity* (London: Goldsmiths College, 2005).

Morris, Brian, 'Review of Paul Cudenec, *The Anarchist Revelation: Being What We Are Meant to Be*', *Anarchist Studies*, 23 (2015), 111–15.

Mueller, Justin, 'Anarchism, the State, and the Role of Education', in *Anarchist Pedagogies: Collective Actions, Theories, and Critical Reflections on Education*, ed. by Robert H. Haworth (Oakland, CA: PM Press, 2012), pp. 14–31.

Myers, Ched, *Binding the Strong Man: A Political Reading of Mark's Story of Jesus* (Maryknoll, NY: Orbis Books, 1988).

Myers, Ched 'Forward', in Mark Van Steenwyk, *That Holy Anarchist: Reflections on Christianity & Anarchism* (Minneapolis, MN: Missio Dei, 2012), pp. 1–11.

Neusner, Jacob, *Recovering Judaism: The Universal Dimension of Jewish Religion (Philadelphia, PA:* Fortress Press, 2001).

Newman, Saul, *From Bakunin to Lacan: Anti-Authoritarianism and the Dislocation of Power* (Lanham, MD: Lexington Books, 2001).

Nietzsche, Friedrich Wilhelm, 'Der Antichrist', in *Nietzsches Werke: Der Fall Wagner; Götzen-Dämmerung; Nietzsche contra Wagner; Der Antichrist; Gedichte* (Leipzig: C. G. Naumann, 1895), VIII, pp. 211–313.

Novakovic, Lidija, '4Q521: The Works of the Messiah or the Signs of the Messianic Time?', in *Qumran Studies*, ed. by Michael Thomas Davis and Brent A. Strawn (Cambridge: Eerdmans, 2007), pp. 208–231.

Overing, Joanna, 'Images of Cannibalism, Death and Domination in a "Nonviolent" Society', *Journal de la Société des Américanistes*, 72 (1986), 133–156.

Patterson, Stephen J., *The God of Jesus: The Historical Jesus and the Search for Meaning* (Valley Forge, PA: Trinity Press International, 1998).

Patterson, Stephen J., 'The Gospel of Thomas and Historical Jesus Research', in *Coptica – Gnostica – Manichaica*, ed. by Louis Painchaud and Paul-Hubert Poirier (Quebec: Les Presses de l'Université Laval, 2006), pp. 663–684.

Peabody, Francis, 'New Testament Eschatology and New Testament Ethics', *Harvard Theological Review*, 2 (1909), 50–57.

Peirats, José, *The CNT in the Spanish Revolution*, ed. by Chris Ealham, 3 vols. (Oakland, CA: PM Press, 2011).

Porter, Stanley E., *The Criteria for Authenticity in Historical-Jesus Research: Previous Discussion and New Proposals* (Sheffield: Sheffield Academic Press, 2000).

Preston, Paul, *The Spanish Holocaust: Inquisition and Extermination in Twentieth-century Spain* (London: HarperPress, 2012).

Proudhon, Pierre-Joseph, *Qu'est-ce que la propriété? Ou recherches sur le principe du droit et du gouvernment* (Paris: Librairie de Prévot, 1840).

Proudhon, Pierre-Joseph, *Jésus et les origines du christianisme* (Paris: G. Havard fils, 1896).

Proudhon, Pierre-Joseph, *Ecrits sur la religion*, ed. by M. Ruyssen (Paris: M. Rivière, 1959).

Reimarus, Herman S., *Fragments,* ed. by C. H. Talbert (Philadelphia: Fortress, 1970 [1774–7]).

Rohrbaugh, Richard L., 'Ethnocentrism and Historical Questions About Jesus', in *The Social Setting of Jesus and the Gospels*, ed. by Wolfgang Stegemann (Minneapolis, MN: Augsburg Fortress, 2003), pp. 27–43.

Rosenblum, Jordan D., *Food and Identity in Early Rabbinic Judaism* (Cambridge: Cambridge University Press, 2010).

Ruel, Malcolm, *Belief, Ritual and the Securing of Life: Reflective Essays on a Bantu Religion* (Leiden: Brill, 1997).

Runesson, Anna, *Exegesis in the Making: Postcolonialism and New Testament Studies* (Leiden: Brill, 2010).

Saller, Richard P., *Personal Patronage Under the Early Empire* (Cambridge: Cambridge University Press, 2002).

Sanders, E. P., *Jesus and Judaism* (London: SCM Press, 1985).

Sanders, E. P., *Judaism: Practice and Belief, 63 BCE-66 CE* (London: SCM Press, 1992).

Sandford, Michael J., *Poverty, Wealth, and Empire: Jesus and Postcolonial Criticism* (Sheffield Phoenix Press, 2014).

Sandt, Huub van de, and Jürgen K. Zangenberg, *Matthew, James, and Didache: Three Related Documents in Their Jewish and Christian Settings* (Atlanta, GA: Society of Biblical Literature, 2008).

Scheidel, Walter, 'From the "Great Convergence" to the "First Great Divergence": Roman and Qin-Han State Formation and Its Aftermath', in *Rome and China: Comparative Perspectives on Ancient World Empires*, ed. by Walter Scheidel (Oxford: Oxford University Press, 2009), pp. 11–23.

Schinkel, Willem, *AspE. P. Sanders, Judaism: Practice and Belief, 63 BCE-66 CE (London: SCM Press, 1992)ects of Violence: A Critical Theory* (Basingstoke: Palgrave, 2010).

Schmidt, Michael, *Cartography of Revolutionary Anarchism* (Oakland, CA: AK Press, 2013).

Schweitzer, Albert, *Von Reimarus zu Wrede: eine Geschichte der Leben-Jesu-Forschung* (Tübingen: Mohr Siebeck,1906).

Schweizer, Bernard, *Hating God: The Untold Story of Misotheism* (Oxford: Oxford University Press, 2010).

Scott, Bernard Brandon, *Hear Then the Parable: A Commentary on the Parables of Jesus* (Philadelphia, PA: Fortress Press, 1989).

Scott, James C., *The Art of Not Being Governed: an Anarchist History of Upland Southeast Asia* (New Haven, CT: Yale University Press, 2009).

Segers, Mary C., 'Equality and Christian Anarchism: The Political and Social Ideas of the Catholic Worker Movement', *The Review of Politics,* 40 (1978), 196–230.

Seidman, Michael, *The Imaginary Revolution: Parisian Students and Workers in 1968* (New York, NY: Berghahn Books, 2004).

Shpayer-Makov, Haia, 'Anarchism in British Public Opinion 1880–1914', *Victorian Studies,* 31 (1988), 487–516.

Sim, David C., and Boris Repschinski, eds, *Matthew and his Christian Contemporaries* (Edinburgh: T&T Clark, 2008).

Snodgrass, Klyne, 'From Allegorizing to Allegorizing: a History of the Interpretation of the Parables of Jesus', in *The Challenge of Jesus' Parables*, ed. by Richard Longenecker (Grand Rapids, MI: Eerdmans, 2000), pp. 3–29.

Steenwyk, Mark Van, *That Holy Anarchist: Reflections on Christianity & Anarchism* (Minneapolis, MN: Missio Dei, 2012).

Stirner, Max, *The Ego and His Own* (New York, NY: Benj. R. Tucker, 1907).

Suissa, Judith, *Anarchism and Education: A Philosophical Perspective*, 2nd edn (Oakland, CA: PM Press, 2010).

Temin, Peter, *The Roman Market Economy* (Princeton, NJ: Princeton University Press, 2012).

Theissen, Gerd, 'Gruppenmessianismus: Überlegungen zum Ursprung der Kirche im Jüngerkreis Jesu', *Jahrbuch für Biblische Theologie*, 7 (1992), 101–123.

Theissen, Gerd and Annette Merz, *The Historical Jesus: a Comprehensive Guide* (London: SCM Press, 1998).

Theissen, Gerd, and Dagmar Winter, *The Quest for the Plausible Jesus: the Question of Criteria* (Louisville, KY: Westminster John Knox Press, 2002).

Thompson, E. P., *The Making of the English Working Class* (London: Victor Gollancz, 1963).

Thompson, Thomas L., and Thomas S. Verenna, *Is This Not the Carpenter?: The Question of the Historicity of the Figure of Jesus* (Sheffield: Equinox, 2012).

Tolstoy, Leo, *Church and State and Other Essays: Including Money; Man and Woman: Their Respective Functions; The Mother; A Second Supplement to the Kreutzer Sonata* (Boston, MA: B. R. Tucker, 1891).

Tolstoy, Leo, '*The Kingdom of God Is within You': Christianity Not as a Mystic Religion but as a New Theory of Life*, trans. by Constance Garnett, 2 vols. (London: William Heinemann, 1894).

Vaage, Leif E, 'Beyond nationalism: Jesus the "holy anarchist"? : the cynic Jesus as eternal recurrence of the repressed', in *Jesus Beyond Nationalism: Constructing the Historical Jesus in a Period of Cultural Complexity*, ed. by Halvor Moxnes, Ward Blanton and James G. Crossley (London: Equinox, 2009), pp. 79–95.

Verhey, Allen, *The Great Reversal: Ethics and the New Testament* (Exeter: Paternoster, 1984).

Vermes, Geza, *The Religion of Jesus the Jew* (London: SCM Press, 1993).

Viviano, Benedict, 'Eschatology and the Quest for the Historical Jesus', in *Oxford Handbook of Eschatology*, ed. by Jerry L. Walls (New York, NY: Oxford University Press, 2008), pp. 73–90.

Walter, Nicholas, *About Anarchism*, 2nd edn (London: Freedom Press, 2002).

Weber, Max, *The Theory of Economic and Social Organizations*, trans. by A. M. Henderson and Talcott Parsons (New York, NY: Free Press, 1964).

Weber, Max, *Weber: Political Writings*, ed. by Peter Lassman and Ronald Spiers (Cambridge: Cambridge University Press, 1994).

Wedderburn, Alexander J. M., *Jesus and the Historians* (Tübingen: Mohr Siebeck, 2010).

Western, Simon, 'Autonomist Leadership in Leaderless Movements: Anarchists Leading the Way', *Ephemera: Theory & Politics in Organization*, 14 (2014), 673–698.

Wilde, Oscar, *The Soul of Man Under Socialism* (London: Privately Printed, 1891).

Williams, Kristian, 'The Soul of Man Under . . .Anarchism?', *New Politics*, 8 (2011). <http://newpol.org/content/soul-man-under-anarchism> [accessed 31 July 2015]

Willitts, Joel, 'Presuppositions and Procedures in the Study of the Historical Jesus: Or, Why I Decided Not to Be a Historical Jesus Scholar', *Journal for the Study of the Historical Jesus*, 3 (2005), 61–108.

Wink, Walter, 'Neither Passivity nor Violence: Jesus' Third Way (Matt 5:38//Luke 6:29–30)', in *The Love of Enemy and Non-Retaliation in the New Testament*, ed. by Willard M. Swartley (Louisville, KY: Westminster John Knox Press, 1992), pp. 102–125.

Woodcock, George, *Anarchism*, 2nd edn (Harmondsworth: Penguin, 1986).

Wright, N. T., *Jesus and the Victory of God* (London: SPCK, 1996).

Zerbe, Gordon, *Non-retaliation in Early Jewish and New Testament Texts: Ethical Themes in Social Contexts* (Sheffield: JSOT, 1993).

Zimmermann, Ruben, 'How to Understand the Parables of Jesus: A Paradigm Shift in Parable Exegesis', *Acta Theologica*, 29.1 (2009), 157–182.

A Reflection on Mystical Anarchism in the Works of Gustav Landauer and Eric Voegelin

Franziska Hoppen

University of Kent, UK

While German anarchist philosopher Gustav Landauer and American political scientist Eric Voegelin have each inspired significant scholarly comment, these two figures have not yet been brought into contact with one another. This paper seeks to draw attention to the similarities in their work, exploring Landauer's and Voegelin's mystical anarchism, the foundation of their critique of politics, and visions of what they describe as a true, anti-political community. According to both thinkers, the cornerstone for community is the essential unity between an individual's direct, unmediated experience of being, and its knowledge of being, forming its most primary reality. Politics, they state, only becomes necessary when this unity is separated, functioning to maintain the separation by foreclosing experience and externalising knowledge. Thus, politics creates a substitutional, second reality and a particularist society, which encompasses a people's new self-interpretation. While the two thinkers have identified this substitutional reality in need of constant self-defence as the basis for 20th-century totalitarian politics, they also argue that primary reality can at all times be remembered. Through a process which Landauer refers to as "separation" and Voegelin as "anamnesis", the individual may re-access primordial reality, radiating its knowledge into, and thereby transforming, second reality.

This paper is a personal reflection on anarchism from a mystical perspective, guided by the works of German anarchist philosopher Gustav Landauer (1870–1919) and American political scientist Eric Voegelin (1901–1985), focussing specifically on their

How to cite this book chapter:
Hoppen, F. 2017. A Reflection on Mystical Anarchism in the Works of Gustav Landauer and Eric Voegelin. In: Christoyannopoulos, A. and Adams, M. S. (eds.) *Essays in Anarchism and Religion: Volume 1*. Pp. 198–237. Stockholm: Stockholm University Press. DOI: https://doi.org/10.16993/bak.f. License: CC-BY

conception of community. Although seemingly little connects those two thinkers, an exploration of their respective critiques of political practice and science, both rooted in mystical philosophy,[1] reveals a significant degree of cohesion. Since their work has not yet been brought into contact with one another, this chapter seeks to articulate a comprehensive outline of the above theme. While there exist differences in aim, scope and argumentation between Landauer and Voegelin, differences that invite further investigation, the following reflections focus on the similarities and general coherence in their work, with the aim of thereby contributing to a discussion on mystical anarchism.

At the centre of Landauer's and Voegelin's critique of politics lies a theme reoccurring throughout their works: the separation of the *experience* of being from the *knowledge* of being, severing the direct link that connects the individual to the world within which she finds herself. Politics, both thinkers argued, emerges from this situation of separation to create, through a system of thought and practices, a second, imaginary reality that encompasses a people's new interpretation of the world. Simultaneously, politics seeks to ensure, through its various norms, discourses and techniques, the foreclosure of reality so that a restoration of the link between experience and knowledge remains deferred. Politics thus functions as a surrogate for what both Landauer and Voegelin identified as the true commune of the individual with herself, others and the world. Consequently, the condition of politics can only be overcome through deep *experience* of the individual's unmediated relationship with reality. Both Landauer and Voegelin based this argument on the claim of a unity of existence, whose multiplicity of existents issues from a single, common source[2] which reveals itself within each being and the world and yet extends infinitely beyond it. As the world is already within each being, the quest for order does not lead via ordering the world from the outside through politics, but inside the self, becoming the world. Community, from this perspective, is not situated in the particularity of an extrinsic self-interpretation, but is, rather, the situating "alliance of the plenty"[3] originating within the cosmos.[4] This chapter argues that anarchism in the works of Landauer and Voegelin is concentrated in the argument that the self is the primary reality by which the individual comes to know all other realities, and that the self is the starting point in the struggle for change. This claim is read as mystical to the extent that the experience of the self involves the rediscovery of a primary or originary union with the world.

A short introduction to Landauer and Voegelin

At first sight, the anarchist-socialist revolutionary Landauer, considered to be the "most influential German anarchist intellectual of the twentieth century,"[5] and German born American political scientist Eric Voegelin, known for his philosophy of consciousness, seem to have little in common. Landauer promoted anarchism,[6] Voegelin was highly critical of it; Landauer sought to overcome not just the state but politics altogether,[7] Voegelin seemingly considered it a necessary evil; Landauer participated in the revolutionary Bavarian Council Republic, Voegelin held a deep-seated mistrust of the masses and utopian ideas. There is no evidence of any personal connection between the two philosophers, and Voegelin does not appear to have read Landauer. However, Voegelin might have studied Landauer's translations of German mystic Meister Eckhart's sermons, while researching the latter, or his translations of Bakunin, Tolstoy or Kropotkin, when he formulated his criticism of their anarchism. Moreover, Voegelin studied the works of Jewish philosopher, and friend of Landauer, Martin Buber[8] whose work was partly influenced by Landauer and *vice versa*.[9]

A short summary of Landauer's and Voegelin's respective biographies shows how, despite their writing within different historical contexts and challenging different forces of authoritarian oppression, a common concern and thread of investigation nonetheless emerges in their work. Beneath Landauer's various anarchist projects, practical as well as literary, can be found a common unifying theme that "We are piteously divided."[10] Landauer referred to the division between society and politics, to the division between members of an increasingly atomised society and, most importantly, to the division of the individual from herself. This theme remained prominent throughout Landauer's life, thought and activism, forming the centre of his work. Already as a young student, Landauer felt that his desire for "purity, beauty and fulfilment" found resonance neither in the school curriculum nor the political scene, but only in the world of "theatre, music and especially books." Thus, he argued, "the reason for my opposition to society, as well as the reason for my continued dreams and my outrage, was not class identity or even compassion, but the permanent collision of romantic desire with philistine limitation."[11] As a literary Bohemian in Berlin during the early 1890s Landauer received a Marxist education and grew aware of the divisions between politicians' words and deeds. He then joined a radical group called *Verein Unabhängiger Sozialisten* (Association of Independent Socialists, short *Die Jungen*),[12] wrote for their journal *Der Sozialist,* of which he would later become editor, and campaigned against the *Social Democratic Party of Germany* (SPD). Yet, Landauer soon grew disillusioned with what he perceived as a tendency amongst the workers to merely await a revolution led by political elites, rather than organise in the here and now. Simultaneously, Landauer distanced himself from fellow anarchists and socialists, who fought amongst each other instead of for the common cause. With his program of anarchism-socialism, declaring that "anarchism is the goal.... socialism is the means..." he alienated both groups alike and began to focus on consumer-producer cooperatives and the non-industrial sector, arguing for a return to the countryside and meaningful labour.[13]

After a year-long prison term in 1899, during which Landauer translated parts of German medieval mystic Meister Eckhart's sermons into modern German[14], and edited the linguist Fritz Mauthner's *Beiträge zu einer Kritik der Sprache* (*Contributions to a Critique of Language*), Landauer began to formulate matured, explicitly mystical texts, focussing on the possibility of retrieving true community through mystical access to the world and its natural order. Using and developing the theories of Mauther and, implicitly,[15] Meister Eckhart, these texts include *Durch Absonderung zur Gemeinschaft* (*Through Separation to Community,* 1900), *Anarchische Gedanken über Anarchismus,* (*Anarchic Thoughts on Anarchism,* 1901), *Skepsis und Mystik,* (*Scepticism and Mysticism,*1903), *Revolution* (1907) and *Aufruf zum Sozialismus,* (*Call to Socialism,* 1911).

After 1901, Landauer re-immersed himself in political activism, attempting to realise his envisioned community in various projects. Notably, he founded the *Sozialistische Bund* (Socialist Union) in 1908, seeking to create small, independent, artistic cooperatives and settlements as the basic cells of a new, socialist culture. Yet, like most of his projects, the *Sozialistische Bund* was dissolved in 1914 due to lack of commitment amongst its members. Landauer's probably best known and more ambiguous activist involvement was his participation in the Bavarian Democratic and Social Republic,[16] following the German Revolution. Despite his *Antipolitik* he became the Minister of Culture and even drafted the constitution of the Bavarian Council Republic.[17] Landauer appears to have hoped that Bavaria could become the germ cell for the federalised Germany he envisioned, based on grass-roots democracy and communities that would form according to historical and cultural background, and in which all members of the public could be involved in decentralised councils. Yet, his enthusiasm soon gave way to disillusionment when he realised that many participants merely sought to prepare for the dictatorship of the proletariat. In 1919, the SPD sent military units into Munich to arrest the opposition, and Landauer was assassinated on May 2, 1919.

Voegelin's life, at first sight, appears to be antonymous to that of Landauer. Having lived through World War I as an adolescent, through Austria's political, economic and cultural turmoil as a doctoral candidate under Hans Kelsen, and through the rise of Nazism in Germany and Austria, Voegelin tasked himself with the exploration of the causes of what he considered to be the twentieth century's great spiritual degeneration,[18] made manifest in the various forms of political violence and ideological mass movements. Decisive for Voegelin's later work was his encounter with common sense philosophy during a scholarship in America in 1924. While political science at the University of Vienna was preoccupied with methodological questions about epistemology, common sense philosophy confirmed Voegelin's assumption that the reality of experience was self-interpretive.[19] He argued that all people share a type of rationality based on the ordinary, direct experience of reality without any technical apparatus, being the everyman's natural ability to grasp truth and order, which is then expressed in symbols. From 1924 onwards experience was at the centre of Voegelin's thought, and he became occupied with exploring the trails of such symbolisms.

In 1933, the year Hitler came to power, Voegelin published *Race and State* and *The History of the Race Idea,* investigating the symbols of race science and the emergence of the Nazi ideology's racist idea of the state.[20] Therein, he clarified that the authoritarian state was not a theoretical concept but a political symbol which rested on the dogmatic reduction of the human experience of reality to its physical dimensions, discounting mind, spirit and history, thereby radically mutilating the unity of the human form. Unsurprisingly, the works were banned in Germany almost immediately.

In 1938 Voegelin fled to the United States, where he became a citizen in 1944. His project for the coming decades was the formulation of an extensive history of political ideas, as a side effect of which Voegelin developed his philosophy of consciousness, a maturation of his previous explorations of experience and its symbols. At its centre and at the heart of his future philosophical endeavours was the explication of the experience of consciousness as the first reality, one that is forever caught between immanent and transcendent poles of existence.[21] After World War II Voegelin used this argument to theorise that political ideologies, especially totalitarian politics, were quests for an absolute reality, one in which the in-between state of consciousness could be overcome. Yet, as the search for certainty requires eliminating evidence of the contrary, the desire for absolute reality limits the individual's view of human reality. The resulting alienation from reality can only be overcome, Voegelin argued, through the creation of an alternative, "second reality", which would make the individual's curtailed vision of reality appear absolute.

In 1958 Voegelin returned to Munich University, taking up a chair in political science. In his famous lecture series "Hitler and the Germans" he argued that the refusal of some Germans to accept their responsibility for Nazism was a dramatic example of such a second reality. Voegelin returned to America in 1969, joining Stanford University and the Hoover Institution, where he remained until his death.

Voegelin's life work was dedicated to philosophy, which he considered the critical clarification of the present disorder, bringing to consciousness the true order of reality and persuading others to join in the quest, forming communities of the spirit which may, eventually, achieve social effectiveness.[22]

At the core of both philosophers' projects lies the attempt to restore order through experience of and participation in the locus of the world's self-revelation within oneself. Landauer's work was predominantly concerned with the political perpetuation of the division between the individual's personal experience of reality, its desire for "purity, beauty and fulfilment" on the one hand, and the exterior, political circumstances with their "philistine limitations" on the other, with which it "permanently collided."[23] Landauer found, in other words, a reality within the individual, and one outside of it, both disconnected by (and outside reality governed by) political regiment. Similar to Landauer, Voegelin's work revolved around the separation between two realities: the first reality which society refused to apperceive (the reality in between whose existential poles consciousness is caught) and the second reality created from within this refusal with the purpose to permanently separate imaginary reality from reality, so that the imaginary could become absolute. Politics, for Landauer and Voegelin, is merely symptomatic of the individual's division from reality. Thus, both dealt, albeit in various ways that will be explored below, with the separation of experiencing reality from knowing about reality, and with the role politics plays in upholding that separation. The following section will highlight how Landauer and Voegelin envisioned politics, in particular the state and political ideology, as imaginary reality and how they concluded that its true purpose lay in separating the individual's experience from its knowledge of reality.

Politics and political science as imaginary reality:

Disappointed with the theories and practices of contemporary anarchists, Landauer published an essay critiquing the misconception of the state as a reified institution that can be overcome by violent revolution. Published in 1910 as *Schwache Staatsmänner, schwächeres Volk* (*Weak statesmen, weaker people*), the essay contains Landauer's most widely quoted statement:

> A table can be overturned and a window can be smashed. However, those who believe that the state is also a thing or a fetish that can be overturned or smashed are sophists and believers in the Word. The state is a social relationship; a certain way of people relating to one another. It can be destroyed by creating new social relationships; i.e., by people relating to one another differently. The absolute monarch said: I am the state. We, who we have imprisoned ourselves in the absolute state, must realise the truth: we are the state! And we will be the state as long as we are nothing different; as long as we have not yet created the institutions necessary for a true community and a true society of human beings. [24]

Landauer's anarchist critique was not directed against the illegitimate rule of the state (*archein*), rather it recognised that the state, far from being a singular centre of top-down power and domination, consists of the micro-power and network structures of each member. Power, for Landauer, lay in the hands of the oppressed as well as of the oppressors, its front line running through each individual. It is precisely because "we are the state", that *we* have the power to organise differently, though it requires, and is only possible if, we first recognise that it was we who have "imprisoned ourselves", that there is no state to be overcome, but only ourselves. [25]

The essential problem to which Landauer's political struggle drew attention was the difference between the state as an ideological excuse on the one hand, and lived reality on the other. He argued that "we speak of the state without thinking. This word designates nothing but a definite condition of a public-legal nature in which we persist with our wills. It is the reification of what are in fact fluid and spiritual relations; it does injury to our perception because we take an expedient for naked reality." [26] What Landauer effectively argued was that no such thing as "the state" exists, that it is only language creating an illusion in which the state *appears* as a "thing or a fetish" It is a reified institution and central unity, constructing out of the openness and fluidity of social relationships order, norms, practices, discourses, technologies and essential identities.

Yet, we "persist in this definite condition" with our will. The state is "no reality that exists independently from the people. There is no 'state' on the one hand, and people who live in it on the other. The 'state' much rather belongs to what people do and understand. People do not live in the state. The state lives in the people."[27] It is not the state which creates a people but a people which create and organise symbols and ideological systems as their mode of self-interpretation, shaping social relationships accordingly. In other words, the state is the externalisation of the self when its internal reference points cease to have meaning, functioning as its substitute.[28] The state is there,

> to create order and the possibility to continue living amid all this spiritless nonsense, confusion, hardship and degeneracy. The state, with its schools, churches, courts, prisons, workhouses, the state with its army and its police; the state with its soldiers, officials and prostitutes. Where there is no spirit and no inner compulsion, there is external force, regimentation, the state. Where spirit is, there is society. Where unspirit is, there is the state. The state is the surrogate for spirit.[29]

It is "not a particular type of the state that causes oppression, but self-coercion, self-denial, and the worst of all emotions: mistrust towards others and oneself. All this is engrained in the notion of the state itself..."[30] Thus, Landauer asked, "Is it not like a game of echo? What are the people afraid of? The people. Who obstructs the masses? The masses. You are your own enemy!"[31] Eventually, Landauer argued, symbolic reality is substituted for reality itself. While the state is a human creation, it requires its creator's constant service in order to maintain itself, on account of not being an invention made at a single point in time, but a continuous process of self-denial. Repetition, ultimately, consolidates.[32] Therefore Landauer described the state as an illusory construction (*Scheingebilde*),[33] a "perfected nothingness,"[34] and its politics as an illusion of reality (*Schein der Wirklichkeit*).[35] His critique was not directed against *archos,* the ruler, but against *arche*, which, as Benjamin Tucker writes, "comes to mean a *first principle*, an element; then *first place, supreme power, sovereignty, dominion, command, authority*; and finally a *sovereignty, an empire, a realm, a magistracy, a government office.*"[36] *Arche* is the creation of a world of appearances, curtailing open and fluid reality with the aim to obliterate it. The state is merely symptomatic of *arche*. In fact, Landauer reiterated that he opposed *any arche*, "any fight that is led for or against word-constructs as if they were reality."[37]

Voegelin discussed a similar problem in his 1933 work *Race and State*.[38] Therein, he argued that the particular community, for example the racially defined community, is not constituted through an outside (such as the state), but that, on the contrary, particularity begins as an idea. Just as Landauer found that the state consists of social relationships, Voegelin argued that the particular community is "a thought construct in the minds of the people sharing in it, and precisely by appearing in the subjective idea the community also becomes objective reality."[39] Like Landauer, who argued that the state emerges as a solution out of "spirit-lessness and chaos," arising when experience no longer produces meaningful knowledge, Voegelin found that the particular community emerges as an expression of a feeling of separation from humanity and of a lack of essential social experience. The loss of the unity of humanity under God,[40] he argued, gave rise to the first institutions that sought to conserve at least partial unity and provide meaning under the banner of a certain particularity. However, as particularity always contains the experience of a loss of the world, each people sees their own particularity reflected in that of other communities, and begins to flee from this sight "by claiming for itself the status of the 'world' and regarding all others as 'non world'". Fear of the other, then, becomes "the deepest root of the new idea of community", and the claim of superiority and uniqueness grows ever more exaggerated.[41] Only later, during his *Hitler and the Germans* lectures, did Voegelin refer to this false image of reality, or *Ersatz*-reality which eclipses genuine reality, as "second reality."[42] Simply put, a second reality is the construction of a system; but "since reality has not the character of a system, a system is always false; and if it claims to portray reality, it can only be maintained with the trickery of an intellectual swindle."[43]

Voegelin's 1936 publication *The Authoritarian State* discussed to what extent political and legal sciences were complicit in this intellectual swindle, when they researched the phenomenon of the state. Scholarly discussion of political subjects, Voegelin argued, while being concerned with developing sharply defined concepts of their subjects, ignored the fact that their definitiveness did not hold in reality. Methodology, Voegelin stated, had replaced ontology, so that the scientific method falsely constituted the object of its science, guaranteeing the unity of the scientific object by the unity of a methodological system of categories. The object of research that concerned a certain segment of reality, such as the state, was subordinated to the method used to approach reality, and since methodology was a closed system of categories, so the object was determined by it. Hence, he urged political science to distinguish between political symbol on the one hand and theoretical concept on the other, and not simply attempt to assign to a political symbol an epistemologically correct meaning. Thus,

> By recognising political language for what it is, we integrate it into the reality of the state as one of its components. Refusing to misunderstand the creation of a political symbol as an act of perception, renouncing the assumption that the political symbol has to mean something and not just be something, allows us to understand it as a symbol in the full richness and force of its expression.... The elements of the situation in which the political symbol has its place become visible only when we do not act as if the perspective of the concept were identical with the perspective of the symbol.[44]

Voegelin's analysis of the contradictions both within Nazi race ideology and political science's methodological preoccupations can be read, like Landauer's analysis of the state, as a critique of *arche*, substituting imaginary reality for reality itself.

Landauer, in turn, described what he considered the original purpose of science. In order to generate knowledge about the meaning of its experiences, he argued, the individual has to explore the world, providing her senses with objective data for her soul to interpret.[45] Yet, being is not only experienced by the senses, but also by the spirit, non-linguistically and non-rationally.[46] It follows that the world cannot be explained materialistically alone, for the emergence of the spirit from material is mystery. [47] Rather, Landauer argued, the purpose of science is to contemplate experience so that practice can be meaningfully attuned to knowledge.[48] This type of science is an existential, lifelong process, which, despite the awareness that ultimate knowledge is impossible, *resists* escaping through *arche*. This conception of science resembles the philosophy of common sense which influenced Voegelin. Both are intuitive, the everyday person's experience of self-reflective reality, and both seek order and resistance against indoctrination and dogma.

However, Landauer also argued that the purpose of modern science has become radically different. He dated the root of that change back to the Middle Ages, when the sacred texts and traditions of Christianity underwent a divorce from their symbolic meaning.[49] As scripture was reduced to literal meaning and opaque facts, the Christian community split into the Church on the one hand, seeking knowledge through literary interpretation, and into mystics and heretics on the other, seeking to protect symbolism from rationalist analysis. The principle of the unity of existence and common spirit, as they were revealed through those symbolisms[50], were thenceforth no longer valid as a community's ordering force. Its surrogate became a new form of science, focusing on the natural world to generate meaning.[51] Subjective input was eliminated, and sciences based on the immediate datum of experience were declared superstition. As knowledge was objectified, producing mental abstractions and mechanical laws, the individual came to be viewed as an isolated body whose existence in the world was accidental, without further meaning or purpose. Humanity no longer considered itself a part of the universe it could only become its conqueror, transforming science into the method to achieve power and domination, instead of knowledge, to disguise its lack thereof. Landauer stated,

> But they do not have you [spirit], and therefore they replace you. Therefore they concoct their illusory counterfeit, the surrogate product of their historical patch work and their scientific laws: they recognize only one convincing general principle that forms, correlates and coordinates details and connects scattered facts, namely: science. Indeed science is spirit, order, unity and solidarity: when it is science. But when it is a swindle and monkey-business, when the supposed man of science is only a journalist in disguise… when statistically formulated heaps of facts…claim to be a sort of higher mathematics of history and an infallible instruction-manual

for future life then this so-called science is unspirit, an impediment to the intellect.[52]

This type of science, while producing facts, cannot and must not provide knowledge in the sense of traditional science, because it is, like politics, symptomatic of *arche*. Landauer then contrasted the representative of such scientific thinking, referred to as "professor", whose mind is closed to reality, with the "prophet", whose spirit is fully open and who serves the creation of a future which raises true community from its potentiality within symbols to actuality.[53] While the prophet warns of foreclosing reality, the professor does precisely that, and is, thereby, the statesman's ally.

Both thinkers then proceeded to explain the detrimental effects of *arche*, its statesmen and professors, on the community. As the previous section showed, to maintain itself and the appearance of reality as a system, fluidity and openness, which are natural to social relationships, are hidden and destroyed. Society becomes an infinite deferral of direct engagement[54] in a complex network of expedient reality. Its order is a collection of separated individualities, attributes and representations,[55] coexisting within their enclosed, segmented spaces as, in Landauer's words, "a mad cluster of purposes,"[56] force and self-constraint, interacting alongside the governed nodal points of legislated existence. This rigidification is ultimately incompatible with life, for Landauer argued, "there is clarity only in the land of appearances and words. Where life begins, systems end"[57], so that, "death is the atmosphere between us."[58] Because *arche* requires repetition, society grows ever more dehumanising. Totalitarian politics and the ideological mass movements which Landauer and Voegelin encountered in Wilhelmine Germany and the Third Reich respectively, appear to be not an aberration from politics, but, rather, the logical path of *arche*. To explore, in contrast to this society, the possibilities for *true* community, *this* differentiation between substitute and reality must be restored.

Returning to reality

The starting point Landauer and Voegelin appear to agree, is the individual herself and, more precisely, her spirit (Landauer) or consciousness (Voegelin),[59] constituting for both thinkers the most primary reality which generates knowledge before any intermediary, such as politics, could interfere with its experience. For Voegelin, to break the illusion of imaginative second reality was possible because,

> There is no imaginative oblivion without remembrance…There is, furthermore, no remembrance or oblivion without the existential consciousness to which the acts in reflective distance pertain. And finally, there is no existential consciousness without the reality in which it is conscious of occurring…[60]

In other words, reality can merely be *hidden* through oblivion, but it cannot be *destroyed*. The nature of reality is such that the fact of existence itself will arouse remembrance of it- usually when the symbols of imaginative reality, e.g. the racist state, cease to have meaning in the reality in which they occur, revealing the limits of their doctrinal truths. Reality re-asserts itself by penetrating the experience of being, for example through encounters or events whose meaning transcends the logical and fathomable realm of senses and reason, and, as unfathomable mystery, arouses "awe" within consciousness. "The total being", Voegelin wrote, "is an apex of mind, animal and vegetative animation, inanimate matter. Death, sleep, dream, illness, fear, ecstasy, mystical submersion to God, spiritual self-involvement of meditation, all of which serve as a vantage point for speculation."[61] According to Voegelin mystery, which raises questions about the "what for?", "where from and to?" and "why?" of existence, is a basic every day experience of reality. Thus, he stated,

> Man is not a self-created, autonomous being carrying the origin and meaning of his existence within himself. He is not a divine *causa sui;* from the experience of his life in precarious existence within the limits of birth and death there rather arises the wondering question about the ultimate ground, the *aitia* or *proto arche*, of all reality and specifically his own…this questioning is inherent in man's experience of himself at all times.[62]

Landauer described this speculative moment and the awakening of individual spirit in a similar way, especially in his philosophical masterpiece *Skepsis und Mystik*.[63] While being in the world implies the continuous generation of new and different sense experiences, reflected in language metaphors, he argued, experience also transcends the grasp of senses and language. He identified the *Seelenhafte,* the "function of the endless universe"[64] within the individual as the locus of the universe's self-revelation and the individual's non-linguistic, non-rational, mystical access to the world, disclosing the unattainability of absolute knowledge of the world. Through its *Seelenhafte* the individual is united with the world, yet only to the extent that the individual grows to know that it cannot know its essence. While the root of human existence lies within the world, the world also mysteriously transcends it, so that all reality can be experienced at once as being and beyond being.[65] This mystical access cannot be lost, but only forgotten, for "the connection is never broken, but our superficial mind cannot remember its origins, cannot recognise the ever-present source in ourselves, and not allow it to flourish."[66] Spirit then creates a new *Weltanschauung* from *both* of these levels of experience as the foundation for action in the world.[67]

For both Landauer and Voegelin, therefore, the key to overcoming the separation of knowing and being lies, quite simply, in "unprecedented, intense, deep experience."[68] According to Landauer experience reveals that "[e]verything that appears to us as separated, is in the reality of infinite space und infinite time only a single, large connected whole."[69] The feeling that humanity is simply the sum of its individual components is but "human perception as it is served by the individual organs of our senses."[70] Nothing, least of all the individual, could be summoned under the principle of *arche*. Hence, he decided that,

> I leave behind the only thing that seems certain within myself; I now float into the uncertain world of hypotheses and fantasies. I reject the certainty of my I so that I can bear life. I try to build myself a new world, knowing that I do not really have any ground to build it on...Just like someone who jumps into the water to kill himself, I jump into the world- but instead of death, I find life.[71]

Instead of transforming the world "into the spirit of man, or into the spirit of our brain,"[72] which had dragged the world down to that which could be grasped by reason and the senses, Landauer sought to raise himself to the world. The world is "unfathomably rich," he wrote, "the world is without language. Language, the intellect, cannot serve us in bringing the world closer. But as a speechless part of nature the human being transforms itself into everything, because it touches everything. This is where mysticism begins."[73] Mysticism is a deep, intense experience of being, of letting oneself "be grasped and seized by it. Until now everything has been divided into a poor, weak, active I and an unapproachable rigid, lifeless, passive world. Let us instead be the medium of the world, both active and passive."[74] The human being does not just perceive the world as a reality that lies outside of it, she is herself already the world. This will be experienced "by all who…are able to recreate the original chaos in themselves and to become spectators at the drama of their own desires and deepest secrets."[75]

Landauer's argument of "becoming the medium of the world" resonates with what Voegelin described as "participation in the ground of being whose logos has to be brought to clarity through the meditative exegesis of itself. The illusion of a 'theory' had to give way to the reality of the meditative process; and this process had to go through its phases of increasing experience and insight."[76] Just like Landauer advised not to limit knowledge of the world to that which the "brain" can grasp, Voegelin warned of wanting to create objectively verifiable theories and generically valid propositions regarding the ground of being,[77] because its structure can only truly be verified experientially, through personal experience and a reflective-meditative process. Both Landauer and Voegelin concluded that the "world" or "ground of being", implicating those realms that lie beyond sense experience, intellect and reason, is not something *outside* of the individual that can be explored from the separated position of the observer, but that it is, rather, already *within* the individual. The experience of being the world, of participating in the ground of being, renders a distinction between an inside and outside, objective and subjective superfluous.

The deeper the individual dives into herself, becoming the world, the more she also *separates* herself from the *arche* of reality, with its supposedly isolated, concrete and autonomous bodies that form society; it is an *an-archist* inward movement. Landauer referred to this process of re-uniting with true reality as "separation" from false reality, which constitutes, simultaneously, a form of self-annihilation, because the imaginative "I kills itself so that the world-I can live."[78] An anarchist kills only himself, Landauer wrote, "in the mystical sense, in order to be reborn after having descended into the depths of their soul".[79] An anarchist is someone who, through separation, becomes a nobody in the terms of society, moving beyond all names, race, colour, country or nation and who yet becomes a somebody in the highest, spiritual sense of the term by reconnecting to true community. The specific quality of the anarchist's "world-I" is that it has no quality, because the annihilated soul that has become conscious to itself knows that it cannot know itself fully, and that no attributes can serve to characterise its own or any other individual's being. Thus,

> The way to a newer, higher form of human society passes by the dark, fatal gate of our instincts and the *terra abscondita*- the "hidden land" of our soul, which is our world. This world can only be constructed from within. We can discover this land, this rich world, if we're able to create a new kind of human being through chaos and anarchy, through unprecedented, intense, deep experience. Each one of us has to do this.[80]

This process of separation is reflected in Voegelin's description of the re-uniting of knowing and being, to which he gave the Greek term *anamnesis*, or remembrance.[81] According to Voegelin, *anamnesis* is to bring to the presence of knowledge that which has wrongly been forgotten, revealing it as knowledge in the mode of oblivion, where it has aroused such existential unrest that it had to be raised to knowledge through remembrance. Precisely, *anamnesis* is the remembrance of experiences that have "opened sources of excitation, from which issue the urge to further philosophical reflection", such as experiences of transcendence in space, time, matter, dreams, etc. Through its recalling of truths about the immanent and transcendent structure of the real or about the "order of reality", *anamnesis* constitutes a process of unlearning and unknowing of the imaginative limitations of the second reality, recovering "the human condition revealing itself in consciousness, when it is smothered by the debris of opaque symbols."[82]

For both Landauer and Voegelin the process of re-connection is an experiential descending into consciousness, or spirit, with the aim of clearing out, in Voegelin's words, "all ideological junk to make the *conditio humana* visible once again."[83] In particular, Voegelin proposed the method of recounting childhood or pre-reflective experiences that had raised questions about mind and reality, moments of awareness "that cause one to apprehend some part of reality as opaque, as something that calls for interpretation."[84] However, the interpretation of awe inducing moments does not remain a purely personal and individual endeavour, but the interpretation of consciousness also implies a re-interpretation of one's relationships to reality. According to Voegelin, one remembers moments that impel

> toward reflection and do so because they have excited consciousness to the "awe" of existence. The nature of the irrupting experiences and of the excitations they induce, together with the result of an "attunement" of consciousness to its "problems" seem to me to be the determinants on which depend the radicalism and the breadth of philosophical reflection.[85]

Hence, Voegelin considered *anamnesis* to be the precondition for philosophy, as only "recapturing reality in opposition to its contemporary deformation…"[86] made possible a genuine, unmediated and direct reflection on reality.

It is precisely within Landauer's and Voegelin's theorisation of respectively the soul and consciousness, which, both urged, needs to be actively reclaimed from the influence of the second reality and can only be done so by the individual herself that a common, anarchic claim can be found. It begins with Voegelin's insistence that to search for an operational definition of consciousness and of the experience of consciousness would defeat the purpose of its exploration. This is because generically valid propositions about the experience of consciousness cannot, by the virtue of consciousness being the very first reality of personal experience, be given from another or from the outside. By virtue of it experiencing not only immanent but also transcendent, unfathomable reality consciousness lies beyond the reach of rational and formal logic.[87] Hence,

All philosophising about consciousness is an event in the consciousness of the philosopher and presupposes this consciousness
together with its structures. Inasmuch as the consciousness of
philosophising is not "pure" consciousness, but rather the consciousness of a human being, all philosophising is an event in the
philosopher's life history; an event in the history of the community
with its symbolic language; an event in the history of mankind, and
of the cosmos. No "human" in his reflection on consciousness and
its nature can make consciousness an "object" to be confronted;
the reflection is rather an orientation within consciousness with
which he can push to its limits but never cross them.[88]

Consciousness, in other words, can only be understood through
the experience of the person to whom it belongs, allowing only
the individual herself direct and unmediated insight into reality
and stepping out of the second reality. These new insights arising
from consciousness have a fundamental impact on the concep-
tualisation of the possibilities and aims of community and are
worthwhile to be explored in more detail.

According to Voegelin, consciousness appears situated within
and contained by the body, functioning to make its specific external reality intelligible.[89] And yet, the concept of body, matter,
or corporeality itself is also already contained *within* consciousness, so that consciousness is ultimately experienced no less real
than reality itself. Accordingly, it is not a mere thing, but rather a
mysterious force somehow distinguished from thingness. It both
"intends reality" as its object and makes reality "luminous"[90] by
experiencing and philosophising about the "awe of existence."[91]
Consciousness is enclosed from the cosmos surrounding it, as
well as being itself a cosmic principle.[92] Through this particular
"in-betweenness" consciousness experiences additional being that
is other than the existent things and which, therefore, can only
be known in its attributes, but not in its essence. To describe this
peculiar structure of consciousness, Voegelin used the Greek term
metaxy, designating an intermediary and intermediate reality.[93]
Anamnesis, then, really refers to the remembrance of *metaxy*, of
the lasting tension between the intelligible and the unattainable,
"between life and death, immortality and mortality, perfection
and imperfection, time and timelessness, between order and disorder, truth and untruth, sense and senselessness."[94]

When consciousness becomes explicit to itself, Voegelin argued, it unsurprisingly provokes fundamental bewilderment, because

> At the centre of his existence man is unknown to himself and must remain so…this situation of ignorance with regard to the decisive core of existence is more than disconcerting: it is profoundly disturbing for from the depth of this ultimate ignorance wells up the anxiety of existence.[95]

Moreover, "[r]eality is not a static order of things given to a human observer once and for all; it is moving, indeed, in the direction of the emergent truth."[96] Because the beyond has an indefinite number of meanings, revealing itself to every person differently, constituting, "different events in the philosopher's life,"[97] meaning does not repeat itself but reality remains in constant motion. Thus, everyone undergoes constant change and flux as moments of reality's disclosure follow one upon another, producing continuous becoming and difference. The "I" is in a constant process of unfolding, being new in every moment of its existence, so that selfhood never comes to an end and ultimately cannot be achieved, making attempts for reification superfluous and revealing multiplicity as something that not only occurs between, but within human beings, whose substance is essential instability. From the realisation that this flux of being constitutes being in the sense that one cannot exempt oneself from it, the belief that human beings are merely being added to reality, or objects that simply exist within reality is no longer tenable and the safety that came with that view dissolves.

Landauer was aware of this, too, when he stated, "I leave behind the only thing that seems certain within myself. I now flood out into the uncertain world of hypotheses and fantasies."[98] To make reality luminous through consciousness or spirit is not to find *arche,* a first principle or firm ground, but it is, on the contrary, to realise that the "why?" and "what for?" that aroused the quest remain unintelligible and must do so. While the horizon of the beyond lures to be made intelligible, Voegelin argued, it withdraws itself with every step that the seeker advances.[99] Hence, when Voegelin spoke of the luminosity of the reality of being he did not refer to reaching an objective fact of truth. Rather, he meant the movement from suffering from estrangement from the prevalent

order toward suffering from bewilderment about the "order of being."[100] In short, to be conscious of one's existence is to know that
one knows nothing at all, that no further answer is possible.[101]

A first implication of Landauer's and Voegelin's argument is
a certain democratisation of mystical experience, which, rather
than being an elitist affair of a few select individuals, appears to
be a universally accessible, natural component of conscious everyday experience. Voegelin scholar Morrissey summarised the
situation as such:

> These experiences cannot be proved any more than sense experience
> can be proved. Yet there is nothing esoteric about such experiences.
> Insofar as everyone experiences reality, everyone has experiences of
> transcendence, at least on a limited level. A philosopher who experi-
> ences his or her consciousness as transcending discovers the ground
> of philosophizing, and no special belief is required to substantiate
> it, for it is self-evident. To deny the self-transcending nature of one's
> consciousness would be to deny one's own experience. Such a denial
> is certainly possible, but then one would not be operating rationally;
> one would be closed to the reality one is trying to investigate. One
> may arrive at a number of different conclusions but one cannot in
> good faith deny the nature of transcending consciousness.[102]

Thus, it can be argued that the shared anarchist element in
Landauer and Voegelin is precisely their emphasis on both grasp-
ing one's own life and search, one's direct and unmediated relationship with reality as the primary instrument in the quest for reality, and this relationship being accessible, theoretically, to every
consciousness. This is also the reason why Landauer, when seeking to define anarchism, strictly warned against considering it a
system of thought and action to be brought to all of humanity. For
Landauer this constituted an imposition of one's own idea of freedom on others that was no different from the violence anarchists
sought to oppose. Rather, he stated, anarchism was a mode of
being, "a matter of how one lives" in the present here and now.[103]

While it has been argued that Voegelin was highly critical of anarchism, his essays on the topic, dealing with Bakunin, Kropotkin,
Tolstoy, Gandhi and Warren, reveal that he, rather, shared the same
criticism which Landauer raised against anarchists of the deed.[104]

Both Voegelin and Landauer, though Landauer has not criticised the particular anarchists named above, considered naive the belief in the perfectibility of the human situation, which assumes that the destruction of the state would release a natural instinct for freedom and peace. According to Voegelin this belief failed to recognise that the state and its politics are symbols created to overcome the *metaxy's* tension, which, defining the human situation, cannot be overcome. Voegelin's criticism thus targeted a specific misconception, which attached concrete problems of injustice, inequality and violence to an imaginary and generalised evil, rather than anarchism *per se*.[105] Likewise, Voegelin's criticism of utopian thought did not simply condemn radically idealistic thought, but the creations of blueprints which, rather than seeking luminous knowledge from within the *metaxy*, built their visions of an ideal society on the eradication of either pole of existence, thereby limiting, rather than fostering, society's becoming.[106] Consequently, Voegelin's mistrust of the masses was the fear that, rallied under such promises, liberation might turn totalitarian.

Yet, Voegelin did not promote political quietism. On the contrary, he argued,

> One can, indeed, not root out traditional vices at a moment's notice; but there is a limit beyond which delay is impermissible. And that all men are not good and therefore all things cannot be well, is sound admonition to a perfectionist; but it easily can become a cover for condoning crimes. What makes this argument so flat is the renunciation of the spirit as the ultimate authority beyond the temporal order and its insufficiencies.[107]

Much in line with Landauer, Voegelin stated that genuine change could occur only from embracing the nature of reality in the *metaxy* and proceeding in a process of trial and error, or, as Landauer argued, experimentation and learning. Through failure one learns and fails better. According to Voegelin, axioms, principles or categorical imperatives, as they occurred, for example, in the sacred texts which Gandhi and Tolstoy used, had no bearing in reality. Rather, they exposed *human imperfection* and its failures that result from conscious participation in the tension of existence. Voegelin's major criticism of Christianity, thus, concerned its disengagement of the life of the spirit from the conditions of any particular society, resulting in political and social passivity,[108] failing to adequately address the problems of concrete, mundane existence.[109] In an explication of the Sermon of the Mount, Voegelin argued,

> We have to recall that the Sermon of the Mount is not a code for the life in the "world"; it is addressed to men who live in between the worlds of eschatological expectation. In historical existence, entangled in the network of social obligations... If he is struck on the right cheek, he will not turn his left, but hit back in defence of his life, his family and his community. But in hitting back, he will do good, as a Christian, to remember the Sermon, and to be aware that in defence he is involved in guilt...[110]

Yet, the anarchists which Voegelin criticised had dealt with the question of change in abstraction, not from the position of a participant in reality, but from that of a spectator, tempted by the unattainable "magic" of perfection.[111] Like Voegelin, Landauer emphasised that his ideas for community creation were "little beginnings, nuclei, cells,"[112] because "reality lies in movement and true socialism is always only beginning, is always only one which moves."[113] He did not "... approach the absolute. A religion, which connects us all, is not be expected. What I call socialism is not perfection, perfection exists only in our words..."[114] Neither from Voegelin nor Landauer a blueprint for community could be expected.

The *an-archist* Community:

Both philosophers conceptualised true community not as being situated in a particular context, it is already everywhere, but as situating. It can only be made intelligible through experience. Only when the link between experience and knowledge of the world is restored can the realisation of its natural community be attempted. According to Landauer, only when one has consciously felt "unprecedented, intense, deep experience", then "anarchists and anarchy exist, in the form of scattered individuals, everywhere. And they will find each other."[115] It follows that,

Whoever brings the lost world in himself to life – to individual life – and whoever feels like a true part of the world and not as a stranger: he will be the one who arrives not knowing where from, and who leaves not knowing where to. To him the world will be what he is to himself. Men such as this will live with each other in solidarity – as men who belong together. This will be anarchy.[116]

While Voegelin appears more pessimistic, his vision resonates with Landauer's, stating that the building block for change is not the masses, but the individual, which, reinterpreting its relationship to the world, also affects social relationships. He stated,

We know what the life of reason and the good society are; we can cultivate the former and try, by our actions, to bring about the latter. We can restate the problem: the formation of the psyche by encouraging participation in transcendent reason... And that is all one can do; whether or not this offer is accepted depends on the Spirit that blows where It pleases. Collectively, as a society, there is at the moment little, if anything, we can do...[117]

Through experience, Landauer and Voegelin argued, the individual gives up the certainty of its particular self, instead opening itself to the universe, or reality, and to the infinite possibilities for existence. When the "world-I" replaces the "I" bewilderment, loss of direction and perplexity replace the simplistic limitations and reductive images which the "I" used to confine its self, others and the world to attune to its imagination. The more one moves inward the more one realises oneself and others not to be pure, undivided individuals, but rather "points of passage, electrical sparks of something greater,"[118] namely the "unbreakable chain that comes from infinite and proceeds to the infinite,"[119] toward the "most ancient and most complete community."[120] Landauer's true anarchist community proceeds from this unbreakable community, that one finds "in the deepest depths of our selves".[121] "Our most individual", he continued, "is our ever most common."[122] Humanity is but the term for an "alliance of the plenty".[123]

For Voegelin, as already established above, the tension of the *metaxy* and the continuous motion of existence constituted the universal structure of consciousness. "Man" Voegelin argued, "is man insofar as he is *Imago Dei,* and insofar as he is *Imago*

Dei are all men equal as participating in the reality of God..."[124] Consequently, "the existence of man becomes existence in community. In the openness of the common spirit there develops the public life of society."[125] In other words,

> With regard to the transcendent source of order in the soul, all men are equal. The discovery of transcendent divinity as the source of order is paralleled by the discovery of mankind. 'Mankind' in this sense is not a particular group of human beings at any given time, but indeed the 'open society' of all men extending into the unknown future. The idea of 'mankind' has nothing to do with the idea of a 'world-government' established over a group of contemporaneously living human beings.[126]

Voegelin's "open society", influenced by Henri Bergson's "Open Society,"[127] is not a concrete society existing in the world, but a "symbol which indicates man's consciousness of participating, in his earthly existence, in the mystery of a reality which moves towards its transfiguration. Universal mankind [or the open society] is an eschatological index."[128] For Voegelin the open society was a guideline for being in the world, shaped by awareness of the *metaxy*. It opens the individual toward transcendent reality and the community of universal mankind, as opposed to the particular, pathologically closed society. It is a form of order that is "knowable only from the perspective of participation in it"[129] because

> The experience of being activates man to the reality of order in himself and in the cosmos... The background of the experience of being is the primary experience of the cosmos in which man is consubstantial with the things of his environment, a partnership that in philosophy is heightened to the wake consciousness of the community of order uniting thought and being.[130]

Voegelin suggested a departure from the model of the polis towards "the *politeia* in the soul, with the perspective that this course opens into existence in a spiritual community beyond temporal organization of government".[131]

Finally, then, the purpose of the *an-archist* community is not merely to transcend the rigidity of second reality and create conditions that allow for multiplicity and becoming, but it is, rather, to increase knowledge of reality. According to Voegelin, "the ultimate, essential ignorance is not complete ignorance. Man can achieve considerable knowledge about the "order of being", and not the least part of that knowledge is the distinction between the knowable and unknowable."[132] While the ultimate essence of reality, which has neither cause, matter, form, nor attributes, cannot be known by humans, the knowledge that *can* be gained is that of seeing the world no longer as self-subsistent truth, but understanding that its various phenomena and events refer to and reflect the reality that belongs to the realm of mystery.[133] The thingness of the world conceals and reflects the metaphysical truth beyond and a higher level of meaning. Voegelin's *Anamnesis* and Landauer's *Separation* are the processes by which these levels of meaning can gradually be unveiled, moving from outwardness to inwardness, penetrating into what appears as fact to move beyond the purely external level of meaning and reach inner significance. The true community, then, not only allows for infinite becoming in a mysterious universe, but for making it more intelligible through direct experience.

Conclusion

This meditation on the works of Landauer and Voegelin serves to suggest a common line of argumentation in two thinkers whose works have not yet been brought into contact with one another, and thereby aims to contribute to a discussion on mystical anarchism. The focus of this meditation was Landauer's and Voegelin's critique not just of a particular type of politics, but of politics as such, constituting a surrogate for true community. Initially, Landauer and Voegelin each sought diagnosis and therapy for the political ills of their respective societies. Yet, rather than finding a particular type of politics to be at fault, they argued that politics *as such* was symptomatic of a more profound disorder. Only when the relationship between direct experience and knowledge of reality was lost did politics arise with the purpose to create a new, imaginary reality in which this loss was hidden and, ultimately, through conserving and protecting the division between experience and knowledge, forgotten. Community, in reality based on openness and fluidity, was replaced with its rigid surrogate, society. Consequently, they argued, the condition of politics can only be overcome through deep experience of reality to restore knowledge of the world and unlearn the illusions of imaginary reality. Landauer referred to this process as "separation", for one leaves behind the particular, closed society, Voegelin as *anamnesis*, or remembrance of the primary reality that had been pushed into oblivion. Landauer's and Voegelin's mysticism is their argument that the multiplicity of existents issues from a single source that is within and yet infinitely transcends the individual, allowing each individual access to her source, but only to the extent that she grows to know that she cannot know her ultimate essence. The potentiality for human community, then, is to be found not in external ordering via politics, but precisely within each individual herself as she becomes the world. The shared anarchic element in Landauer and Voegelin is their argument that only the individual herself has direct, unmediated access to the world with which no intermediary, such as politics, can interfere and therefore has the power, in the present here and now, to reconnect the link between *experience* and *knowledge*.

Notes

1. Landauer has been considered a "Jewish-Christian-Atheist" mystic, Voegelin self identifies as mystical philosopher, arguably in the Christian tradition. Both conceive of mystery not as an object of the external world to be confronted with, but as something knowable only through participation in it. Landauer identifies *spirit,* Voegelin *consciousness* as the locus of reality's self-revelation, which paradoxically experiences reality as an object intended, while also itself occurring in reality. Thus, the human situation is characterised by its participation in a reality that is a mysterious, known unknown. Landauer and Voegelin consider mystery existential; Philosophy is their existential project of expressing this basic experience and seeking adequacy.

2. Voegelin, rather than referring to a common source, speaks of the "ground", *aition,* as it occurs in the philosophy of Plato and Aristotle. Accordingly, "the ground" is not a spatially distant thing but a divine

presence that becomes manifest in the experience of unrest and the desire to know…" *Anamnesis* (Columbia: University of Missouri Press, 1989), 32f. Landauer speaks of an "eternal source." See, for example, "Through Separation to Community", in *Revolution and Other Writings: A Political Reader,* ed. Gabriel Kuhn (Oakland: PM Press, 2010), 106.

3. Gustav Landauer, "Zum Beilis Prozess", in *Der werdende Mensch, Aufsätze über Leben und Schrifttum,* ed. Martin Buber (Weimar: Gustav Kiepenheuer Verlag 1921), 33.

4. Voegelin commonly uses the word "cosmos" to refer to the whole of ordered reality, including animate and inanimate nature and the gods. Eugene Webb, *Eric Voegelin: Philosopher of History* (Seattle: University of Washington Press, 1981), 279.

5. Paul Avrich, *Anarchist Portraits* (Princeton: Princeton University Press, 1988), 248.

6. Kuhn and Wolf cite a letter sent by Landauer to Margarethe Faas-Hardegger in 1908, concerning the description of the *Sozialist's* editors' collective: "You can choose any of the following: 'Socialist-Anarchists' (my favourite), 'Socialists', 'Anarchists' or simply 'Comrades.'" In *Revolution and Other Writings : A Political Reader* (Oakland: PM Press, 2010), 32.

7. According to Kuhn and Wolf several Landauer scholars refer to his ideas as *Antipolitik,* to Landauer as *Anti-Politiker.* Landauer began to refer to himself as such during the late 1890s with reference to Friedrich Nietzsche's critique of politics in *Ecce Homo.* In *Revolution and Other Writings: A Political Reader* (Oakland: PM Press, 2010), 25. In 2010, Wolf edited two volumes entitled *Antipolitik,* a collection of newspaper articles, speeches, letters and essays dealing with the theme. Gustav Landauer, *Antipolitik: Gustav Landauer, Ausgewählte Schriften, Band 3.1* (and *3.2.*), ed. Siegbert Wolf (Lich/Hessen: Verlag Edition AV, 2010).

8. Buber is frequently cited by Voegelin, in particular his biblical studies. See, for example, *Israel and Revelation* (Baton Rouge: Louisiana State University Press, 2001).

9. After Landauer's death, Buber edited his articles into the books *Der werdende Mensch* (1921), *Beginner* (1924), *Gustav Landauer, sein Lebensgang in Briefen* (1929).

10. Gustav Landauer, "Goethe's Politik", in *Der Werdende Mensch, Aufsätze über Leben und Schrifttum,* ed. Martin Buber (Weimar: Gustav Kiepenheuer Verlag, 1921), 142, my translation.

11. Gustav Landauer, "Twenty Five Years later, on the Jubilee of Wilhelm II", in *Revolution and Other Writings: A Political Reader,* ed. Gabriel Kuhn (Oakland: PM Press, 2010), 64. Landauer continues, "This is why I was (without knowing the word at the time) an anarchist before I was a socialist, one of the few who had not taken a detour via social democracy."

12. *Die Jungen (Young Ones)* opposed the SPD, which had transformed into a mass party, setting the tone in national socialist politics. They criticised its bureaucratic and centralised authority, its passivity and tactical reformism. Instead, *Die Jungen* proposed a libertarian alternative to state politics. Banned from the opposition they formed the *Verein unabhängiger Sozialisten,* which subsequently campaigned in favour of anti-parliamentarism and anarchism. See, for example, Eugene Lunn, *Prophet of Community* (Santa Barbara: University of California Press, 1973), 55ff.

13. ibid, 80ff.

14. Hochheim, Eckhart, and Gustav Landauer, *Meister Eckhart's Mystische Schriften: In Unsere Sprache Übertragen von Gustav Landauer,* ed. Gustav Landauer (Leipzig: Insel Verlag, 1991).

15. Joachim Willems explores the extent to which Landauer relies on the ideas of Meister Eckhar in *Religiöser Gehalt des Anarchismus und anarchistischer Gehalt der Religion, die jüdisch-christich-atheistische Mystik Gustav Landauers zwischen Meister Eckhart und Martin Buber* (Albeck: Verlag Ulmer Manuskripte, 2001).

16. During the *November Revolution* after WWI members of the Independent SPD (USPD) under leadership of Landauer's friend Kurt Eisner overthrew the Bavarian monarchy in 1918 and declared Bavaria the first German state to become a republic. The USPD established thousands of councils across Bavaria through which groups with various interests, such as workers, peasants, soldiers or students, self-governed.

17. Charles Maurer, *Call to Revolution: The Mystical Anarchism of Gustav Landauer* (Detroit: Wayne State University Press, 1971), 180.

18. Eric Voegelin, *Published Essays 1966–1985* (Baton Rouge: Louisiana State University Press, 1990), 55.

19. Ellis Sandoz, *The Voegelinian Revolution* (Baton Rouge: Louisiana State University Press, 1981), 22.

20. Eric Voegelin, *Race and State* (Baton Rouge: Louisiana State University Press, 1977*), The History of the Race Idea* (Baton Rouge: Louisiana State University Press, 1998).

21. Clifford F. Porter, "Eric Voegelin on Nazi Political Extremism," *Journal of the History of Ideas* 63 (2002): 151, 156.

22. John J. Ranieri, *Eric Voegelin and the Good Society* (Columbia: University of Missouri Press, 1995), 204.

23. Gustav Landauer, "Twenty Five Years Later: On the Jubilee of Wilhelm II," in *Revolution and Other Writings: A Political Reader,* ed. Gabriel Kuhn (Oakland: PM Press, 2010), 64.

24. Gustav Landauer, "Weak Statesmen, weaker people", in *Revolution and Other Writings: A Political Reader,* ed. Gabriel Kuhn (Oakland: PM Press, 2010), 214.

25. Landauer's view of power was influenced by his reading and translation of French, 16th century philosopher Étienne de La Boétie's *Discours sur la Servitude Volontaire.* Boétie argued that a tyrant's oppression of the people required the people's voluntary subservience. All it needed to overcome servitude was the individual's will to be free. Instead of overthrowing the tyrant the task was to stop obeying it. "Revolution" in *Revolution and Other Writings* (Oakland: PM Press, 2010), 155f.

26. Gustav Landauer, "Die Botschaft der Titanic", in *Der werdende Mensch, Aufsätze über Leben und Schrifttum,* ed. Martin Buber (Weimar: Gustav Kiepenheuer Verlag, 1921), translated in Eugene Lunn, *Prophet of Community* (University of California Press, 1973), 158.

27. Gustav Landauer, "Tucker's Revelation", in *Revolution and other Writings: A Political Reader,* ed. Gabriel Kuhn (Oakland: Pm Press, 2010), 249.

28. The reason for this lack of meaning will be discussed in the third section.

29. Gustav Landauer, "Call to Socialism", http://theanarchistlibrary. org/library/gustav-landauer-call-to-socialism, 17.

30. Gustav Landauer, "Revolution", in *Revolution and Other Writings: A Political Reader,* ed. Gabriel Kuhn (Oakland: PM Press, 2010), 173.

31. Gustav Landauer, "Das erste Flugblatt: Was will der kapitalistische Bund?", in *Antipolitik: Gustav Landauer, Ausgewählte Schriften, Band 3.1,* ed. Siegbert Wolf (Lich/Hessen: Verlag Edition AV, 2010), 140.

32. Gustav Landauer, "Revolution" in *Revolution and Other Writings: A Political Reader,* ed. Gabriel Kuhn (Oakland: PM Press, 2010), 135.

33. Gustav Landauer, "Sind das Ketzergedanken", in *Der werdende Mensch, Aufsätze über Leben und Schrifttum,* ed. Martin Buber (Weimar: Gustav Kiepenheuer Verlag, 1921), 142.

34. Gustav Landauer, "Volk und Land, Dreissig sozialistische Thesen", in *Antipolitik: Gustav Landauer, Ausgewählte Schriften, Band 3.1,* ed. Siegbert Wolf (Lich/Hessen: Verlag Edition AV, 2010), 121.

35. Gustav Landauer, "Sind das Ketzergedanken", in *Der werdende Mensch, Aufsätze über Leben und Schrifttum,* ed. Martin Buber (Weimar: Gustav Kiepenheuer Verlag, 1921), 142.

36. Benjamin Tucker, *Instead of a Book: By a Man too Busy to Write One: A Fragmentary Exposition of Political Anarchism* (Vulgus Press, 2011), 112, Tucker's emphasis.

37. Gustav Landauer, "Einkehr", in *Antipolitik: Gustav Landauer, Ausgewählte Schriften, Band 3.1,* ed. Siegbert Wolf (Lich/Hessen: Verlag Edition AV, 2010), 108.

38. Eric Voegelin, *Race and State* (Baton Rouge: Louisiana State University Press, 1977).

39. ibid, 150.

40. The third section will explore Voegelin's claim about the importance of humanity having been created as *Imago Dei* in more detail.

41. Eric Voegelin, *Race and State* (Baton Rouge: Louisiana State University Press, 1977), 152.

42. Eric Voegelin, *Hitler and the Germans* (Columbia: University of Missouri Press 2003), 108.

43. ibid.

44. ibid, 58.

45. Gustav Landauer, "Through Separation to Community" in *Revolution and Other Writings* (Oakland: PM Press, 2010), 100.

46. This non-linguistic, non rational experience will be explained in further detail in the next section.

47. Gustav Landuer, "Through Separation to Community" in *Revolution and Other Writings* (Oakland: PM Press, 2010), 99.

48. ibid, 100.

49. As in Voegelin, "symbol" refers to the expression of the experience of being, which, because it contains non-rational and non-linguistic elements, can only be metaphorical and open.

50. This will also be explained in more detail in the next section.

51. ibid, "Revolution", 136f.

52. Gustav Landauer, "Call to Socialism", http://theanarchistlibrary.org/library/gustav-landauer-call-to-socialism, 24.

53. ibid.

54. Gustav Landauer, "Vom geistigen Privileg", in *Antipolitik. 3.1,* ed. Siegbert Wolf (Lich/Hessen: Verlag Edition AV, 2010), 89.

55. Eugene Lunn, *Prophet of Community, The Romantic Socialism of Gustav Landauer* (Berkeley: University of California Press, 1973), 106. Landauer distinguishes between *Gemeinschaft* (community), possible only when people come together freely through spirit, and *Gesellschaft* (society), a mechanistic sum of individuals that occurs within the state.

56. Gustav Landauer, "Volk und Land. Dreissig sozialistische Thesen", in *Antipolitik. 3.1,* ed. Siegbert Wolf (Lich/Hessen: Verlag Edition AV, 2010), 117.

57. Gustav Landauer, "Anarchic Thoughts on Anarchism," in *Revolution and other Writings,* ed. Gabriel Kuhn (Oakland: PM Press, 2010), 91.

58. Gustav Landauer, "Call to Socialism", http://theanarchistlibrary. org/library/gustav-landauer-call-to-socialism, 12.

59. Further investigation into the different conceptualisations of soul and consciousness may be required. Landauer's conception of soul is detailed in "Revolution," *Revolution and Other Writings: A Political Reader*, ed. Gabriel Kuhn (Oakland: PM Press, 2010); Voegelin's conception of consciousness is detailed in *In Search of Order* (Columbia: University of Missouri Press, 2000), a short introduction follows below.

60. Eric Voegelin, *In Search of Order* (Columbia: University of Missouri Press, 2000), 56.

61. Eric Voegelin, *Race and State* (Baton Rouge: Louisiana State University Press, 1977), 19.

62. Eric Voegelin, *Anamnesis* (Columbia: University of Missouri Press, 2002), 92ff.

63. Gustav Landauer, "Skepsis und Mystik, Versuche im Anschluss an Mauthner's Sprachkritik", http://www.weltrevolution.net/zeit/ Landauer2.htm.

64. ibid, my translation.

65. Gustav Landauer, "Through Separation to Community", in *Revolution and Other Writings: A Political Reader*, ed. Gabriel Kuhn (Oakland: PM Press, 2010), 106.

66. ibid, 211.

67. See, for example, Gustav Landauer, "Revolution", in *Revolution and Other Writings: A Political Reader*, ed. Gabriel Kuhn (Oakland: PM Press, 2010), 136.

68. ibid, "Anarchic Thoughts on Anarchism", 88.

69. Gustav Landauer, "Zur Entwicklungsgeschichte", in *Signatur G.L. Gustav Landauer im Sozialist (1892–1899)*, ed. Ruth Link Salinger (Frankfurt am Main: Surhkamp, 1995), 330, my translation.

70. ibid, 329, my translation.

71. Gustav Landauer, "Through Separation to Community", in *Revolution and Other Writings: A Political Reader*, ed. Gabriel Kuhn (Oakland: PM Press, 2010), 97.

72. ibid, 98.

73. Gustav Landauer, *Skepsis und Mystik,* Versuche im Anschluss an Mauthner's Sprachkritik", http://www.weltrevolution.net/zeit/Landauer2.htm p. 6, my translation.

74. Gustav Landauer, "Through Separation to Community", in *Revolution and Other Writings: A Political Reader,* ed. Gabriel Kuhn (Oakland: PM Press, 2010), 98.

75. ibid, "Anarchic Thoughts on Anarchism", 88.

76. Eric Voegelin, *Anamnesis* (Columbia: University of Missouri Press, 1989), 33.

77. See footnote 2, further clarification below.

78. Gustav Landauer, "Through Separation to Community", in *Revolution and Other Writings: A Political Reader,* ed. Gabriel Kuhn (Oakland: PM Press, 2010), 96.

79. ibid, "Anarchic Thoughts on Anarchism," 89

80. ibid, 88.

81. Eric Voegelin, *Anamnesis* (Columbia: University of Missouri Press 2002), 84ff.

82. Eric Voegelin, "Hurried over the Face of the Earth", in *Robert B. Heilman and Eric Voegelin: A Friendship in letters, 1944–1984,* ed. Robert B. Heilman (Columbia: University of Missouri Press, 2004), 242.

83. Eric Voegelin, *Hitler and the Germans* (Columbia: University of Missouri Press, 1999), 72.

84. Keulman, Kenneth, *The Balance of Consciousness: Eric Voegelin's Political Theory* (University Park: University of Pennsylvania Press, 1990), 56.

85. Eric Voegelin, *Anamnesis* (Columbia: University of Missouri Press, 2002), 84.

86. Eric Voegelin, *Autobiographical Reflections* (Columbia: University of Missouri Press, 2006), 121.

87. ibid, 33.

88. Eric Voegelin, *Anamnesis* (Columbia: University of Missouri Press, 2002), 81.

89. Eric Voegelin, *In Search of Order* (Columbia: University of Missouri Press, 2000), 29.

90. ibid.

91. ibid, 30.

92. Eric Voegelin, *Plato and Aristotle* (Columbia: University of Missouri Press, 2000), 16.

93. Eric Voegelin, *In Search of Order* (Columbia: University of Missouri Press, 2000), 30ff.

94. Eric Voegelin, *Published Essays 1966–1985* (Baton Rouge: Louisiana State University Press, 1990), 176.

95. Eric Voegelin, *Israel and Revelation* (Columbia: University of Missouri Press, 2001), 1.

96. Eric Voegelin, *The Ecumenic Age* (Columbia: University of Missouri Press, 1980), 217.

97. ibid, 133f.

98. Gustav Landauer, "Through Separation to Community", in *Revolution and Other Writings: A Political Reader,* ed. Gabriel Kuhn (Oakland: PM Press, 2010), 96.

99. Eric Voegelin, "Wisdom and the magic of the extreme", in *Published Essays 1966–1985* (Baton Rouge: Louisiana State University Press, 1990), 326.

100. ibid, 318.

101. ibid, 337.

102. Michael P. Morrissey, *Consciousness and Transcendence: The Theology of Eric Voegelin* (Notre Dame: University of Notre Dame Press, 1994), 43.

103. Gustav Landauer, "Anarchic Thoughts on Anarchism", in *Revolution and other writings: A Political Reader,* ed. Gabriel Kuhn (Oakland: PM Press, 2010), 86.

104. Eric Voegelin, "Revolutionary Existence: Bakunin" and "Bakunin: The Anarchist", in *From Enlightenment to Revolution,* ed. John H. Hallowell (Durham: Duke University Press, 1975), Eric Voegelin, "On John R. Commons", in *On the Form of the American*

Mind (Baton Rouge: Louisiana State University Press, 1995). See the section "Politics and political science as imaginary reality" above.

105. ibid.

106. Eric Voegelin, "More's *Utopia*", in *Published Essays, 1940–1952*, ed. Ellis Sandoz (Baton Rouge: Louisiana State University Press, 2000).

107. ibid, 203.

108. Eric Voegelin, *Israel and Revelation* (Baton Rouge: Louisiana State University Press, 2001), 227f.

109. A more detailed discussion of this can be found in Ranieri's *Eric Voegelin and the Good Society* (Columbia: University of Missouri Press, 1995).

110. Eric Voegelin, *Crisis and the Apocalypse of Man* (Baton Rouge: University of Missouri Press, 1999), 281.

111. Eric Voegelin, "Wisdom and the Magic of the Extreme: A Meditation", in *Published Essays 1966–1985* (Baton Rouge: Louisiana State University Press, 1990).

112. Gustav Landauer, "Das erste Flugblatt: Was will der sozialistische Bund?", *Antipolitik: Gustav Landauer, Ausgewählte Schriften, Band 3.1*, ed. Siegbert Wolf (Lich/Hessen: Verlag Edition AV, 2010), 139.

113. Gustav Landauer, "Das dritte Flugblatt: Die Siedlung", in *Antipolitik 3.1*. ed Siegbert Wolf (Lich/Hessen: Verlag Editino AV, 2010), 60.

114. Gustav Landauer, "Fragen und Antworten", in *Der werdende Mensch, Aufsätze über Leben und Schrifttum* ed. Martin Buber (Weimar: Gustav Kiepenheuer Verlag, 1921), 32, my translation.

115. Gustav Landauer, "Revolution", in *Revolution and other writings: A Political Reader,* ed. Gabriel Kuhn (Oakland: PM Press, 2010), 88.

116. ibid, 89.

117. Eric Voegelin, "Industrial Society in Search of Reason", in *World Technology and Human Destiny,* ed. Raymond Aron (Ann Arbor: University of Michigan Press, 1963), 43. Quoted in John J. Ranieri, *Eric Voegelin and the Good Society* (Columbia: University of Missouri Press, 1995), 201.

118. Gustav Landauer, "Through Separation to Community", in *Revolution and other writings: A Political Reader,* ed. Gabriel Kuhn (Oakland: PM Press, 2010), 101.

119. ibid, 103.

120. ibid, 95.

121. ibid, 105.

122. ibid.

123. Gustav Landauer, "Zum Beilis Prozess", in *Der werdende Mensch, Aufsätze über Leben und Schrifttum,* ed. Martin Buber (Weimar: Gustav Kiepenheuer Verlag 1921), 33.

124. Eric Voegelin, *Hitler and the Germans* (Columbia: University of Missouri Press, 1999), 205.

125. Eric Voegelin, "The German University and the Order of Society", in *Published Essays 1966–1985* (Baton Rouge: Louisiana State University Press, 1990), 7.

126. Eric Voegelin, *Nature of the Law and Related Legal Writings* (Baton Rouge: Louisiana State University Press, 1991), 76ff.

127. Henri Bergson, *Les deux sources de la morale et de la religion* (Paris: Presses universitaires de France, 1932).

128. Eric Voegelin, "Immortality: Experience and Symbol", in *Harvard Theological Review* 60 (1967), 239.

129. Eric Voegelin, *Israel and Revelation* (Columbia: University of Missouri Press, 2001), 1.

130. Eric Voegelin, *Anamnesis* (Columbia: University of Missouri Press, 2002), 80.

131. Eric Voegelin, *Plato and Aristotle* (Columbia: University of Missouri Press, 2000), 171.

132. Eric Voegelin, *Israel and Revelation* (Columbia: University of Missouri Press, 2001), 40ff.

133. Eric, Voegelin, *The New Science of Politics* (Chicago: University of Chicago Press, 1987), 61.

References

Avrich, Paul. *Anarchist Portraits*. Princeton: Princeton University Press, 1988.

Bergson, Henri. *Les deux sources de la morale et de la religion*. Paris: Presses universitaires de France, 1932.

Hinz, Thorsten. *Mystik und Anarchie, Meister Eckhart und seine Bedeutung im Denken Gustav Landauers*. Berlin: Karin Kramer, 2000.

Hochheim, Eckhart and Gustav Landauer. *Meister Eckhart, mystische Schriften: In Unsere Sprache Übertragen von Gustav Landauer*. Leipzig: Insel Verlag, 1991.

Hyman, Ruth Link-Salinger. *Gustav Landauer, Philosopher of Utopia*. Indianapolis: Hackett Pub. Co, 1977.

Keulman, Kenneth. *The Balance of Consciousness: Eric Voegelin's Political Theory.*University Park: Pennsylvania State University Press, 1990.

Landauer, Gustav. *Der werdende Mensch, Aufsätze über Leben und Schrifttum*. Edited by Martin Buber. Weimar: Gustav Kiepenheuer Verlag, 1921.

Landauer, Gustav. *Skepsis und Mystik, Versuche im Anschluss an Mauthners Sprachkritik*. Münster: Büchse der Pandora, 1978.

Landauer, Gustav. *Der Todesprediger*. Münster: Verlag Büchse der Pandora, 1978.

Landauer, Gustav. *Signatur G.l. Gustav Landauer im Sozialist (1892–1899)*. Edited by Ruth Link-Salinger Hyman. Frankfurt am Main: Surhkamp, 1995.

Landauer, Gustav. *Revolution and other writings, a political reader*. Edited and translated by Gabriel Kuhn. Oakland, PM Press, 2010.

Landauer, Gustav. *Antipolitik: Gustav Landauer, Ausgewählte Schriften, Band 3.1*. Edited by Siegbert Wolf. Lich (Hessen): Verlag Edition AV, 2010.

Landauer, Gustav. *Antipolitik: Gustav Landauer, Ausgewählte Schriften, Band 3.2*. Edited by Siegbert Wolf. Lich (Hessen): Verlag Edition AV, 2010.

Landauer, Gustav. "Call to Socialism". http://theanarchistlibrary.org/library/gustav-landauer-call-to-socialism.

Landauer, Gustav. "Skepsis und Mystik, Versuche im Anschluss an Mauthner's Sprachkritik". http://www.weltrevolution.net/zeit/Landauer2.htm.

Lunn, Eugene. *Prophet of Community, the romantic socialism of Gustav Landauer.* Santa Barbara: University of California Press, 1973.

Maurer, Charles B. *Call to Revolution: The Mystical Anarchism of Gustav Landauer.* Detroit: Wayne State University Press, 1971.

Morrissey, Michael P., *Consciousness and Transcendence: The Theology of Eric Voegelin.* Notre Dame: University of Notre Dame Press, 1994.

Porter, Clifford F. "Eric Voegelin on Nazi Political Extremism." *Journal of the History of Ideas* 63 (2002): 151–171.

Ranieri, John J. *Eric Voegelin and the Good Society.* Columbia: University of Missouri Press, 1995.

Sandoz, Ellis. *The Voegelinian Revolution.* Baton Rouge: Louisiana State University Press, 1981.

Tucker, Benjamin. *Instead of a Book: By a man too busy to write one: A Fragmentary Exposition of Political Anarchism.* Vulgus Press, 2011.

Voegelin, Eric. "Immortality: Experience and Symbol". In *Harvard Theological Review* 40 (1967):235–279.

Voegelin, Eric. *From Enlightenment to Revolution.* Edited by John H. Hallowell. Durham: Duke University Press, 1975.

Voegelin, Eric. *The Ecumenic Age.* Columbia: University of Missouri Press, 1980.

Voegelin, Eric. *The New Science of Politics.* Chicago: University of Chicago Press, 1987.

Voegelin, Eric. *Published Essays 1966–1985.* Baton Rouge: Louisiana State University Press, 1990.

Voegelin, Eric. *Nature of the Law and Related Legal Writings.* Baton Rouge: Louisiana State University Press, 1991.

Voegelin, Eric. *On the Form of the American Mind*. Baton Rouge: Louisiana State University Press, 1995.

Voegelin, Eric. *Race and State*. Baton Rouge: Louisiana State University Press, 1997.

Voegelin, Eric. *The Authoritarian State: an Essay on the Problem of the Austrian State*. Columbia: University of Missouri Press, 1999.

Voegelin, Eric. *Crisis and the Apocalypse of Man*. Baton Rouge: University of Missouri Press, 1999.

Voegelin, Eric. *Hitler and the Germans*. Columbia: University of Missouri Press, 1999.

Voegelin, Eric. *Published Essays 1940–1952*. Columbia: University of Missouri Press, 2000.

Voegelin, Eric. *Plato and Aristotle*. Columbia: University of Missouri Press, 2000.

Voegelin, Eric. *In Search of Order*. Columbia: University of Missouri Press, 2000.

Voegelin, Eric. *Israel and Revelation*. Columbia: University of Missouri Press, 2001.

Voegelin, Eric. *Anamnesis: On the Theory of History and Politics*. Columbia: University of Missouri Press, 2002.

Voegelin, Eric, and Robert Bechtold Heilman. *Robert B. Heilman and Eric Voegelin: A Friendship in Letters, 1944–1984*. Edited by Charles R. Embry. Columbia: University of Missouri Press, 2004.

Voegelin, Eric. *Autobiographical Reflections*. Columbia: University of Missouri Press, 2006.

Webb, Eugene. *Eric Voegelin: Philosopher of History*. Seattle: University of Washington Press, 1981.

Willems, Joachim. *Religiöser Gehalt des Anarchismus und anarchistischer Gehalt der Religion? : die jüdisch-christlich-atheistische Mystik Gustav Landauers zwischen Meister Eckhart und Martin Buber*. Albeck: Verlag Ulmer Manuskripte, 2001.

The Anarchē of Spirit: Proudhon's Anti-theism & Kierkegaard's Self in Apophatic Perspective

Simon D. Podmore
Liverpool Hope University, UK

This essay explores the possibility of an avowedly theological anarchē through a reading of Søren Kierkegaard's (1813–55) theology of "the self before God" in relation to the "anti-theism" of his contemporary, Pierre-Joseph Proudhon (1809–65). In doing so it establishes an apophatic dialectic between their two positions in which human idols of 'God' are continually un-known in the search for an unknowable God. Such a Wholly Other God, it is suggested, provides a kenotic (self-limiting) model of power which subverts anthropomorphic projections of Providential omnipotence, typically imagined as mastery over the other. A truly apophatic mode of divine power, by contrast, is one which establishes a primal and inviolable gift of human freedom and autonomy which is central to Kierkegaard's theism, Proudhon's anti-theism, and to the apophatic dialectic which continually emerges in the struggle between both impulses. Reading with and against both Kierkegaard and Proudhon, I propose that each provides a prescient prophetic voice against the abuses of Divine Providence and human freedom. In concluding, I gesture towards an anti/theology of apophasis and anarchē which is inspired by the negations and antagonisms as well as the synergies which exist between these two great strugglers with God.

Introduction: The Anarchy of Spirit

"The wind blows where it wills, and you hear the sound thereof, but cannot tell from where it came, and where it goes: so is everyone that is born of the Spirit."

—John 3:8

How to cite this book chapter:
Podmore, S. D. 2017. The Anarchē of Spirit: Proudhon's Anti-theism & Kierkegaard's Self in Apophatic Perspective. In: Christoyannopoulos, A. and Adams, M. S. (eds.) *Essays in Anarchism and Religion: Volume 1*. Pp. 238–282. Stockholm: Stockholm University Press. DOI: https://doi.org/10.16993/bak.g. License: CC-BY

"Spirit is the self"/ "The self is freedom"
—Søren Kierkegaard, *The Sickness unto Death*[1]

The freedom of the self is an inviolable principle of *possibility* to which, in a profound and scandalous sense, *even God submits*. God surrenders to the self's freedom out of a kenotic[2] freedom: a divine freedom which sacrifices itself in the name of human freedom. This upholding of the freedom of the self—including the freedom to refuse God, to choose the unfreedom of despair—is nonetheless a source of ineffable divine sorrow. It is a wound of a sacred Love which gives itself in the only manner it can, without overpowering the freedom of the beloved.[3] God does not, perhaps even *cannot*, remove from creation the possibility of saying 'no' to God, even though the sustenance of this possibility constitutes an "unfathomable grief" of divine love.[4] In this horizon of possibility, in which freedom is free even to the point of negating itself, there emerges what Kierkegaard discerns as a struggle between faith and that which faith names as "despair". This same despair is, nonetheless, named by itself as an expression of ultimate human autonomy.

However, as both Søren Kierkegaard (1813–55) and Pierre Joseph Proudhon (1809–65) recognise in their own diverse ways, even the denial of God's existence or goodness is caught within a dialectical relationship towards positive assertions about God. Negation exists in irresolvable tension with the affirmation it denies. Atheism, as identified by Kierkegaard as a rejection of God, therefore reveals an implicit even insentient dependence upon the very idea of God it seeks to negate.[5] It is in recognition of this unconscious relationship that Proudhon asserts a more consciously explicit negation of theism (understood as the *idea* of the existence of God) in the form of his notion of *anti-theism* (denial or negation of this idea): a perennial process of destructive antinomy (contradiction) between affirmation and denial of the idea of God.[6]

For Proudhon and Kierkegaard, theism would generally include the idea that God is somehow a creative force within human history, to the problematic extent that God's Will can be invoked in support of human structures remaining as they are (rather than acting as a radical challenge to the world). This is a particular idea of a *God of Providence* (divine oversight and ordering of human order) which, as explored below, Proudhon rejects as unjust and Kierkegaard critiques as a convenient projection of bourgeois Christendom and a betrayal of true Christianity. Kierkegaard does so, I contend, by drawing a distinction between theistic *ideas of God* and *the living God* who is beyond and sometimes at odds with even avowed Christians' constructions of such ideas. To an extent, Proudhon also proposes a distinction along similar lines. However, an essential departure between Proudhon and Kierkegaard resides in the difference between Proudhon's conviction that such a God is ultimately unknowable, and thereby irrelevant (rather than to be venerated for its mystery), and Kierkegaard's belief that the unknowable God has given Godself in saving revelation.

This essay represents an attempt to think Kierkegaard's and Proudhon's readings of this dialectical relationship between the affirmation and denial of 'God' together in creative dialogue. While in this essay I will risk an experiment in thinking both with and against Kierkegaard[7] as well as Proudhon, I suggest that the seeds of a dialectical reading of theistic thought in relation to its antagonists is already present in Kierkegaard's own reading of Feuerbachian atheism. Kierkegaard provocatively suggests that Feuerbach's exposé of theology as disguised anthropology might serve Christianity as a critique against the all-too domesticated anthropomorphic idols of Christendom's portrayal of 'God'. Listening to the voice of Feuerbach is akin to receiving "*ab hoste consilium*" [advice from the enemy] even though this enemy may be a "*malitieus dæmon*" [evil daimon].[8] Although talk of Proudhon as "the French Feuerbach" was somewhat erroneous,[9] he stands alongside, and at times against Feuerbach[10] as a demonic-prophetic voice opposing the theistic idol of a certain God of Providence: the projected God-image who supposedly endorses and upholds the status quo of Christendom for the benefit of those already empowered by it. In referring to Feuerbach's assertion that "the true sense of Theology is Anthropology"[11] as advice from a demon, Kierkegaard implicitly affirms the dialectical value of atheism as a critical iconoclastic force against the delusions of bourgeois Christendom. Feuerbach, in other words, exposes the theistic notion of a God who is 'on our side' as nothing other than a dangerous projection of a decadent Christendom which legitimises its privileging of certain types of men: specifically the men currently enjoying the power of State-sponsored modern Christendom. As such, this essay seeks to think about theism and anti-theism in light of the *apophatic*[12] possibility of a God existing beyond all human idols of power and imagination: a God whose own kenotic (self-abdicating) relationship with power subverts human ideals of power and powerlessness in the name of Divine Love.[13]

This essay therefore explores the possibility of an avowedly theological *anarchē* through a reading of Kierkegaard's theology of "the self before God" (*coram Deo*; in contrast to selfhood as defined *coram hominibus*, "before the crowd") in a de/constructive dialectic with the "anti-theism" of his contemporary, Proudhon. This comparison was initially proposed, though not elaborated, by the French Jesuit theologian Henri de Lubac who suggested an affinity between the divine-human antagonism of Proudhon's "anti-theism" and Kierkegaard's statement that "there is a life and death battle between God and man; God hates man just as man hates God."[14] Both Kierkegaard and Proudhon are identified by de Lubac as anti-Hegelians[15] each opposed (albeit for conflicting reasons) to any Feuerbachian sublimation of the agonistic infinite qualitative difference between humanity and divinity.[16] A similar comparison between Kierkegaard and Proudhon on this same point of divine-human enmity is also proposed by Françoise Meltzer:

> There are affinities between Kierkegaard and Proudhon: the former's conviction that 'against God we are always in the wrong,' for example; or Kierkegaard's view of the either/or as 'explosive'. Proudhon, however, much less radical conceptually, and armed with a reductio ad absurdum grasp of Hegelianism, always sees the synthesis as the solution (which he provides) to dangerous contradiction.[17]

Furthermore, Proudhon's *Justice in the Revolution and the Church* (1858) is referred to by George Woodcock as:

sired of a long line of inspiration that begins with the Jewish
prophets and brings Proudhon into contact at more than one
point with the personalist tradition that embraced Kierkegaard
and Dostoevsky [...] In the last resort the author of *Justice* has less
in common with Charles Bradlaugh than with Kierkegaard, who
as Father de Lubac has pointed out, called God 'the mortal enemy'
and declared 'Christianity exists because there is hatred between
God and man'.[18]

Contrasting the dialectical "systematic negation" of Proudhon's
"practical atheism" with Kierkegaard's un-sublated dialectic of
the "infinite qualitative difference" between the human and the
divine, this essay seeks an effectively *apophatic* theological critique of *Power*, established in the kenotic (self-emptying) and loving divine gift of human freedom, and realised through individual
self-becoming as *Spirit*. In appealing to Proudhon and Kierkegaard,
this essay explores the potential effectiveness of apophatic theology and *anti-theism* for negating harmful ideas of divine power:
idols of divine omnipotence which are established via the projection of human notions of power in terms of mastery and subjugation. However, as shall be seen, whereas Kierkegaard's negation of
power is established upon a positive (*kataphatic*) affirmation of a
notion of divine omnipotence revealed through freedom as God's
love for creation, Proudhon undertakes a perennial negation of
the idea of "God" as a necessary requisite for the affirmation of
human justice.

Juxtaposing the dialectics of Kierkegaard's agonistic "self before
God" and Proudhon's antagonistic "anti-theism", I suggest that each
might contribute towards an apophatic critique of theistic accounts
of Divine Providence which model God's power according to human projections of worldly power—a mundane form of power understood as mastery over "the other". While both assert the primacy
of human freedom in relation to God, Proudhon's "anti-theism" is,
I ultimately suggest, nonetheless vulnerable to a Kierkegaardian critique which views "anti-theism" as a form of "offence" towards the
kenosis (self-negation) of the "self before God". However, while in
Kierkegaardian perspective Proudhon expresses the enslavement of
"despair", "anti-theism" nonetheless remains an inexorable "possibility" divinely ensured by the inviolable and primal gift of anarchic

human freedom. In other words, though God may "grieve" over the "offense" of *anti-theism*, divine power is truly manifest in God's kenotic (self-sacrificial) love as the refusal to negate, or over-power, its possibility. As such, God's love preserves the struggle between the agonistic self before God and the antagonistic anti-theistic self in despair.

Furthermore, insofar as it partakes in an agonistic and apophatic struggle against idols of "God", *anti-theism* represents a more vitalised—if despairingly misdirected—expression of the freedom of "*Spirit*" (*Ånd*) than is found in the sedative "spiritless-ness" (*Åndløsheden*) of bourgeois Christendom. In this respect, Kierkegaard is read as implicitly valuing Proudhon's *anti-theism* as a potential ally in the *via negativa* (way of negation) towards a more authentic understanding of the relationship between human freedom and divine omnipotence. Theology, by attending to the voice of *anti-theism* (even within itself), is reminded of the pro-phetic task of speaking truth to power. Theology is also reminded of a God whose self-revelation is a subversion of such power, and one whose love connotes an unfathomable grief over the victims of the self-apotheosis of that power.

Kierkegaard: The Anarchy of Interpretation and the Untruth of Crowds

> "To be *spirit* is to be *I*. God desires to have *I*s, for God desires to be loved [...] 'Christendom' is a society of millions—all in the third person, no *I*."
>
> —Kierkegaard, *Journals and Papers*[19]

In proposing this reading of Kierkegaard and Proudhon, this es-say may, from its beginning, already be guilty of a hermeneutic anarchy—albeit an anarchy of (mis-)reading which Kierkegaard's own *an-archē* of authorial authority has itself made think-able. The elliptical evasions, pseudonymous self-effacements, polyvalences, and ironic mis-directions of Kierkegaard's liter-ary styles elicit the possibilities and temptations of an anarchic hermeneutic. In other words, by opening his works to be free-ly (mis-)appropriated in the name of existential subjectivity, does Kierkegaard bequeath the right to (re)interpret his works, even in spite of any implicit protestations to the contrary? Even when—perhaps *precisely when*—writing more "directly" about that which is avowedly most sacred to him, Kierkegaard confesses himself to be "without authority"[20] before his solitary readers.[21] Yet while his texts permit, even at times reward, high degrees of hermeneutical freedom, I am also mindful of interpreting Kierkegaard's writings within the orbit of what he avowed to be most central to his authorship: namely, the task of becoming a Christian in Christendom. As such, I read Kierkegaard as addressing the hermeneutic question of what is meant, or required, in becoming oneself as an individual *before God*; yet subjected to the illusory heteronomy of a State-Church which behaves as if it possessed the keys to the kingdom of heaven. What is required, according to Kierkegaard's prophetic and Socratic discourse, is to disillusion oneself of this theatrical heteronomy, to become an individual "self before God", to become "Spirit" within—yet not subject to—Christendom's rule of "Spiritlessness". Only in this is one enabled to resist Christendom's subtle and insidious opiate against the very task of personally realising selfhood as individualised Spirit.

I also remain mindful that I may stretch Kierkegaard's arc of essential concern beyond that with which he himself would have been entirely comfortable. In pressing this horizon, I do not wish to invoke the already self-renounced authority of "Kierkegaard" by speaking in his name nor imposing views upon him which do injustice to his own autonomy. In light of this caveat, it is not my contention, for example, to reprise Vernard Eller's impassioned vision of Kierkegaard as an anarchist per se. I imagine that Kierkegaard himself would have been uneasy, on a number of levels, about being proposed as providing leadership for a twentieth-century "Neo-Sectarianism," or "Kierkegaardian Sectarianism." Nonetheless, I empathise with Eller's diagnosis that "Not the creedal system of a Barth nor the philosophic-theological system of a Tillich, but the free and unstructured approach of a Kierkegaard is the only method appropriate to radical discipleship."[22] However, while I esteem Eller's prophetic tonality and his emphasis upon the "infinite qualitative difference" between the human and the divine, my suspicion is that Kierkegaard himself remained politically conservative and ultimately too profoundly horrified by the European revolutions of 1848 to have been comfortable with Eller's appellation of "that ancient anarchist".[23]

Kierkegaard's personal anxiety about revolutionary Europe, the death of King Christian VIII and the end of absolute monarchy in Denmark, along with his reaction against the Hegelian leadership of the new post-1848 Danish People's Church, are also in alignment with his critical stance towards the notion of a bourgeois state—itself ensuing from a suspicion towards the wisdom of "the crowd" which he describes as essentially an expression of "untruth".[24] Under the gaze of Kierkegaardian solitude, "the crowd" evokes not only the revolutionary mob, but the primal image of the cacophonic crowd who howl for the crucifixion of Jesus—while also signifying the folly of the State trial of Socrates (an image which itself tempers any Hegelian romanticisation of the mythical Greek state).[25] In contrast to Eller's reading, Perkins thus explicitly considers Kierkegaard's critique of "the crowd" as actually tantamount to a critique of anarchy itself:

> Kierkegaard's point is that any popularly based government cannot govern in the interest of the crowd because the party is the creature of the crowd at the same time that it manipulates the crowd. For Kierkegaard, the development of popular government answerable to the crowd was the way to anarchy [...] As Kierkegaard perceives the facade of the modern liberal state it is a mask for the grossest anarchistic hedonism imaginable. Everything in modern politics depends on who manipulates the crowd.[26]

As Perkin's reading demonstrates, Kierkegaard ostensibly elides hedonism with both anarchy and egotism: "In the modern state, aesthetic egotism instead of being merely destructive of the single person, as presented in *Either/Or,* has become a politics of egotism, avariciousness, and anarchy." In other words, an aesthete's life of hedonic self-indulgence expresses the way in which even the ostensibly individualistic libertine easily becomes a cell within a collective ego-State. Kierkegaard's view, as Perkins observes, "is that a state which possesses a power base only in the crowd, its whims, and ill-defined but boundless desires has no rational and essential unity."[27]

As an expression of "human egotism on a large scale and in great dimensions", the state organises and subordinates all "individual egotisms" in such a way "that these must egotistically understand that egotistically it is the most prudent thing to live in the state." Kierkegaard thus labels the state as "a calculus of egotisms".[28] If the state, as expressing *Sittlichkeit* (Hegel's "ethical order", embodied in the ideal State), is the manifestation of a collective Spirit (*Geist*), then it stands in tension with Kierkegaard's notion of Spirit (*Ånd*) as individual selfhood, as singular freedom before God. But even this individual self before God does not stand above, on top of, or in violation of others. Rather it stands alongside in radical equality with all other singular selves, who are themselves equally entitled to Spirit. "*Before God*" becomes the paradigm of all individuality and equality which is, as divine, never mine to ascribe or refuse but is always and already God's gift given in love.

Therefore, as a derivative of *theonomy*, individual equality is no one's to bestow or deny. It is a divine command which binds all individuals together as equal in God's love: not simply as "the other" but as "the neighbour".[29] Kierkegaard therefore rejects the quasi-Providential human notion of a "pyramid-union" of humanity, at the peak of which stands "a super-king" who is the closest to God, who has the ear of God, even to the inevitably revolutionary point of being able to dethrone God. Christianity, according to Kierkegaard, teaches that God opposes, even despises, this pyramid structure of power. By contrast, "Christianly, God chooses and is closest to the despised, the castoffs of the race, one single sorry abandoned wretch, a dreg of humanity." Since "God is infinite love", God "readily sees how cruel this human pyramid-idea can easily become toward the unfortunate, the ignored, and the like in the human race". In defence of those who bear the weight of the base of the pyramid, and in opposition to the self-apotheosis of the one who stands at its pinnacle, "God pushes over the pyramid and everything collapses", though lamentably "a generation later man begins the pyramid business again".[30]

In contrast to this hubris of the pyramidal state, Kierkegaard asserts the theological meaning of Spirit as individual and personalised *freedom*. "Voluntariness is the precise form for qualitatively being spirit".[31] The freedom of will as Spirit is expressed through "this fundamental idea in Christianity, that which makes it what it is: transformation of the will".[32] The struggle of wills with God is not, however, a struggle against a God who stands "in the external, palpable sense [as] a power who, face to face with me, asserts his rights." Rather, the God-relationship is such that the divine will is revealed in the Word of God—a disempowered Word which one is free and responsible to read as one wills, which one is free even to reject. As the Word which is spoken or read, "God is not an external, palpable power who bangs the table in front of me when I want to alter his will and says: No, stop! No, in this sense it is almost as if he did not exist. It is left up to me".[33] The individual is left free to respond to the Word, according to the autonomy of human subjectivity. God withdraws, almost to the point of non-existence.

Christendom, however, betrays such a vision of Christianity by transposing its concern from the sphere of the *Will* and "into the sphere of the intellectual" where it sublimates the subjective struggles of the will into intellectual strivings with doctrine. While Christendom supposes itself to have raised Christianity to the ostensibly objective sphere of the intellect, it chooses to forget that it is ultimately towards the change of will "where Christianity aims its deadly blow. But Christendom deftly dodges the blow—and transposes everything into intellectuality".[34] Within the sphere of intellectuality, the existential freedom of the single individual as subjective Spirit becomes absorbed within the speculative ideal of objective Spirit, which Christendom's intellectuals have inherited from the Hegelian dream of viewing all providence *sub species aeternitatis* (under the aspect of eternity). Christendom, as the delusion of State Christianity, thereby betrays the New Testament concern with the subjective freedom of the self before God by "elevating" Spirit to the rarefied realm of intellect and objectivity.

Mindful of the extent to which Kierkegaard was aghast at the excesses of the revolutionary mob, I wish now to move towards a constructive reading of Kierkegaard in relation to his contemporary, Proudhon—a reading which elicits a potential spirit of anarchy, or perhaps more aptly an anarchism of Spirit within Kierkegaard's writings. *Christian* anarchism, as Eller would have it, is concerned with "theonomy" rather than "autonomy": the *arky* of God rather than the rule of the self. However, as I shall explore below, the 'power' of this theonomy is not ultimately the crushing heteronomy of the Wholly Other Master who reduces the self to nothingness. A Kierkegaardian vision of divine omnipotence, and its concomitant notion that "God *is* that all things are possible"[35] (even the freedom of creation before the gaze its creator) are not reducible to the Master-Slave dialectic which marks human struggles for empowerment through recognition.[36] In contrast to human struggles for the possession of being-in-and-for-itself, I suggest that Kierkegaardian theonomy can be understood as the law of Love which names Spirit as freedom, a freedom in which Spirit is truly realised through the transfiguration of *self* before a divine gaze which does not base its being-as-Master on recognition from the abject other-as-slave.

Reciprocally, I suggest that while subjectivity is established in the sphere of the Will, authentic human selfhood is not realised by struggling, unto death and despair, to will one's own autonomy over-against the heteronomous gaze of the Wholly Other. The freedom of the Will is finally realised in the paradox of willing to become oneself, as nothing, *before* and even *in* God. Self as *Spirit* is the transfiguration of the *self before God*, the *self* as it *"rests transparently in God"*[37]: the omnipotent Creator whose gift of being and becoming to the self is the original gift of freedom in a love which neither needs nor coerces recognition.

While divine love is understood as a gift which, as gratuity, is not dependent upon reciprocity or recognition, this does not mean that God is indifferent to being loved by the other. On the contrary, God *desires*, though does not *need*, to be loved. And since love can only truly be free, God desires only to be loved from a heart of subjective freedom. "To be *spirit* is to be *I*. God desires [*vil*] to have *Is*", Kierkegaard affirms, "for God desires to be loved."[38] But God's Will is not coercive. The love which God desires can only, by definition, be love which is freely given *ex nihilo*: created from nothing, and therefore independent and autonomous. Love therefore discovers it origin in the divine act of an independent creation which makes freedom possible.

In this agapeistic, even erotic, cosmogony, an inexorable, even tragic gift of freedom arises at the heart of Kierkegaard's vision of the self-God relationship. Divine omnipotence is expressed, indirectly, by human freedom. As such, God's true and gracious omnipotence is revealed in creating human beings as free *ex nihilo*, because only free beings can truly love without coercion. This freedom, however, also begets anxiety—fear and desire of freedom and the nothingness of non-being—and the possibility to say 'No', or even to say nothing at all, to the gift of divine love. Such freedom is the possibility of offence: "the unfathomable grief of [divine] love"[39] in which God is wounded by God's own refusal to deny the autonomy of the human self. This grief of divine love is even essentially tragic insofar as human freedom, by subjecting itself to the heteronomy of the crowd, rejects and crucifies the God of love. Creation *ex nihilo* is sustained in the true sense of the Providence (*preservatio*) of crucified Love. Such *preservatio* of *ex nihilo* freedom also maintains the possibility to say "No" to divine power, even to being itself—a "No" which is dialectically expressed by the *anti-theism* of Proudhon.

Anarchist Dialectics: Proudhon's Anti-Theism as Eternal Via Negativa

"Humanity is a spectre to God, just as God is a spectre to humanity; each of the two is the other's cause, reason, and end of existence."
—Proudhon, *The Philosophy of Misery*[40]

"My criticism of the idea of God is [...] a systematic negation, which is meant to come to a higher affirmation, equally systematic."
—Proudhon, Letter to abbé X., Jan. 22nd 1849[41]

While Proudhon's "offence" and Kierkegaard's "faith" may appear dialectically related, the search for a synthesis between Proudhon's *anti-theism* and Kierkegaard's theism is problematized by the suggestion that Kierkegaard also subverts central assumptions of traditional Christian theism and Church sovereignty which Proudhon himself resists. Nevertheless, while the individualistic freedom at the heart of Kierkegaard's "self before God" refutes the voluntaristic (*will*-centred) mastery of "the other", it ultimately discovers its true freedom in the *free submission* of the self-will to the Holy Other: that is, to a God who is revealed through kenotic love as otherwise than the God of Providential theism against which Proudhon struggles. However, this free submission is not tantamount to total abjection. As the self before God is consummated in relationship with others—a relation grounded in the liberating grace of love—so too does Kierkegaardian submission to God (becoming nothing *before God*; or resting transparently *in God*) also entail *becoming something in relation to God*. This *something* is namely a self in freedom, a self as *Spirit*.

Before proceeding further, however, certain caveats ought to be noted. For one, it should be observed that Kierkegaard's own knowledge of Proudhon's thought is extremely modest.[42] While Kierkegaard may have heard the dreadful echoes of Proudhon's promethean judgement that "God is evil",[43] he gives no sense that he is cognisant of its ultimately dialectical meaning.[44] Nonetheless, in a profound sense Kierkegaard also struggles in his darkest moments with a similar abyssal possibility: how is one to uphold faith in divine love when it *appears* that God is evil? However, whereas Proudhon's practical yet dialectically provocative philosophy intends the negation of *the idea of "God"* in the name of human justice, Kierkegaard's agonistic spiritual interiority seeks to affirm the Absolute yet subjective reality of God in the name of a fearful and trembling faith. In other words, while Kierkegaard's ultimate concern is with the subjective *self-God-relationship*, Proudhon is essentially engaged with indicting the theistic conception of the God of Providence (an objective ideal in which, for Kierkegaard, the single individual becomes lost).

According to what might be called Proudhon's quasi apophatic anti-theology, God (if there is such a "being") remains essentially unknowable, whether by *kataphasis* (positive assertions) or *apophasis* (negation). Consequently, "God" cannot be meaningfully invoked within human ethical concerns: "we cannot legitimately deny anything or affirm anything of the absolute; that is one of the reasons why I rule the divine concept out of morality."[45] This radical anti-theological position allows Proudhon to evacuate God from "the alpha and omega" of his argument: *Justice.*[46] "If God is outside knowledge for us," Proudhon infers that "he must remain outside practical matters [...] When religion, through its theology, its revelations and its cult, brings God out of the absolute, it drives man out of morality."[47] Humanity and divinity are so radically different that "God", as beyond human knowledge, must remain irreducibly wholly other than ethics. Proudhon thus regards it as his duty to struggle against the *idea* of the transcendental God of ecclesiastical Providence: a "God" whose intrusion into human morality serves to maintain the unjust status quo of tyranny and poverty. This idea of the God of Providential theism is the God of evil who disrupts the possibility of true inter-personal and systemic human justice.[48]

This evil God of theism is diagnosed by Proudhon as an idolatrous construct of anthropomorphism: "the theology of infancy and poesy" which projects the idea of God in the image of Man. By attempting to mediate or sublate the wholly otherness of the Absolute, Man attempts to reduce an unknowable Absolute to an object which can then be wielded according to the aggrandising desires of Man's self-apotheosis:

> But having made God in his own image, man wished to appropriate him still farther; not satisfied with disfiguring the Almighty, he treated him as his patrimony, his goods, his possessions. God, pictured in monstrous forms, became throughout the world the property of man and of the State. Such was the origin of the corruption of morals by religion, and the source of pious feuds and holy wars.[49]

The discipline of theology, in Proudhon's verdict, becomes the "the *science of the infinitely absurd*"[50] which, through the idea of God, enslaves humanity in miserable self-alienation, leaving it with the "eternally antagonistic" vision of "Man [...] at war with himself".[51] Only *anarchy* as "the absence of a master, or a sovereign" can exorcise the spectre of theology and emancipate true human justice from the regime of theonomy. "Liberty is anarchy", Proudhon asserts, "[...] the balance of rights and duties. To make a man free is to balance him with others, —that is to put him on their level".[52] Such anarchistic equality frees humanity from the necessarily imbalanced heteronomy of subjection to a Wholly Other God.[53]

Proudhon affirms that true anarchic justice is only realisable at the inter-human level, without the intrusion of metaphysics.

Within this strict horizon, "*Équité*, justice, and society, can exist only between individuals of the same species", and therefore "They form no part of the relations of different races to each other,—for instance, of the wolf to the goat, of the goat to man, of man to God, much less of God to man".[54] If God is as Wholly Other as some projections of theism would postulate then there can be no relationship of justice between humanity and divinity, since the notion of true justice demands both equality and reciprocity. "The attribution of justice, equity, and love to the Supreme Being is pure anthropomorphism", Proudhon therefore contends, "[...] God can be regarded as just, equitable, and good, only to another God. Now, God has no associate; consequently, he cannot experience social affections, —such as goodness, *équité*, and justice".[55]

While rejecting the anthropomorphic construction of theism's idea of a Wholly Other God of Providence, Proudhon nonetheless retains a "social" idea of God as a cypher to the past, present, and even the future of humanity. In contradistinction to the theist's projection of the God of Providence, Proudhon speaks of "God, the great unknown" as "an hypothesis [...] a necessary dialectical tool" which in its social context "[...] is much more a collective act of faith than an individual conception".[56] Unlike Kierkegaard's concern with the individual self-God-relation, Proudhon's hypothetical "God" performs a collective social function. Nonetheless, at the same time as he dismantles the theistic construct of the God of Providence, Proudhon also confesses that belief in God "is a fact as primitive, an idea as inevitable, a principle as necessary as are the categorical ideas of a cause, substance, time, and space to our understanding".[57] By virtue of this necessity, Proudhon treats the "hypothesis of God" as the dialectical social *a priori* of *anti-theism*.[58] Without the idea of "a God or master-builder" the universe, and humanity itself, cannot be conceived to exist. Proudhon calls this rather deistic conception (a deity who is not regarded as intervening in creation) "the social profession of faith." In tension with the thought that existence without God as its first cause seems inconceivable, however, Proudhon asserts the notion that "also without man God would not be thought, or—to clear the interval—God would be nothing".[59] In other words, whether in deism, theism, or *anti-theism*, the thought of God and humanity appear within a mutually inter-dependent configuration.

Though *anti-theism* seeks the negation of the theistic idea of God, Proudhon tempers his polemic with the avowal that his "criticism of the idea of God [theism] is similar to all the criticisms I have made of authority, property, etc.; it is a systematic negation, which is meant to come to a higher affirmation, equally systematic."[60] In striving for an almost *apophatic* negation Proudhon desires a further dialectical *via negativa* which rises above the self-delusions of *atheism's* denial of God's existence. In Proudhon's eyes, atheism attempts a self-apotheosis which thinks itself "intelligent and strong", but which, by failing to discover a higher systematic negation of both the idea of "God" and of itself, is in reality merely "stupid and timid."[61] Proudhon and Kierkegaard are allied in discerning an unconscious irony in atheism's denial of the existence of God. Despite its self-aggrandising claims to a Promethean form of freedom, humanist atheism merely seeks to re-internalise the idea of God which it had projected and alienated from itself.[62] As such, atheism's negation of the idea of God cannot aspire towards a higher systematic affirmation beyond itself, as sought by Proudhon's *anti-theism*.

However, *anti-theism* operates under the caveat that consummate realisation of this "higher affirmation" remains eternally elusive. The dialectic is never resolved, the system is never complete; and so the struggle continues. *Anti-theism* will not find rest with the distant God of deism, according to which "God" serves a merely hypothetical or social purpose. While it may strive beyond atheism's deicidal re-appropriation of theism (as Feuerbach sought to reclaim statements about God as statements about Man), Proudhon's *anti-theism* itself is motivated by an irascible sense of *Misotheism* (hatred of God[63]). In contrast to the late revolutionary deistic beliefs of *théophilanthropie* (a sect affirming friendship of God and man), *anti-theism* is unmoved by the promise of rapprochement, preferring instead to struggle against the God of Providence "like Israel against Jehovah [Genesis 32], until death."[64] However, by desiring its own elusive higher systematic negation, *anti-theism*, developing Proudhon's principle, also seeks something beyond itself which in turn struggles against it. As such, *anti-theism* aspires beyond the despairing hubris and egoism of humanistic atheism at the same moment in which it struggles for the negation of the God of theism. Humanity, in Proudhon's system, actually surpasses itself, not by re-assimilating the "God" who symbolises its self-alienation, but by continuing to engage in an eternal dialectical struggle against all ideas of "God". Proudhon opposes "God" in a spirit of *misotheism* dialectically compelled by the belief that "God is man's adversary, and Providence a misanthrope".[65]

Theology's myth of divine Providence, the consoling yet desolating thought of a cosmic harmony presiding over human order, stands in direct violation to the visceral sufferings of the humanity it stands over: "the bread, kneaded in blood and tears, upon which you [God] have fed us".[66] The all-seeing eye of Providence is tragically blind to the suffering and injustice which announce its negation. Far from being the perfection or idealisation of humanity, the classical Divine Attributes thus express the negation of human values: "God is contradictory of man, just as charity is contradictory of justice".[67] Rather than aspiring to a sublation of the human and the divine, Proudhon's *anti-theism* asserts a "radical antinomy" between humanity and God:

> *Antinomy*, literally *counter-law*, means opposition in principle or antagonism in relation [...] antinomy is the conception of a law with two faces, the one positive, the other negative.[68]

Within this antagonism of the positive and the negative there is a tendency towards reciprocal negation. "An antinomy is made up of two terms, necessary to each other, but always opposed, and tending to mutual destruction"; and yet, in *anti-theism*'s systematic negation a higher affirmation arises: "from the combination of these two zeros unity springs forth, or the idea which dispels the antinomy".[69]

This affirmation, inevitably, is itself vulnerable to its own systematic negation, thereby continuing the eternal struggle, perpetuating "the insoluble antinomy between God and man".[70] Any affirmation which emerges from this antinomy is itself always vulnerable to further negation. As such, a sublation of humanity and divinity is never attained within the eternal antinomy of *theism* and *anti-theism*. In radical and perennial struggle, the human and the divine retain an inexorable *alterity* (a radical otherness irreducible to sameness or reconciliation). In terms of Kierkegaard's own refusal of Hegelian sublation (*Aufheben*), there remains an "infinite qualitative difference" between humanity and divinity. Or, in Proudhon's words, there remains a refusal to "make God into humanity", a sublation which, after all, "[...] would be slander of both".[71] Yet while Kierkegaard aspires towards a restless "synthesis" of the human and the divine realised through a self-God relationship which retains the agonistic tension of infinite *alterity*, Proudhon refuses any spiritual horizon of reconciliation between the human and the divine. "God and man hold each other in perpetual check and continually avoid each other".[72]

Whereas Kierkegaard hopes for a personalised relationship between self and God beyond the realm of ideality, Proudhon remains within the principle of irascible antinomy. Divinity and humanity are each the shadow-side of the other: "Humanity is a spectre to God, just as God is a spectre to humanity; each of the two is the other's cause, reason, and end of existence".[73] Each is incomplete without the other who it both haunts and is haunted by; and yet, according to the eternal antinomy, the other will never complete it nor reconcile it to itself.[74] God may be "the complement of man",[75] but God is also the contradiction of Man. While Kierkegaard contemplates the revelation of an impossible reconciliation of the infinite qualitative difference in personal relationship with the paradox of Christ, Proudhon remains within a principle of justice which continues to regard God and humanity as mutually, antagonistically, and irreconcilably wholly other.[76]

To recapitulate: Proudhon's refusal to reconcile the antinomy of *anti-theism* is ultimately a struggle against theism and atheism, as well as a refusal of the benign concessions of deistic *théophilanthropisme*. In its striving to re-appropriate the image of God, Proudhon discerns that atheist humanism merely expresses the desire to sublate theism. In light of this desire, "Humanism" becomes nothing but "the most perfect theism".[77] Opposing both atheism and theism (which are implicitly just two sides of the same coin), Proudhon's asserts *anti-theism* as a struggle in which "God is inexhaustible, and our contest eternal."[78] In its intentional rejection of humanistic atheism, of Providential theism, and of transcendentally indifferent deism (*théophilanthropisme*), *anti-theism* can be read as an apophatic struggle against all forms of ideology and authority which manufacture idols from ideals of "God" or "Man". By refusing to resolve this struggle, *anti-theism* can help ensure that humanity remains free from the totalising *archē* of either. *Anti-theism* refuses the metaphysical discourse between theism and atheism on the existence of God, preferring instead to critique the idolatry of *essence*.[79] Proudhon asserts *anti-theism* as an expression of "practical atheism" as the struggle against providential theism and atheistic humanism's re-appropriation of power.[80] Since the divine essence is beyond human knowledge, *anti-theism*'s apophatic "first duty of man" is "[...] to continually hunt the idea of God out of his mind and conscience", even in its moralist and deistic forms, insofar as "[...] every step we take in advance is a victory in which we crush Divinity".[81] Through *anti-theism*'s struggles in the name of justice, the idol of divinity is "dethroned and broken [...] For God is stupidity and cowardice; God is hypocrisy and falsehood; God is tyranny and misery; God is evil".[82]

But it should not be forgotten that such statements are avowed by Proudhon as systematic negations *aspiring towards*—though never arriving at—a higher synthesis. Such denials of "God" are themselves vulnerable to future negations. They are spoken within the eternal struggle to think humanity and think God within the same horizon of freedom. It is, I suggest, in such openness to future negation that *anti-theism* becomes a voice—even a prophetic-demonic voice—to which theology might constructively attend. At the very least, as Kierkegaard observes, "the demonic always contains the truth in reverse".[83]

Towards an Anti/Theology: An Apophatic Struggle with "God"

> "[T]hat God could create human beings free over against himself is the cross which philosophy could not bear but upon which it has remained hanging."
>
> —Kierkegaard, *Journals and Papers*[84]

By gesturing towards a notion of *anti/theology*, I intend a course of dialectical struggle between the embrace and rejection of theological thinking about God: a continuous apophatic process which struggles in the name of both human and divine freedom. This entails a dialogical approach to thinking about God which is mindful of the antipathy as well as the sympathy with which the human relates to the divine. In order to resist the temptation to sublate *anti-theism* into theology, however, it must be recognised that when Proudhon appeals to the notion that God is beyond knowledge he is not consciously aligning himself to the devotional *via negativa* (negative way) of mystical theology. Even negative theology's confession of the unknowable nature of God, as Feuerbach similarly implored, can be rejected as representing a mere subterfuge and mystification of the idea of God. The *denial* of qualities to God, according to Feuerbach, renders God as nothing more than "a negative being" and, as such, is merely a symptomatic "offspring of recent times, a product of modern unbelief."[85]

Historically and conceptually untenable as Feuerbach's dismissal may be, his identification of negative theology with implicit atheism contains a powerful critique of the temptations of employing the *via negativa* as a strategy for theological mystification. However, by inscribing 'negation' within a dialectical relationship to 'affirmation', Feuerbach fails to appreciate the extent to which the negation of positive predicates is only an initial stage on the way of apophatic theology. *Apophasis* does not merely rest with the dialectical negation of the *via eminentiae* (the way of eminence; also *via positiva*) by the *via negationis* (way of negation; also *via negativa*). *Apophasis* negates the dialectical negation between positive and negative statements about God in order to move towards a higher sense of God *beyond affirmation and negation*.[86] Feuerbach remains unable to escape the dialectical relationship between divine and human attributes, as reflected in his rejection of the theological distinction between "what God is in himself and what he is for me". Feuerbach cleaves to his notion that God's nature is identical to the anthropocentric standpoint: "I cannot know whether God is something else in himself or for himself than he is for me; what he is to me is to me all that he is [...] his very nature".[87] In doing so Feuerbach denies in advance the apophatic possibility of a God *beyond* or *otherwise* than human conception. This is further reflected in his insistence on referring to God in terms of *a* being, "the Highest Being" in reference to the human being.[88] For mystical theology, by contrast, God is *hyperousious*: beyond, before, or otherwise than the category of 'being' itself. As the classic illustration of Pseudo-Dionysius leads us: the affirmation that 'God is light' is negated by the denial that 'God is darkness'. The negation between these two is, however, transcended by the notion that 'God is dazzling darkness': a statement which carries one beyond the limited dialectical thinking of affirmation and denial.

Although Proudhon would surely suspect such moves of mystification, I suggest that his notion of *anti-theism* is actually more consistent with apophatic technique (if not its motivation or goal) than that of Feuerbach's atheism. As Proudhon recognises, atheism (as the denial of the existence of the God of theism) remains unconsciously dependent upon the idea of God it seeks to negate. *Anti-theism*, however, aspires beyond atheism by negating the idea of God in order to perpetuate the eternal struggle between theism and itself: a struggle which perpetuates the endless antinomy between God and humanity. While theism may affirm that 'God is good', *anti-theism* denies this goodness by stating that 'God is evil'. However, *anti-theism* would not rest content with an apophatic sublation of these statements. *Anti-theism* refuses the synthesis offered by such a mystical statement as 'God is beyond good and evil'. *Anti-theism* would rise up again against this statement, denying the idea of a God who is *beyond* accountability to morality in the name of visceral human justice.

This, I suggest, is precisely where the voice of Proudhon's *anti-theism* speaks most deeply to theology (even at its mystical edge), from the outside, as *"ab hoste consilium"* [advice from the enemy] who may be a *"malitieus dæmon"* [evil daimon]. More than this, *anti-theism*, especially in its critique of the God of Providence in the name of human suffering, offers a powerfully *prophetic* voice against the power-plays which linger within many strands of theology. *Anti-theism* itself reminds us that the struggle between theism and *anti-theism* remains unresolved, even by the consolations of mystical theology: consolations which for some will appear more like desolation and mystification than a resolution to the problems of human suffering. From the dialectical struggle between theism and *anti-theism*, I suggest, a new expression of theism may emerge (perhaps even a new mystical theology). But this new form does not dispel the antinomy. So too must a new *anti-theism* arise against every new expression of theism. In maintaining this perpetual struggle, consolation is always countered by the spectre of desolation. The idea that 'God is beyond good and evil' does not resolve the anti-theistic agony of the statement that 'God is evil'. All it does is challenge it to re-assert itself in a manner which struggles authentically with its antagonist. Theology should be willing to express the goodness of God in a mode which is capable of struggling with the concomitant sense of the darkness of God.[89]

The ongoing deferral of sublimation which arises from this method may, furthermore, actually be more apposite to the strategy of *apophasis* itself. Even the statement that 'God is dazzling darkness' is vulnerable to the charge of mystification, just as a mystical theodicy of a God of Providence 'beyond good and evil' remains vulnerable to the antagonistic reality of unjust suffering. In other words, even the most apophatic of negative theologies must struggle against the *practical* assertion, as exemplified by Proudhon, that the *idea of God* can become far removed from cries of human justice. Mystical theology must contend with the temptation to occupy itself solely with a "God" who is "beyond" to the point of mystifying detachment from the cries for justice of those in suffering. The "practical" denials of Proudhon's *anti-theistic* struggle against God in the name of human suffering and social justice cannot be fully negated, cannot be reduced to silence by any totalising *apophasis*. Theism and *anti-theism* struggle in the space between the affirmation and negation of God, between the Kierkegaardian polarities of "faith" and "offence". Such is the indeterminate space in which the agonistic and apophatic dialectics of *anti/theology* might operate: a space marked by the unsettling and unresolved cry "My God, my God, why have you forsaken me?".[90]

In seeking to clear such a space for *anti/theology* I return finally to Kierkegaard who I suggest provides theistic grounds for upholding the voice of *anti-theism*, even though it is a voice he ultimately identifies as a cry of despair. The fact that the last word goes to Kierkegaard discloses the notion that this nascent vision of *anti/theology* operates within a provisionally theological framework. It is as if *anti-theism* is finally viewed via the diagnostic lens of theism itself—albeit a form of theism which privileges human and divine freedom as related in Love rather than Power. While I conclude here with this sense, it is important to regard such a view as provisional, as potentially anarchic, as open to the struggles with a higher *anti-theism*—which in turn drives both onwards in Love.

From Kierkegaard's avowedly theological perspective, the *possibility* of *anti-theism* is itself implicitly sustained by an account of divine and human freedom grounded in the nature of God's omnipotence as *love*. This is an account of divine omnipotence as the Love of God which is itself critical of both theistic notions of divine Providence and of human constructs of power. That is not to say that Kierkegaard evokes an image of harmony. As Proudhon urges an eternal struggle against God, Kierkegaard elicits the presence of an inexorable struggle between the human and the divine at the genesis of his own dialectical vision. This struggle is itself a symptomatic expression of the relationship between both divine and human freedom: freedom understood as a divine gift of omnipotent love which God, even in God's unfathomable grief, will not violate. Kierkegaard seeks to evoke and also to provoke this existential tension by declaring that "God is man's most redoubtable enemy, thy mortal enemy; He would that thou shouldst die, die unto the world".[91]

If one is only willing to gaze deeply into the abyss of existence, then we will see that the world does not express the Providence of God transmitted through benign ecclesial hierarchy. Rather, we should discern the ancient and perennial struggle between "Spirit" (*Ånd*) and "spiritlessness" (*Åndløsheden*) which promises to awaken us to the realization that "there is a life and death battle between God and man; God hates man just as man hates God."[92] In eliciting a struggle of alterity at the heart of this relationship, Proudhon and Kierkegaard each regards the relation between the divine and the human as irreducible to either the sublation

(*Aufheben*) of Hegelian *Geist* in history or the sublimation of Feuerbachian humanist atheism.

However, the decisive point of departure for Kierkegaard's relational theism from Proudhon's antinomous *anti-theism* is found in Kierkegaard's account of divine omnipotence expressed in love's irrevocable gift of freedom—a freedom which, nonetheless, sustains the possibility of *anti-theism* as the freedom of "offence". In other words, the freedom to negate the idea of "God" in the name of offence is itself an expression of a God-given freedom which the divine itself refuses to negate. God's refusal to negate the one who struggles against God expresses a notion of divine omnipotence opposed to the a/theistic projection of human ideas of "power" as "mastery over the other". Instead, divine omnipotence becomes a kenotic expression of God's love for an other who remains free to refuse the very love which creates its being and its freedom. The human individual, as freely-created *ex nihilo* (out of nothing), is ultimately free to refute the cause of its own being (since it depends upon nothing). As *ex nihilo* the creature is free to will itself; or even to will its own nothingness. It is free to not be. What is more, as Kierkegaard describes in one of his most extensive and remarkable journal entries from 1846, this grounding of divine omnipotence in kenotic love implies a redefinition of the relationship between God and evil—one which contrasts profoundly with Proudhon's assertion of the God of Providence as the God of evil:

> The whole question of the relation of God's omnipotence and goodness to evil (instead of the differentiation that God accomplishes the good and merely permits the evil) is resolved quite simply in the following way. The greatest good, after all, that can be done for a being, greater than anything else that one can do for it, is to make it free. In order to do just that, omnipotence is required. This seems strange, since it is precisely omnipotence that supposedly would make [a being] dependent. But if one will reflect on omnipotence, one will see that it also must contain the unique qualification of being able to withdraw itself again in a manifestation of omnipotence in such a way that precisely for this reason that which has been originated through omnipotence can be independent.[93]

The vision of freedom and independence presented here seeks to exceed human notions of inter-subjectivity, insofar as they are typically enslaved to a dialectic approximate to Hegel's account of the relation between Master and Slave (*Herrschaft und Knechtschaft* – or "Lordship and Bondage"[94]):

> This is why one human being cannot make another person wholly free, because the one who has power is himself captive in having it and therefore continually has a wrong relationship to the one whom he wants to make free. Moreover, there is a finite self-love in all finite power (talent etc.). Only omnipotence can withdraw itself at the same time it gives itself away, and this relationship is the very independence of the receiver. God's omnipotence is therefore his goodness [rather than the evil Proudhon identifies with the God of Providence]. For goodness is to give away completely, but in such a way that by omnipotently taking oneself back one makes the recipient independent. All finite power makes [a being] dependent; only omnipotence can make [a being] independent, can form from nothing [creation *ex nihilo*] something that has its continuity in itself through the continuous withdrawing of omnipotence. Omnipotence is not ensconced in a relationship to another, for there is no other to which it is comparable [Proudhon may agree with this point]—no, it can give without giving up the least of its power, that is, it can make [a being] independent.[95]

Such a vision, however, conflicts with merely mundane capacities for relative dependence and independence, as habitually encountered in the world:

> It is incomprehensible that omnipotence is able not only to create the most impressive of all things—the whole visible world—but is able to create the most frail of all things—a being independent of that very omnipotence. Omnipotence, which can handle the world so toughly and with such a heavy hand, can also make itself so light that what it has brought into existence receives independence. Only a wretched and worldly conception of the dialectic of power holds that it is greater and greater in proportion to its ability to compel and to make dependent.[96]

Omnipotence is not expressed, as human power typically is, in the mastery of slaves or even as a direct Providence which macro-manages the worldly status quo of suffering and injustice, or evil.

> No, Socrates had a sounder understanding; he knew that the art of power lies precisely in making another free [insofar as Socrates, as a maieutic and incidental teacher, helps deliver the individual of a truth which liberates them from heteronomous delusion and into the light of their own autonomy]. But in the relationship between individuals this can never be done, even though it needs to be emphasized again and again that this is the highest; only omnipotence can truly succeed in this. Therefore if a human being had the slightest independent existence over against God (with regard to *materia*) then God could not make him free. Creation out of nothing is once again the Omnipotent One's expression for being able to make [a being] independent. He to whom I owe absolutely everything, although he still absolutely controls everything, has in fact made me independent. If in creating man God himself lost a little of his power, then precisely what he could not do would be to make a human being independent.[97]

In other words, whereas the powerful tend to crave greater and greater power over others, only true divine omnipotence has the power to make another free. Kierkegaard thus interprets divine omnipotence as kenotic love and as a gift of freedom which creates *ex nihilo* the space for a self to become itself as truly independent. The self truly becomes itself, not in sole relation to the others, nor to the State, none of whom can make it free. The self becomes itself *before God* in relation to whom it becomes conscious of itself as "Spirit"—Spirit realised as individuated freedom.

At this moment, however, Kierkegaard and Proudhon assume their stands even further apart. While Proudhon may regard theism as a necessary dialectical agonist for *anti-theism*, Kierkegaard's theism validates the possibility of Proudhon's negation of "God" as an inexorable, yet ultimately grievous, expression of the freedom of *offence*. Under Kierkegaard's theological dialectic, therefore, Proudhon's *anti-theism* becomes an expression of *despair*: specifically "In Despair to will to Be Oneself: Defiance".[98] While *anti-theism* is made *possible* by freedom, its expression ultimately leads away from the realisation of freedom as Spirit and down into the abyssal un-freedom of despair. In struggling against God, anarchistic *anti-theism* refuses to submit to God as Master, nor to any other as Master. Yet according to Kierkegaard's diagnosis of such defiant despair, the self which refuses all external powers and wills to become its own Master is itself doomed to internalise and thereby to enslave itself to the power dialectic of Master-Slave.[99] Such a self is essentially master over nothing (reflecting its creation *ex nihilo*) because it has become enslaved to the unrealisable ideal of mastery, of power, of itself.[100] Even without the *archē* of God or the other, the *anti-theist* cannot escape the fall into slavery at the hands of its own self. For Kierkegaard, unless the self becomes itself as Spirit, one will always deprive oneself of one's own freedom because one is fatally flawed by the desire to master oneself. Even the single anarchist cannot become free from this self-enslaving power of the self—the despair which Kierkegaard names as *the sickness unto death*.

Anti/Conclusion: Neither/Nor?

"Do I step forward as one who in God's behalf, so to speak, has orders to reduce Christendom in rank? O, no, I am without authority. Stirred by the ideal myself, I find a joy in being reduced in rank myself, and I strive "without authority" to stir others to the same."
—Kierkegaard, *Journals and Papers*[101]

Kierkegaard's verdict is intense. *Anti-theism* is made possible by divine freedom; but it expresses itself as despair, and despair is a turning away from freedom—a turning inward into nothingness. The anarchic self is never free from itself; autonomy descends into self-incarceration. Under the heteronomous rubric of Kierkegaard's diagnosis, Proudhon's *anti-theism* discovers itself inscribed within the categories of "defiance" and "demonic rage", under the bondage of which the self labours in the unfreedom of "despair".[102] The despair of defiant *anti-theism* is demonic: "the will of unfreedom".[103] But Kierkegaard is himself open to the inverted wisdom of the demonic enemy. What is more, Kierkegaard identifies the despair of offense as symptomatic of a rise in consciousness from spiritlessness to Spirit itself.[104] As such, there is hope that for dialogue beyond this apparent impasse. It is, furthermore, pertinent to the *anarchē* of Proudhon's position that while *anti-theism* refuses the heteronomy of theism, it simultaneously invites a systematic negation of itself which may raise thinking up to a higher affirmation in the eternal struggle between the human and the divine. Kierkegaard, for his part, might suggest of Proudhon that insofar as it is continually re-assigning itself within this eternal struggle, *anti-theism* cannot, or will not, break itself free from the imagery of a religion which it professes to despise. Proudhon's ultimate despair may reside in the fact that he cannot say that God does not exist. He does not believe *in* God; but he cannot free himself from the idea of "God" which resides as an insidious presence within the human imagination.[105]

In Proudhon's demonic antagonism of theology, however, "God" effectively becomes "Satan": the adversary, the evil one against whom one struggles in the name of the human good.[106] As Proudhon may wish to retain some dialectical notion of "God", I wish to uphold the freedom of *anti-theism*'s "offence" against evil perpetrated in the name of a "God" who appears more demonic than divine. In such cases, the cry of the *anti-theist*, as Proudhon himself sensed, can speak prophetic truth to the idols of power. Latent in Proudhon's demonic struggles against God, Meltzer, like Marx, suspects a nostalgia for religion which recurs in Proudhon's enduring rhetoric of redemption and in "a style of dialectics professing to 'cure' contradiction through ascension (with vestigial religious undertones) rather than *Aufhebung* [sublation]."[107] In this respect, Proudhon's preference for renewed antinomy over sublation can be compared with Kierkegaard's preference for the unresolved tension of a paradoxical "synthesis" which nonetheless refuses to sublate the "infinite qualitative difference" between humanity and divinity.[108] Furthermore, both Kierkegaard and Proudhon oppose any idea of "God" which upholds the providence of the powerful over the weak, the impoverished, and the oppressed: namely, the God of evil.

However, insofar as it exposes Christendom's construct of a God of Providence as a projection of human delusions of power, I suggest that Kierkegaard's theology might offer a higher negation of Proudhon's *anti-theism*. Both the *theism* of Christendom and the *anti-theism* of Proudhon are ultimately realised via Kierkegaard's lens as manifestations of *despair*. And yet, in the irrepressible spirit

of *anarchē* as well as *apophasis*, I suggest that Kierkegaard's negation is itself laid open to even higher negations by renewed forms
of *anti-theism*—forms which perhaps break free of despair, forms
which we have yet to see.

Insofar as it seeks for a higher *theonomy*, the aspiration of this
dialectic is ultimately theological—albeit a theological *apophasis*
which remains dialectically open to its negation by anti-theology.
In this respect, such an anarchistic and apophatic theology understands its struggle with God somewhat differently from Proudhon.
Whereas Proudhon wages eternal war against the idea of the God
of Providence in the name of justice, Kierkegaard urges Christianity
to struggle against the idols of the mind, incarnate in the illusion
of state Christendom, which imagine divine omnipotence to be
an infinite projection of finite human power. Unlike Proudhon,
Kierkegaard discerns that at the ground of all freedom there is
the revelation of a hidden, silent lake—even a secret abyss—of
unfathomable divine love. Ultimately the self is enabled to struggle
with God because, out of the omnipotence of love, God gives the
ground of freedom from which struggle becomes possible.

Furthermore, God has given Godself to be struggled with: as
an other whose omnipotence does not subjugate, re-assimilate,
or annihilate the self, but who desires the self to become itself
(and no other) in freedom as Spirit. To an extent, Proudhon and
Kierkegaard agree that God is Wholly Other; but for Kierkegaard
this is only one side of a deeper dialectic. God is ultimately the
Holy Other who also descends—as well as withdraws—in the gracious gift of a divine love which offers itself in the space of alterity.
For Kierkegaard, while struggle is free to express itself in despair,
defiance, offence, love, or even indifference, such struggles are ultimately stages on the way to a higher synthesis: the struggle of
restless Spirit, as self, as freedom, realising itself as the image of
God, in faith willing to become itself, resting transparently in God.

In Genesis thirty-two's image of Jacob's conflict with the mysterious divine stranger to which both Proudhon and Kierkegaard
appeal, de Lubac discerns "the condition of all greatness, and it
may be the means—but here Proudhon would no longer follow
us—of a purer submission."[109] Such "purer submission" involves
a self-denial which consummates the loving struggle with God

by reconciling itself in faith's vow, "nevertheless, not my will, but your will be done" (Luke 22:42). Denying its claim to be its own *archē*, the restless self surrenders its despairing will-to-power[110] in order, paradoxically, to will to be itself as resting transparently in God.[111] In doing so, the self surrenders itself to a God who, through the primal creative *kenosis* (self-giving) of love, has already surrendered what humanity would imagine to be absolute power in the creative gift of freedom.

The Spirit, once again, is freedom. And freedom is also manifest in the possibility to negate "God"—a possibility of despairing negation which, out of wounded love and with "unfathomable grief", God does not negate. As such, the *kenosis* of the human self as Spirit is a free response to grace: the primal *kenosis* of divine omnipotence, sacrificed to the inviolable divine gift of human freedom. So long as the human imagination remains inventive and evasive in its construction of theological idols to subsidise its own desire for power, however, theological thinking does well to heed Proudhon's demonic-prophetic profession that "God is inexhaustible, and our contest eternal".[112] Until it discovers final rest in God, the restless Spirit is destined to struggle against and with God; against "God" and with God. Perhaps in a spirit of *anarchē* and *agonia* as well as *apophasis*, theology should struggle against the idols of despair, continually renewing the spirit sought by one of its greatest mystics: "Therefore let us pray to God that we may be free of God".[113]

Notes

1. *The Sickness Unto Death*, ed. and trans. Howard V. Hong and Edna H. Hong (Princeton, New Jersey: Princeton University Press, 1983), p. 13, p. 29 (hereafter SUD).

2. Deriving from the theological notion of *kenosis*: the self-emptying or self-eclipsing of God invoked with reference to the act of incarnation (Philippians 2:7). On the wider role of this idea as a defining motif in Kierkegaard's thought see David R. Law, *Kierkegaard's Kenotic Christology* (Oxford: Oxford University Press, 2013).

3. Kierkegaard elaborates this tension between love and freedom further in *Philosophical Fragments*, ed. and trans. Howard V. Hong and

Edna H. Hong (Princeton, New Jersey: Princeton University Press, 1985), p. 30.

4. SUD, 126.

5. Kierkegaard, *Christian Discourses, The Crisis and a Crisis in the Life of an Actress,* ed. and trans. Howard V. Hong and Edna H. Hong (Bloomington: Indiana University Press, 1997), p. 66–67.

6. Proudhon, *System of Economical Contradictions or, The Philosophy of Misery,* trans. Benjamin R. Tucker (New York: Arno Press, 1972), pp. 83–5 (hereafter PM).

7. Cf. the comment of Joakim Garff, 'The Eyes of Argus: The Point of View and Points of View on Kierkegaard's Work as an Author', in *Kierkegaard: A Critical Reader,* ed. Jonathan Rée and Jane Chamberlain (Malden MA: Blackwell, 1998), p. 77. For critique of this approach see Sylvia Walsh, 'Reading Kierkegaard With Kierkegaard Against Garff', *Søren Kierkegaard Newsletter 38* (July 1999), p. 4–14. My tactic of reading with and against Kierkegaard and Proudhon is, however, not a hermeneutic of mistrust towards authorial/autobiographical intention or self-determination but is rather an experimental attempt to think dialectically with the theistic and anti-theistic ideas they present.

8. Søren Kierkegaard, *Journals and Papers,* 7 volumes, ed. and trans. By Howard V. Hong and Edna H. Hong (Bloomington, Indiana: Indiana University Press, 1967–1978), volume 6, entry 6523. Hereafter referred to as JP by volume and entry number (e.g. JP 6:6523).

9. He was dubbed such by Karl Grün. See further Paul Thomas, *Karl Marx and the Anarchists* (Abingdon & New York: Routledge, 2010), p. 176.

10. Particularly as Proudhon is critical of atheism as not sufficiently conscious of its dialectical relationship to theism. See further below.

11. Ludwig Feuerbach, *The Essence of Christianity,* trans. George Elliot (New York: Prometheus Books, 1989), p. xvi.

12. Apophatic theology is a form of negative theology which acknowledges the limits of language in relation to the otherness of God. It appeals to the technique of *Apophasis:* meaning 'to deny', 'to speak away from'; contrasted with *Kataphasis:* meaning 'to affirm', 'to speak down', or bring down to the level of language. Key to this

dialectic is the relationship between the kataphatic assertion 'God is light', and its apophatic denial 'God is not light' or 'God is dark', in which the contradiction between these two statements is transcended by the apophatic vision of God as 'dazzling darkness'. The seminal mystical theologian Pseudo-Dionysius proposes the notion of God as "dazzling darkness" as a violation and sublation of the law of logical non-contradiction. Pseudo-Dionysius' *The Mystical Theology* seeks contemplation of the "mysteries of God's word" which lie "beyond unknowing and light", hidden "in the brilliant darkness of a hidden silence" and "beyond assertion and denial." Pseudo-Dionysius, 'The Mystical Theology', Chapter 1.1, *The Complete Works*, trans. Colm Luibheid (New York: Paulist Press, 1987), 135, 141. For a helpful treatment of the relation between *apophasis* and anarchism see Christopher R. Williams, 'Anarchic Insurgencies: The Mythos of Authority and the Violence of Mental Health', in *Psychological Jurisprudence: Critical Explorations in Law, Crime, and Society*, ed. by Bruce A. Arrigo (Albany: State University of New York, 2004), pp. 46–53. Williams writes that "To suggest that a spirit of *apophasis* runs throughout anarchism's search for a more human social order is to suggest that humanity and justice require a stripping away, a negation, of that which subjugates the affirmative in life [...] the apophatic indirectly seeks the affirmation of life through the negation of that which inhibits it. In a word, the apophatic seeks justice" (p. 47).

13. This reading of kenosis as subversively emptying human forms of power and empowering forms of vulnerability is indebted in part to Sarah Coakley, 'Kenosis and Subversion: On the Repression of 'Vulnerability' in Christian Feminist Writing', ed. Daphne Hampson, *Swallowing a Fishbone?: Feminist Theologians Debate Christianity* (London: SPCK, 1996), 82–111. See further my *Struggling With God: Kierkegaard and the Temptation of Spiritual Trial* (Cambridge: James Clarke & Co., 2013), p. 263–5.

14. JP 4:4711.

15. The relative relationships of Kierkegaard and Proudhon to Hegel would demand a substantial study in itself. I have addressed Kierkegaard's critical stance towards the Hegelian sublation of what Kierkegaard upholds as a paradoxical and inviolable "infinite qualitative difference" between the human and the divine elsewhere (*Struggling With God*, p. 219–226). The scholarship on

this relation is extensive. In particular, see further Mark C. Taylor, *Journeys to Selfhood: Hegel and Kierkegaard* (California: University of California Press, 1989); Niels Thulstrup, Kierkegaard's Relation to Hegel, trans. George L. Stengren (Princeton: Princeton University Press, 1980); and *Kierkegaard's Relation to Hegel Reconsidered* (Cambridge: Cambridge University Press, 2003) in which Stewart contends that Kierkegaard's ire is directed more towards contemporary Hegelian thought than towards Hegel himself. On Proudhon's relation to Hegel, see further René Berthier, *Études proudhoniennes, L'Économie politique* (Paris: Éditions du Monde libertaire, 2009). Berthier shows how Proudhon's ambivalent and often second-hand knowledge of Hegel was more significant than many, particularly owing to Karl Marx, have given credence for. Both Marx and his enemy Karl Grün had attempted to train Proudhon in Hegelianism. I am grateful to an anonymous reviewer of this essay for providing me with a translation of Berthier's chapter on 'Proudon and German Philosophy'.

16. Henri de Lubac, *The Un-Marxian Socialist: A Study of Proudhon*, trans. R. E. Scantlebury (London: Steed and Ward, 1948), p. 178.

17. Françoise Meltzer, *Seeing Double: Baudelaire's Modernity* (Chicago/London: University of Chicago Press, 2011), p. 51 n.69. However, since Proudhon did not read German, and since by the decisive date of 1848 Hegel's works had not yet been translated into French, his knowledge of Hegelian thought was formed principally from conversations with Charles Grün, "a German, who had come to France to study the various philosophical and socialistic systems." J. A. Langlois, 'P. J. Proudhon: His Life and His Works', *What is Property? An Inquiry into the Principle of Right and of Government*, trans Benj. R. Tucker (New York: Dover, 1970), p. xxxvi.

18. *Pierre-Joseph Proudhon: His Life and Work* (New York: Schocken Books, 1972), p. 205.

19. JP 4:4350.

20. "I am without authority. I make no proposal in relation to the established order, not a single one. I think that for the sake of the cause it can continue as it stands, except that each individual should make a confession before God and compel oneself to remember it." *Kierkegaard's Journals and Notebooks: Volume 7, Journals*

NB15-NB20, ed. and trans. Bruce Kirmmse et al (Princeton, New Jersey: Princeton University Press, 2014), *Journal* NB19: 28 1850, p. 356.

21. The canonical text in the field of Kierkegaardian hermeneutics remains Roger Poole, *Kierkegaard: The Indirect Communication* (Charlottesville and London: University Press of Virginia, 1993). It is notable that Proudhon's own dramatic style rendered him vulnerable to readings which go against the subtleties of his own intention. His frustrations concerning this abound in his response to the misunderstandings which arise from his scandalous proclamations that "property is theft", and "God is evil", which George Woodcock calls "a phrase to startle and provoke the world." *Pierre-Joseph Proudhon*, p. 99.

22. See 'Chapter XIV: What Shall We Do With S.K.?', *Kierkegaard and Radical Discipleship: A New Perspective*. Princeton, New Jersey: Princeton University Press, 1968.

23. See Vernard Eller, *Kierkegaard and Radical Discipleship: a New Perspective* (Princeton, NJ: Princeton University Press, 1968) and Vernard Eller, *Christian Anarchy: Jesus' Primacy Over the Powers* (Grand Rapids, Michigan: Wm. B. Eerdmans Publishing Company, 1987). See also Richard A. Davis's more recent insightful reading which "suggests one way in which the Danish philosopher theologian Søren Kierkegaard can be understood as an anarchist. It suggests that Kierkegaard advocates neither love nor hatred of the state, but indifference, the fruit of a truly Christian life. The argument begins by explaining how anarchism can be understood as indifference." 'Love, Hate, and Kierkegaard's Christian Politics of Indifference', in Alexandre J. M. E. Christoyannopoulos (ed.), *Religious Anarchism: New Perspectives* (Newcastle upon Tyne: Cambridge Scholars Publishing, 2009), pp. 82–105, at p. 82.

24. For example, JP 3:2932, 3:2942, 3:2946, 3:2951.

25. Robert L. Perkins, 'Kierkegaard's critique of the bourgeois state', *Inquiry: An Interdisciplinary Journal of Philosophy*, (1984) 27:1–4, p. 212–13. And yet, though offering individualistic responses to certain problems, Kierkegaard is neither unequivocally anti-social nor anti-community. Kierkegaard juxtaposes "the individual" to "the crowd" and even to the State, but not necessarily to the community (particularly the community of believers). The individual who may

become the victim of the State is nonetheless treasured and upheld in love by the community of individuals before God: "the other" thus becomes "the neighbour" made intimate through the communion of divine love. Kierkegaard, *Works of Love*, ed. and trans. Howard V. Hong and Edna H. Hong (Princeton, New Jersey: Princeton University Press, 1995), p. 37. See also Perkins, 'Kierkegaard's critique of the bourgeois state', pp. 207–218. See further George Pattison and Steven Shakespeare (eds.), *Kierkegaard: The Self in Society* (Basingstoke and London: Macmillan Press, 1998); Simon D. Podmore, 'Between Sociology, Anthropology, and Psychology: The Insider/Outsider Self', in Jon Stewart (ed.), *The Blackwell Companion to Kierkegaard* (Oxford: Blackwell, 2015), pp. 415–434.

26. Perkins, p. 214.

27. Perkins, p. 214.

28. JP 4:4238.

29. *Works of Love*, p. 253, p. 37.

30. JP 4:4231.

31. JP 2:1259.

32. JP 4:4953.

33. JP 2:1273.

34. JP 4:4953.

35. SUD, p. 40.

36. As paradigmatically outlined by G. W. F. Hegel, *Phenomenology of Spirit*, B, IV, 187, trans. A.V. Miller (Oxford: Oxford University Press, 1977), p. 111–119.

37. SUD, p. 83 (my emphasis).

38. JP 4:4350.

39. SUD, p. 126.

40. PM, p. 465.

41. Cited in de Lubac, *The Un-marxian Socialist*, 177.

42. Published treatments of Kierkegaard and Proudhon are scarce. On the relationship between the thought of Kierkegaard and Proudhon

see further Simon D. Podmore, 'Struggling With God: Kierkegaard/ Proudhon', *Acta Kierkegaardiana Vol II: Kierkegaard and Great Philosophers*, ed. by C. Diatka and R. Králik (Mexico City/Barcelona/ Sala: Sociedad Iberoamericana de Estudios Kierkegaardianos, University of Barcelona, Kierkegaard Society in Slovakia, 2007), pp. 90–103. See also Simon D. Podmore, *Kierkegaard and the Self Before God: Anatomy of the Abyss* (Bloomington: Indiana University Press, 2011), pp. 97–101. See also Jean Blum, 'Pierre-Joseph Proudhon et Søren Kierkegaard', *La Revue Scandinave*, no.4 (1911), April, pp. 276–87. On the reception of Kierkegaard in France see Jon Stewart, 'France: Kierkegaard as a Forerunner of Existentialism and Poststructuralism', in *Kierkegaard's International Reception Tome I: Northern and Western Europe*, ed. by Jon Stewart (Farnham: Ashgate, 2009) pp. 421–476. There are passing comparisons between Kierkegaard's and Proudhon's treatments of irony in Winfield E. Nagley, 'Søren Kierkegaard's *The Concept of Irony*', *Journal of the History of Ideas*, 29: 3 (1968), p. 464 (pp. 458–464) and Pierre Schoentjes, 'Ironie et anarchie : De l'éthique à l'esthétique', *Revue d'histoire littéraire de la France*, 99: 3 (1999), p. 493 (pp. 485–497), along with a mention of both figures in Joseph A. Dane's *The Critical Mythology of Irony* (Athens: University of Georgia Press, 2011), p. 9. There is a brief reference to Proudhon in relation to Kierkegaard's attitude towards mysticism and atheism in Régis Jolivet, 'Le problème de la religion de Kierkegaard', *Revue Philosophique de Louvain*, Troisième série, Tome 47, N°13 (1949), p. 138 (pp. 137–142).

43. As Gregor Malantschuk observes, Kierkegaard most likely gleaned some acquaintance of French socialism, including Proudhon, from discussions in the Danish newspapers. Gregor Malantschuk, *The Controversial Kierkegaard*, trans. Howard and Edna Hong (Ontario: Wilfrid Laurier University Press, 1980) p. 11 n.36.

44. "If a man continues with this purely human outlook, then the unconditioned is the devil, or God is the evil, as modern French philosophy [Proudhon?] maintains, God is the evil in the sense that he is guilty of all man's unhappiness; if we could only eliminate the unconditioned, knock all ideals out of our heads, everything would go well – but God makes us unhappy, he is the evil" (JP 4:4911). "But as a matter of fact it is the eternal that is needed. Some stronger evidence is needed than socialism's belief that God is the evil, and so it

says itself, for the demonic always contains the truth in reverse" (JP 6:6256).

45. *De la Justice dans la Révolution et dans L'Eglise*, volume i, p. 448. Cited in de Lubac, *The Un-marxian Socialist*, p. 265 n.1.

46. "Justice, nothing else; that is the alpha and omega of my argument". Pierre-Joseph Proudhon, *What is Property? An Inquiry into the Principle of Right and of Government*, p. 14 (hereafter WP).

47. *De la Justice dans la Révolution et dans L'Eglise*, volume iii, p. 302. Cited in de Lubac, *The Un-marxian Socialist*, p. 271 n.28.

48. WP, p. 22.

49. WP, p. 23.

50. WP, p. 30.

51. WP, p. 24.

52. WP, p. 281.

53. There may be some resonance at this point between Proudhon's exclusion of God from morality and Emmanuel Levinas' plea for ethics as inter-subjective response to the face of the human (wholly) other, rather than as the vertical response to the heteronomous Divine Command of a Wholly Other God issued from "beyond". For a recent treatment of Levinasian ethics of anarchism—though one which does not draw significantly on Proudhon—see Simon Critchley, *Infinitely Demanding: Ethics of Commitment, Politics of Resistance* (London and New York: Verso, 2007).

54. WP, p. 245. On this question of ontological difference and relationality between the human and the divine see further my 'Struggling with God: Kierkegaard/Proudhon', pp. 94–95.

55. WP, p. 245.

56. PM, p. 2.

57. WP, p. 22.

58. PM, pp. 17–31.

59. PM, p. 7.

60. Letter to abbé X., Jan. 22nd 1849. Cited in de Lubac, *The Un-marxian Socialist*, 177.

61. *De la Justice dans la Révolution et dans L'Eglise*, volume iii, 179. Cited in de Lubac, *The Un-marxian Socialist*, 265.

62. Proudhon asserts that "Providence in God is a contradiction within a contradiction; it was through providence that God was actually made in the image of man; take away this providence, and God ceases to be man, and man in turn must abandon all his pretensions to divinity" (PM, p. 462). Through this Proudhon also affirms a critique of Feuerbach's own scandalous assertion that "Consciousness of God is self-consciousness, knowledge of God is self-knowledge." *The Essence of Christianity*, p. 12. For Proudhon "[H]umanism is a religion as detestable as any of the theisms of ancient origin" (PM, p. 457). See further my 'Struggling with God: Kierkegaard/Proudhon', pp. 95–96.

63. See further the erudite discussion of Proudhon in Bernard Schweizer, *Misotheism: The Untold Story of Hating God* (Oxford: Oxford University Press, 2011), pp. 40–47. Schweizer refers to Proudhon's 1846 *Philosophie de la misère* as the "earliest and possibly the most radical and shocking manifestation" of a "politically inspired misotheism" (p. 40) and Proudhon himself as "a titan of misotheism" (p. 46).

64. *Philosophie de la misère*, volume ii, p. 253. Cited in de Lubac, *The Un-marxian Socialist*, p. 179.

65. PM, p. 137.

66. PM, p. 450.

67. PM, p. 458.

68. PM, p. 83.

69. PM, pp. 84–5.

70. Woodcock, *Pierre-Joseph Proudhon*, p. 205.

71. PM, p. 461.

72. PM, pp. 463–4.

73. PM, p. 465. "If God and man are opposed to each other, they are by that very fact necessary to each other". Letter to Guillaumin, Nov. 21st 1846. Cited in *The Un-Marxian Socialist*, pp. 177–178.

74. "[N]either is more than the other; they are two incomplete realities, which have not the fullness of existence." Notebook (1846). Cited in de Lubac, *The Un-Marxian Socialist*, p. 178 n.48.

75. Woodcock, *Pierre-Joseph Proudhon*, p. 99.

76. PM, p. 452.

77. PM, p. 461. Humanity must instead recognise God, not as man's reflection, but as "his antagonist. And this last consideration will suffice to make us reject humanism also, as tending invincibly, by the deification of humanity, to a religious restoration. The true remedy for fanaticism [...] is to prove to humanity that God, in case there is a God, is its enemy" (PM, pp. 467–8).

78. *De la Justice dans la Révolution et dans L'Eglise*, volume ii, p. 253. Cited in de Lubac, *The Un-marxian Socialist*, p. 289.

79. This is not equivalent to a denial of the existence of God (which would be to lapse into the discourse of theism and atheism). Rather, "A prejudice relative to the divine essence has been destroyed [e.g. Providence]; by the same stroke the independence of man is established: that is all. The reality of the divine Being is left intact, and our hypothesis still exists" (PM, p. 451).

80. PM, p. 468.

81. PM, p. 448.

82. PM, p. 450.

83. JP 6:6256.

84. JP 2:1237.

85. Feuerbach, *The Essence of Christianity*, p. 14 (see further p. 14–18).

86. See note 13 above.

87. *The Essence of Christianity*, p. 16

88. *The Essence of Christianity*, p. 17.

89. I elaborate the possible nature of such theological struggle between contrary views of God in my *Struggling With God*.

90. Psalm 22:1; Matthew 27:46. I explore the ambivalence of this further in 'My God, My God, Why Have You Forsaken Me? Between Consolation & Desolation', in Christopher C.H. Cook (ed.), *Spirituality, Theology & Mental Health: Multidisciplinary Perspectives* (London: SCM Press, 2013), pp. 193–210.

91. 'The Instant', No. 5, July 27, 1855, *Kierkegaard's Attack Upon 'Christendom'*, trans. Walter Lowrie (Princeton: Princeton University Press, 1968), p. 157.

92. JP 4:4711. Kierkegaard proposes "Spirit" as the paradoxical "synthesis" of opposites which retains the alterity that he interprets as lost within Hegelian "mediation" or "sublation" (*Aufheben*)—a reconciliation which ultimately sublimates what Kierkegaard maintains as an irreducible "infinite qualitative difference" between the human and the divine. See Mark C. Taylor, *Journeys to Selfhood: Hegel and Kierkegaard* (Berkeley and Los Angeles, California and London: University of California Press, 1980), pp. 170–171.

93. JP 2:1251.

94. I discuss this further in *Kierkegaard and the Self Before God*, 160–165.

95. JP 2:1251.

96. JP 2:1251.

97. JP 2:1251.

98. SUD, p. 68.

99. SUD, pp. 68–70. See further my *Kierkegaard and the Self Before God*, pp. 159ff.

100. This is analogous to Hegel's view of the Unhappy Consciousness as the internalisation of the Master-Slave dialectic: "the duplication which formerly was divided between two individuals, the lord and the bondsman, is now lodged in one […] the *Unhappy Consciousness* is the consciousness of self as a dual-natured, merely contradictory being." Hegel, *Phenomenology of Spirit*, trans. A. V. Miller (Oxford: Oxford University Press, 1977), 'B. Self-Consciousness', IV, B, 206, p. 126. See further my *Kierkegaard and the Self Before God*, pp. 160–164.

101. JP 6: 6761.

102. SUD, p. 72.

103. *The Concept of Anxiety*, ed. and trans. Reidar Thomte in collaboration with Albert B. Anderson (Princeton, New Jersey: Princeton University Press, 1980), p. 143*.

104. SUD, p. 116.

105. Schweizer notes that while Proudon "still held a vestigial belief" in "a personal God" he vehemently opposed "any divine object of worship" (*Misotheism*, p. 50), equally so if this object, or idol, be a humanist idea of Man himself. See David Nicholls, *Deity and Domination: Images of God and the State in the Nineteenth and Twentieth Centuries* (London: Routledge, 2005), pp. 204–213, for a lucid account of Proudhon's development "from a critical acceptance of Christianity, through a kind of deism to anti-theism" (p. 204), motivated by a growing political rejection of political and religious authority which culminated in a declaration of total war on God by the pacifist anarchist.

106. In this defiant sense Proudhon's thought had a significant influence on Baudelaire's poetic idea of "the demonic" (see further Meltzer, *Seeing Double: Baudelaire's Modernity*, pp. 45–65).

107. Meltzer, *Seeing Double: Baudelaire's Modernity*, pp. 52–53.

108. I discuss this further in *Struggling With God*, pp. 220–224.

109. *The Un-Marxian Socialist*, p. 275.

110. For a compelling and critical comparison of Nietzsche's will-to-power and Kierkegaard's view of power in relation to Christ see J. Keith Hyde, *Concepts of Power in Kierkegaard and Nietzsche* (Farnham: Ashgate, 2010). Hyde argues "that Kierkegaard's theory of power is more coherent and consistent than Nietzsche's position [which Hyde regards as undermined by inconsistency and contradiction], which he foresaw and "forswore" with uncanny accuracy" (p. 7). Nonetheless, Hyde also suggests that had Kierkegaard been able to read Nietzsche, he would have esteemed him "for openly expressing his antagonism against divine authority" and for pursuing "a tragic bid for freedom" which shames "the deplorable ways that the church, grace, and compassion had been used to buttress political power in state Lutheranism" (p. 183).

111. SUD, p. 82.

112. *De la Justice dans la Révolution et dans L'Eglise*, volume ii, p. 253. Cited in de Lubac, *The Un-marxian Socialist*, p. 289.

113. Meister Eckhart, *The Complete Mystical Works of Meister Eckhart*, trans. Maurice O'C Walshe (New York: Crossroad, 2009) Sermon Eighty-Seven, p. 422.

References

Berthier, René, *Études proudhoniennes, L'Économie politique* (Paris: Éditions du Monde libertaire, 2009).

Blum, Jean, 'Pierre-Joseph Proudhon et Søren Kierkegaard', *La Revue Scandinave*, no.4 (1911), April, pp. 276–87.

Coakley, Sarah, 'Kenosis and Subversion: On the Repression of 'Vulnerability' in Christian Feminist Writing', in *Swallowing a Fishbone?: Feminist Theologians Debate Christianity*, ed. by Daphne Hampson, (London: SPCK, 1996), pp. 82–111.

Critchley, Simon, *Infinitely Demanding: Ethics of Commitment, Politics of Resistance* (London and New York: Verso, 2007).

Dane, Joseph A., *The Critical Mythology of Irony* (Athens: University of Georgia Press, 2011).

Davis, Richard A., 'Love, Hate, and Kierkegaard's Christian Politics of Indifference', in *Religious Anarchism: New Perspectives*, ed. by Alexandre J. M. E. Christoyannopoulos, (Newcastle upon Tyne: Cambridge Scholars Publishing, 2009).

Eller, Vernard, *Christian Anarchy: Jesus' Primacy Over the Powers* (Grand Rapids, Michigan: Wm. B. Eerdmans Publishing Company, 1987).

_____, *Kierkegaard and Radical Discipleship: A New Perspective*. Princeton, New Jersey: Princeton University Press, 1968.

Feuerbach, Ludwig, *The Essence of Christianity*, trans. by George Elliot (New York: Prometheus Books, 1989).

Garff, Joakim, 'The Eyes of Argus: The Point of View and Points of View on Kierkegaard's Work as an Author', in *Kierkegaard: A Critical Reader*, ed. by Jonathan Rée and Jane Chamberlain (Malden MA: Blackwell, 1998).

Hegel, G. W. F., *Phenomenology of Spirit*, trans. by A.V. Miller (Oxford: Oxford University Press, 1977).

Hyde J., Keith, *Concepts of Power in Kierkegaard and Nietzsche* (Farnham: Ashgate, 2010).

Jolivet, Régis, 'Le problème de la religion de Kierkegaard', *Revue Philosophique de Louvain*, Troisième série, Tome 47, N°13 (1949), pp. 137–142.

Kierkegaard, Søren, *Christian Discourses, The Crisis and a Crisis in the Life of an Actress*, ed. and trans. by Howard V. Hong and Edna H. Hong (Bloomington: Indiana University Press, 1997)

———, *The Concept of Anxiety*, ed. and trans. by Reidar Thomte in collaboration with Albert B. Anderson (Princeton, New Jersey: Princeton University Press, 1980).

———, *Journals and Papers*, 7 volumes, ed. and trans. by Howard V. Hong and Edna H. Hong (Bloomington, Indiana: Indiana University Press, 1967–1978).

———, *Kierkegaard's Attack Upon 'Christendom'*, trans. by Walter Lowrie (Princeton: Princeton University Press, 1968).

———, *Kierkegaard's Journals and Notebooks: Volume 7, Journals NB15-NB20*, ed. and trans. by Bruce Kirmmse et al (Princeton, New Jersey: Princeton University Press, 2014).

———, *Philosophical Fragments*, ed. and trans. by Howard V. Hong and Edna H. Hong (Princeton, New Jersey: Princeton University Press, 1985).

———, *The Sickness Unto Death*, ed. and trans. by Howard V. Hong and Edna H. Hong (Princeton, New Jersey: Princeton University Press, 1983).

———, *Works of Love*, ed. and trans. by Howard V. Hong and Edna H. Hong (Princeton, New Jersey: Princeton University Press, 1995).

Langlois, J. A., 'P. J. Proudhon: His Life and His Works', *What is Property? An Inquiry into the Principle of Right and of Government*, trans by Benj. R. Tucker (New York: Dover, 1970).

Law, David R., *Kierkegaard's Kenotic Christology* (Oxford: Oxford University Press, 2013).

de Lubac, Henri, *The Un-Marxian Socialist: A Study of Proudhon*, trans. by R. E. Scantlebury (London: Steed and Ward, 1948).

Malantschuk, Gregor, *The Controversial Kierkegaard*, trans. by Howard and Edna Hong (Ontario: Wilfrid Laurier University Press, 1980).

Meister Eckhart, *The Complete Mystical Works of Meister Eckhart*, trans. by Maurice O'C Walshe (New York: Crossroad, 2009).

Meltzer, Françoise, *Seeing Double: Baudelaire's Modernity* (Chicago/London: University of Chicago Press, 2011).

Nagley, Winfield E., 'Søren Kierkegaard's *The Concept of Irony*', *Journal of the History of Ideas*, 29: 3 (1968), pp. 458–464.

Nicholls, David, *Deity and Domination: Images of God and the State in the Nineteenth and Twentieth Centuries* (London: Routledge, 2005).

Perkins, Robert L., 'Kierkegaard's critique of the bourgeois state', *Inquiry: An Interdisciplinary Journal of Philosophy*, (1984) 27:1–4, p. 212–13.

Pattison, George and Steven Shakespeare (eds.), *Kierkegaard: The Self in Society* (Basingstoke and London: Macmillan Press, 1998).

Podmore, Simon D., 'Between Sociology, Anthropology, and Psychology: The Insider/Outsider Self', in *A Companion to Kierkegaard*, ed. by Jon Stewart, (Oxford: Blackwell, 2015), pp. 415–434.

_____, *Kierkegaard and the Self Before God: Anatomy of the Abyss* (Bloomington: Indiana University Press, 2011).

_____, 'My God, My God, Why Have You Forsaken Me? Between Consolation & Desolation', in *Spirituality, Theology & Mental Health: Multidisciplinary Perspectives*, ed. by Christopher C.H. Cook (London: SCM Press, 2013), pp. 193–210.

_____, 'Struggling With God: Kierkegaard/Proudhon', *Acta Kierkegaardiana Vol II: Kierkegaard and Great Philosophers*, ed. by C. Diatka and R. Králik (Mexico City/Barcelona/Sala: Sociedad Iberoamericana de Estudios Kierkegaardianos, University of Barcelona, Kierkegaard Society in Slovakia, 2007), pp. 90–103.

_____, *Struggling With God: Kierkegaard and the Temptation of Spiritual Trial* (Cambridge: James Clarke & Co., 2013).

Poole, Roger, *Kierkegaard: The Indirect Communication* (Charlottesville and London: University Press of Virginia, 1993).

Proudhon, Pierre-Joseph, *System of Economical Contradictions or, The Philosophy of Misery*, trans. by Benjamin R. Tucker (New York: Arno Press, 1972).

_____, *What is Property? An Inquiry into the Principle of Right and of Government*, trans. by Benjamin R. Tucker (New York: Dover Publications, 1970).

Pseudo-Dionysius, 'The Mystical Theology', *The Complete Works*, trans. by Colm Luibheid (New York: Paulist Press, 1987).

Schoentjes, Pierre, 'Ironie et anarchie: De l'éthique à l'esthétique', *Revue d'histoire littéraire de la France*, 99: 3 (1999), pp. 485–497.

Schweizer, Bernard, *Hating God: The Untold Story of Misotheism* (Oxford: Oxford University Press, 2011).

Stewart, Jon, 'France: Kierkegaard as a Forerunner of Existentialism and Poststructuralism', in *Kierkegaard's International Reception Tome I: Northern and Western Europe*, ed. by Jon Stewart (Farnham: Ashgate, 2009), pp. 421–476.

_____, *Kierkegaard's Relation to Hegel Reconsidered* (Cambridge: Cambridge University Press, 2003).

Taylor, Mark C., *Journeys to Selfhood: Hegel and Kierkegaard* (California: University of California Press, 1989).

Thomas, Paul, *Karl Marx and the Anarchists* (Abingdon & New York: Routledge, 2010).

Thulstrup, Niels, *Kierkegaard's Relation to Hegel*, trans. by George L. Stengren (Princeton: Princeton University Press, 1980).

Walsh, Sylvia, 'Reading Kierkegaard With Kierkegaard Against Garff', *Søren Kierkegaard Newsletter 38* (July 1999), p. 4–14.

Williams, Christopher R., 'Anarchic Insurgencies: The Mythos of Authority and the Violence of Mental Health', in *Psychological Jurisprudence: Critical Explorations in Law, Crime, and Society*, ed. by Bruce A. Arrigo (Albany: State University of New York, 2004), pp. 46–53.

Woodcock, George, *Pierre-Joseph Proudhon: His Life and Work* (New York: Schocken Books, 1972).

Does religious belief necessarily mean servitude? On Max Stirner and the hardened heart

Hugo Strandberg
Åbo Akademi University, Finland

A common view of morality and religion is that they demand self-denial. The starting point is me in isolation, to which we then ought to add a moral concern which restricts my doings, or, according to the self-professed egoist, ought not to add. The moral difficulty is hence about forcing oneself to renounce the things one wants, even parts of oneself. Religious belief means servitude, and we have to choose between it and freedom. In this chapter, the intricacies of this picture of morality and religion are critically discussed. In this discussion, Max Stirner is used as the main interlocutor. Another understanding of morality and religion is contrasted to the egoist one, a contrasting understanding in which it is egoism that is the result of self-denial: the egoist must harden his or her heart, that is, must renounce love. According to this contrasting understanding, religious belief is thus positively related to freedom.

In John Milton's *Paradise Lost*, Satan says: "Better to reign in Hell, than serve in Heav'n."[1] And "Here at last / We shall be free".[2] Or as the anarchist would say: "no gods, no masters".[3] According to this well-known anarchist slogan, all servitude should be rejected.[4] That slogan suggests that anarchism does not only affect the political realm narrowly understood, but also has a religious import: all gods should be eliminated too, not only all earthly masters. Religious faith means servitude and is therefore antithetical to freedom.

Such a general rejection of religion can be easily countered by pointing out that it is only possible to claim that religious

---

How to cite this book chapter:
Strandberg, H. 2017. Does religious belief necessarily mean servitude? On Max Stirner and the hardened heart. In: Christoyannopoulos, A. and Adams, M. S. (eds.) *Essays in Anarchism and Religion: Volume 1*. Pp. 283–307. Stockholm: Stockholm University Press. DOI: https://doi.org/10.16993/bak.h. License: CC-BY

belief necessarily mean servitude if you have surveyed *all* religious possibilities, including all imagined, not yet actual ones. In other words, it is not enough just to point to specific historical forms of religion, many of which are no doubt incompatible with anarchism. Answering the question whether religious belief necessarily means servitude in the affirmative would hence be a strange thing to do.

However, such a criticism of the "no gods, no masters" slogan is too superficial. The mistake is not simply an undue generalization. What is imperative is, instead, to get to grips with the thinking which lies behind it: what picture holds me captive when I definitely rule out all religious possibilities as 'servitude'?[5] In this paper I will only discuss one such picture, and my discussion is therefore by no means exhaustive. In the anarchist tradition there have been many critics of religion, but that criticism seldom occupies centre stage. Max Stirner's *Der Einzige und sein Eigentum* (1844) is in this respect very different.[6] His book can be read as an extensive discussion of the "no gods, no masters" slogan (even though he never uses that phrase) in that it is an attempt at spelling out what it would mean to reject servitude in general. There is thus an obvious picture of the above kind at work in it. This is the picture my discussion will be centred around. What makes Stirner's criticism of religion interesting for my purposes is that it is much more general than only restricted to religious belief: it is based on a picture of human life in its entirety. Focusing on that picture means that religious faith will not be the main focus of my discussion, but indirectly my discussion will suggest possibilities in which religious faith and anarchism are compatible, even though that is not my primary goal.

Since my starting point is a specific question – does religious belief necessarily mean servitude? – and since what my discussion will be centred around is a specific picture at work in Stirner's text, my focus will not be Stirner's text itself and its historical context. Scholarly exegeses of Stirner's works can be found elsewhere.[7] Stirner will here be used as an interlocutor in order for us to learn something as regards the main question. This could basically be done in two ways: either by turning something he says into a positive contribution to the answering of the question or by disentangling mistakes he makes in a way which makes it possible for us to gain better insight into the principal issue. In none of these two cases is his text or his historical context something to which we have to be faithful. Instead, the philosophical aim of this paper is to turn something seemingly dead into something that is still able to speak to us. One of my tasks is therefore to establish connections between Stirner's text and what is existentially relevant, positively or negatively, that is, to discuss the picture at work in it.

1. Stirner and the rejection of religious belief

Not knowing anything about Stirner, one might suppose that his criticism of religion is the usual one: religion is unreasonable. But what characterises the Young Hegelian criticism of religion is that it is not so much a criticism as an interpretation of religious belief from a position already more or less distant to it. *Der Einzige und sein Eigentum* should be understood as a radicalization of that approach and thus as a criticism of the way in which it has been carried out previously, for example in Feuerbach's *Das Wesen des Christentums* (1841, 2nd edn 1843). According to Stirner it is not only the religious believer who believes in "ghosts": reason is a ghost too and the belief in it just another form of religious belief. Stirner writes: "Whether the church, the bible or reason […] is the holy authority makes no essential difference."[8]

What is then, according to Stirner, the common problem? "Everything holy is a bond, a fetter."[9] This could be understood as a summarizing definition of the holy. Anything that binds me in this way is religious, even if it is not normally presented in that way. "Alienness is a criterion of the 'holy'. In everything holy there is something 'uncanny' [*Unheimliches*], i.e. alien, in which we are not quite at home [*heimisch und zu Hause*]. What is holy to me, is to me *not my own*".[10]

The problem, as Stirner sees it, is a problem pertaining to *any* ideal, no matter whether it is expressed in religious terms or not. An ideal is something I must strive toward but cannot ever reach. Ideals thus create the alienation they, superficially considered, might seem to be the solution to.[11] "Atheists" are in this regard no different than religious believers but only believe in other gods:[12] reason, truth, man, the good, justice, humanity, freedom.[13]

This is a crucial point in Stirner's line of thought but at the same time one that is hard to fathom. What, exactly, is it that Stirner criticises? What is an "ideal"? As I understand Stirner, it is not attempting to achieve something in general he finds problematic. What is it he finds problematic? The problem, if there is one, becomes especially poignant when failure to live up to the ideal is inevitable: since it is not possible to *be* reason, the good, humanity, or, for that matter, God, my life, if I made these ideals central to it, would, according to Stirner, always be a failure.[14] But what makes failure so bad? What Stirner finds problematic is, as I understand him, hence rather one possible attitude to failure: when I relate to myself as to a possible object of disrespect and self-contempt.

One way of explaining this is by means of an example. A good one could be one in which the ideals are ideals of etiquette. I try to become a refined person, but if those ideals of refinement I have adopted are impossible to live up to, I will always, though to different degrees, see myself as vulgar and shabby. And even if they are not impossible to live up to, and even if I succeed in living up to them, this will not be a permanent accomplishment: I will always need to keep up this refinement, against the risk of sinking into vulgarity. Here we have a case where the ideals apparently create the possibility of refinement but in fact only create alienation.

Of course, a more sophisticated form of etiquette will not make its distinctions in terms that are obviously empty and vain. On the contrary, taking clothes and superficial manners to be essential to etiquette could be seen as vulgar. So the more sophisticated form of etiquette will make its distinctions in other terms, for example moral ones. The alienation is created when I relate my distance to the moral ideal to myself. Hurting somebody is thus here understood not as something I do to her but as something I do to myself: I fail to live up to the ideal. And doing good to her is not something I do for her sake but for the sake of the good, that is for the sake of the ideal. Stirner writes:

Not τοὺς ἀνθρώπους, human beings, but τὸν ἄνθρωπον, man, the philanthropist carries in his heart. He certainly cares for each individual, but only because he wants to see his dear ideal realised everywhere. So there is no question of care for me, you, us[15]

Since he however does not pay much respect to what you are privatim – indeed, if he follows his principle strictly, attaches no value at all to that – he sees in you only what you are generatim. In other words: he sees in you not *you*, but the *species*, not Peter or Paul, but man, not the real one or the individual, but your essence or your concept, not the living one, but the *spirit*.[16]

And at bottom – this is the reason why the ideal, or any formulated principle, never touches upon what is essential – you and I are not conceptual: "neither I nor you are sayable, we are unspeakable".[17]

In other words, the problem with ideals is, first, to relate what one is doing to oneself, as if what I cared about was not the one I am trying to help but at bottom only about myself or about my ideal self; second, to see others as just potential instances of something general which my helping them really concerns. And these two problems are of course connected: understanding things in terms of etiquette, that is, understanding them in terms of my potential refinement and vulgarity, means understanding what I do as concerning who *I* am, and that in relation to the ideals I try to live up to, not to the one I am, say, rude to.

This, however, goes beyond anything Stirner actually says or even could have said. By trying to picture the situation in which what he says is actually connected to something important I have made his point far less general than it is for him, even distorted it. I will come back to that; this far I have only tried to create a sense of what he is up to by showing that he is on to something when he wants to get rid of ideals. Even if I will criticise him in what follows, there are things he is right about, but to see what these are we have to depart from his general way of thinking.

So, to sum up, what Stirner criticises all previous forms of criticism of religious belief for is that they have not touched upon the fundamental problem. In fact they have even reinforced that problem although the terms used are not so obviously religious anymore:

> To be sure, you could say, with Feuerbach and others, that religion
> has taken what is human out of man and placed it into a beyond
> so that it there, unattainable, has its existence as something per-
> sonal for itself, as a "God". But [...] you could certainly let fall
> the personality of the removed human, could transform God into
> the divine, and you would still remain religious. For the religious
> consists in being dissatisfied with *present* man, i.e. in setting up a
> *"perfection"* to be striven for[18]

The ideal, the perfection to be striven for, promises refinement,
were I to live up to it. But what it does not say is that I would not
understand myself in terms of vulgarity and would not be dissatisfied with myself, were it not for the ideal. So the road away from
alienation and to being at home in the world does not consist
in fulfilling the ideal, which I would nevertheless fail to do, but
in rejecting the ideal. The first kind of life only means servitude
to something alien. The second kind of life would not even be a
"kind", for this word would only suggest a new ideal.

This summary leaves us with a question: how come I submit to
something which only makes me dissatisfied with myself? Stirner
explains this by saying that I have become "possessed" by the
ideal.[19] In other words, it is not mine. If it were mine, it would not
alienate me and make me feel dissatisfied, for then I would be free
in relation to it and would be able to live in accordance with it or
not care about it, as I would see fit. But, in fact, this is not what
an ideal means, for an ideal is precisely that which I cannot alter
as I please. Expressed in Stirner's terms: an ideal is real only if you
are *possessed* by it. The problem begins "[p]recisely when an end
ceases to be *our* end and our *property*, which we as proprietors
can control at pleasure".[20] But this means that what I said above,
that there is a difference between doing good to someone for her
sake and for the sake of the good, is something Stirner would protest against. If I do something for any other sake than for my own
sake, this means that I cannot do as I please with that end. I am
possessed by the ideal and if I do not live up to it, it will turn
against me, judge me, and make me discontent with myself. This
feeling of discontent I am not able to get rid of, for I am not able to
dispose of the ideal. The end is, in short, not in my own power.[21] So
the alternative to the life of alienation and servitude, that is to the

obviously religious or merely apparently atheist life, is egoism.[22] (Stirner's alternative to the life of servitude to something alien is thus nonetheless a specific kind of life, a fact which will serve as a starting point for my critical discussion in the next section.)

This conclusion could be seen as a result of a reflection on moral autonomy. Only those ends I have set myself are mine; any other end means servitude. Of course, Kant believes that autonomously set ends really do bind me – that they really form *nomous* – but it is easy to see what Stirner would say about that. Connecting to the second formulation of the categorical imperative:[23] the respect to be paid to reason, in myself and generally, only means dividing me into an essential part and an inessential part,[24] means alienation, and means forgetting that I, as a corporeal existing being, that is not as thought, always go beyond all determinations.[25] In short, "autonomy" is a contradictory concept: a duty is precisely what I cannot do as I please with.

2. The possibility of complete control

If we accept this, there are different conclusions to draw. One would be to say that that kind of independence Stirner wants is impossible and that there always will be ends set by others to which you have to adapt yourself.[26] As a human being you are almost totally helpless as a newborn and therefore dependent on your parents, or others, and the ends they set for your life. But this Stirner would accept: those connections of dependence become looser as we grow up, and if they do not ever vanish completely, that only means that I should take command over my own life to the extent this proves to be possible.[27] Another conclusion would be to say that in the choice between servitude and egoism we should choose servitude. There are after all more important things than myself and to those I should submit. This is the price I have to pay. And a third conclusion would be that Stirner is completely right.

But all these conclusions presuppose that Stirner is right concerning the relation of what we, to sum up, could call "morality" (including religious faith) and myself.[28] According to Stirner there is necessarily a conflict here, for the first one always means servitude and self-denial. But is this really so? This is what the rest of this paper will, in different ways, try to question.

When questioning Stirner's point it would however be easy to misread him and take him to deny the many ways in which our lives are connected. But, as I pointed out, Stirner does not deny that. Stirner tries to show that what we often take to be a form of moral behaviour is in fact motivated egoistically: when doing something for my friend, I do something for what is mine, that is for myself.[29] Saying this risks making the term "egoism" meaningless, since there seems now not to be any contrast to it. But there is after all one thing that Stirner wants to combat: being possessed by something. When you are possessed, you are not doing what you are doing for egoist reasons and for your own sake, for you are not in control and able to skip doing it as you please. Stirner does not claim that morality is the only thing which gives rise to servitude and self-denial. For example, greed is according to Stirner a good example of being possessed, for I am here bound to the things I want to get in possession of in a way in which I am not able to control.[30] But even though he does not claim that morality is the only thing which gives rise to servitude and self-denial, love is still his paradigmatic example. Love is a kind of symbol for everything he sees as problematic.[31] Love is what you are not able to control and dispose of as you please. Love binds me and I am not able to control it. Love means servitude and self-denial.

A real situation in which I am possessed by ideas destructive to myself shows however rather the opposite of what Stirner is saying. Think of a voice of self-contempt: here it is clear that the ideas are destructive. But that very clarity would, if Stirner was right, testify that I am still in the grips of some ideas, namely those ideas that form the basis of my realization that the contemptuous voice is destructive. If I were able to stand free in relation to those ideas, the clarity would not be there anymore. And that is after all what the voice of self-contempt could be saying. In other words, I am able to say that these ideas are clearly destructive only in so far as the applicability of the terms by means of which I say this is not possible to decide to reject. And the same goes for the distinction between my own voice and the voice which has taken possession of me. If this were not so and that distinction were one which I could draw in any way I please – but which I? and what does "please" here mean? – I would never be able to tell which of the voices were mine and which of them were destructive.

Furthermore, trying to stand free in relation to all alternatives and have all of them in one's power is also a kind of life, and living that life thereby means renouncing all other alternatives. The word "renouncing" is here apt, for those other kinds of life I could not have dropped by choosing their alternative in a situation in which I stand free in relation to both them and their alternative, for this would mean being already decided in favour of the latter.

3. Love as a contrast both to control and servitude

These objections are however too clever and do not get hold of the fundamental problems. Let us instead examine some of Stirner's examples of what it means to have one's ends in one's power. Love is, as I said, the typical example of being possessed. What form should our relations have instead, according to Stirner? Of course, the basis must be found in myself: I do not relieve your suffering for your sake but in order to relieve that suffering which I feel when seeing you suffer.[32] Such an example is however unconvincing. If I were able to dispose of any end when I want to, it would certainly be easier to relieve my pain in that way than by helping you. So if I help you, that shows that I am possessed by you, if we use Stirner's terminology. It would be more convincing to express this in positive terms: by means of other people I acquire things I am not able to acquire on my own. And then we come to love, or to the only kind of love Stirner accepts: "love is […] as each of my feelings, *my property*. *Earn*, i.e. buy my property, then I let you have it."[33] And vice versa:

> A friend and a service of friendship […] society cannot procure for you. And yet you will at all moments be in need of such a service and on the slightest occasions need someone who is helpful to you. Therefore do not rely on society but see to it that you have the means to buy the fulfilment of your wishes.[34]

Buying and selling is here the best example of a relation where no ties are created between us and where we will consequently not be possessed by each other. No doubt Stirner is abstracting from the contexts in which buying and selling takes place in real life – that the cashier in the grocery store says good afternoon may be company regulations, but if you meet every other day it may turn into something fairly personal – but such an abstraction is perhaps acceptable here. Since he talks about love and friendship – what society cannot do for you – he is not talking about situations like the one in the grocery store, where these abstractions are easily made. So if Stirner happens to meet the prostitute he visited the night before, who gave him all that society cannot procure for him in terms of comfort, consolation, and sex, what will be his reaction? Of course, he may see himself in the light of society's view of prostitution and react with shame if its view demands that. But if he does not, or if the society in which he lives does not support such a view, would that really mean that the abstraction is easily made? Will he not find the situation, say, awkward, and act as if he did not recognise her? In other words, if he manages to isolate the night before from the rest of his life so that their lives are not weaved together in any way, that will precisely be an accomplishment, an ideal he is trying to live up to by denying parts of himself.

This is not a sad fact about human existence, as if this were akin to the fact that as a newborn, and also later, you are dependent on others for your physical survival, that is, that you need the things society can procure for you. To society, I am just a particular instance of the general, and if society distinguishes me, it distinguishes me because of my properties, that is, because of something general, which means that I am nevertheless substitutable; what society therefore cannot do is recognize me in my singularity. This is how Stirner sees it,[35] but what he forgets is that this means that only to the extent that I do not believe that my friend is my friend simply because of my money, that is, because of something general, friendship is something society cannot procure for me. In other words, what society cannot procure for me is my being recognised as someone not possible to dispose of at pleasure. But if my friend is not able to dispose of me at pleasure, I may still be able to dispose of him at pleasure, that is, the threads by which our lives are weaved together only run in one direction. But is this really so? Of course, initially he may be anybody to me, but the extent to which he remains one is the extent to which what we are talking about when we meet is not important to me, is the extent to which the consolation he affords me is not one I am in great need of, in short, is the extent to which I see his place in my life as an isolated and superficial one. The extent to which he is not able to dispose of me at pleasure is the extent to which I will not be able to dispose of him at pleasure. The life Stirner wants to live would thus be deprived of all such relations. The point is not that such a life is impossible – that would be another question[36] – but that it would be a life of renunciation, of trying to live up to an ideal. Stirner wants to control his feelings – himself be "able to get away from or renounce"[37] any feeling – but is this not a prime example of asceticism?

Since the kind of life Stirner wants to live is, in fact, a life of renunciation, of trying to live up to an ideal, he could, to use his own terminology, be said to be possessed by an idea. Stirner would of course deny this and say that this is an idea he is in control of and that he is able to dispose of it at pleasure, but saying this would prove the very opposite. Again a perhaps too clever comment: by controlling his ideal of control, he succumbs to it. That he is possessed by an idea shows in his insistence on concepts and pictures of power, control, and self-interest. These constitute the screen through which everything is seen. And here we come to something much more interesting, especially in relation to the topic of this paper: one has not rejected power if one has rejected the power of "God, men, authorities, law, state, church" to the benefit of the power of "myself"[38]. Autarchy is not anarchy. Liberation would mean rejecting this way of thinking in its entirety, not, as Stirner, only turning up another side to it. This, however, does not mean that we should celebrate being possessed by something: when I love someone, neither do I say "here I stand, I can do otherwise", nor "here I stand, I cannot do otherwise" – "the principal motto of all possessed"[39] – for both would be to relate to my love (in both senses of the word) in an external way.

The close relation of egoism and ideals became in fact visible already in the beginning of our discussion. When discussing ideals of etiquette, especially that more sophisticated form of etiquette which makes its distinctions in moral terms, it became evident that it is precisely when I relate what I am doing to myself that alienation starts. Trying to live up to ideals could, in fact, be seen as an advanced form of self-centredness: the ideal demands that I look at myself with the ideal as a mirror. What takes me out of that circle is doing something for someone else's sake. The sorrow I may feel is then not about my own failure to relieve her pain – the self-contempt I feel when not being as skilful as I ought to be – but precisely about her. In the first case an infinite striving for control and mastery starts; in the second case the affection I feel is certainly not something I control, but that is not a control I see myself as lacking, and I may certainly try to learn more about, say, first aid, but that does not mean that the meaning of what I know and do not know is its contribution to my self-admiration and self-contempt.[40]

4. A contrasting understanding of morality and religion

A common picture is that morality demands self-denial. The starting point is me in isolation, to which we then ought to add a moral concern which restricts my doings, or, according to Stirner, ought not to. The moral difficulty is hence about forcing oneself to renounce the things one wants, even parts of oneself. The struggle could be seen as a struggle between servitude and freedom. And goodness is then connected to strength and control, badness to weakness. The task of philosophy and reason is here to add to that strength; in the light of its results badness is only possible in the form of stupidity or (temporary) insanity.

But the above discussion points in a very different direction. What we had there was a person who denied parts of himself, strove for control, and submitted to an ideal. But the very point of this was to achieve the egoist life, by fighting the ways in which his life is weaved together with the lives of others. In other words, if the moral difficulty according to the common picture is about forcing oneself to deny parts of oneself, the moral difficulty is here about *not* denying parts of oneself, about not making things difficult for oneself. The starting point is not me in isolation but the concern for others I feel, a concern which I then, possibly, renounce; since badness is renunciation of that concern, the condition of possibility of the moral distinctions is not amoral. The egoist life demands that I deny parts of myself by changing myself in the direction of an ideal, and therefore it is that life which requires strength and control. Doing things for my own sake in terms of motivation – trying to live the egoist life – is precisely not to do things for my own sake in terms of outcome. The moral struggle could in this case, if one wants to, be seen as a struggle between servitude and freedom, that is, between serving oneself or letting oneself be free. And the latter does not need the help of philosophy, for there is no strength here to add anything to. If there is a task for philosophy, it is merely to disclose the attempt of the former to confuse the situation by self-deceptively describing itself as freedom and the latter as servitude and self-denial, and to show that what the former tries to deny it still presupposes and that the renunciation therefore cannot be more than by halves; trying to show the stupidity and insanity of moral badness risks on the contrary to contribute to that very badness by appealing to that sense of shamefulness which only directs one's gaze at how one appears in the light of the ideal.

When we now have two ways of understanding the relation of morality to myself – a common picture and something that points in a very different direction – it can be tempting to try to determine which of them, if any, is right, in general or by describing those cases the one is right about and those the other is right about. But this would, as I see it, be a mistake, for reasons I will come to.[41] Instead we will investigate that understanding which points in a very different direction in order to understand its meaning, see what possibilities it offers, and what light it sheds.

What am I then doing, in the light of this other understanding, when trying to live the egoist life? Ostensibly I am repudiating serving, but what I really do is hardening my heart. What does this mean? It means trying not to listen to, trying not to hear, that is, trying not to understand, an address directed at me. What is that address about? That things concern me, say, sometimes in both senses of the word. But whereas I am certainly able to decide not to respond to the address, I am not able to decide not understanding it. And therefore there is always some sort of response of understanding, however distorted it might be: for example, later on I might realise that the repugnance, even rage, I felt against someone was in fact compassion for him, compassion I did not want to acknowledge. So if understanding something is something you cannot decide not to do, that means that the origin of the address is not to be placed there, in my power of decision. If that were the place it came from there would be no need of hardening one's heart against it. But the address cannot be said to be forced upon me either. If it were, there would be no need of hardening one's heart against it, for being forced to do something means precisely that your heart is not in what you are doing. So the address is not the result of, or some form of, social pressure. On the contrary, a social pressure is one of the sources of a felt need of hardening one's heart, obviously when whom my care concerns is a member of an outcast group and strongly felt when the consequences of that address involves my confrontation with that sociality the pressure expresses. Just as the contrast between egoism and self-denial is merely apparent, the same goes for the contrast between egoism and sociality.

What all this means is that what we are left with when having repudiated servitude is not a bare self; that bare self belongs, on the contrary, to the side of servitude. "Being oneself" is not to return to some self hidden beneath that which covered it, for example that which took possession of me; it is to enter into that extending movement which I am and which the egoist life is an attempt to put an end to. For what we are left with when having repudiated servitude is that which we hardened our hearts against, those relations of care – or more positively expressed: of love – which the above address is about, which therefore cannot definitely be placed either inside or outside me, and which here is the starting point of morality and not something that should be achieved by means of it.

A religious believer could here see God as not only one possible object to harden one's heart against but also what I harden my heart against as soon as I harden it against anything. According to this believer, the religious difficulty is not about denying parts of oneself in order to create a place for God, a God I consequently do not have anything to do with to begin with but have to force

myself into wanting to establish a relation to; the religious difficulty is about not denying oneself, for by doing so one destroys
the already existing relations to God. For this believer, atheism
would be chastity and asceticism, that is, an attempt at denying
oneself dimensions, possibilities and abundances of human life.

This means that submitting to the authority of God could be
understood in two very different ways. In the first one, that submission is identical to self-denial. According to the believer I have
tried to give voice to here, this submission means turning one's
back on God; the problem with this form of submission is then
not that it is too severe but that it is too tempting, that its severity
is tempting. In the second one, submitting to the authority of God
is what I do when I do not submit to any authority, including my
own.[42] The slogan "no gods, no masters" would thus according to
this believer be mistaken, for it is precisely by seeing God as master I do away with *all* authoritarian thinking. The believer I have
tried to give voice to could talk in that way, but it is also possible
that she finds this way of talking too dangerous in that it invites
misunderstandings, also and above all in herself, for only if one
understands that talking in this way means rejecting "submission"
and "authority" completely, not only having given them a new application, has one understood it. No matter what, that believing in
God for her means not submitting to any authority means that for
her there is a freedom which logically precedes all political free-
doms, including religious freedom, for the latter ones are granted
by the state in that the state, so to speak, restricts itself. And that
freedom, the most basic and original, is for her religious.

5. An example: Martin Andersen Nexø's *Pelle Erobreren*

In order to let you see how some of this shows, especially in relation
to political struggle, I will in this section connect to *Pelle Erobreren*
(1906–10), a novel by the Danish author Martin Andersen Nexø.
The third and fourth parts of the novel, which are the ones I will
discuss, depict the political awakening of the protagonist, Pelle, his
marriage and having children, his commitment and work for the
union, his time in prison, and the political work he is engaged in
after his release. No doubt there are many problems in the novel's

perspective on the political and existential questions it deals with, but these problems will not bother me here.

After having come to Copenhagen, from an agrarian, almost feudal, environment to an industrial one, Pelle hardens his heart:

> the capital was simply a battleground, where army upon army had rushed forward and miserably foundered. Everywhere were heaps of fallen, the town was built over them as on top of a cemetery; you had to tread upon them in order to be able to move – and harden your heart. This was basically the lot of life; and you closed your eyes[43]

But this "had to" is after all an illusion. In fact, it is only with open eyes one can give this description. So Pelle's political awakening could be described as the opening of his eyes, as the softening of his hardened heart. But this is not the result of some decision or intellectual process. It happens quite spontaneously, and his growing political commitment is a result of that, rather than what makes it happen. Pelle simply becomes involved in the life of his neighbours and it is only then, that is, for their sake, that he feels a need to change things; on his own and isolated he is passive and accepts things as they are.[44] This conflict repeats itself several times, especially in relation to his wife and children; on the one hand his new family opens up his concern, on the other hand it restricts it to a definite unit. The conflict is however not symmetrical: restricting himself to himself (and to his family) involves rationalization and self-persuasion, whereas his involvement in the life of those he encounters happens without his decision, quite spontaneously.[45]

All this has an explicitly religious dimension, a religious belief born in and out of the political struggle.[46] The climax occurs in prison, where Pelle, having hardened his heart against all those whom he feels have forsaken him, has a revelation of God.[47] After his release he returns to Copenhagen, but many years have passed and much has changed. One of the first things he does is to go to a political celebration and improvising a speech:

> His [Pelle's] words became a greeting to them from a world they did not yet know, that great solitude in which you have to travel alone – without loud-voiced companions to brace one up – and listen for the way ahead, until you hear your own heart beat

inside. He sits in a cell again, as in the first original germ of life – alone and forsaken, above him a spider spins its skilful web. In the beginning he is angry with the busy animal and tears the web apart, but the animal indefatigably begins again. And this suddenly becomes a consolatory lesson about never giving up; he becomes fond of this little vigilant creature, which spins its web really skilfully, as though it had a great responsibility [...] He bitterly regrets his ravaging and would give much for a sign that the little animal is not angry with him; for no one can afford to push away another [...] And one day as he sits reading and the spider is busy with carrying a thread just past him, it comes down intimately and uses his shoulder as a temporary hold. Never before had such trust despite everything been showed him, the little animal knew how a hardened prisoner should be taken. It taught him that he had both a heart and a soul to take care of! – A greeting to the comrades from that great stillness, waiting to speak to them one by one.[48]

The speech is a failure, however. The crowd meets him with indifference and they do not listen to what he is saying. Two different worlds stand against each other: on the one hand Pelle, the lone one who listens to his own heart, and his message of solidarity, on the other hand the crowd, during the last years more and more shaped by bourgeois individualism. Pelle is happy with that economical development which has made this possible, but most of all he deplores this shift of mood: the lost feeling for the miraculous and incomprehensible and that lost solidarity this gives rise to, in particular on the part of the established working class with the new groups coming to the city and becoming pauperised.[49] By listening inward you will find everyone, the whole world, and that which cannot be comprehended.[50] But by being part of the crowd you succumb to one or the other of its ideologies, for example individualism, an ideology which hence means renunciation both of oneself and of the life together, and the one by means of the other.

6. Concluding discussion

"But is it not, after all, better to be able to dispose of that which pains one? Perhaps you are right in that caring only for oneself means renunciation, but caring for others means that I would feel their pain, and believing that it is possible to relieve all pain in the world is utopian. So I choose the lesser evil and care only for myself. That renunciation is after all the smaller one."

The problem this imaginary interlocutor formulates seems to be possible to solve in two different ways: either by ceasing to care for others or by creating a heaven on earth. And the questions we then seem to have to answer are whether the one or the other is possible, which of the solutions is the easier one, and which of the two renunciations is the smaller one. And after having answered these questions we are able to choose the one or the other of the two solutions. But this is, after all, an illusion. The terms in which any comparison of that kind could be made are taken from the two solutions themselves, so it is only after having chosen the one or the other you could say which of the two renunciations is the smaller one. What content could the concept of renunciation have that is not dependent on any of these two solutions but, nevertheless, makes it possible to determine which of them is the better one? But, to be strict, they could not even be seen as two different solutions to a common problem. This is obvious from the perspective of that understanding pointing in a very different direction I described in section 4. The starting point there is not me in isolation but the concern for others I feel, a concern which I then, possibly, renounce, which means that there is no choice to be made prior to this very starting point. And furthermore, since your caring for others is here not understood as merely a part of yourself, it is not possible to renounce that part and have another part left, which means that choosing that solution will never be made more than by halves. But that they could not even be seen as two different solutions to a common problem is obvious also from the other perspective: caring for others could here not even be seen as a possibility, for seeing it is a possibility would mean that you actually do care for others. In other words, since they could not even be seen as two different solutions to a common problem – the problem being understood in different ways and the other solution not being understood as even a possibility – it would be a mistake to try to determine which of them is right. Trying to determine which of them makes it possible for me to "be myself" is for example not possible, for the terms in which I try to evaluate this will already be biased in favour of the one or the other. This does not mean that there is not anything to be said about the issue, but what is to be said depends, as I said, on where one stands and that standpoint already involves some stance or other on the issue.

"Here at last / We shall be free [...] Better to reign in Hell, than serve in Heav'n."[51] That Satan understands religious faith to mean servitude and lack of freedom is hence not surprising. The only possibility is for him one of power and the question then simply concerns who shall have it. So he is the prime example of an authoritarian figure. What he says could thus be understood as a self-deceptive attempt at confusing the situation by describing that renunciation and self-denial serving oneself means as freedom. That freedom Satan contrasts servitude to is a freedom of reigning; the concept of power is not rejected and *this* freedom is thus not won.

One way of concluding is to say that I have not showed that Stirner's way of thinking should be rejected, only that there is no necessary conflict between religious faith and freedom. Religious faith does not necessarily mean servitude, for I have described a possibility in which it does not. But this is, in fact, both to over- and underestimate the consequences of what I have said. It is to overestimate them, for Stirner could say that he does not understand what I have said at all and that he finds it completely incomprehensible. It is to underestimate them, for if he does understand what I have said and sees it as a possibility, that means that his own possibility does not exist anymore. For seeing caring for others as a possibility means caring for others; seeing it as a possibility means that the address I talked about above is understood, although not necessarily actively responded to. So when having understood that the life Stirner wants to live is a life of self-denial, it is not possible anymore to choose it as the lesser evil, for having understood this is in fact having rejected it as a possibility. This does however not mean that the "understanding that points in a very different direction" and the understanding of the believer I tried to give voice to necessarily are the only possibilities. Whether that is another question or not, is another question.

Notes

1. John Milton, *Paradise Lost*, in *The Complete Poems*, ed. by John Leonard (London: Penguin, 1998), I. 263.

2. Milton, I. 258–59.

3. Coined by Blanqui, the slogan soon became so closely associated with anarchism that writers distant to anarchism often referred to it as a typical example of anarchist thinking. See e.g. Friedrich Nietzsche, *Jenseits von Gut und Böse: Vorspiel einer Philosophie der Zukunft*, in *Kritische Studienausgabe*, ed. by Giorgio Colli and Mazzino Montinari, 15 vols (Berlin: de Gruyter, 1988), V, 125 (§ 202); Joseph Conrad, *The Secret Agent: A Simple Tale* (London: Penguin, 2007), 242.

4. The conference session this book grew out of had the heading "'No Master but God?' Exploring the Compatibility of Anarchism and Religion" and the subsequent call for papers stated "many anarchists insist that religion is fundamentally incompatible with anarchism, recalling that anarchism calls for 'no gods, no masters'".

5. Cf. Ludwig Wittgenstein, *Philosophical Investigations*, 4th edn (Chichester: Wiley-Blackwell, 2009), § 115.

6. Max Stirner, *Der Einzige und sein Eigentum*, ed. by Ahlrich Meyer (Stuttgart: Reclam, 1981). Since the tone of the rest of Stirner's writings (collected in *Kleinere Schriften*, ed. by John Henry Mackay, 2nd edn (Treptow bei Berlin: Bernhard Zack, 1914)) is in fact quite different and what I am interested in is not Stirner but the kind of picture mentioned above, I will only make references to those writings when they are in line with *Der Einzige und sein Eigentum*, not when they differ from it.

7. For some examples, with their respective strengths and weaknesses, see Karl Löwith, *Das Individuum in der Rolle des Mitmenschen* (Munich: Drei Masken Verlag, 1928); Karl Löwith, *Von Hegel zu Nietzsche: Der revolutionäre Bruch im Denken des 19. Jahrhunderts*, 7th edn (Hamburg: Felix Meiner, 1978); Hans G. Helms, *Die Ideologie der anonymen Gesellschaft: Max Stirners ›Einziger‹ und der Fortschritt des demokratischen Selbstbewußtseins vom Vormärz bis zur Bundesrepublik* (Köln: M. DuMont Schauberg, 1966); R. W. K. Paterson, *The Nihilistic Egoist: Max Stirner* (Oxford: Oxford University

Press, 1971); Michael Maier, *Scheiternde Titanen: De Maistres Papst, Stirners Einziger, Jean Pauls Himmelsstürmer* (Paderborn: Ferdinand Schöningh, 2006); John F. Welsh, *Max Stirner's Dialectical Egoism: A New Interpretation* (Lanham: Lexington Books, 2010); *Max Stirner*, ed. by Saul Newman (Basingstoke: Palgrave Macmillan, 2011); Maurice Schuhmann, *Radikale Individualität: Zur Aktualität der Konzepte von Marquis de Sade, Max Stirner und Friedrich Nietzsche* (Bielefeld: transcript, 2011).

8. Stirner, *Der Einzige und sein Eigentum*, p. 387. All translations from works not originally written in English are mine.

9. Stirner, *Der Einzige und sein Eigentum*, p. 237.

10. Stirner, *Der Einzige und sein Eigentum*, p. 40.

11. This kind of criticism has its origin in the section on unhappy consciousness in Hegel's *Phänomenologie des Geistes* (G. W. F. Hegel, *Gesammelte Werke* (Hamburg: Felix Meiner, 1968-), IX: *Phänomenologie des Geistes*, ed. by Wolfgang Bonsiepen und Reinhard Heede (1980), esp. pp. 122–23, 125–27; see also pp. 327–28). In the end the need for sublating religion is motivated in those terms; see p. 420–21.

12. Stirner, *Der Einzige und sein Eigentum*, pp. 31–32, 40, 42, 50–52, 62, 141, 202–203, 269, 320–21, 387–88; Stirner, *Kleinere Schriften*, pp. 358, 362.

13. For examples of such new gods, see Stirner, *Der Einzige und sein Eigentum*, e.g. pp. 3, 46, 79, and Stirner, *Kleinere Schriften*, p. 282.

14. See Stirner, *Der Einzige und sein Eigentum*, e.g. pp. 33–34, and Stirner, *Kleinere Schriften*, pp. 366–67.

15. Stirner, *Der Einzige und sein Eigentum*, p. 84

16. Stirner, *Der Einzige und sein Eigentum*, p. 189. See also, e.g., pp. 87, 321.

17. Stirner, *Der Einzige und sein Eigentum*, p. 348. See also p. 201, and Stirner, *Kleinere Schriften*, pp. 345, 348–49. However, and as we will see, this is in the end not true as to the you; see e.g. Stirner, *Der Einzige und sein Eigentum*, p. 381.

18. Stirner, *Der Einzige und sein Eigentum*, pp. 268–69. For examples of what Stirner criticises in Feuerbach, see Ludwig Feuerbach,

Das Wesen des Christentums (Stuttgart: Reclam, 1969), pp. 37–40, 54, 64–65, and Ludwig Feuerbach, *Grundsätze der Philosophie der Zukunft*, in *Werke*, ed. by Erich Thies, 5 vols (Frankfurt a.M.: Suhrkamp, 1975–76), III (1975), 247–322 (p. 321).

19. See Stirner, *Der Einzige und sein Eigentum*, p. 47 and *passim*.

20. Stirner, *Der Einzige und sein Eigentum*, pp. 65–66.

21. Cf. Stirner, *Der Einzige und sein Eigentum*, pp. 66, 187.

22. See Stirner, *Der Einzige und sein Eigentum*, p. 4 and *passim*.

23. Immanuel Kant, *Grundlegung zur Metaphysik der Sitten*, in *Werkausgabe*, ed. by Wilhelm Weischedel, 12 vols (Frankfurt a.M.: Suhrkamp, 1968), VII, 7–102 (pp. 60–61 (AA 4:428–29)).

24. Stirner, *Der Einzige und sein Eigentum*, p. 34.

25. Stirner, *Der Einzige und sein Eigentum*, p. 139; Stirner, *Kleinere Schriften*, pp. 346–51, 384.

26. This is basically Feuerbach's answer to Stirner's criticism. Whether I like it or not, I will always have ideals (Ludwig Feuerbach, *Über das* »Wesen des Christentums« *in Beziehung auf den* »Einzigen und sein Eigentum«, in *Werke*, ed. by Erich Thies, 5 vols (Frankfurt a.M.: Suhrkamp, 1975–76), IV (1975), 69–80, 454–63, (pp. 461–62)) and I will always understand myself by comparing myself with others and them by comparing them with each other (pp. 74–76).

27. Stirner, *Der Einzige und sein Eigentum*, pp. 202, 342, 344. This issue is however more complicated than as just presented. There is another strain to Stirner's text that, in the end, would deny *all* kinds of dependence, when he writes that "[o]nly *I am* not abstraction alone [...] I am no mere thought" (p. 381) and describes the I in terms by which God is described in philosophical theology: perfect, self-sufficient, creator *ex nihilo* (pp. 5, 39, 378–79, 412). But if this strain of Stirner's text were the only one you would emphasise a very one-sided picture would be the result; that I leave it out of account is however due to the fact that it is not that relevant as to the theme of this paper.

28. For examples of Stirner's "immorality", see *Kleinere Schriften*, pp. 271–72, 279–80, 293.

29. Stirner, *Der Einzige und sein Eigentum*, e.g. pp. 4, 45, 324–25.

30. Stirner, *Der Einzige und sein Eigentum*, pp. 64, 81–82, 324, 335; Stirner, *Kleinere Schriften*, p. 292.

31. Stirner, *Der Einzige und sein Eigentum*, e.g. pp. 285–86, 320; Stirner, *Kleinere Schriften*, pp. 274–77.

32. Stirner, *Der Einzige und sein Eigentum*, pp. 324–25.

33. Stirner, *Der Einzige und sein Eigentum*, p. 326.

34. Stirner, *Der Einzige und sein Eigentum*, pp. 304–305.

35. Stirner, *Der Einzige und sein Eigentum*, p. 304. What he says here is of course heavily dependent on Hegel's view of society as about the general, of the family (most obvious in the relation of brother and sister) as about the singular; see Hegel, pp. 241–44, 247–48.

36. As we will see in section 6 however, this is after all *not* another question.

37. Stirner, *Der Einzige und sein Eigentum*, p. 330. Stirner has taken this understanding of feelings from Feuerbach (*Das Wesen des Christentums*, p. 50) but comes to a very different conclusion.

38. Stirner, *Der Einzige und sein Eigentum*, p. 187.

39. Stirner, *Der Einzige und sein Eigentum*, p. 66.

40. For additional discussion of the issues in this section, see Hugo Strandberg, *Self-Knowledge and Self-Deception* (Basingstoke: Palgrave Macmillan, 2015), esp. ch. 11; Hugo Strandberg, "Is Pure Evil Possible?", in *The Problem of Evil: New Philosophical Directions*, ed. by Benjamin W. McCraw and Robert Arp (Lanham: Lexington Books, 2016), 23–34.

41. See section 6.

42. For more about this use of "not … any" and "nothing", see Gareth Moore, *Believing in God: A Philosophical Essay* (Edinburgh: T&T Clark, 1988), *passim*, e.g. ch. 4.

43. Martin Andersen Nexø, *Pelle Erobreren: Bind 2*, 15th edn (Copenhagen: Gyldendal, 2006), p. 58.

44. Nexø, pp. 58–61.

45. See Nexø, e.g. pp. 171–72, 176, 241, 394.

46. See Nexø, e.g. pp. 187, 210, 214.

47. Nexø, pp. 342–43.

48. Nexø, p. 357.

49. Nexø, pp. 358, 383.

50. Nexø, p. 396.

51. Milton, I. 258–59, 263.

References

Conrad, Joseph, *The Secret Agent: A Simple Tale* (London: Penguin, 2007).

Feuerbach, Ludwig, *Das Wesen des Christentums* (Stuttgart: Reclam, 1969).

_____, *Über das* »Wesen des Christentums« *in Beziehung auf den* »Einzigen und sein Eigentum«, in *Werke*, ed. by Erich Thies, 5 vols (Frankfurt a.M.: Suhrkamp, 1975–76), IV (1975), 69–80, 454–63.

_____, *Grundsätze der Philosophie der Zukunft*, in *Werke*, ed. by Erich Thies, 5 vols (Frankfurt a.M.: Suhrkamp, 1975–76), III (1975), 247–322.

Hegel, G. W. F., *Gesammelte Werke* (Hamburg: Felix Meiner, 1968–), IX: *Phänomenologie des Geistes*, ed. by Wolfgang Bonsiepen und Reinhard Heede (1980).

Helms, Hans G., *Die Ideologie der anonymen Gesellschaft: Max Stirners ›Einziger‹ und der Fortschritt des demokratischen Selbstbewußtseins vom Vormärz bis zur Bundesrepublik* (Köln: M. DuMont Schauberg, 1966).

Kant, Immanuel, *Grundlegung zur Metaphysik der Sitten*, in *Werkausgabe*, ed. by Wilhelm Weischedel, 12 vols (Frankfurt a.M.: Suhrkamp, 1968), VII, 7–102.

Löwith, Karl, *Das Individuum in der Rolle des Mitmenschen* (Munich: Drei Masken Verlag, 1928).

_____, *Von Hegel zu Nietzsche: Der revolutionäre Bruch im Denken des 19. Jahrhunderts*, 7th edn (Hamburg: Felix Meiner, 1978).

Maier, Michael, *Scheiternde Titanen: De Maistres Papst, Stirners Einziger, Jean Pauls Himmelsstürmer* (Paderborn: Ferdinand Schöningh, 2006).

Milton, John, *Paradise Lost*, in *The Complete Poems*, ed. by John Leonard (London: Penguin, 1998), 119–406.

Moore, Gareth, *Believing in God: A Philosophical Essay* (Edinburgh: T&T Clark, 1988).

Newman, Saul, ed., *Max Stirner* (Basingstoke: Palgrave Macmillan, 2011).

Nexø, Martin Andersen, *Pelle Erobreren: Bind 2*, 15th edn (Copenhagen: Gyldendal, 2006).

Nietzsche, Friedrich, *Jenseits von Gut und Böse: Vorspiel einer Philosophie der Zukunft*, in *Kritische Studienausgabe*, ed. by Giorgio Colli and Mazzino Montinari, 15 vols (Berlin: de Gruyter, 1988), v, 9–243.

Paterson, R. W. K., *The Nihilistic Egoist: Max Stirner* (Oxford: Oxford University Press, 1971).

Schuhmann, Maurice, *Radikale Individualität: Zur Aktualität der Konzepte von Marquis de Sade, Max Stirner und Friedrich Nietzsche* (Bielefeld: transcript, 2011).

Stirner, Max, *Der Einzige und sein Eigentum*, ed. by Ahlrich Meyer (Stuttgart: Reclam, 1981).

_____, *Kleinere Schriften*, ed. by John Henry Mackay, 2nd edn (Treptow bei Berlin: Bernhard Zack, 1914).

Strandberg, Hugo, "Is Pure Evil Possible?", in *The Problem of Evil: New Philosophical Directions* , ed. by Benjamin W. McCraw and Robert Arp (Lanham: Lexington Books, 2016), 23–34.

_____, *Self-Knowledge and Self-Deception* (Basingstoke: Palgrave Macmillan, 2015).

Welsh, John F., *Max Stirner's Dialectical Egoism: A New Interpretation* (Lanham: Lexington Books, 2010).

Wittgenstein, Ludwig, *Philosophical Investigations*, 4th edn (Chichester: Wiley-Blackwell, 2009).

Contributors

Matthew S. Adams is Lecturer in Politics, History and Communication at Loughborough University. He is the author of *Kropotkin, Read, and the Intellectual History of British Anarchism* (Palgrave, 2015), and editor of *Anarchism, 1914–1918* (Manchester University Press, 2017). He has also published, amongst others, in the journals *History of Political Thought, Journal of Political Ideologies, Journal of the History of Ideas, History of European Ideas* and *Historical Research*. He is currently working on the idea of the 'anarchist public intellectual' in the context of Cold War cultural politics, and editing *The Palgrave Handbook of Anarchism* with Carl Levy. A full list of publications is available via http://orcid.org/0000–0002-5440–4866.

Alexandre Christoyannopoulos is Senior Lecturer in Politics and International Relations at Loughborough University, which he joined in 2010. He is the author of *Christian Anarchism: A Political Commentary on the Gospel* (Imprint Academic, 2010) as well as a number of articles, chapters and other publications on religious anarchism and on Leo Tolstoy, including *Religious Anarchism: New Perspectives* (Cambridge Scholars Publishing, 2009). A full list of publications is available via http://orcid. org/0000–0001-5133–3268. He is currently writing a monograph on Tolstoy's political thought, and editing the next volumes of the present collection of essays on anarchism and religion. He also runs https://socratichive.wordpress.com/, and acts as Treasurer of the Anarchist Studies Network and moderator of the ASIRA mailing list on religious anarchism.

Enrique Galván-Álvarez is a lecturer at Universidad Internacional de La Rioja-UNIR. His doctoral research was focused on the English-language poetry written by diaspora and exiled Tibetans. His post-doctoral research has been largely concerned with

Buddhist anarchism, both as an explicit product of Buddhist modernity and as a theoretical and retrospective exploration of libertarian themes in the history of Buddhist traditions. Enrique has published a monograph on modern Indian fiction and its connections to the pre-modern and pre-colonial, along with many journal articles and book chapters on postcolonial nation building and the use of religious narratives to legitimate or resist the state. Some of his recent projects involve studying the performative nature of sovereignty within the Syrian war and the transnational history of anti-colonial anarchism in the Canary Islands.

Franziska Hoppen's research interests lie at the intersection of politics and religion. The working title of her PhD thesis is "Critiques of modern Western politics from the perspective of twentieth century mystical philosophy." It examines and compares critiques by mystical philosophers Eric Voegelin, Gustav Landauer, Simone Weil, and Vaclav Havel, as well as their normative visions for community. Franziska began her doctoral studies in political thought, funded by the Economic and Social Research Council, at the University of Kent in 2012.

Ruy Llera Blanes, anthropologist, is currently Ramon y Cajal Fellow at the Institute of Heritage Sciences (CSIC), in Spain. His current research site is Angola, where he has been conducting research on religion, mobility (diasporas, transnationalism, the Atlantic), politics (leadership, charisma, repression, resistance, utopia), and temporalities (historicity, memory, heritage, expectations). He is co-editor of the journal *Religion and Society: Advances in Research*, published by Berghahn. His recent publications include *A Prophetic Trajectory: Ideologies of Time and Space in an Angolan Religious Movement* (Berghahn, 2014), and *The Social Life of Spirits* (Chicago UP, 2013)., co-edited with Diana Espírito Santo.

Justin Meggitt is Senior Lecturer in the Critical Study of Religion at the University of Cambridge and Visiting Researcher at the Department of Ethnology, History of Religions and Gender studies at Stockholm University. He has published widely on the historical Jesus, the origins of Christianity, magic in antiquity, and early modern transcultural encounters, including the books *Paul, Poverty and Survival* (1998) and *Early Quakers and Islam: Slavery, Apocalyptic and Christian-Muslim Encounters in the Seventeenth Century* (2013). He is one of the founders of the newly established Centre for the Critical Study of Apocalyptic and Millenarian Movements based in Bedford, UK

Benjamin J. Pauli is Assistant Professor of Social Science at Kettering University in Flint, Michigan, USA. His research interests include the study of political ideologies, particularly anarchism, as well as religion and politics and urban politics. He is the editor of Radical Religion: Contemporary Perspectives on Religion and the Left and the author of several articles and book chapters on 20th-century anarchist thought in Britain and the United States. He has been active in the popular mobilization around the Flint Water Crisis and is currently at work on a book project that frames the struggle for clean water in Flint as part of a broader struggle for democracy in the city and beyond.

Simon D. Podmore is Senior Lecturer in Systematic Theology at Liverpool Hope University. He is the author of *Struggling With God: Kierkegaard and the Temptation of Spiritual Trial* (Cambridge: James Clarke & Co., 2013) and K*ierkegaard and the Self Before God: Anatomy of the Abyss* (Bloomington: Indiana University Press, 2011); and co-editor of *Exploring Lost Dimensions in Christian Mysticism: Opening to the Mystical* (Farnham: Ashgate, 2013), *Christian Mysticism and Incarnation Theology: Between Transcendence and Immanence* (Farnham: Ashgate, 2013), and *Mystical Theology and Continental Philosophy: Interchange in the Wake of God* (London/New York: Routledge, 2017). His research explores the relationships between constructive, philosophical, and mystical theology, psychotherapy, and the arts. He is co-convenor of The Mystical Theology Network.

Hugo Strandberg is Senior Lecturer in Philosophy at Åbo Akademi University, Finland. His latest books are *Self-Knowledge and Self-Deception* (Palgrave Macmillan, 2015), *Love of a God*

of Love: Towards a Transformation of the Philosophy of Religion (Continuum, 2011), *Escaping My Responsibility: Investigations into the Nature of Morality* (Peter Lang, 2009), and *The Possibility of Discussion: Relativism, Truth and Criticism of Religious Beliefs* (Ashgate, 2006).

Index

Lightning Source UK Ltd.
Milton Keynes UK
UKHW010751131218
333948UK00014B/1156/P